IMPROVE YOUR
SPELLING

IMPROVE YOUR
SPELLING

BLOOMSBURY

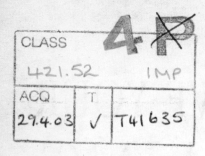
First published in 2002 by
Bloomsbury Publishing Plc
38 Soho Square
London W1D 3HB

Copyright © Bloomsbury Publishing Plc 2002

A copy of the CIP data entry for this book is available
from the British Library.

ISBN 0 7475 5913 9

10 9 8 7 6 5 4 3 2 1

Typeset by Hewer Text Ltd, Edinburgh
Printed in Great Britain by Clays Ltd, St Ives plc

CONTENTS

INTRODUCTION

How to use the dictionary

Spelling can be difficult. To use a spelling dictionary effectively, you need to be able to make a good guess at how a word might be spelt in order to find a likely place to look it up – and this is not always easy.

This book gives you three different types of help to make spellings easier to find:

- a list is given below of common alternative spellings for sounds may be written in different ways. If you do not find the word initially in the dictionary you should try these alternative spellings.

- where a group of words has an unusual or unexpected spelling, a note is given at the expected spelling to direct you to the unexpected one. For example, at the group of words beginning with the letters **fol . . .**, which includes words like **follow**, a note directs you to look at **fal . . .** for words like **false** and **falter**.

- for many words whose spelling is particularly difficult to guess, common incorrect spellings are given that direct you to the correct spelling. Incorrect spellings may either be misspellings like ~~medecine~~ (correctly spelt **medicine**) or ~~opthalmic~~ (correctly **ophthalmic**), or they may reflect the sound of the word, like ~~diffrent~~ (correctly **different**) or ~~goverment~~ (correctly **government**). Incorrect spellings are shown with a line through them.

Note also that American spelling is not covered in this dictionary, so a spelling such as **gray** is not given here although it would be correct in American English.

How to look up a word whose spelling you do not know

The main alternative spellings for consonant and vowel sounds are given below. If you cannot find the word you want in the first place you look for it, look at the examples below to find different possible spellings that you could try.

Introduction

CONSONANTS

Consonants are all the letters of the alphabet except **a**, **e**, **i**, **o**, **u**, and sometimes **y**. Consonants in English can generally be doubled except for **h**, **j**, **q**, **w**, and **x**. If you cannot find the word with a doubled consonant, try a single one.

ALTERNATIVE SPELLINGS FOR CONSONANTS

Sound	Alternative spellings			
ch sandwi**ch** **ch**in	**tch** ki**tch**en pa**tch**	**tu** punc**tu**re sta**tue**		
f de**f**end **f**air	**ph** dol**ph**in **ph**one	**gh** rou**gh**		
j ca**j**ole **j**am	**g** (before **e**, **i**, or **y**) **g**em lo**g**ic ed**g**y	**dg** ba**dg**e ju**dg**e		
k **k**itten	**c** **c**rowd	**ck** chi**ck**en	**qu** opa**qu**e	**ch** **ch**aos te**ch**nique
n **n**ow do**n**e	**gn** **gn**aw campai**gn**	**kn** **kn**eel ac**kn**owledge		
qu li**qu**id **qu**ick	**cqu** a**cqu**ire	**kw** aw**kw**ard		
s **s**end ba**s**e	**c** (before **e**, **i**, or **y**) **c**entre a**c**id jui**c**y	**sc** **sc**ent a**sc**end	**ss** profe**ss**or confe**ss**	
sh **sh**op ca**sh**	**ss** pa**ss**ion proce**ss**ion	**ti** pa**ti**ence cau**ti**ous		

w forward	**u** (before vowel) persuade		
x taxi	**ks** thanks	**xc** except	**cs** physics
z daze marzipan	**s** (before vowel) please easy	**x** anxiety xylophone	

There is also a sound somewhere between **z** and **sh** for which there is no consonant. It is usually spelt **su**, as in **pleasure** or **casual**, but can also be spelt **si**, as in **vision** or **precision**.

VOWELS

The vowels in the alphabet are **a, e, i, o, u**, and sometimes **y**. All the vowels have a 'long' vowel sound and a 'short' vowel sound. The 'long' sound is the sound of the letter as it would be pronounced if you were reciting the alphabet. The 'short' sounds are those in b**a**d, b**e**d, b**i**d, b**o**dy, and b**u**d. The letter **y** has the long and short sound of **i**, as in c**y**cle and bic**y**cle.

A vowel on its own (between two consonants or at the beginning of a word) can have either the long or short sound. A vowel before a double consonant will have the short sound, as in **latter** (compare **later**) or **hopping** (compare **hoping**).

LONG VOWELS

In general a vowel followed by a single consonant and then an **e** (with the **e** not pronounced) is a long vowel, eg

spade, these, bite, phone, prune, style

ALTERNATIVE SPELLINGS FOR THE LONG VOWELS **A, E, I, O, U**

Sound	Alternative spellings			
a make amiable	**ai** complaint aim	**ay** day	**ea** great	**ei** rein eight
e lethal even	**ee** sheep	**ea** peace	**ie** believe	**ei** ceiling

ix

Introduction

i Friday ice	**igh** l**igh**t	**ie** p**ie**	**y** cr**y**		
o gh**o**st **o**ver	**oa** r**oa**st **oa**ts	**ow** sh**ow** **ow**n	**oe** h**oe**	**ou** alth**ou**gh	
u r**u**de **u**nion	**ew** gr**ew** f**ew**	**ue** gl**ue** d**ue**	**oo** g**oo**s	**ou** gr**ou**p	

ALTERNATIVE SPELLINGS FOR THE SHORT VOWELS **E, I, U**

Sound	Alternative spellings		
e b**e**d **e**lephant	**ea** r**ea**dy		
i h**i**m **i**nk	**y** g**y**m		
u h**u**ndred **u**nder	**o** d**o**zen	**oo** bl**oo**d	**ou** t**ou**ch

ALTERNATIVE SPELLINGS FOR OTHER VOWELS

Sound	Alternative spellings					
aw str**aw** **aw**ful	**al** **al**ter f**al**l	**or** f**or**k **or**der	**au** fr**au**d **au**thor	**oo** d**oo**r	**ore** sh**ore**	**ough** **ough**t
air p**air**	**ar** c**ar**e v**ar**ious					
ar h**ar**m **ar**tist	**al** c**al**m **al**mond	**a** f**a**ther	**oir** boud**oir** mem**oir**			
ier f**ier**ce	**eer** b**eer** **eer**ie	**ea/ear** id**ea** **ear**drum	**ere** sev**ere**			

oo	u				
fo**oo**t	p**u**sh				

oor	ur	eur			
p**oor**	c**ur**e	**eur**o			

ow	ou				
c**ow**	r**ou**nd				
sh**ow**er	s**ou**r				

oy	oi				
t**oy**	v**oi**ce				
	oil				

ur	er	ir	ear		
c**ur**ve	m**er**ge	b**ir**th	p**ear**l		
urgent			**ear**n		

Sounds like '**uh**'
The very short vowel sound '**uh**' is so short it is almost not pronounced at all. It can be written as **e**, **a**, **i**, **o**, or **u**, as in barr**e**l, mis**e**rable, ref**e**ree, **a**bout, turb**a**n, defin**i**te, respons**i**ble, comm**o**n, p**u**rsue, and circ**u**s.

WORD ENDINGS

Sound like	Possible spellings				
el	**le**	**al**			
	catt**le**	dent**al**			
er	**er**	**or**	**re**	**ar**	**eur**
	driv**er**	act**or**	lust**re**	burgl**ar**	chauff**eur**
i	**y**	**ie**	**ey**		
	happ**y**	calor**ie**	mon**ey**		
idj/ij	**age**	**ege**	**idge**		
	man**age**	privil**ege**	cartr**idge**		
ius	**ious**	**eous**			
	delir**ious**	hid**eous**			
jus	**geous**	**gious**			
	coura**geous**	presti**gious**			
shul	**tial**	**cial**			
	substan**tial**	commer**cial**			

Introduction

shun	tion	sion	cion
	posi**tion**	man**sion**	coer**cion**
shus	tious	cious	scious
	cau**tious**	pre**cious**	con**scious**
sul	stle	sle	sel
	ca**stle**	tus**sle**	mus**sel**
ul	el	le	al
	barr**el**	catt**le**	dent**al**
us	ous		
	jeal**ous**		

- Endings sounding like **ible** may also be spelt **able**
- Endings sounding like **ent** may also be spelt **ant**
- Endings sounding like **ence** may also be spelt **ance**

SILENT LETTERS AND MISSPELLINGS
There are some silent consonants and vowels that are not pronounced and that can easily be forgotten when we are spelling certain words.

SILENT LETTERS

Sound	Silent in:
d	han**d**kerchief, suppose**d** to
e	desperat**e**ly, int**e**rest, sev**e**ral
g	desi**g**n, len**g**th, reco**g**nize
h	diarr**h**oea, eig**h**th, ex**h**ibition, r**h**ythm
n	condem**n**, enviro**n**ment, gover**n**ment
r	adve**r**tise, Feb**r**uary, gove**r**nor, su**r**prise
u	g**u**arantee, g**u**ard, Portug**u**ese

Main spelling rules

1. Adding **s** or **es** for plurals and verbs
The regular plural ending for nouns and the 3rd person singular ending for verbs is an added **s**.
Words ending in **ch**, **s**, **sh**, **x**, and **z** add **es** in the plural and 3rd person singular:

cat, cats
beech, beeches
batch, batches
boss, bosses
bush, bushes
fox, foxes
waltz, waltzes

Words ending in **f** or **fe** sometimes add **s** and sometimes change to **ves**:

scarf, scarves

Exceptions: the plural of **gas** is **gases** but the 3rd person singular of the verb 'to gas' is **gasses**.
The plurals of **hero**, **potato**, and **tomato** end in **es** rather than **s**.

2. Changing **y** to **ie**

Words that end in **y** keep the **y** before **ing** but change to **ies** and **ied** for the noun plural, the 3rd person present singular and the past tense of verbs, and before the **er** and **est** form of adjectives:

worry, worries, worried, worrying
try, tries, tried, trying
happy, happier, happiest

Names of people and places that end in **y** keep the **y** and just add **s** in the plural, eg Mr and Mrs **Perry**, the **Perrys**.

Exceptions: words that end in a vowel and **y** keep the **y** before **s, ed, er**, and **est**:

play, plays, played, playing
grey, greyer, greyest

3. Verbs ending in **ie**

Verbs like **lie, tie**, and **die** replace **ie** with **y** in the present participle:

lie, lies, lied, lying
die, dies, died, dying

Note the difference between **die** above and **dye, dyes, dyed, dyeing**.

Introduction

4. Dropping **e** before **ing**
Words that end in a consonant and **e** generally lose the **e** before **ing** (also before **ise**, **ize**) and **ed** (also before **er**):

hike, hikes, hiked, hiking, hiker

Exceptions are the present participles of **singe** (= burn), which is **singeing** (to avoid confusion with 'singing'), and **age**, which can be spelt **ageing** or **aging**. Note also **swingeing** (= large), spelt with an **e** to avoid confusion with 'swinging'.

5. Words ending in **c**
Words ending in **c** add **k** before **ed** and **ing**:

panic, panics, panicked, panicking

An exception is **arc,** for which the participles are **arced** and **arcing**.

6. Doubling the consonant before **ed**, **ing**, **er**
Single-syllable words that end in a single vowel and a consonant usually double the consonant before **ed, ing, er**, and **est**:

pot, pots, potted, potting, potter
fit, fitter, fittest

Words that end in a single vowel and a consonant and are stressed on the last syllable usually double the consonant before **ed** and **ing**:

regret, regrets, regretted, regretting
omit, omits, omitted, omitting

Compare these examples with **benefit** and **target**, which are stressed on the first syllable:

benefit, benefits, benefited, benefiting
target, targets, targeted, targeting

7. **ie**, **ei**
The well-known rule 'i before e except after c' applies when the vowel sound rhymes with 'sheep':

shriek, niece, 'i before e'
ceiling, deceit, 'except after c'

There are some exceptions such as **seize, weird,** and the names **Sheila** and **Keith.**

8. Verbs ending in **ise** or **ize**

Although the traditional spelling of verbs like **characterise** is usually **ise**, many publications, including this dictionary, now use the American **ize** spelling. However, the following verbs are only ever spelt **ise:**

advertise	excise
advise	exercise
apprise	improvise
arise	merchandise
chastise	prise (open)
circumcise	revise
comprise	rise
compromise	supervise
despise	surmise
devise	surprise
enfranchise	televise

Capsize, prize, and **size** are only ever spelt **ize**. Note also that **analyse** is spelt **yse**, not **yze**.

Alternative spellings

This list gives possible alternative spellings for some common word beginnings:

acs try **acc:**	accelerate
air try **aer:**	aerial
ca try **cha:**	character
ce try **che:**	chemical
clor try **chlor:**	chlorine
co try **cho:**	cholera
cr try **chr:**	Christmas
ecs try **ex:**	exercise
ef try **af:**	affection, afraid
egs try **exh:**	exhaust
fer try **fur:**	furry
fol try **fal:**	false
for try **four:**	fourteen
gi try **gui:**	guilt
hi try **high:**	higher
ho try **who:**	whole

Introduction

meca try mecha: mechanic
na try kna: knack, knave
ne try kne: knee, knell
ni try kni: knife, knit
no try kno: knob, know
nur try neur: neurosis
nut try neut: neutral
ocs try ox: oxygen
pel try pol: polite
per try pur: purple, pursue
pre try pro: provide
quo try qua: qualification, quarrel
ra try wra: wrap
re try wre: wreck
ri try wri: wriggle, write
ro try wro: wrong, wrote
se try sce: scene, scent
si try sci: science, scissors
sic try psych: psychology
sosh try soci: social
spesh try speci: special, species
squo try squa: squabble, squad
uf try euph: euphoria
uph try euph: euphoria
ur try eur: Europe
vial try viol: violin
wa try wha: whack, whale
wawl try wal: walnut
we try whe: when, wheel
wi try whi: which, while
wo try wa: wander, wash
wor try wa: water
wur try wor: work

A

aardvark
aback
abacus
  abacuses
abaft
abalone
abandon
  abandons
  abandoned
  abandoning
abandoned
abandonment
abase
  abases
  abased
  abasing
abasement
abashed
abate
  abates
  abated
  abating
abattoir
~~abbatoir~~ = abattoir
abbé
  abbés
abbess
  abbesses
abbey
  abbeys
abbot
abbreviate
  abbreviates
  abbreviated
  abbreviating
abbreviation
abdicate
  abdicates
  abdicated
  abdicating
abdomen
abdominal
abdominally
abduct
  abducts
  abducted

  abducting
abduction
abductor
abecedarian
abed
Aberavon
Aberdeen
Abergavenny
aberrant
aberration
Abertillery
Aberystwyth
abet
  abets
  abetted
  abetting
abeyance
abeyant
abhor
  abhors
  abhorred
  abhorring
abhorrence
abhorrent
abide
  abides
  abode *or*
  abided
  abiding
ability
  abilities
abject
abjection
abjectly
abjure
  abjures
  abjured
  abjuring
ablative
ablaut
ablaze
able
able-bodied
ablution
ably
abnegate

abnegates
abnegated
abnegating
abnormal
abnormality
  abnormalities
abnormally
aboard
abode
abolish
  abolishes
  abolished
  abolishing
abolishable
abolisher
abolishment
abolition
A-bomb
abominable
abominably
abominate
  abominates
  abominated
  abominating
abomination
aboriginal
aborigine
abort
  aborts
  aborted
  aborting
abortion
abortionist
abortive
abound
  abounds
  abounded
  abounding
about
above
abracadabra
abrade
  abrades
  abraded
  abrading
abrasion

abrasive
abrasively
abreast
~~abreviation~~ =
  abbreviation
abridgable
abridge
  abridges
  abridged
  abridging
abridgement
abridgment
abroad
abrogate
  abrogates
  abrogated
  abrogating
abrupt
abruptly
abruptness
abscess
  abscesses
abscond
  absconds
  absconded
  absconding
absconder
abseil
  abseils
  abseiled
  abseiling
absence
  absences
absent
  absents
  absented
  absenting
~~absense~~ = absence
absentee
absenteeism
absently
absentminded
absinth (plant)
absinthe (drink)
absolute
absolutely

1

absolution
absolutism
absolvable
absolve
　absolves
　absolved
　absolving
absolver
absorb
　absorbs
　absorbed
　absorbing
absorbability
absorbable
absorbency
absorbent
absorbent
absorbing
absorbtion =
　absorption
absorption
absorptive
abstain
　abstains
　abstained
　abstaining
abstemious
abstemiously
abstemiousness
abstention
abstinence
abstract
　abstracts
　abstracted
　abstracting
abstracted
abstractedly
abstraction
abstruse
abstrusely
abstruseness
absurd
absurdity
　absurdities
absurdly
absurdness
abundance
abundant
abundantly
abuse
　abuses
　abused
　abusing
abuser

abusive
abusively
abusiveness
abut
　abuts
　abutted
　abutting
abuzz
abysmal
abysmally
abyss
　abysses
acacia
academe
academia
academic
academically
academician
academy
　academies
acanthus
　acanthi *or*
　acanthuses
ACAS
a cappella
accede
　accedes
　acceded
　acceding
acceder
accelerate
　accelerates
　accelerated
　accelerating
acceleration
accelerative
accelerator
accent
　accents
　accented
　accenting
accentuate
　accentuates
　accentuated
　accentuating
accentuation
accept
　accepts
　accepted
　accepting
acceptability
acceptable
acceptableness
acceptably

acceptance
accepted
acceptence =
　acceptance
accepter
access
　accesses
　accessed
　accessing
accessibility
accessible
accessibly
accession
accessional
accessory
　accessories
accidence
accident
accidental
accidentally
accidently =
　accidentally
acclaim
　acclaims
　acclaimed
　acclaiming
acclaimer
acclamation
acclamatory
acclimatisation
acclimatise
　acclimatises
　acclimatised
　acclimatising
acclimatization
acclimatize
　acclimatizes
　acclimatized
　acclimatizing
acclivity
　acclivities
accolade
accommodate
　accommodates
　accommodated
　accommodating
accommodatingly
accommodation
accomodate =
　accommodate
accomodation =
　accommodation
accompaniment

accompanist
accompany
　accompanies
　accompanied
　accompanying
accomplice
accomplish
　accomplishes
　accomplished
　accomplishing
accomplishable
accomplishment
accord
　accords
　accorded
　according
accordance
according
accordingly
accordion
accordionist
accost
　accosts
　accosted
　accosting
account
　accounts
　accounted
　accounting
accountability
accountable
accountably
accountancy
accountant
accounting
accoustic = acoustic
accoutrement
Accra
accredit
　accredits
　accredited
　accrediting
accreditation
accross = across
accrue
　accrues
　accrued
　accruing
accumulable
accumulate
　accumulates
　accumulated
　accumulating
accumulation

accumulative
accumulatively
accumulativeness
accumulator
accuracy
  accuracies
accurate
accursed
accursedly
accursedness
accusal
accusation
accusative
accusatively
accuse
  accuses
  accused
  accusing
accuser
accusing
accusingly
accustom
  accustoms
  accustomed
  accustoming
accustomed
AC/DC
ace
acephalous
acerbate
  acerbates
  acerbated
  acerbating
acerbic
  acerbically
acerbity
acessory = accessory
acetate
acetic
acetone
ache
  aches
  ached
  aching
acheive = achieve
achier
achiest
achievable
achieve
  achieves
  achieved
  achieving
achievement
achiever

aching
achy
acid
acidhead
acidic
acidification
acidifier
acidify
  acidifies
  acidified
  acidifying
acidity
  acidities
acidly
acidometer
acknowledge
  acknowledges
  acknowledged
  acknowledging
acknowledgement
acknowledgment
acme
acne
acolyte
acommodate =
  accommodate
acommodation =
  accommodation
acompany =
  accompany
aconite
acording = according
acorn
acoustic
acoustically
acoustician
acoustics
acquaint
  acquaints
  acquainted
  acquainting
acquaintance
acquaintanceship
acquainted
acquiesce
  acquiesces
  acquiesced
  acquiescing
acquirable
acquire
  acquires
  acquired
  acquiring
acquirer

acquisition
acquisitive
acquisitively
acquisitiveness
acquit
  acquits
  acquitted
  acquitting
acquittal
acquittance
acre
acreage
acrid
acridity
acridness
acrilic = acrylic
acrimonious
  acrimoniously
  acrimoniousness
acrimony
  acrimonies
acrobat
acrobatic
acrobatically
acrobatics
acronym
acronymous
acrophobia
across
across-the-board
acrostically
acrylic
acs try acc
act
  acts
  acted
  acting
action
actionable
activate
  activates
  activated
  activating
active
actively
activism
activist
activity
  activities
actor
actress
  actresses
actual
actualise

actualises
actualised
actualising
actuality
  actualities
actualize
  actualizes
  actualized
  actualizing
actually
actuarial
actuary
  actuaries
actuate
  actuates
  actuated
  actuating
acuity
acumen
acupressure
acupuncture
acupuncturist
acurate = accurate
acute
acutely
acuteness
acyclic
AD
adage
adagio
  adagios
adamant
adapt
  adapts
  adapted
  adapting
adaptability
adaptable
adaptableness
adaptation
adapter
adaptive
adaptor
add
  adds
  added
  adding
addendum
  addenda
adder
addict
addiction
addictive
adding

addition
additional
additionally
additive
addle
  addles
  addled
  addling
add-on
address
  addresses
  addressed
  addressing
addressee
adduce
  adduces
  adduced
  adducing
adduceable
adducible
Adelaide
adenoid
adenoidal
adenoidectomy
  adenoidectomies
adept
adeptly
adeptness
adequacy
  adequacies
adequate
adequately
adequatly = adequately
adhere
  adheres
  adhered
  adhering
adherence
adherent
adhesion
adhesive
adhesively
adhesiveness
ad hoc
adict = addict
adieu
  adieus or
  adieux
ad infinitum
adios
adipose
adjacency
adjacent
adjacently

adjectival
adjective
adjoin
  adjoins
  adjoined
  adjoining
adjourn
  adjourns
  adjourned
  adjourning
adjournment
adjudge
  adjudges
  adjudged
  adjudging
adjudicate
  adjudicates
  adjudicated
  adjudicating
adjudication
adjudicative
adjudicator
adjunct
adjure
  adjures
  adjured
  adjuring
adjust
  adjusts
  adjusted
  adjusting
adjustable
adjuster
adjustment
adjutant
ad-lib
  ad-libs
  ad-libbed
  ad-libbing
ad-libber
admeasure
  admeasures
  admeasured
  admeasuring
admin
administer
  administers
  administered
  administering
administrate
  administrates
  administrated
  administrating
administration

administrative
administratively
administrator
admirable
  admirably
admiral
admiralty
  admiralties
admiration
admire
  admires
  admired
  admiring
admirer
admiringly
admision = admission
admissable =
  admissible
admissibility
admissible
admission
admit
  admits
  admitted
  admitting
admittance
admittedly
admixture
admonish
  admonishes
  admonished
  admonishing
admonition
ad nauseam
ad nauseum = ad
  nauseam
ado
adobe
adolescence
adolescent
adolesent = adolescent
Adonis
adopt
  adopts
  adopted
  adopting
adopted
adoption
adoptive
adorable
adorably
adoration
adore
  adores

adored
adoring
adorer
adoring
adoringly
adorn
  adorns
  adorned
  adorning
adornment
adrenal
adrenaline
adress = address
Adriatic
adrift
adroit
adroitly
adroitness
adulation
adulatory
adult
adulterate
  adulterates
  adulterated
  adulterating
adulteration
adulterer
adulteress
  adulteresses
adulterous
adulterously
adultery
  adulteries
adulthood
advance
  advances
  advanced
  advancing
advanced
advancement
advances
advancingly
advantage
  advantages
advantageous
advantageously
advent
Advent
adventitious
adventure
  adventures
adventurer
adventurism
adventurous

adventurously
adverb
adverbial
adverbially
adversarial
adversary
　adversaries
adverse
adversely
adversity
　adversities
advert
advertise
　advertises
　advertised
　advertising
advertisement
advertisment =
　advertisement
advertiser
advertising
advice
advisability
advisable
advisableness
advisably
advise
　advises
　advised
　advising
advised
advisedly
adviser
advisor
advisory
advocaat
advocacy
　advocacies
advocate
　advocates
　advocated
　advocating
adze
　adzes
Aegean
Aegean Sea
aegis
aeon
　aeons
aerate
　aerates
　aerated
　aerating
aeration

aerial
aerobatics
aerobic
aerobics
aerodrome
　aerodromes
aerodynamic
aerodynamics
aerofoil
aerogram
　aerograms
aerogramme
　aerogrammes
aeronautical
aeronautics
aeroplane
aerosol
aerospace
aesthete
aesthetic
aesthetically
aesthetician
aestheticism
aesthetics
aether
aethereal
afar
affability
affable
affair
affect
　affects
　affected
　affecting
affectation
affected
affectedly
affectedness
affection
affectionate
affectionately
affidavit
　affidavits
affiliate
　affiliates
　affiliated
　affiliating
affinity
　affinities
affirm
　affirms
　affirmed
　affirming
affirmation

affirmative
　affirmatives
affirmatively
affix
　affixes
　affixed
　affixing
afflict
　afflicts
　afflicted
　afflicting
affliction
affluence
affluent
afford
　affords
　afforded
　affording
affordability
affordable
afforest
　afforests
　afforested
　afforesting
afforestation
affray
affront
　affronts
　affronted
　affronting
affusion
afghan
Afghan
Afghanistan
aficionado
　aficionados
afield
afloat
aflutter
afoot
aforementioned
aforesaid
afraid
afresh
African
African-American
Afrikaans
Afrikaner
Afro
　Afros
aft
after
afterbirth
aftercare

afterdeck
aftereffect
afterglow
afterlife
　afterlives
aftermath
afternoon
afterpains
afters
aftershave
　aftershaves
aftershock
aftertaste
afterthought
afterwards
afterword
Aga
　Agas
again
against
agape (= wide open)
Agape (= Christian
　love)
agate
　agates
age
　ages
　aged
　ageing or
　aging
aged
ageing
ageism
ageless
agency
　agencies
agenda
　agendas
agent
agentive
agent provocateur
　agents provocateurs
ages
agglomerate
　agglomerates
　agglomerated
　agglomerating
agglomeration
aggrandisement
aggrandizement
aggravate
　aggravates
　aggravated
　aggravating

aggravation
aggregate
  aggregates
  aggregated
  aggregating
aggregation
aggregative
aggression
aggressive
aggressively
aggressiveness
aggressor
aggrieve
  aggrieves
  aggrieved
  aggrieving
aggrieved
aggrievedly
aggro
aghast
agile
agility
agin
aging
agism
agist
agitate
  agitates
  agitated
  agitating
agitated
agitatedly
agitation
agitato
agitator
AGM
agnostic
agnosticism
ago
agog
agonise
  agonises
  agonised
  agonising
agonize
  agonizes
  agonized
  agonizing
agonizingly
agony
  agonies
agoraphobia
agoraphobic
agrarian

agrarianism
agree
  agrees
  agreed
  agreeing
agreeable
agreeableness
agreeably
agreed
agreeing
agreement
agrees
agression = aggression
agressive = aggressive
agribusiness
  agribusinesses
agricultural
agriculturalist
agriculture
agrochemical
agronomist
agronomy
aground
ague
  agues
ah
aha
ahead
ahem
ahoy
AI
aid (= help → aide)
  aids
  aided
  aiding
aide (= military
  officer → aid)
aide-de-camp
  aides-de-camp
aide-mémoire
  aides-mémoire
AIDS
aikido
ail (= be unwell
  → ale)
ails
ailed
ailing
ailerons
ailing
ailment
aim
  aims
  aimed

aiming
aimless
aimlessly
aimlessness
ain't
äioli
air try aer
air (= let in air
  → e'er, ere, heir)
airs
aired
airing
airborne
airbrick
Airbus
aircraft
  aircraft
aircraftman
  aircraftmen
aircraftsman
  aircraftsmen
aircrew
airdrop
Airedale
airfield
airier
airiest
airily
airiness
airing
airless
airlift
  airlifts
  airlifted
  airlifting
airline
  airlines
airliner
airlock
airmail
airman
  airmen
airplane
airport
airs
airship
airshow
airsick
airspace
airspeed
airstrip
airtight
airtime
airwaves

airway
airworthy
airy (= open to the air
  → eyrie)
  airier
  airiest
aisle (= passage or
  corridor → isle)
  aisles
aitch
  aitches
aitchbone
  aitchbones
ajar
akimbo
akin
aknowledge =
  acknowledge
alabaster
à la carte
alack
alacritous
alacrity
à la mode
alarm
  alarms
  alarmed
  alarming
alarmed
alarming
alarmingly
alarmism
alarmist
alas
Albania
Albanian
albatross
  albatrosses
albeit
albinism
albino
  albinos
album
albumen
albumin
alchemist
alchemy
  alchemies
alcohol
alcoholic
alcoholise
  alcoholises
  alcoholised
  alcoholising

alcoholism
alcoholize
　alcoholizes
　alcoholized
　alcoholizing
alcove
　alcoves
Aldeburgh
aldehyde
　aldehydes
alder
alderman
　aldermen
ale (= beer → ail)
　ales
alehouse
~~alein~~ = alien
alert
　alerts
　alerted
　alerting
alertly
alertness
alewife
　alewives
Alexander
Alexandra
Alexandrian
Alexandrine
alfalfa
　alfalfas
alfresco
algae
algal
algebra
　algebras
algebraic
Algeria
Algerian
algicide
algorithm
alias
　aliases
alibi
　alibis
alien
alienable
alienate
　alienates
　alienated
　alienating
alienation
alight
　alights

alighted *or*
alit
　alighting
align
　aligns
　aligned
　aligning
alignment
　alignments
alike
aliment
alimentary
alimentation
alimony
　alimonies
alit
alive
alkali
　alkalis *or*
　alkalies
alkaline
alkalinity
alkaloid
all (= every one of
　→ awl)
Allah
allargando
allay
　allays
　allayed
　allaying
~~alledged~~ = alleged
allegation
allege
　alleges
　alleged
　alleging
alleged
allegedly
allegiance
　allegiances
~~allegience~~ = allegiance
allegorical
allegorise
　allegorises
　allegorised
　allegorising
allegorize
　allegorizes
　allegorized
　allegorizing
allegory
　allegories
allegretto

allegrettos
allegro
　allegros
alleluia
allergen
allergic
allergist
allergy
　allergies
alleviate
　alleviates
　alleviated
　alleviating
alleviation
alleviative
alley
alleyway
All Hallows
alliance
allied
allies
alligator
alliterate
　alliterates
　alliterated
　alliterating
alliteration
alliterative
~~allmost~~ = almost
allocate
　allocates
　allocated
　allocating
allocation
allocution
allopath
allopathic
allopathy
allot
　allots
　allotted
　allotting
allotment
allow
　allows
　allowed
　allowing
allowable
allowably
allowance
　allowances
alloy
~~allready~~ = already
allspice

~~allthough~~ = although
allude
　alludes
　alluded
　alluding
allure
　allures
　allured
　alluring
alluring
alluringly
allusion
alluvial
alluvion
alluvium
~~allways~~ = always
ally
　allies
　allied
　allying
alma mater
　alma maters
almanac
almightily
almightiness
almighty
Almighty
almond
almost
alms (= gifts for the
　poor → arms)
almshouse
　almshouses
Alnwick
aloe
　aloes
aloft
alone
along
alongside
aloof
aloud
alpaca
　alpacas
alpha
　alphas
alphabet
alphabetical
alphabetically
alphabetise
　alphabetises
　alphabetised
　alphabetising
alphabetize

alphabetizes
alphabetized
alphabetizing
alpha-fetoprotein
alpine
alpinist
already
alright
Alsatian
also
alstroemeria
　alstroemerias
altar (= structure in
　church → alter)
altarpiece
alter (= change
　→ altar)
　alters
　altered
　altering
alteration
altercate
　altercates
　altercated
　altercating
altercation
alternate
　alternates
　alternated
　alternating
alternately
alternation
alternative
　alternatives
alternatively
alternativeness
alternator
although
altimeter
altissimo
altitude
alto
　altos
altogether
Altrincham
altruism
altruistic
altruistically
alum
aluminium
alumna
　alumnae
alumnus
　alumni

always
am
a.m.
AM
amalgam
amalgamate
　amalgamates
　amalgamated
　amalgamating
amalgamation
amanuensis
　amanuenses
amaryllis
amass
　amasses
　amassed
　amassing
amateur
amateurish
amatory
~~amatuer~~ = amateur
amaze
　amazes
　amazed
　amazing
amazement
amazing
amazingly
Amazon
ambassador
ambassadorial
ambassadorship
amber
ambergris
ambidextrous
ambience
ambient
ambiguity
　ambiguities
ambiguous
ambiguously
ambiguousness
ambit
ambition
ambitious
ambitiously
ambitiousness
ambivalence
ambivalent
amble
　ambles
　ambled
　ambling
ambrosia

ambrosian
ambulance
ambulant
ambulatory
ambuscade
ambush
　ambushes
　ambushed
　ambushing
ameliorable
ameliorate
　ameliorates
　ameliorated
　ameliorating
amelioration
amen
Amen
amenability
amenable
amend (= put right
　→ emend)
　amends
　amended
　amending
amendable
amendment
amends
amenity
　amenities
amenorrhoea
American
Americana
Americanise
　Americanises
　Americanised
　Americanising
Americanism
Americanize
　Americanizes
　Americanized
　Americanizing
Amerindian
amethyst
amiability
amiable
amiably
amicable
amicably
amid
amidships
amidst
amigo
amino acid
Amish

amiss
amity
　amities
ammeter
ammo
ammonia
　ammonias
ammonite
ammonium
ammunition
amnesia
amnesiac
amnesty
　amnesties
amniocentesis
　amniocenteses
amniotic
amoeba
　amoebae or
　amoebas
amoebic
amok
among
amongst
amontillado
　amontillados
amoral
amorality
amorous
amorphous
amorphously
amorphousness
amortise
　amortises
　amortised
　amortising
amount
amour
amp
amperage
ampere
ampersand
amphetamine
amphibian
amphibious
amphitheatre
ampicillin
ample
amplification
amplifier
amplify
　amplifies
　amplified
　amplifying

amplitude
amply
ampoule
amputate
amputates
amputated
amputating
amputee
amuck
amulet
amuse
amuses
amused
amusing
amusement
amusing
amusingly
an
Anabaptist
anabolic
anachronic
anachronism
anachronistic
anachronistically
anaconda
anaemia
anaemic
anaerobic
anaesthesia
anaesthetic
anaesthetics
anaesthetise
anaesthetises
anaesthetised
anaesthetising
anaesthetist
anaesthetization
anaesthetize
anaesthetizes
anaesthetized
anaesthetizing
Anaglypta
anagram
anal
analgesia
analgesic
analog
analogous
analogously
analogue
analogues
analogy
analogies
analyse

analyses
analysed
analysing
analysis
analyses
analyst
analytic
analytical
anaphoric
anarchic
anarchical
anarchically
anarchism
anarchist
anarchy
anarchies
anastigmatic
anathema
anathematise
anathematises
anathematised
anathematising
anathematize
anathematizes
anathematized
anathematizing
Anatolian
anatomical
anatomist
anatomy
anatomies
ANC
ancestor
ancestral
ancestry
ancestries
anchor
anchors
anchored
anchoring
anchorage
anchorite
anchorman
anchormen
anchovy
anchovies
ancient
ancillary
ancillaries
and
andante
andantes
andantino
andiron

androgynous
androgyny
android
anemometer
anemone
anencephalic
anencephaly
anenome = anemone
aneroid
anesthetic
anew
angel
angelfish
angelic
angelica
angelically
Angelus
anger
angers
angered
angering
angina
angle
angles
angled
angling
angler
Anglesey
Anglian
Anglican
Anglicanism
anglicise
anglicises
anglicised
anglicising
Anglicism
anglicize
anglicizes
anglicized
anglicizing
angling
Anglo
Anglophile
Anglophobe
Anglophone
Angola
angora
angry
angrier
angriest
angst
anguish
anguished
angular

angularity
anihilation =
annihilation
anima
animal
animate
animates
animated
animating
animated
animatedly
animation
animato
animator
animosity
animosities
aniseed
ankle
anklebone
anklet
ankylosaur
ankylosis
annals
annelid
annex (= take control
of → annexe)
annexes
annexed
annexing
annexation
annexe (= building
→ annex)
annihilate
annihilates
annihilated
annihilating
annihilation
annihilator
anniversary
anniversaries
anno Domini
anonymous =
anonymous
annotate
annotates
annotated
annotating
annotation
announce
announces
announced
announcing
announcement
announcer

annoy
  annoys
  annoyed
  annoying
annoyance
annoyer
annoyingly
annual
annuity
  annuities
annul
  annuls
  annulled
  annulling
annulment
Annunciation
anode
anodise
  anodises
  anodised
  anodising
anodize
  anodizes
  anodized
  anodizing
anodyne
anoint
  anoints
  anointed
  annointing
anointer
anointment
anomalous
anomalously
anomalousness
anomaly
  anomalies
anon
anonymity
anonymous
anonymously
anonymousness
anorak
anorexia
anorexic
another
Anschluss
answer
  answers
  answered
  answering
answerable
ant
antacid

antagonise
  antagonises
  antagonised
  antagonising
antagonism
antagonist
antagonistic
antagonistically
antagonize
  antagonizes
  antagonized
  antagonizing
Antarctic
Antartic = Antarctic
ante- (= before
    → anti-)
anteater
antecedent
antechamber
antedate
  antedates
  antedated
  antedating
antediluvian
antelope
antemeridian
antenatal
antenna
  antennae (= part of
    insect) or
  antennas (= aerial)
antepenultimate
anterior
anteriority
anteroom
anthem
anther
anthological
anthology
  anthologies
Anthony
anthracite
anthrax
anthropic
anthropocentric
anthropogenesis
anthropoid
anthropological
anthropology
anthropomorphic
anthropomorphism
anti try ante
anti- (= against
    → ante-)

antibiotic
antibody
  antibodies
antic
Antichrist
anticipate
  anticipates
  anticipated
  anticipating
anticipation
anticlimactic
anticlimax
  anticlimaxes
anticlockwise
anticoagulant
anticonvulsant
antics
anticyclone
  anticyclones
anticyclonic
antidepressant
antidote
antifreeze
antigen
antiglobulin
antihero
  antiheroes
antihistamine
anti-inflammatory
antilogarithm
antimacassar
antimagnetic
antimalarial
antimatter
antinuclear
antioxidant
antipasto
  antipastos
antipathetic
antipathy
  antipathies
antiperistalsis
antipersonnel
antiperspirant
antipodean
antipodes
antiquarian
antiquary
  antiquaries
antiquated
antique
antiquity
  antiquities
antirrhinum

antirrhinums
anti-Semite
antiseptic
antiserum
antisocial
antithesis
  antitheses
antitoxin
antitrust
antler
Antony
antonym
antonymous
anus
  anuses
anvil
anxiety
  anxieties
anxious
anxiously
any
anybody
anyhow
anymore
anyone
anyplace
anyroad
anything
anyway
anywhere
Anzac
AOB
A-OK
A-okay
A-one
aorta
  aortae or
  aortas
aortal
aortic
apace
Apache
apalling = appalling
aparatus = apparatus
aparent = apparent
aparently = apparently
apart
apartheid
apartment
apathetic
apathy
ape
apear = appear
apeman

apemen
apéritif
apéritifs
aperture
apery
aperies
apetite = appetite
apex
apexes *or*
apices
APEX
aphid
aphids
aphis
aphrodisiac
apiarist
apiary
apiaries
apices
apiece
apish
aplenty
aplomb
apocalypse
apocalypses
apocalyptic
apocalyptically
apocryphal
apolitical
apologetic
apologetically
apologia
apologise
apologises
apologised
apologising
apologist
apologize
apologizes
apologized
apologizing
apology
apologies
apoplectic
apoplexy
apostasy
apostasies
apostate
apostatical
a posteriori
apostle
apostolic
apostrophe
apostrophise

apostrophises
apostrophised
apostrophising
apostrophize
apostrophizes
apostrophized
apostrophizing
apothecary
apothecaries
apotheosis
apotheoses
appal
appals
appalled
appalling
Appalachian
appallingly
Appaloosa
apparantly =
apparently
apparatus
apparatus *or*
apparatuses
apparel
apparent
apparently
apparition
appartment =
apartment
appassionato
appeal
appeals
appealed
appealing
appealing
appealingly
appear
appears
appeared
appearing
appearance
appearence =
appearance
appeasable
appease
appeases
appeased
appeasing
appeasement
appellant
appellate
appellation
append
appends

appended
appending
appendage
appendicectomy
appendicectomies
appendicitis
appendix
appendixes *or*
appendices
appertain
appertains
appertained
appertaining
appetiser
appetising
appetite
appetizer
appetizing
applaud
applauds
applauded
applauding
applauding
applaudingly
applause
apple
Appleby
applecart
applejack
appliance
applicable
applicant
application
applicator
applied
appliqué
appoint
appoints
appointed
appointing
appointee
appointees
appointment
appologize = apologize
appology = apology
apportion
apportions
apportioned
apportioning
apportionment
apposite
apposition
appraisal
appraise

appraises
appraised
appraising
appraiser
appreciable
appreciably
appreciate
appreciates
appreciated
appreciating
appreciation
appreciative
appreciatively
apprehend
apprehends
apprehended
apprehending
apprehension
apprehensive
apprentice
apprenticeship
apprise
apprises
apprised
apprising
apprize
apprizes
apprized
apprizing
approach
approaches
approached
approaching
approachability
approachable
approachableness
approbation
approch = approach
appropriacy
appropriate
appropriates
appropriated
appropriating
appropriately
appropriateness
appropriation
approval
approve
approves
approved
approving
approved
approx.
approximate

approximates
approximated
approximating
approximately
approximation
approximative
approximatly =
   approximately
appurtenance
APR
apreciate = appreciate
après-ski
aproximately =
   approximately
apricot
April
a priori
apron
apropos
apse
apt
aptitude
aquaduct = aqueduct
aquaerobics
aquaint = acquaint
aquaintance =
   acquaintance
aqualung
aquamarine
aquaphobia
aquaplane
  aquaplanes
  aquaplaned
  aquaplaning
aquarist
aquarium
Aquarius
aquatic
aquatics
aquatint
aqueduct
aqueous
aquifer
aquilegia
aquiline
aquire = acquire
aquit = acquit
arabesque
Arabian
Arabic
arable
arachnid
arachnophobia
Araldite®

Aran
arbiter
arbitrage
arbitrageur
arbitrarily
arbitrariness
arbitrary
arbitrate
  arbitrates
  arbitrated
  arbitrating
arbitration
arboreal
arboretum
arboriculture
arbour
arc
arcade
Arcadian
arcane
arcanely
arcaneness
arch
  arches
  arched
  arching
archaeological
archaeology
archaic
archaically
archaism
archangel
archbishop
archbishopric
archdeacon
archdeaconry
  archdeaconries
archdiocese
  archdioceses
archducal
archduchess
  archduchesses
archduchy
  archduchies
archduke
  archdukes
arched
archeological
archeology
archer
archery
archetype
archetypical
archfiend

archimandrite
Archimedes
arching
archipelago
architect
architectural
architecturally
architecture
architrave
archival
archive
archivist
archly
archway
arcs
Arctic
ardent
ardently
ardour
arduous
are
area
arena
aren't
areola
areolar
areolate
areole
arête
argent
Argentina
argie-bargie
argon
Argonaut
argot
arguable
arguably
argue
  argues
  argued
  arguing
argueing = arguing
arguement = argument
argument
argumentation
argumentative
Argus
argy-bargy
  argy-bargies
Argyll
aria
arid
aridity
Aries

aright
arise
  arises
  arose
  arisen
  arising
aristocracy
  aristocracies
aristocrat
aristocratic
arithmetic
arithmetical
arithmetically
arithmetician
ark
Ark
arm
  arms
  armed
  arming
armada
armadillo
  armadillos
Armageddon
Armagh
Armagnac
Armalite®
armament
armature
armband
armchair
armed
Armenia
Armenian
armful
armhole
arming
armistice
  armistices
armoire
armour
armoured
armoury
  armouries
armpit
armrest
arms (= weapons
  → alms)
army
  armies
arnica
aroma
  aromas
aromatherapist

aromatherapy
aromatic
aromaticity
arose
around
arousal
arouse
  arouses
  aroused
  arousing
arpeggio
  arpeggios
arraign
  arraigns
  arraigned
  arraigning
arraignment
arrange
  arranges
  arranged
  arranging
arrangement
arranger
arrant
array
  arrays
  arrayed
  arraying
arrears
arrest
arrestingly
arrhythmia
arrival
arrive
  arrives
  arrived
  arriving
arrivederci
arrivisme
arriviste
arrogance
arrogant
arrogantly
arrogate
  arrogates
  arrogated
  arrogating
arrow
arrowroot
arrows
arse
arsehole
arsenal
arsenic

arson
art
artefact
arterial
arterially
arteriosclerosis
  arterioscleroses
artery
  arteries
Artex®
artful
artfully
artfulness
arthritic
arthritis
arthropod
Arthurian
artic
Artic = Arctic
artichoke
article
articulacy
articulate
  articulates
  articulated
  articulating
articulately
articulation
articulatory
artier
artiest
artifact
artifice
  artifices
artificial
artificialise
artificiality
artificially
artillery
artilleryman
  artillerymen
artisan
artisanal
artist (= painter, etc.
  → artiste)
artiste (= performer
  → artist)
artistic
artistically
artistry
artless
artlessly
arts
artwork

arty
  artier
  artiest
arty-crafty
Arundel
Aryan
as
asafetida
asafoetida
a.s.a.p.
asbestos
asbestosis
ascend
  ascends
  ascended
  ascending
ascendancy
ascendant
ascendency
ascendent
ascending
ascension
Ascension
ascent
ascertain
  ascertains
  ascertained
  ascertaining
ascetic
ascetically
asceticism
ASCII
ascot
ascribable
ascribe
  ascribes
  ascribed
  ascribing
ASEAN
aseptic
asexual
asexually
ash
  ashes
ashamed
ashamedly
ashen
ashes
ashore
ashphalt = asphalt
ashram
ashtray
ashy
Asia

Asian
Asiatic
aside
asinine
asininity
ask
  asks
  asked
  asking
askance
askew
asleep
ASLEF
asociation =
  association
asp
asparagus
aspect
aspen
asperity
  asperities
aspersion
asphalt
  asphalts
  asphalted
  asphalting
asphyxia
asphyxiate
  asphyxiates
  asphyxiated
  asphyxiating
asphyxiation
aspic
aspidistra
  aspidistras
aspirate
  aspirates
  aspirated
  aspirating
aspiration
aspire
  aspires
  aspired
  aspiring
aspirin
asprin = aspirin
asquint
ass
  asses
assail
  assails
  assailed
  assailing
assailable

assailant
assam
assasin = assassin
assassin
assassinate
  assassinates
  assassinated
  assassinating
assassination
assault
  assaults
  assaulted
  assaulting
assay
  assays
  assayed
  assaying
assemblage
assemble
  assembles
  assembled
  assembling
assembly
  assemblies
assent
  assents
  assented
  assenting
assert
  asserts
  asserted
  asserting
assertion
assertive
assertively
assertiveness
assess
  assesses
  assessed
  assessing
assessment
assessor
asset
assiduity
assiduous
assiduously
assign
  assigns
  assigned
  assigning
assignable
assignation
assignment
assimilable

assimilate
  assimilates
  assimilated
  assimilitating
assimilation
assimilative
assimilatory
assist
  assists
  assisted
  assisting
assistance
assistant
assister
assizes
associate
  associates
  associated
  associating
associateship
association
associative
assonance
assort
  assorts
  assorted
  assorting
assorted
assortment
assuage
  assuages
  assuaged
  assuaging
assumable
assume
  assumes
  assumed
  assuming
assumed
assumption
Assumption
assurance
assure
  assures
  assured
  assuring
assuredly
assuredness
Assyrian
aster
asterisk
  asterisks
  asterisked
  asterisking

astern
asteroid
asthma
asthmatic
asthmatically
astigmatic
astigmatism
astir
astonish
  astonishes
  astonished
  astonishing
astonishingly
astonishment
astound
  astounds
  astounded
  astounding
astoundingly
astrakhan
astral
astray
astride
astringence
astringency
astringent
astrologer
astrological
astrologist
astrology
astronaut
astronomer
astronomical
astronomically
astronomy
astrophysics
astute
astutely
astuteness
asunder
asylum
asymmetric
  asymmetrical
  asymmetrically
asymmetry
asymptomatic
asymptomatically
at
atavism
atavistic
ate (= consumed food
  → eight)
atempt = attempt
atheism

atheist
atherosclerosis
athiest = atheist
athlete
athletic
athletically
athleticism
athletics
athwart
atilt
atitude = attitude
Atlantic
atlas
  atlases
atmosphere
atmospheric
atmospherically
atmospherics
atoll
atom
atomic
atomise
  atomises
  atomised
  atomising
atomiser
atomize
  atomizes
  atomized
  atomizing
atomizer
atonal
atonality
atonally
atone
  atones
  atoned
  atoning
atonement
atop
atopic
atrium
atrocious
atrociously
atrocity
  atrocities
atrophy
  atrophies
  atrophied
  atrophying
attaboy
attach
  attaches
  attached

attaching
attaché
attached
attachment
attack
  attacks
  attacked
  attacking
attackable
attacker
attain
  attains
  attained
  attaining
attainability
attainable
attainment
attempt
  attempts
  attempted
  attempting
attemptable
attend
  attends
  attended
  attending
attendance
attendant
attention
attentive
attentively
attentiveness
attenuate
  attenuates
  attenuated
  attenuating
attenuation
attest
  attests
  attested
  attesting
attestable
attestation
attested
attic
attire
attitude
Attlee, Clement
attorney
  attorneys
attorneyship
attract
  attracts
  attracted

attracting
attractant
attraction
attractive
attractively
attractiveness
attractor
attributable
attribute
  attributes
  attributed
  attributing
attribution
attributive
attributively
attrition
attune
atypical
atypically
auberge
aubergine
aubretia
aubrietia
auburn
Auchterader
Auchtermuchty
Auckland
auction
  auctions
  auctioned
  auctioning
auctioneer
audacious
audaciously
audacity
~~audiance~~ = audience
audibility
audible
audibly
audience
audio
audiogram
audiotypist
audiovisual
audit
  audits
  audited
  auditing
audition
auditor
auditorium
  auditoria or
  auditoriums
auditory

au fait
Augean
auger (= tool
  → augur)
aught
augment
  augments
  augmented
  augmenting
augmentation
augmentative
augur (= be a sign of
  → auger)
  augurs
  augured
  auguring
augury
august
August
auk
auld
aunt
auntie
aunty
  aunties
aura
  auras or
  aurae
aural
aureole
au revoir
auricle
auricular
aurora
  aurorae or
  auroras
aurora borealis
auroral
auspices
auspicious
Aussie
Austen, Jane
austere
austerely
austerity
Australasia
Australasian
Australia
Australian
Austria
Austrian
autarchic
autarchy
  autarchies

authentic
authentically
authenticate
  authenticates
  authenticated
  authenticating
authentication
authenticator
authenticity
author
  authors
  authored
  authoring
authoress
  authoresses
authorial
authorisation
authorise
  authorises
  authorised
  authorising
authoritarian
authoritarianism
authoritative
authoritatively
authority
  authorities
authorize
  authorizes
  authorized
  authorizing
authorship
autism
autistic
auto
  autos
autobahn
autobiographical
autobiography
  autobiographies
autocracy
  autocracies
autocrat
autocratic
autocross
auto-da-fé
  autos-da-fé
autograph
  autographs
  autographed
  autographing
autoimmune
automate
  automates

automated
automating
automatic
automation
automaton
automobile
automotive
autonomous
autonomously
autonomy
  autonomies
autopilot
autopsy
  autopsies
autoroute
  autoroutes
autos-da-fé
~~autum~~ = autumn
autumn
autumnal
auxiliary
  auxiliaries
~~auxillary~~ = auxiliary
avail
  avails
  availed
  availing
availability
available
availably
~~availible~~ = available
avalanche
  avalanches
avant-garde
avarice
avaricious
avariciously
avatar
avenge
  avenges

avenged
avenging
avenger
avenue
aver
  avers
  averred
  averring
average
  averages
  averaged
  averaging
  averagely
averment
averred
averring
averse
aversely
aversion
avert
  averts
  averted
  averting
avgolemono
avian
aviary
  aviaries
aviation
aviator
avid
avidity
avidly
avocado
  avocados
avocation
avocet
avoid
  avoids
  avoided
  avoiding

avoidable
avoidably
avoidance
avoider
avoirdupois
avow
  avows
  avowed
  avowing
avowal
avowed
avuncular
await
  awaits
  awaited
  awaiting
awake
  awakes
  awaked *or*
  awoke
  awaked *or*
  awoken
  awaking
awaken
  awakens
  awakened
  awakening
awakes
awaking
award
  awards
  awarded
  awarding
awardable
aware
awareness
awash
away
awe (= feeling of
  wonder → oar, or, ore)

awes
awed
awing
~~aweful~~ = awful
awesome
awful
awfully
awfulness
awkward
awl (= tool → all)
awkward
awkwardness
awning
awoke
awoken
AWOL
awry
axe
  axes
  axed
  axing
axeman
  axemen
axes
axiom
axiomatic
axis
  axes
axle
ay try eye
ay
ayah
ayatollah
aye (= yes → eye)
Aylesbury
Ayr
azalea
Azerbaijan
Aztec
azure

B

BA
baa
  baas
  baaed
  baaing
baba
babble
  babbles
  babbled
  babbling
babbler
babe
Babel
baboon
babushka
  babushkas
baby
baby-boomer
Baby-bouncer™
babyhood
babyish
Babylonian
babysit
  babysits
  babysat
  babysitting
babysitter
baccalaureate
baccarat
bacchanal
bacchanalia
bacchanalian
Bacchic
baccy
Bach, Johann
  Sebastian
bachelor
bacillary
bacillus
  bacilli
back
  backs
  backed
  backing
backache
backbeat

backbench
backbencher
backbiter
backbiting
backboard
backbone
backbreaking
backchat
backcloth
  backcloths
backcomb
  backcombs
  backcombed
  backcombing
backdate
  backdates
  backdated
  backdating
backdown
backdrop
backed
backer
backfill
  backfills
  backfilled
  backfilling
backfire
  backfires
  backfired
  backfiring
backgammon
background
backhand
backhanded
backhander
backing
backlash
backlog
backpack
  backpacks
  backpacked
  backpacking
backpedal
  backpedals
  backpedalled
  backpedalling

backscratcher
backside
backslapping
backslide
  backslides
  backslid
  backsliding
backspace
backspin
backstage
backstairs
backstitch
backstreet
backstroke
backtrack
  backtracks
  backtracked
  backtracking
backup
backward
backwardation
backwards
backwash
backwater
backwoods
backwoodsman
  backwoodsmen
baclava
bacon
bacteria
bacterial
bactericide
bacteriological
bacteriologically
bacteriologist
bacteriology
bacterium
  bacteria
Bacup
bad
  worse
  worst
baddie
  baddies
baddy
  baddies

bade
badge
badger
  badgers
  badgered
  badgering
badinage
badlands
badly
badminton
badmouth
  badmouths
  badmouthed
  badmouthing
baffle
  baffles
  baffled
  baffling
bafflement
bag
  bags
  bagged
  bagging
bagatelle
bagel
baggage
  baggages
bagged
bagging
baggy
  baggier
  baggiest
bagpipes
bags
baguet
baguette
bah
Bahamiam
Bahraini
Bahreini
bail (= money; empty
  out water → bale)
  bails
  bailed
  bailing
bailey

baileys
bailiff
bain-marie
  bains-marie
bairn
bait (= try to catch;
  torment → baked)
  baits
  baited
  baiting
baize
bake
  bakes
  baked
  baking
Bakelite®
baker
bakery
  bakeries
baking
baklava
baksheesh
balalaika
  balalaikas
balance
  balances
  balanced
  balancing
balanced
balcony
  balconies
bald
  balder
  baldest
balderdash
baldheaded
balding
baldy
baldness
bale (= bundle; jump
  out of aircraft → bail)
  bales
  baled
  baling
Balearic
baleen
baleful
balefully
balence = balance
baler
balk
  balks
  balked
  balking

Balkan
ball (= round object
  → bawl)
ballad
balladeer
ballast
ballerina
  ballerinas
ballet
balletic
ballistic
ballistics
balloon
  balloons
  ballooned
  ballooning
ballooning
balloonist
ballot
  ballots
  balloted
  balloting
ballpark
ballpoint
ballroom
balls
bally
ballyhoo
balm
balmier
balmiest
balmy (= warm
  → barmy)
  balmier
  balmiest
baloney
baloon = balloon
balsa
balsam
balsamic
Baltic
balustrade
bambino
  bambinos or
  bambini
bamboo
bamboozle
bamboozles
bamboozled
bamboozling
bamboozler
ban
bans (= forbid
  → banns)

banned
banning
banal
banality
  banalities
banally
banana
  bananas
bancrupcy =
  bankruptcy
band
  bands
  banded
  banding
bandage
  bandages
  bandaged
  bandaging
bandana
bandanna
bandicoot
bandier
bandies
bandiest
bandit
bandmaster
bandoleer
bandolier
bandsman
  bandsmen
bandstand
bandwagon
bandy
  bandies
  bandied
  bandying
bandy-legged
bane
baneful
banefully
bang
  bangs
  banged
  banging
banger
Bangkok
Bangladesh
Bangladeshi
bangle
banish
  banishes
  banished
  banishing
banishment

banisters
banjo
bank
  banks
  banked
  banking
bankable
banker
banking
banknote
bankroll
  bankrolls
  bankrolled
  bankrolling
bankrupt
  bankrupts
  bankrupted
  bankrupting
bankruptcy
  bankruptcies
banksman
  banksmen
banlieue
  banlieues
banned
banner
banning
bannisters
bannock
banns (= for a
  wedding → bans)
banquet
  banquets
  banqueted
  banqueting
banshee
bantam
bantamweight
banter
  banters
  bantered
  bantering
Bantu
banyan
baobab
bap
baptise
  baptises
  baptised
  baptising
baptism
baptismal
Baptist
baptize

baptizes
baptized
baptizing
bar
  bars
  barred
  barring
Bar
barb
Barbadian
barbarian
barbarianism
barbaric
barbarically
barbarise
  barbarises
  barbarised
  barbarising
barbarism
barbarity
  barbarities
barbarize
barbarous
barbarously
barbecue
  barbecues
  barbecued
  barbecuing
barbed
barbed wire
barbell
barbeque = barbecue
barber
barbershop
barbican
barbie
  barbies
barbiturate
bard
bare (= without a
  covering → bear)
  bares
  bared
  baring
  barer
  barest
bareback
barefaced
barefacedly
barefoot
barely
bareness
bargain
  bargains

bargained
bargaining
barge
  barges
  barged
  barging
bargee
  bargees
bargepole
bargin = bargain
baric
baritone
barium
bark (= make noise
  like a dog → barque)
  barks
  barked
  barking
barley
  barleys
barleycorn
barmaid
barman
barmen
barmy (= mad
  → balmy)
  barmier
  barmiest
barn
barnacle
barney
  barneys
Barnsley
Barnstaple
barnstorm
  barnstorms
  barnstormed
  barnstorming
barnyard
barometer
barometric
barometry
baron (= nobleman
  → barren)
baronage
baroness
  baronesses
baronet
baronetcy
  baronetcies
baronial
barony
  baronies
baroque

baroscope
baroscopic
barperson
  barpersons
barque (= sailing ship
  → bark)
barrack
  barracks
  barracked
  barracking
barracks
barracuda
  barracuda or
  barracudas
barrage
barred
barrel
barrelchested
barrelful
barren (= unfruitful
  → baron)
barrette
barricade
  barricades
  barricaded
  barricading
barrier
barring
barrio
barrister
barrow
barrowful
bars
bartender
barter
  barters
  bartered
  bartering
bartsia
basal
basalt
basaltic
base
  bases
  based
  basing
baseball
baseboard
Basel
baseless
baseline
basely
baseman
  basemen

basement
baseness
bases
bash
  bashes
  bashed
  bashing
bashful
bashfully
bashfulness
basic
basically
basicly = basically
basics
basil
basilica
basilisk
basin
basinful
basis
  bases
bask
  basks
  basked
  basking
basket
basketball
basketful
basketry
basketwork
Basque
bas-relief
  bas-reliefs
bass
  basses
basset
bassinet
bassist
bassoon
bassoonist
bast
bastard
bastardisation
bastardise
  bastardises
  bastardised
  bastardising
bastardization
bastardize
  bastardizes
  bastardized
  bastardizing
bastardy
baste

bastes
basted
basting
bastinado
basting
bastion
bat
  bats
  batted
  batting
~~batallion~~ = battalion
batch
  batches
  batched
  batching
~~batchelor~~ = bachelor
bated (= bated breath
  → bait)
bath
  baths
  bathed
  bathing
bathe
  bathes
  bathed
  bathing
bather
bathers
bathing
bathos
bathrobe
bathroom
baths
bathtub
bathyscaph
bathysphere
batik
batiste
batman
  batmen
baton
bats
batsman
  batsmen
battalion
~~battallion~~ = battalion
batted
batten
  battens
  battened
  battening
batten
Battenburg
batter

batters
battered
battering
batterer
battering
battery
  batteries
battik
batting
battle
  battles
  battled
  battling
battledress
battlefield
battlement
battleship
batty
  battier
  battiest
batwing
batwoman
  batwomen
bauble
baud (= measure of
  speed → bawd,
  bored)
baulk
bauxite
bavarois
bawbee
bawd (= prostitute
  → baud, bored)
bawdier
bawdiest
bawdy
  bawdier
  bawdiest
bawl (= shout → ball)
  bawls
  bawled
  bawling
bay
  bays
  bayed
  baying
bayonet
  bayonets
  bayoneted *or*
  bayonetted
  bayoneting *or*
  bayonetting
bayou
bazaar

bazar
~~bazar~~ = bazaar
bazooka
  bazookas
be
  am
  are
  is
  was
  were
  been
  being
beach (= land on
  shore → beech)
  beaches
  beached
  beaching
beachcomber
beachhead
beacon
bead
  beaded
  beadier
  beadiest
  beading
beadle
beadwork
beady
  beadier
  beadiest
beagle
beak
  beaked
beaker
beam
  beams
  beamed
  beaming
bean
beanbag
beanfeast
beano
  beanos
beanpole
beanstalk
bear (= animal; carry;
  put up with → bare)
  bears
  bore
  born *or*
  borne
  bearing
bearable
bearably

beard
  beards
  bearded
  bearding
beardless
bearer
bearing
bearish
bearishly
Béarnaise
bears
bearskin
beast
beastie
beastly
  beastlier
  beastliest
beat (= defeat
  → beet)
  beats
  beat
  beaten
  beating
beaten
beater
beatific
beatifically
beatification
~~beatiful~~ = beautiful
beatify
  beatifies
  beatified
  beatifying
beating
beatitude
  Beatitudes
beatnik
Beatrice
beats
beau
  beaus *or*
  beaux
Beaujolais
Beaulieu
beaus
beaut
beauteous
beautician
beautification
beautiful
beautifully
beautify
  beautifies
  beautified

beautifying
beauty
  beauties
beaux
beaux-arts
beaver
  beavers
  beavered
  beavering
bebop
becalmed
became
because
beck
Becket, Thomas à
Beckett, Samuel
beckon
  beckons
  beckoned
  beckoning
become
  becomes
  became
  become
  becoming
becoming
becomingly
becomingness
becquerel
bed
  beds
  bedded
  bedding
bedaub
  bedaubs
  bedaubed
  bedaubing
bedazzle
  bedazzles
  bedazzled
  bedazzling
bedazzlement
bedbug
bedchamber
bedclothes
beddable
bedded
bedder
bedding
bedeck
  bedecks
  bedecked
  bedecking
bedevil

bedevils
bedevilled
bedevilling
bedevilment
bedewed
bedfellow
bedlam
bedlamite
Bedouin
bedpan
bedpost
bedraggled
bedridden
bedrock
bedroll
bedroom
beds
bedside
bedsitter
bedsore
bedspread
bedstead
bedtime
bedwetting
bee
bees
Beeb
beech (= tree
  → beach)
  beeches
beechnut
beef
  beefs
  beefed
  beefing
beefburger
beefcake
beefeater
beefier
beefiest
beefs
beefsteak
beefy
beehive
beekeeper
beeline
Beelzebub
been
beep
  beeps
  beeped
  beeping
beer (= drink → bier)
beerier

beeriest
beery
beeswax
beet (= vegetable
  → beat)
Beethoven, Ludwig van
beetle
  beetles
  beetled
  beetling
beetle-browed
beetroot
beezer
befall
befit
  befalls
  befell
  befallen
  befalling
befitting
befittingly
befog
  befogs
  befogged
  befogging
before
beforehand
beforetime
befoul
  befouls
  befouled
  befouling
befriend
  befriends
  befriended
  brefriending
befuddle
  befuddles
  befuddled
  befuddling
befuddlement
beg
  begs
  begged
  begging
begad
began
begat
  begets
  begat or
  begot
  begot or
  begotten
  begetting

begetter
beggar
  beggars
  beggard
  beggaring
beggarly
beggary
begged
begger = beggar
begging
begin
  begins
  began
  begun
  beginning
begining = beginning
beginner
beginning
begone
begonia
  begonias
begorra
begot
begotten
begrudge
  begrudges
  begrudged
  begrudging
  begrudgingly
begs
beguile
  beguiles
  beguiled
  beguiling
beguilement
beguiler
beguiling
beguilingly
begun
behalf
behave
  behaves
  behaved
  behaving
behaviour
behavioural
behaviourism
behaviourist
behead
  beheads
  beheaded
  beheading
beheld
behemoth

behest
behind
behindhand
behold
  beholds
  beheld
  beholding
beholden
beholder
behove
  behoves
  behoved
  behoving
beige
beigel
Beijing
being
Beirut
bejabers
bejewelled
belabour
  belabours
  belaboured
  belabouring
Belarus
belated
belatedly
belatedness
belch
  belches
  belched
  belching
beleaguer
  beleaguers
  beleaguered
  beleaguering
~~beleif~~ = belief
~~beleive~~ = believe
belfry
  belfries
Belgian
Belgium
belie
  belies
  belied
  belying
belief
believability
believable
believably
believe
  believes
  believed
  believing

believer
believing
~~beligerent~~ = belligerent
belittle
  belittles
  belittled
  belittling
belittlement
bell
belladonna
bellboy
belle
  belles
belles-lettres
bellflower
bellicose
bellicosity
belligerence
belligerency
belligerent
bellow (= shout
  → below)
  bellows
  bellowed
  bellowing
bellows
belly
  bellies
bellyache
  bellyaches
  bellyached
  bellyaching
bellybutton
bellyful
belong
  belongs
  belonged
  belonging
belonging
belongings
Belorussian
beloved
below (= underneath
  → bellow)
belt
  belts
  belted
  belting
beltway
beluga
belvedere
bemoan
  bemoans
  bemoaned

bemoaning
bemused
bemusedly
ben
Ben Nevis
bench
  benches
bend
  bends
  bent
  bending
bender
bendier
bendiest
bends
bendy
beneath
Benedictine
benediction
benefaction
benefactor
  benefactoress
  benefactoresses
beneficence
beneficent
beneficently
beneficial
beneficiary
  beneficiaries
benefit
  benefits
  benefited
  benefiting
benevolence
benevolent
benevolently
Bengali
~~benificial~~ = beneficial
~~benifit~~ = benefit
benighted
benightedly
benign
benignity
benignly
bent
bentonite
benumb
  benumbs
  benumbed
  benumbing
bequeath
  bequeaths
  bequeathed
  bequeathing

bequeather
bequest
berate
  berates
  berated
  berating
Berber
berberis
bereave
  bereaves
  bereaved
  bereaving
bereavement
bereft
beret
berg
bergamot
beriberi
berk
Berkhampstead
berm
berme
Bern
berry (= small fruit
  → bury)
  berries
berserk
berth (= dock in
  mooring place
  → birth)
  berths
  berthed
  berthing
Berwick
beseech
  beseeches
  besought or
  beseeched
  beseeching
beseecher
beseeching
beseechingly
beset
  besets
  beset
  besetting
beside
besides
besiege
  besieges
  besieged
  besieging
besmear
  besmears

besmeared
besmearing
besmirch
  besmirches
  besmirched
  besmirching
besom
besotted
besought
bespangled
bespattered
bespeak
  bespeaks
  bespoke
  bespoken
  bespeaking
bespectacled
bespoke
besprinkled
best
bestial
bestiality
  bestialities
bestially
bestiary
  bestiaries
bestir
  bestirs
  bestirred
  bestirring
bestow
  bestows
  bestowed
  bestowing
bestowal
bestrew
  bestrews
  bestrewed
  bestrewed *or*
  bestrewn
  bestrewing
bestride
  bestrides
  bestrode
  bestridden
  bestriding
bet
  bets
  bet *or*
  betted
  betting
beta
betablocker
betacarotene

betake
  betakes
  betook
  betaken
  betaking
betel
bête noire
  bêtes noires
bethink
  bethinks
  bethought
  bethinking
bethought
betide
betimes
bêtise
  bêtises
betoken
  betokens
  betokened
  betokening
betook
betray
  betrays
  betrayed
  betraying
betrayal
betrayer
betrothal
betrothed
bets
betted
better
betterment
betting
between
betwixt
b̶e̶u̶t̶i̶f̶u̶l̶ = beautiful
bevel
  bevels
  bevelled
  bevelling
beverage
bevies
bevy
bewail
  bewails
  bewailed
  bewailing
beware
bewhiskered
bewilder
  bewilders
  bewildered

  bewildering
bewildering
bewilderingly
bewilderment
bewitch
  bewitches
  bewitched
  bewitching
bewitching
bewitchingly
beyond
bezique
bhajee
  bhajees
bhaji
  bhajis
bhang
biannual
biannually
bias
  biases *or*
  biasses
  biased *or*
  biassed
  biasing *or*
  biassing
biathlon
biaxial
bib
Bible
biblical
Biblicist
bibliographic
bibliography
  bibliographies
bibliomania
bibliophile
bibulous
bicameral
bicarb
bicarbonate
bicentenary
  bicentenaries
biceps
Bicester
bichloride
bicker
  bickers
  bickered
  bickering
bickie
  bickies
bicolour
bicoloured

bicycle
bid
  bids
  bade *or*
  bid
  bid *or*
  bidden
  bidding
biddable
bidden
bidder
bidding
biddy
  biddies
bide
  bides
  bided *or*
  bode
  bided
  biding
bidet
biding
bidirectional
biennial
biennially
bier (= table for dead
  body → beer)
bierkeller
biff
  biffs
  biffed
  biffing
bifocal
bifocals
bifurcate
  bifurcates
  bifurcated
  bifurcating
  bifurcation
big
  bigger
  biggest
bigamist
bigamous
bigamy
b̶i̶g̶e̶r̶ = bigger
bigger
biggest
bighead
bighearted
bight
bigot
bigotry
bigwig

bijou
bike
  bikes
  biked
  biking
biker
bikini
  bikinis
bilabial
bilateral
bilaterally
bilberry
  bilberries
bile
bilge
bilharzia
bilinear
bilingual
bilingualism
bilingually
bilious
  biliousness
bilirubin
bilk
  bilks
  bilked
  bilking
bill
  bills
  billed
  billing
billabong
billboard
Billericay
billet
  billets
  billeted
  billeting
billet-doux
  billets-doux
billfold
billhook
billiard
  billiards
billing
billion
billionaire
billow
  billows
  billowed
  billowing
billowy
billposter
billy

billies
billycock
billyo
bilobate
biltong
bimbo
  bimbos
bimonthly
bin
  bins
  binned
  binning
binary
bind
  binds
  bound
  binding
binder
binding
bindweed
binge
  binges
  binged
  bingeing or
  binging
bingo
binman
  binmen
binning
binocular
  binoculars
binomial
binomially
bins
bio-
biochemical
biochemistry
biodegradable
biodegradation
biodiversity
biodynamics
biofeedback
biographer
biographical
biographically
biography
  biographies
biological
biologically
biologist
biology
biomass
bionic
biophysicist

biophysics
biopic
biopsy
  biopsies
biorhythm
biosphere
biotechnological
biotechnology
bipartisan
bipartite
biped
biplane
birch
  birches
  birched
  birching
bird
birdbath
birdbrained
birdcage
birdhouse
birdie
  birdies
birdlime
birdman
  birdmen
birdseed
birdshot
birdsong
biretta
biriani
Birmingham
Biro®
birth (= being born
  → berth)
birthday
  birthdays
birthmark
birthplace
birthright
birthstone
biryani
biscuit
bisect
  bisects
  bisected
  bisecting
bisection
bisexual
bisexuality
bisexually
bishop
bishopric
Bismarck, Otto von

bismuth
bison
  bisons or
  bison
bisque
bistro
  bistros
bisulphate
bisulphide
bisulphite
bit
bitch
  bitches
  bitched
  bitching
  bitchier
  bitchiest
bitchy
  bitchier
  bitchiest
bite (= cut with
  mouth → byte)
  bites
  bit
  bitten
  biting
biting
bitten
bitter
bitterly
bitterness
bitters
bittersweet
bitty
  bittier
  bittiest
bitumen
bituminous
bivalve
bivalvular
bivouac
  bivouacs
  bivouacked
  bivouacking
biweekly
biyearly
bizare = bizarre
bizarre
bizarrely
bizarreness
blab
  blabs
  blabbed
  blabbing

24

blabbed
blabber
  blabbers
  blabbered
  blabbering
blabbermouth
blabbing
blabs
black
  blacks
  blacked
  blacking
blackamoor
blackball
  blackballs
  blackballed
  blackballing
blackberry
  blackberries
blackbird
blackboard
blackcap
blackcurrant
blacken
  blackens
  blackened
  blackening
blackface
blackfly
  blackflies
blackguard
blackhead
blacking
blackjack
blackleg
blacklist
  blacklists
  blacklisted
  blacklisting
blackmail
  blackmails
  blackmailed
  blackmailing
blackout
blacksmith
blackthorn
blacktop
bladder
bladderwort
blade
blaeberry
  blaeberries
blah
blame

blames
blamed
blaming
blamed
blameless
blamelessly
blamelessness
blameworthy
blanch
  blanches
  blanched
  blanching
blancmange
bland
  blander
  blandest
blandishments
blank
blanket
  blankets
  blanketed
  blanketing
blankly
blankness
blare
  blares
  blared
  blaring
blarney
blasé
blaspheme
  blasphemes
  blasphemed
  blaspheming
blasphemer
blasphemous
blasphemously
blasphemy
  blasphemies
blasted
blast
  blasts
  blasted
  blasting
blastoff
blatant
blatantly
blather
  blathers
  blathered
  blathering
blaze
  blazes
  blazed

blazing
blazer
blazes
blazon
  blazons
  blazoned
  blazoning
bleach
  bleaches
  bleached
  bleaching
bleachers
bleak
blearier
bleariest
bleary
  blearier
  bleariest
bleary-eyed
bleat
  bleats
  bleated
  bleating
bled
bleed
  bleeds
  bled
  bleeding
bleeder
bleeding
bleep
  bleeps
  bleeped
  bleeping
bleeper
blemish
  blemishes
  blemished
  blemishing
blench
  blenches
  blenched
  blenching
blend
  blends
  blended
  blending
blende
blender
blenny
  blennies
blepharitis
bless
  blesses

blessed *or*
blest
blessing
blessed
blesses
blessing
blest
blet
blether
  blethers
  blethered
  blethering
blew
blight
  blights
  blighted
  blighting
blighter
blimey
blimp
blind
  blinds
  blinded
  blinding
blinders
blindfold
  blindfolds
  blindfolded
  blindolding
blinding
blindworm
blini
  blinis
blink
  blinks
  blinked
  blinking
blinkered
blinkers
blinking
blintz
  blintzes
blintze
  blintzes
blip
bliss
blissful
blisfully
blister
  blisters
  blistered
  blistering
blistering
blisteringly

blithe
blithely
blithering
blithesome
blitz
  blitzes
  blitzed
  blitzing
Blitz
  Blitzes
blitzkrieg
blizard = blizzard
blizzard
bloated
bloater
blob
bloc
block
  blocks
  blocked
  blocking
blockade
  blockades
  blockaded
  blockading
blockader
blockage
blockboard
blockbuster
blockbusting
blocked
blocker
blockhead
blockhouse
blocking
blockish
bloke
blonde
blood
bloodbath
bloodcurdling
blooded
bloodhound
bloodied
bloodier
bloodies
bloodiest
bloodless
bloodlessly
bloodlessness
bloodline
bloodroot
bloodshed
bloodshot

bloodstained
bloodstock
bloodstone
bloodstream
bloodsucker
bloodthirsty
  bloodthirstier
  bloodthirstiest
bloodworm
bloody
  bloodier
  bloodiest
  bloodies
  bloodied
  bloodying
bloody-minded
bloom
  blooms
  bloomed
  blooming
bloomer
bloomers
blooming
blooper
blossom
  blossoms
  blossomed
  blossoming
blot
  blots
  blotted
  blotting
blotch
  blotches
blotted
blotter
blotting
blotto
blouse
blouson
blow
  blows
  blew
  blown
  blowing
blowed
blower
blowfly
  blowflies
blowhard
blowhole
blowier
blowiest
blowing

blowlamp
blown
blowout
blowpipe
blowsier
blowsiest
blowsy
  blowsier
  blowsiest
blowtorch
blowy
  blowier
  blowiest
blowzier
blowziest
blowzy
  blowzier
  blowziest
blub
  blubs
  blubbed
  blubbing
blubber
bludgeon
  bludgeons
  bludgeoned
  bludgeoning
blue
  bluer
  bluest
bluebell
blueberry
  blueberries
bluebird
bluebook
bluebottle
bluefish
  bluefish
bluegrass
blueish
blueprint
bluer
blues
bluest
bluestocking
bluestone
bluethroat
bluetit
bluetongue
blueweed
bluff
  bluffs
  bluffed
  bluffing

bluish
blunder
  blunders
  blundered
  blundering
blunderbuss
blunt
blur
  blurs
  blurred
  blurring
blurb
blurred
blurring
blurt
  blurts
  blurted
  blurting
blush
  blushes
  blushed
  blushing
blusher
bluster
  blusters
  blustered
  blustering
boa
boar (= animal
  → boor, bore)
board
  boards
  boarded
  boarding
boarder (= one who
  boards → border)
boarding
boardroom
boardsailing
boardwalk
boarfish
boast
  boasts
  boasted
  boasting
boastful
boastfully
boastfulness
boat
boater
boathook
boathouse
boating
boatman

boatmen
boatswain
bob
  bobs
  bobbed
  bobbing
bob
bobbed
bobbejaan
bobbin
bobbing
bobble
bobby
  bobbies
bobbydazzler
bobbysoxer
bobcat
bobfloat
boblet
bobotie
bobsled
bobsleigh
bobstay
bobtail
bocage
bod
bode
  bodes
  boded
  boding
bodega
bodge
  bodges
  bodged
  bodging
bodger
bodice
bodiless
bodily
bodkin
body
  bodies
bodyguard
bodysuit
bodywork
Boer
boffin
bog
  bogs
  bogged
  bogging
bogey
  bogeys
bogeyman

bogeymen
boggart
bogged
bogging
boggle
  boggles
  boggled
  boggling
bogie
  bogies
Bogota
bogus
bogwood
bogy
  bogies
boil
  boils
  boiled
  boiling
boiler
boilermaker
boilerplate
boiling
boilover
boisterous
boisterously
boisterousness
bold
  bolder
  boldest
boldface
boldfaced
boldly
boldness
bole
bolero
  boleros
boletus
  boleti or
  boletuses
Bolivia
boll
bollard
bollocking
bollocks
bollworm
bolometer
bolometric
boloney
Bolshevik
bolshie
  bolshier
  bolshiest
bolshy

bolshier
bolshiest
bolster
  bolsters
  bolstered
  bolstering
bolt
  bolts
  bolted
  boting
bolus
bomb
  bombs
  bombed
  bombing
bombard
  bombards
  bombarded
  bombarding
bombardier
bombardment
bombastic
bombastically
bombed
bomber
bombshell
bombsight
bonanza
Bonaparte, Napoleon
bonbon
bonce
bond
  bonds
  bonded
  bonding
bondage
bonded
bondholder
bonding
bondmaid
bondservant
bondsman
  bondsmen
bone
  bones
  boned
  boning
bone-dry
bonehead
boneshaker
boneyard
bonfire
bong
bongo

bongoes or
  bongos
bonhomie
bonier
boniest
bonk
  bonks
  bonked
  bonking
bonkers
bonne
bonnet
bonny
  bonnier
  bonniest
bonsai
bony
bonzer
boo
  boos
  booed
  booing
boob
  boobs
  boobed
  boobing
boo-boo
booby
  boobies
booed
boogie
  boogies
  boogied
  boogieing
boogie-woogie
boohoo
booing
book
  books
  booked
  booking
bookbinder
bookbinding
bookcase
~~bookeeping~~ =
  bookkeeping
bookie
  bookies
booking
bookish
bookishness
booklet
bookmaker
bookmark

27

bookplate
books
bookstall
booksy
bookworm
bool
boom
  booms
  boomed
  booming
boomer
boomerang
boon
boondocks
boor
boorish
boorishly
boorishness
boos
boost
  boosts
  boosted
  boosting
booster
boot
  boots
  booted
  booting
bootblack
booted
bootee (= shoe for a
  baby → booty)
  bootees
booth
booting
bootlace
bootleg
  bootlegs
  bootlegged
  bootlegging
bootlegger
bootless
bootstraps
booty (= stolen goods
  → bootee)
booze
  boozes
  boozed
  boozing
boozer
boozier
booziest
boozy
  boozier

booziest
bop
  bops
  bopped
  bopping
boquet = bouquet
boracite
borage
borax
borazon
Bordeaux
bordel
bordello
  bordellos
border (= frontier
  → boarder)
  borders
  bordered
  bordering
borderer
borderland
borderline
bore (= not interest
  → boar)
  bores
  bored
  boring
boreal
bored (=
  uninteresting
  → bawd, baud)
boredom
borehole
boreing = boring
borer
boric
boride
boring
born (= came to life
  → borne, bourn)
borne (= carried; put
  up with → born,
  bourn)
bornite
boron
boronia
borough
borrow
  borrows
  borrowed
  borrowing
borsch
borscht
borshcht

borstal
borzoi
Bosch, Hieronymus
bosh
bo's'n
Bosnia
bosom
bosomy
boss
  bosses
  bossed
  bossing
bossa nova
bossed
bosses
boss-eyed
bossier
bossiest
bossing
bossy
  bossier
  bossiest
bosun
botanical
botanically
botanise
  botanises
  botanised
  botanising
botanist
botanize
  botanizes
  botanized
  botanizing
botany
botch
  botches
  botched
  botching
botchier
botchiest
botchy
  botchier
  botchiest
botfly
  botflies
both
bother
  bothers
  bothered
  bothering
botheration
bothersome
bothies

bothy
  bothies
Botswana
Botticelli
bottle
  bottles
  bottled
  bottling
bottlebrush
bottled
bottleful
bottleneck
bottler
bottling
bottom
  bottoms
  bottomed
  bottoming
bottomless
bottommost
botulin
botulinus
botulism
bouclé
boudoir
bouffant
bougainvillaea
  bougainvillaeas
bougainvillea
  bougainvilleas
bough (= branch of a
  tree → bow)
bought
bouillabaisse
bouillon
boulder (= large
  stone → bold)
boules
boulevard
bounce
  bounces
  bounced
  bouncing
bouncer
bouncier
bounciest
bouncing
bouncy
  bouncier
  bounciest
bound
  bounds
  bounded
  bounding

boundary
boundaries
bounded
bounden
bounder
boundless
boundlessly
boundlessness
boundry = boundary
bounds
bounteous
bounteously
bounteousness
bountiful
bounty
bounties
Bounty
bouquet
bourbon
bourgeois
bourgeoise
bourgeoisie
bourn (= stream
  → born, borne)
bout
boutique
boutonniere
bouy = buoy
bouyant = buoyant
bovine
bovver
bow (= bend body in
  respect → bough)
  bows
  bowed
  bowing
bowdlerise
  bowdlerises
  bowdlerised
  bowdlerising
bowdlerize
  bowdlerizes
  bowdlerized
  bowdlerizing
bowed
bowel
  bowels
bower
bowfin
bowing
bowknot
bowl
  bowls
  bowled

bowling
bow-legged
bowler
bowlful
bowline
bowling
bowman
  bowmen
bowsaw
bowshot
bowsprit
bow-wow
box
  boxes
  boxed
  boxing
boxcar
boxer
  boxers
boxful
boxing
boxroom
boxwood
boy (= male child
  → buoy)
boycott
  boycotts
  boycotted
  boycotting
boyfriend
boyhood
boyish
boyishly
boyishness
boysenberry
  boysenberries
bra
brace
  braces
  braced
  bracing
bracelet
  braces
brachah
brachial
brachiosaurus
brachium
bracing
bracken
bracket
  brackets
  bracketed
  bracketing

brackish
brackishly
brackishness
bradawl
bradycardia
brae (= hillside
  → bray)
brag
  brags
  bragged
  bragging
braggadocio
braggart
bragged
bragging
Brahman
  Brahmans
Brahmin
  Brahmin or
  Brahmins
Brahms, Johannes
braid
  braids
  braided
  braiding
Braille
brain
  brains
  brained
  braining
brainbox
brainchild
braindead
brainier
brainiest
brainless
brainpower
brainstem
brainstorm
brainstorming
brainteaser
brainwash
  brainwashes
  brainwashed
  brainwashing
brainy
braise
  braises
  braised
  braising
brake (= for stopping
  → break)
  brakes
  braked

braking
bramble
brambling
Bramley
bran
branch
  branches
  branched
  branching
brand
  brands
  branded
  branding
brandish
  brandishes
  brandished
  brandishing
brandy
  brandies
brash
brashly
brashness
Brasilia
brass
  brasses
brasserie
  brasseries
brassica
  brassicas
brassier
brassiere
brassy
  brassier
  brassiest
brat
bratpack
bratwurst
bravado
brave
  braver
  bravest
bravely
bravery
bravissimo
bravo
  bravos
bravura
brawl
  brawls
  brawled
  brawling
brawn
brawnier
brawniest

brawny
  brawnier
  brawniest
bray (= make sound
  like a donkey → brae)
  brays
  brayed
  braying
brazen
  brazens
  brazened
  brazening
Brazil
brazier
Brazilian
breach (= break
  → breech)
  breaches
  breached
  breaching
bread (= food
  → bred)
breadbasket
breadboard
breadcrumb
breadfruit
breadline
breadth
breadthways
breadwinner
breathwise
break (= become
  broken → brake)
  breaks
  broke
  broken
  breaking
breakable
breakage
breakaway
breakdance
breakdown
breaker
breakeven
breakfast
  breakfasts
  breakfasted
  breakfasting
breaking
breakneck
breakthrough
breakwater
bream
  bream or

breams
breast
  breasts
  breasted
  breasting
breastbone
breastpin
breastplate
breaststroke
breastwork
breath
breathalyse
  breathalyses
  breathalysed
  breathalysing
breathalyser
breathalyze
  breathalyzes
  breathalyzed
  breathalyzing
breathalyzer
breathe
  breathes
  breathed
  breathing
breather
breathier
breathiest
breathing
breathless
breathtaking
breathy
  breathier
  breathiest
Brechin
Brecht, Bertolt
Brecon
bred (= produced
  young → bread)
breech (= as in
  breech birth
  → breath)
breeches
breed
  breeds
  bred
  breeding
breeder
breeding
breeks
breeze
  breezes
  breezed
  breezing

breezier
breeziest
breezy
  breezier
  breeziest
brethren
Breton
Breughel, Pieter
breve
breviary
  breviaries
brevity
brew
  brews
  brewed
  brewing
brewer
brewery
briar
bribe
  bribes
  bribed
  bribing
bribery
bric-a-brac
brick
  bricks
  bricked
  bricking
brickbat
brickearth
brickie
  brickies
bricklayer
bricklaying
brickwork
brickyard
bridal
bride
bridegroom
bridesmaid
bridewell
bridge
  bridges
  bridged
  bridging
bridgehead
bridges
bridgework
bridging
bridie
bridle
  bridles
  bridled

bridling
Brie
brief
  briefs
  briefed
  briefing
  briefer
  briefest
briefcase
briefing
brier
brig
brigade
brigadier
brigand
brigantine
bright
  brighter
  brightest
brightens
  brightens
  brightened
  brightening
brighteyed
brightly
brightness
Brighton
brilliant = brilliant
brill
brilliance
brilliant
brilliantine
brilliantly
brills
brim
  brims
  brimmed
  brimming
brimful
brimfull
brimmed
brimming
brimstone
brindled
brine
bring
  brings
  brought
  bringing
brinier
briniest
brink
brinkmanship
briny

brioche
  brioches
briony
  brionies
briquette
Brisbane
brisk
  brisker
  briskest
brisket
briskly
briskness
bristle
  bristles
  bristled
  bristling
bristletail
bristols
Brit
Britain (= country
  → Briton)
Britannia
Britannic
Britanny = Brittany
britches
Briticism
British
Britisher
Briton (= person
  → Britain)
brittle
brittleness
broach (= introduce a
  subject → brooch)
  broaches
  broached
  broaching
broad
  broader
  broadest
broadband
broadbrim
broadbrush
broadcast
  broadcasts
  broadcasted
  broadcasting
broadcloth
broaden
  broadens
  broadened
  broadening
broadleaf
broad-leaved

broadloom
broadminded
broadsheet
broadside
broadsword
brocade
  brocades
  brocaded
  brocading
broccoli
broccoli = broccoli
brochette
brochure
brock
brogue
broil
  broils
  broiled
  broiling
broiler
broke
broken
brokenhearted
broker
brokerage
brolly
  brollies
bromeliad
bromide
bromine
Bromley
bronchia
bronchial
bronchiole
bronchitic
bronchitis
broncho-
bronchopneumonia
bronco
  broncos
Brontë (sisters)
brontosaurus
  brontosauri
bronze
  bronzes
  bronzed
  bronzing
brooch (= piece of
  jewellery → broach)
  brooches
brood
  broods
  brooded
  brooding

brooder
broodier
broodiest
broody
  broodier
  broodiest
brook
  brooks
  brooked
  brooking
brooklet
brookweed
broom (= brush
  → brume)
broomstick
broth
brothel
brother
brotherhood
brotherly
brougham
brought
brouhaha
brow
browband
browbeat
  browbeats
  browbeat
  browbeaten
  browbeating
brown
  browns
  browned
  browning
brownie
  brownies
Brownie
  Brownies
browning
brownout
browse
  browses
  browsed
  browsing
brucellosis
bruin
bruise
  bruises
  bruised
  bruising
bruiser
bruit
  bruits
  bruited

bruiting
brûlé
brume (= mist
  → broom)
Brummie
  Brummies
brunch
  brunches
brunette
brunt
brush
  brushes
  brushed
  brushing
brushmark
brushoff
brushwood
brushwork
brusque
brusquely
brusqueness
Brussels
brutal
brutalise
  brutalises
  brutalised
  brutalising
brutality
  brutalities
brutalize
  brutalizes
  brutalized
  brutalizing
brutally
brute
brutish
brutishly
bryony
  bryonies
BSc
bub
bubble
  bubbles
  bubbled
  bubbling
bubbly
  bubblier
  bubbliest
bubonic
buccaneer
buck
  bucks
  bucked
  bucking

buckaroo
  buckaroos
buckboard
bucket
  buckets
  bucketed
  bucketing
buckeye
buckhorn
buckle
  buckles
  buckled
  buckling
buckler
buckram
buckshee
buckshot
buckskin
buckthorn
bucktooth
  buckteeth
buckwheat
bucolic
bucolically
bud
  buds
  budded
  budding
Buddha
Buddhism
budding
buddleia
  buddleias
buddy
  buddies
budge
  budges
  budged
  budging
budgerigar
budget
  budgets
  budgeted
  budgeting
budgie
  budgies
buff
  buffs
  buffed
  buffing
buffalo
  buffalos
  buffaloes
buffer

buffers
buffered
buffering
buffet
  buffets
  buffeted
  buffeting
buffoon
buffoonery
bug
  bugs
  bugged
  bugging
bugaboo
  bugaboos
bugbear
bugged
bugger
  buggers
  buggered
  buggering
buggery
bugging
buggy
  buggies
bughouse
bugle
bugler
bugloss
build
  builds
  built
  building
builder
building
built
bulb
bulbiferous
bulbous
Bulgaria
Bulgarian
bulge
  bulges
  bulged
  bulging
bulgur
bulimia
bulimic
bulk
bulkhead
bulkier
bulkiest
bulkily
bulkiness

bulky
  bulkier
  bulkiest
bull
bullace
bulldog
bulldoze
  bulldozes
  bulldozed
  bulldozing
bulldozer
bullet
bulletin
bulletproof
bullettin = bulletin
bullfight
bullfighter
bullfighting
bullfinch
  bullfinches
bullfrog
bullheaded
bullheadedly
bullhorn
bullion
bullish
bullishly
bullishness
bullock
bullring
bullshit
  bullshits
  bullshitted
  bullshitting
bully
  bullies
  bullied
  bullying
bullyboy
bulrush
  bulrushes
bulwark
bum
  bums
  bummed
  bumming
bumbailiff
bumble
  bumbles
  bumbled
  bumbling
bumblebee
bumf
bumfreezer

bummed
bummer
bumming
bump
  bumps
  bumped
  bumping
bumper
bumph
bumpier
bumpiest
bumpkin
bumptious
bumptiously
bumptiousness
bumpy
  bumpier
  bumpiest
bun
bunch
  bunches
  bunched
  bunching
bund
bundle
  bundles
  bundled
  bundling
bung
  bungs
  bunged
  bunging
bungalow
bunghole
bungle
  bungles
  bungled
  bungling
bunion
bunk
  bunks
  bunked
  bunking
bunker
bunkhouse
bunkum
bunny
  bunnies
bunt
  bunts
  bunted
  bunting
bunting
buoy (= floating

object → boy)
buoys
buoyancy
buoyant
  buoyantly
bur
Burberry™
  Burberries
burble
  burbles
  burbled
  burbling
burbot
burden
  burdens
  burdened
  burdening
burdensome
burdock
bureau
  bureaux
bureaucracy
  bureaucracies
bureaucrat
bureaucratically
bureaucratisation
bureaucratization
burette
burgeon
  burgeons
  burgeoned
  burgeoning
burger (= round piece
 of meat → burgher)
burgess
  burgesses
burgh
burgher (= person
 who lives in a town
 → burger)
burglar
burglarize
  burglarizes
  burglarized
  burglarizing
burglary
  burglaries
burgle
  burgles
  burgled
  burgling
burgler = burglar
burgomaster
burial

buried
buries
burk
burlap
burlesque
burliness
burly
Burma
Burmese
burn
  burns
  burned or
  burnt
  burning
burner
burnet
burning
burnish
  burnishes
  burnished
  burnishing
burnoose
burnous
burnouse
burnout
burnsides
burnt
burp
  burps
  burped
  burping
burr
burrito
  burritos
burro
  burros
burrow
  burrows
  burrowed
  burrowing
bursar
bursarial
bursary
  bursaries
burst
  bursts
  burst
  bursting
burthen
  burthens
  burthened
  burthening
burton
burweed

bury (= put into the
 ground → berry)
  buries
  buried
  burying
bus
  buses or
  busses
  bused or
  bussed
  busing or
  bussing
busby
  busbies
bused
buses
bush
bushbaby
  bushbabies
bushed
bushel
bushfire
bushfly
  bushflies
bushier
bushiest
Bushman
  Bushmen
bushwhack
  bushwhacks
  bushwhacked
  bushwhacking
bushwhacker
bushy
  bushier
  bushiest
busied
busier
busies
busiest
busily
busines = business
business
  businesses
businesslike
businessman
  businessmen
businesswoman
  businesswomen
busing
busk
  busks
  busked
  busking

busman
  busmen
bussed
busses
bussing
bust
  busts
  bust or
  busted
  busting
bustard
busted
buster
bustier
bustiest
busting
bustle
  bustles
  bustled
  bustling
busty
  bustier
  bustiest
busy
  busies
  busied
  busying
  busier
  busiest
busybody
  busybodies
busying
but
butane
butanol
butch
butcher
  butchers
  butchered
  butchering
butchery
butler
butlery
butt
  butts
  butted
  butting
butte
butter
  butters
  buttered
  buttering
butterbur
buttercup

butterfingers
butterfly
  butterflies
buttermilk
butternut
butterscotch
butterwort
buttery
buttock
button
  buttons
  buttoned
  buttoning
buttonhole
buttress
  buttresses

buttressed
buttressing
butty
  butties
butyl
buxom
buy (= purchase
  → by, bye)
buys
bought
buying
buyer
buying
buyout
buzz
buzzes

buzzed
  buzzing
buzzard
buzzer
by (= near → buy,
  bye)
by-
~~bycicle~~ = bicycle
bye (= goodbye;
  sports match → buy,
  by)
  byes
bye-bye
bye-election
bye-law
by-election

Byelorussian
bygone
bylaw
bypass
  bypasses
  bypassed
  bypassing
byproduct
byre
bystander
byte (= in a computer
  → bite)
byway
byword
Byzantine

C

ca try cha
cab
cabal
cabala
cabalistic
cabaret
cabbage
cabbogy
cabbala
cabbalah
cabbie
  cabbies
cabby
  cabbies
caber
Cabernet Sauvignon
cabin
cabinet
cable
  cables
  cabled
  cabling
cabochon
caboodle
caboose
cabriole
cabriolet
cacao
cacciatore
cache (= hidden store
  → cash)
cachepot
cachet
cachou (= scented
  sweet → cashew)
  cachous
cackhanded
cackle
  cackles
  cackled
  cackling
cacophonous
cacophony
  cacophonies
cactus
  cactuses or

cactuses
cad
cadaver
cadaverous
CADCAM
caddie (= in golf)
  caddies
  caddied
  caddying
caddish
caddy (= tea
  caddy)
  caddies
cadence
cadenza
cadet
cadge
  cadges
  cadged
  cadging
cadmium
cadre
Caernarfon
Caernarvon
Caerphilly
Caesarean
Caesarian
caesium
caesura
café
cafe
cafeteria
cafetiere
caffeine
~~caffiene~~ = caffeine
caftan
cage
  cages
  caged
  caging
cagey
  cagier
  cagiest
cagoule
cahoots
caïque

cairn
Cairo
caisson
Calcutta
California
cajole
  cajoles
  cajoled
  cajoling
cajolery
Cajun
cake
  cakes
  caked
  caking
calabash
calaboose
calabrese
calamine
calamitous
calamitously
calamity
  calamities
calcareous
calceolaria
calciferol
calcification
calcify
  calcifies
  calcified
  calcifying
calcine
  calcines
  calcined
  calcining
calcium
calculable
calculate
  calculates
  calculated
  calculating
calculation
calculator
calculus
caldera
Caledonian

calendar (= to show
  days, weeks, etc.
  → colander)
calender (= machine
  → colander)
calendula
calf
  calves
calfskin
calibrate
  calibrates
  calibrated
  calibrating
calibre
  calices
calico
caliper
  calipers
caliph
caliphate
calix
  calices
call
  calls
  called
  calling
Callanetics
calligrapher
calligraphist
calligraphy
calling
callipers
callisthenics
callosity
callous
callow
callus
calm
  calms
  calmed
  calming
calmative
calomel
calorie
calorific
calumniate

calumniates
calumniated
calumniating
calumny
  calumnies
calvary
  calvaries
calve (= give birth to
  a calf → carve)
  calves
  calved
  calving
Calvinism
Calvinist
calvinistic
calyces
calypso
  calypsos or
  calypsoes
calyx
  calyces or
  calyxes
cam
camaraderie
Camarthen
camber
Cambodia
cambric
camcorder
came
camel
camelia = camellia
camellia
  camellias
Camembert
cameo
  cameos
camera
cameraderie =
  camaraderie
cameraman
  cameramen
Cameroon
camiknickers
camise
camisole
camomile
camoflage =
  camouflage
camouflage
  camouflages
  camouflaged
  camouflaging
camp

camps
camped
camping
campaign
  campaigns
  campaigned
  campaigning
campaigner
campain = campaign
campanile
campanologist
campanology
campanula
  campanulas
Campari™
camper
camphor
campion
campus
  campuses
camshaft
Camus, Albert
can
Canaan
Canaanite
Canadian
canaille
Canada
canal
canalise
  canalises
  canalised
  canalising
canalize
  canalizes
  canalized
  canalizing
canapé
canard
canary
  canaries
canasta
cancan
cancel
  cancels
  cancelled
  cancelling
cancelation =
  cancellation
cancellation
cancer
cancerophobia
candelabrum
  candelabrums or

candelabra
candid
candida
candidacy
  candidacies
candidate
candidature
candied
candle
candlelight
Candlemas
candlestick
candlewick
candour
candy
candyfloss
candytuft
cane
  canes
  caned
  caning
canine
caning
canister
canker
cankerous
cannabis
canned
cannelloni
canner
cannery
  canneries
cannibal
cannibalise
  cannibalises
  cannibalised
  cannibalising
cannibalism
cannibalize
  cannibalizes
  cannibalized
  cannibalizing
cannily
canning
cannon (= large gun
  → canon)
  cannon or
  cannons
  cannons
  cannoned
  cannoning
cannonade
cannonball
cannonry

cannot
canny
  cannier
  canniest
canoe
  canoes
  canoed
  canoeing
canoeist
canon (= law of
  Christian church
  → cannon)
canonical
canonisation
canonise
  canonises
  canonised
  canonising
canonize
  canonizes
  canonized
  canonizing
canoodle
  canoodles
  canoodled
  canoodling
canopy
  canopies
canst
cant
  cants
  canted
  canting
can't
Cantab.
cantaloup
cantaloupe
cantankerous
cantankerously
cantankerousness
cantata
  cantatas
canteen
canteloupe =
  cantaloupe
canter (= gallop
  → cantor)
Canterbury
  canters
  cantered
  cantering
canticle
cantilever
canto

cantos
canton
Cantonese
cantor (= leader of
  singers → canter)
canvas (= thick cloth
  → canvass)
  canvases
canvass (= find out
  opinions → canvas)
  canvasses
  canvassed
  canvassing
canyon
canzonetta
  canzonettas
cap
  caps
  capped
  capping
capability
capable
capacious
capaciously
capaciousness
capacitor
capacity
  capacities
caparison
cape
caper
  capers
  capered
  capering
capercaillie
  capercaillies
capillary
  capillaries
capita
capital
capitalisation
capitalise
  capitalises
  capitalised
  capitalising
capitalism
capitalist
capitalization
capitalize
  capitalizes
  capitalized
  capitalizing
capitation
capitulate

capitulates
capitulated
capitulating
capitulation
capitulatory
capon
capped
capping
cappuccino
  cappuccinos
cappucino =
  cappuccino
capriccioso
caprice
capricious
capriciously
capriciousness
Capricorn
capsicum
  capsicums
capsize
  capsizes
  capsized
  capsizing
capstan
capsule
captain
  captains
  captained
  captaining
caption
captious
  captiously
captivate
  captivates
  captivated
  captivating
captive
captivity
captor
capture
  captures
  captured
  capturing
capuccino =
  cappuccino
Capuchin
capybara
  capybaras
car
Caracas
carafe
caramel
caramelise

caramelises
caramelised
caramelising
caramelize
  caramelizes
  caramelized
  caramelizing
carapace
carat (= measure of
  purity of gold
  → caret, carrot)
Caravaggio
caravan
caravanning
caravanserai
caraway
carbine
carbohydrate
carbolic
carbon
carbonaceous
carbonade
carbonated
carboniferous
carbonise
  carbonises
  carbonised
  carbonising
carbonize
  carbonizes
  carbonized
  carbonizing
carboy
carbuncle
carburation
carburetter
carcase
carcass
  carcasses
carcinogen
carcinogenic
carcinoma
  carcinomas
card
cardamom
cardamum
cardboard
cardiac
cardie
Cardiff
cardigan
cardinal
cardio-
cardiogram

cardiograph
cardiological
cardiology
cardiopulmonary
cardiovascular
cardoon
cards
cardsharp
care
  cares
  cared
  caring
careen
  careens
  careened
  careening
career
careerism
careerist
carefree
careful
carefull = careful
carefully
carefulness
careing = caring
careless
carelessly
carelessness
carer
caress
  caresses
  caressed
  caressing
caressingly
caret (= symbol used
  in printing → carat,
  carrot)
caretaker
careworn
carfare
cargo
  cargoes or
  cargos
cariage = carriage
Caribbean
caribou
  caribou or
  caribous
caricature
  caricatures
  caricatured
  caricaturing
caries
carillon

caring
Carlisle
Carmelite
carmine
carnage
carnal
carnally
carnation
carnelian
carnival
carnivore
carnivorous
carnivorously
carob
carol
  carols
  carolled
  carolling
Carolingian
carotene
carousal (= merry-
  making → carousel)
carouse
  carouses
  caroused
  carousing
carousel (= merry-
  go-round
  → carousal)
carouser
carp
  carps
  carped
  carping
carpel
carpenter
carpentry
carpet
  carpets
  carpeted
  carpeting
carpetbagger
carpeting
carping
carport
carraige = carriage
carreer = career
carrel
carress = caress
carriage
carriageway
Carribean = Caribbean
carrier
carrion

carrot (= vegetable
  → carat, caret)
carroty
carry
  carries
  carried
  carrying
carrycot
carrying-on
  carryings-on
carsick
cart
  carts
  carted
  carting
carte blanche
cartel
cartful
carthorse
cartilage
cartilaginous
cartload
cartographer
cartographic
cartography
carton
cartoon
cartoonist
cartouch
cartouche
cartridge
cartwheel
cartwright
carve (= cut meat
  → calve)
  carves
  carved
  carving
carver
carvery
  carveries
carving
caryatid
casbah
cascade
  cascades
  cascaded
  cascading
case
  cases
  cased
  casing
casebook
casework

cash (= money
  → cache)
  cashes
  cashed
  cashing
cashew (= nut
  → cachou)
cashier
cashless
cashmere
cashpoint
casing
casino
  casinos
cask
casket
casque
cassava
  cassavas
casserole
  casseroles
  casseroled
  casseroling
cassette
cassock
cassoulet
cassowary
  cassowaries
cast
  casts
  cast
  casting
castanets
castaway
caste
castellated
caster (= sugar
  → castor)
castigate
  castigates
  castigated
  castigating
casting
castle
castor (= oil
  → caster)
castrate
  castrates
  castrated
  castrating
castration
castrato
castrator
casual

casually
casualness
casualty
  casualties
casuist
casuistic
casuistical
casuistry
cat
catabolic
cataclysm
cataclysmic
catacomb
catagory = category
Catalan
catalepsy
cataleptic
catalogue
  catalogues
  catalogued
  cataloguing
catalpa
catalysis
catalyst
catalytic
catamaran
catapult
  catapults
  catapulted
  catapulting
cataract
catarrh
catarrhal
catastrophe
catastrophic
catastrophically
catatonic
catcall
catch
  catches
  caught
  catching
catch-22
catcher
catches
catchier
catchiest
catching
catchment
catchword
catchy
  catchier
  catchiest
catechise

catechises
catechised
catechising
catechism
catechist
catechize
catechizes
catechized
catechizing
categorial
categorical
categorically
categorise
categorises
categorised
categorising
categorize
categorizes
categorized
categorizing
category
categories
cater
caters
catered
catering
caterer
catering
caterpillar
~~caterpiller~~ = caterpillar
caterwaul
caterwauls
caterwauled
caterwauling
catfish
catfish *or*
catfishes
catgut
catharsis
catharses
cathartic
cathedra
cathedral
catheter
catheterise
catheterises
catheterised
catheterising
catheterize
catheterizes
catheterized
catheterizing
cathodal
cathode

catholic
catholicisation
catholicise
catholicises
catholicised
catholicising
Catholicism
catholicization
catholicize
catholicizes
catholicized
catholicizing
catkin
catmint
catnap
catnaps
catnapped
catnapping
catnip
cat-o'-nine-tails
Catseye℠
catsuit
cattery
catteries
cattleman
cattlemen
catty
cattier
cattiest
catwalk
Caucasian
caucus
caucuses
caudal
caught
cauldron
cauliflower
caulk (= block up
  cracks in → cork)
caulks
caulked
caulking
causal
causality
causally
causation
causative
causatively
cause
causes
caused
causing
causeway
caustic

cauterise
cauterises
cauterised
cauterising
cauterize
cauterizes
cauterized
cauterizing
caution
cautions
cautioned
cautioning
cautionary
cautious
cautiously
cautiousness
cavalcade
cavalier
cavalry
cavalryman
cavalrymen
cave
caves
caved
caving
caveat
caveman
cavemen
cavern
cavernous
cavernously
caviar
cavil
cavils
cavilled
cavilling
caving
cavity
cavities
cavort
cavorts
cavorted
cavorting
caw
caws
cawed
cawing
cayenne
CB
CD
CD-ROM
ce *try* ca
ce *try* che
ceanothus

ceanothuses
cease
ceases
ceased
ceasing
ceaseless
ceaselessly
cedar
cede (= give up
  → seed)
cedes
ceded
ceding
cedilla
cedillas
Ceefax
ceilidh
ceiling
celandine
celebrant
celebrate
celebrates
celebrated
celebrating
celebration
celebrity
celebrities
celeriac
celerity
celery
celestial
celibacy
celibate
cell (= room in a
  prison; unit of living
  matter → sell)
cellar
cellarage
cellist
cello
cellos
cellphone
cellular
cellulite
celluloid
cellulose
Celsius
Celt
Celtic
cembalo
cembali *or*
cembalos
cement
cements

cemented
cementing
cemetery
　cemeteries
cemetry = cemetery
cenotaph
censor (= take parts
　out of a film, etc.
　→ censure)
　censors
　censored
　censoring
censorious
censoriously
censoriousness
censorship
censure (= express
　disapproval of
　→ censor)
　censures
　censured
　censuring
census
　censuses
cent
centaur
centavo
　centavos
centenarian
centenary
　centenaries
centesimal
centigrade
centigram
centigramme
centilitre
centime
centimetre
centipede
central
centralisation
centralise
　centralises
　centralised
　centralising
centralism
centrality
　centralization
centralize
　centralizes
　centralized
　centralizing
centrally
centre

centres
centred
centring
centrefold
centrepiece
centrifugal
centrifugally
centrifuge
centripetal
centrist
centurion
century
　centuries
cephalic
cephalopod
ceramic
ceramics
ceramist
cereal (= grain crop
　→ serial)
cerebellum
cerebral
cerebrally
cerebration
cerebrum
　cerebra or
　cerebrums
ceremonial
ceremonially
ceremonious
ceremoniously
ceremony
　ceremonies
cerise
cert
certain
certainly
certainty
　certainties
certifiable
certificate
　certificated
certification
certificatory
certified
certify
certifies
certified
certifying
certin = certain
certitude
cerulean
cervical
cervix

cervices or
cervixes
cesium
cessation
cession
cesspool
cetacean
cetologist
cetology
cf
CFC
Chablis
cha-cha-cha
chafe
　chafes
　chafed
　chafing
chaff
　chaffs
　chaffed
　chaffing
chaffinch
　chaffinches
chagrin
chain
　chains
　chained
　chaining
chair
　chairs
　chaired
　chairing
chairman
　chairmen
chairmanship
chairperson
　chairpersons
chairwoman
　chairwomen
chaise
chalenge = challenge
chalet
chalice
chalk
　chalks
　chalked
　chalking
chalkiness
chalky
challenge
　challenges
　challenged
　challenging
chamber

chamberlain
chambermaid
chambers
chambray
chameleon
chammy
chamois
chamomile
champ
　champs
　champed
　champing
champagne
champion
championship
chance
　chances
　chanced
　chancing
chancel
chancellery
chancellor
chancery
chancy
chancier
　chanciest
chandelier
chandler
chandlery
changable =
　changeable
change
　changes
　changed
　changing
changeability
changeable
changeing = changing
changeless
changeling
changeover
channel
　channels
　channelled
　channelling
chant
　chants
　chanted
　chanting
chantry
　chantries
chanty
chaos
chaotic

chaotically
chap
  chaps
  chapped
  chapping
chaparral
chapel
chaperon
  chaperons
  chaperoned
  chaperoning
chaperone
  chaperones
  chaperoned
  chaperoning
chaplain
chaplaincy
chaplet
chapped
chappie
chapping
chaps
chapter
char
  chars
  charred
  charring
charabanc
character
characterisation
characterise
  characterises
  characterised
  characterising
characteristic
characteristically
characterization
characterize
  characterizes
  characterized
  characterizing
charade
charades
charcoal
chard
Chardonnay
~~characer~~ = character
charge
  charges
  charged
  charging
chargeable
chargé d'affaires
  chargés d'affaires

charger
charier
chariest
charily
chariness
chariot
charioteer
charisma
charismatic
charitable
charitably
charity
  charities
charlady
  charladies
charlatan
Charleston
charlie
charm
  charms
  charmed
  charming
charmer
charming
charmingly
charnel
Charolais
Charollais
charred
charring
chart
  charts
  charted
  charting
charter
Chartism
chartist
Chartreuse™
charwoman
  charwomen
chary
  charier
  chariest
chase
chases
chased
chasing
chaser
chasm
chassis
  chassis
chaste
chastely
chasten

chastens
chastened
chastening
chastise
  chastises
  chastised
  chastising
chastisement
chastity
chasuble
chat
  chats
  chatted
  chatting
château
  châteaus or
  châteaux
chatelaine
chatline
chatted
chattel
chatter
  chatters
  chattered
  chattering
chatterbox
  chatterboxes
chatterer
chatting
chatty
  chattier
  chattiest
chauffeur
  chauffeurs
  chauffeured
  chauffeuring
chauffeuse
chauvinism
chauvinist
chauvinistic
chauvinistically
cheap (= not
  expensive → cheep)
cheapen
  cheapens
  cheapened
  cheapening
cheaply
cheapness
cheapo
cheapskate
cheat
  cheats
  cheated

cheating
check (= look for
  mistakes → cheque)
  checks
  checked
  checking
checker
checklist
checkmate
checkout
checkpoint
checkup
cheddar
cheek
  cheeks
  cheeked
  cheeking
cheekbone
cheeky
  cheekier
  cheekiest
cheep (= make noise
  like a bird → cheap)
  cheeps
  cheeped
  cheeping
cheer
  cheers
  cheered
  cheering
cheerful
cheerfully
cheerfulness
cheerier
cheeriest
cheerio
cheerleader
cheerless
cheerlessly
cheers
cheery
  cheerier
  cheeriest
cheese
cheeseboard
cheeseburger
cheesecake
cheesecloth
cheesemonger
cheeseparing
cheesewood
cheesy
  cheesier
  cheesiest

cheetah
chef
chef d'oeuvre
   chefs d'oeuvre
cheif = chief
Chekhov, Anton
chemical
chemically
chemise
chemist
chemistry
chemotherapeutic
chemotherapy
chenille
cheque (= used as
  means of payment
  → check)
chequebook
chequered
chequers
cherish
  cherishes
  cherished
  cherishing
Cherokee
cheroot
cherry
  cherries
cherub
  cherubim or
  cherubs
cherubic
cherubically
cherubim
chervil
chess
chessboard
chessman
  chessmen
chest
chesterfield
chestier
chestiest
chestnut
chesty
  chestier
  chestiest
chevalier
chevron
chew
  chews
  chewed
  chewing
chewy

chewier
chewiest
Cheyenne
chianti
chiaroscuro
chic (= elegant
  → sheikh, sheik)
Chicago
chicanery
chichi
chick
chickadee
chicken
  chickens
  chickened
  chickening
chickenpox
chickpea
chickweed
chicle
chicly
chicory
chide
  chides
  chid or
  chided
  chid or
  chidden
  chiding
chief
chiefly
chieftain
chiffon
chiffonier
chiffonnier
chigger
chignon
chihuahua
chilblain
child
  children
childbirth
childcare
childhood
childish
childishly
childishness
childlike
children
Chile
chill
  chills
  chilled
  chilling

chiller
chilli
  chillies
chilliness
chilly
  chillier
  chilliest
chimaera
chime
  chimes
  chimed
  chiming
chimera
chimerical
chimney
  chimneys
chimneypiece
chimneypot
chimp
chimpanzee
chin
China
china
chinchilla
chine
Chinese
chink
  chinks
  chinked
  chinking
chinless
chino
chinos
chintz
chintzy
  chintzier
  chintziest
chinwag
chior = choir
chip
  chips
  chipped
  chipping
chipboard
chipmunk
chipolata
chipped
chipper
Chippewa
chipping
chippy
  chippies
chiromancy
chiropodist

chiropody
chiropractic
chiropractor
chirp
  chirps
  chirped
  chirping
chirpy
  chirpier
  chirpiest
chisel
  chisels
  chiselled
  chiselling
  chiseller
chit
chitchat
chitin
chitterlings
chitty
  chitties
chivalrous
chivalrously
chivalry
chives
chivvy
  chivvies
  chivvied
  chivvying
chivy
  chivies
  chivied
  chivying
chlorate
chloride
chlorinate
  chlorinates
  chlorinated
  chlorinating
chlorine
chlorite
chlorofluorocarbon
chloroform
chlorophyll
chloroplast
chlorosis
choc
chocaholic
chocalate = chocolate
chock
  chocks
  chocked
  chocking
chocoholic

chocolate
Choctaw
choice
choir (= group of
  singers → coir,
  quire)
choirboy
choirmaster
choke
  chokes
  choked
  choking
choker
chokey
choky
choler
cholera
choleric
cholerically
cholesterol
chomp
  chomps
  chomped
  chomping
choose
  chooses
  chose
  chosen
  choosing
choosy
  choosier
  choosiest
chop
  chops
  chopped
  chopping
chophouse
chopped
chopper
choppers
chopping
choppy
  choppier
  choppiest
chops
chopsticks
chop suey
choral (sung by a choir
  → coral, corral)
chorale
chord (= musical
  notes → cord)
chording
chore

choreograph
  choreographs
  choreographed
  choreographing
choreographer
choreographic
choreography
chorister
chorizo
  chorizos
chortle
  chortles
  chortled
  chortling
chorus
  choruses
  chorused
  chorusing
chose
chosen
choux
chow
chowder
chow mein
Christ
christen
  christens
  christened
  christening
Christendom
christening
Christian
Christianise
  Christianises
  Christianised
  Christianising
Christianity
Christianize
  Christianizes
  Christianized
  Christianizing
Christlike
Christmas
Christmassy
Christmastide
chromate
chromatic
chrome
chromite
chromium
chromosome
chronic
chronically
chronicle

chronicles
chronicled
chronicling
chronicler
chronograph
chronological
chronologically
chronologist
chronology
chrysalis
  chrysalises
chrysanthemum
  chrysanthemums
chubby
  chubbier
  chubbiest
chuck
  chucks
  chucked
  chucking
chuckle
  chuckles
  chuckled
  chuckling
chuffed
chug
  chugs
  chugged
  chugging
chukka
chukker
chum
  chums
  chummed
  chumming
chummy
  chummier
  chummiest
chump
chunk
chunky
  chunkier
  chunkiest
Chunnel
church
  churches
churchgoer
churchier
churchiest
Churchill, Winston
churchman
churchmen
churchwarden
churchwoman

churchwomen
churchy
  churchier
  churchiest
churchyard
churl
churlish
churlishly
churlishness
churn
  churns
  churned
  churning
chute (= slide
  → shoot)
chutney
  chutneys
CIA
ciao
cicada
  cicadas
cicatrice
  cicatrices
cicatrix
  cicatrices
cicerone
CID
cider
~~cieling~~ = ceiling
cig
cigar
cigarette
cigarillo
  cigarillos
ciggy
  ciggies
~~cilinder~~ = cylinder
~~cinamon~~ = cinnamon
cinch
cincture
cinder
cinema
cinematographer
cinematographic
cinematography
cinnabar
cinnamon
Cinzano®
cipher
  ciphers
  ciphered
  ciphering
circa
circadian

circiut = circuit
circle
  circles
  circled
  circling
circlet
circuit
circuitous
circuitously
circular
circularise
  circularises
  circularised
  circularising
circularity
circularize
  circularizes
  circularized
  circularizing
circulate
  circulates
  circulated
  circulating
circulation
circumcise
  circumcises
  circumcised
  circumcising
circumcision
circumference
circumferential
circumflex
circumlocution
circumlocutory
circumnavigate
  circumnavigates
  circumnavigated
  circumnavigating
circumnavigation
circumscribe
  circumscribes
  circumscribed
  circumscribing
circumscription
circumspect
circumspection
circumspectly
circumstance
circumstantial
circumstantially
circumvent
  circumvents
  circumvented
  circumventing

circus
  circuses
cirque
cirrhosis
cirrus
CIS
cissy
  cissies
Cistercian
cistern
citadel
citation
cite (= give as an
  example → site,
  sight)
  cites
  cited
  citing
citizen
citizenry
citizenship
citric
citron
citronella
citrus
  citruses
city
  cities
citywide
civet
civic
civics
civies
civil
civilian
civilisation
civilise
  civilises
  civilised
  civilising
civilised
civility
civilization
civilize
  civilizes
  civilized
  civilizing
civilized
civilly
civvies
civvy
clack
  clacks
  clacked

  clacking
clad
cladding
claggy
  claggier
  claggiest
claim
  claims
  claimed
  claiming
claimant
clairvoyance
clairvoyant
clairvoyantly
clam
  clams
  clammed
  clamming
clamber
  clambers
  clambered
  clambering
clammed
clamming
clammy
  clammier
  clammiest
clamour
  clamours
  clamoured
  clamouring
clamp
  clamps
  clamped
  clamping
clampdown
clan
clandestine
clandestinely
clandestineness
clang
  clangs
  clanged
  clanging
clanger
clank
  clanks
  clanked
  clanking
clannish
  clannishly
  clannishness
clansman
  clansmen

clap
  claps
  clapped
  clapping
clapper
clapperboard
clappers
clapping
claptrap
claque
claret
clarification
clarify
  clarifies
  clarified
  clarifying
clarinet
clarinetist
clarinettist
clarion
clarity
clash
  clashes
  clashed
  clashing
clasp
  clasps
  clasped
  clasping
class
  classes
  classed
  classing
classic
classical
classicism
classicist
classics
classier
classiest
classification
classified
classify
  classifies
  classified
  classifying
classism
classless
classmate
classroom
classy
  classier
  classiest
clatter

clatters
clattered
clattering
clause (= part of a
　sentence → claws)
claustrophobia
claustrophic
clavichord
clavicle
claw (= clutch at with
　hand → clause)
　claws
　clawed
　clawing
clay
claymore
clean
　cleans
　cleaned
　cleaning
clean-cut
cleaner
cleanliness
cleanly
cleanse
　cleanses
　cleansed
　cleansing
cleanser
cleanup
clear
　clears
　cleared
　clearing
clearance
clear-cut
clearing
clearly
clearsighted
clearstory
　clearstories
clearway
cleat
cleavage
cleave
　cleaves
　cleaved or
　clove
　cleaved or
　cleft or
　cloven
　cleaving
cleaver
Cleethorpes

clef
cleft
cleg
clematis
clemency
clement
clementine
clemently
clench
　clenches
　clenched
　clenching
clerestory
　clerestories
clergy
clergyman
　clergymen
cleric
clerical
clericalism
clerically
clerihew
clerk
Cleveland
clever
cleverdick
cleverly
cleverness
clew
clianthus
cliché
clichéd
click
　clicks
　clicked
　clicking
client
clientele
cliff
cliffhanger
climacteric
climacterical
climactic
climactically
climate
climatic
climatically
climatological
climatologically
climatology
climax
　climaxes
climb (= ascend
　→ clime)

climbs
climbed
climbing
climber
clime (= climate
　→ climb)
clinch
　clinches
　clinched
　clinching
clincher
cline
cling
　clings
　clung
　clinging
clingfilm
clinic
clinical
clinically
clinician
clink
　clinks
　clinked
　clinking
clinker
clip
　clips
　clipped
　clipping
clipboard
clipped
clipper
clippers
clipping
clique
cliquish
cliquishness
clitoral
clitoris
　clitorises
cloak
　cloaks
　cloaked
　cloaking
cloakroom
clobber
　clobbers
　clobbered
　clobbering
cloche
clock
　clocks
　clocked

clocking
clockmaker
clockwise
clockwork
clod
cloddish
clodhopper
clog
　clogs
　clogged
　clogging
cloisonné
cloister
　cloisters
　cloistered
　cloistering
clone
　clones
　cloned
　cloning
clop
　clops
　clopped
　clopping
clor try chlor
close
　closes
　closed
　closing
　closer
　closest
close-fisted
close-grained
close-hauled
close-knit
closely
closeness
closet
　closets
　closeted
　closeting
closing
closure
clot
　clots
　clotted
　clotting
cloth
clothe
　clothes
　clothed
　clothing
clothes
clotheshorse

clothesline
clothier
clothing
clotted
cloture
cloud
  clouds
  clouded
  clouding
cloudberry
  cloudberries
cloudburst
cloudier
cloudiest
cloudless
cloudy
  cloudier
  cloudiest
clout
  clouts
  clouted
  clouting
clove
cloven
clover
cloverleaf
clown
  clowns
  clowned
  clowning
cloy
  cloys
  cloyed
  cloying
cloze test
club
  clubs
  clubbed
  clubbing
clubby
clubhouse
cluck
  clucks
  clucked
  clucking
clue
  clues
  clued
  cluing
clued-up
clueless
clump
  clumps
  clumped

clumping
clumsy
  clumsier
  clumsiest
clung
clunk
  clunks
  clunked
  clunking
cluster
  clusters
  clustered
  clustering
clutch
  clutches
  clutched
  clutching
clutter
  clutters
  cluttered
  cluttering
Clwyd
Clyde
cm
c.m.
CND
co try cho
Co.
c/o
coach
  coaches
  coached
  coaching
coachbuilder
coachman
  coachmen
coachwork
coaction
coactive
coactively
coadjutor
coagulable
coagulant
coagulate
  coagulates
  coagulated
  coagulating
coagulation
coagulative
coal
coalesce
  coalesces
  coalesced
  coalescing

coalescence
coalface
coalfield
coalition
coalman
  coalmen
coarse (= rough
  → course)
coarsen
  coarsens
  coarsened
  coarsening
coast
  coasts
  coasted
  coasting
coaster
coastguard
coastline
coat
  coats
  coated
  coating
coating
coauthor
coax
  coaxes
  coaxed
  coaxing
cob
cobalt
cobber
cobble
  cobbles
  cobbled
  cobbling
cobbled
cobbler
cobblers
cobblestone
cobnut
cobra
  cobras
cobweb
coca
cocaine
coccyx
  coccyxes or
  coccyges
cochineal
cochlea
  cochlea or
  cochleae
cock

cocks
cocked
cocking
cockade
cock-a-doodle-doo
cock-a-hoop
cock-a-leekie
cockalorum
cockatiel
cockatoo
  cockatoos or
  cockatoo
cockatrice
cockchafer
cockcrow
cockerel
cockeyed
cockfight
cockhorse
cockier
cockiest
cockiness
cockle
cockleshell
cockney
  cockneys
cockpit
cockroach
cockscomb
cocksure
cocktail
cockup
cocky
  cockier
  cockiest
cocoa
coconut
cocoon
  cocoons
  cocooned
  cocooning
cocotte
cod
coda
  codas
coddle
  coddles
  coddled
  coddling
code
  codes
  coded
  coding
codeine

codename
codeword
codex
  codices
codger
codices
codicil
codification
codify
  codifies
  codified
  codifying
codling
codpiece
codswallop
co-ed
coeducation
coefficient
coelacanth
coeliac
coequal
coequally
coerce
  coerces
  coerced
  coercing
coercion
coercive
coercively
coerciveness
coeval
coexist
  coexists
  coexisted
  coexisting
coexistence
coextensive
coffee
coffeepot
coffer
cofferdam
coffin
cog
cogency
cogent
  cogently
cognac
cognate
cognisance
cognisant
cognition
cognitive
cognitively
cognizance

cognizant
cognomen
cognominal
cognoscenti
cogwheel
cohabit
  cohabits
  cohabited
  cohabiting
cohabitant
cohabitation
cohabiter
cohere
  coheres
  cohered
  cohering
coherence
coherent
coherently
cohesion
cohesive
cohesively
cohesiveness
cohort
coif
coiffed
coiffeur
coiffure
coiffured
coil
  coils
  coiled
  coiling
coin
  coins
  coined
  coining
coinage
coincide
  coincides
  coincided
  coinciding
coincidence
coincident
coincidental
coincidentally
Cointreau
coir (= material used
  for mats, ropes, etc.
  → choir)
coital
coition
coitus
coitus interruptus

coke
col
cola
coleborate =
  collaborate
colander
colateral = collateral
cold
  colder
  coldest
coldblooded
coldhearted
coldly
coldness
Coleraine
coleslaw
coley
  coleys
colic
colicky
coliseum
colitis
collaborate
  collaborates
  collaborated
  collaborating
collaboration
collaborationism
collaborationist
collaborative
collaborator
collage (= picture
  → college)
collagen
collapse
  collapses
  collapsed
  collapsing
collapsibility
collapsible
collar
  collars
  collared
  collaring
collarbone
collard
collate
  collates
  collated
  collating
collateral
collation
collator
colleague

collect
  collects
  collected
  collecting
collectable
collected
collectedly
collection
collective
collectively
collectivisation
collectivization
collector
colleen
college (= place of
  education → collage)
collegial
collegiate
collegium
collide
  collides
  collided
  colliding
collie
  collies
collier
colliery
  collieries
collision
collocate
  collocates
  collocated
  collocating
collocation
colloid
colloquial
colloquialism
colloquially
colloquialness
colloquy
colossal = colossal
collude
  colludes
  colluded
  colluding
collusion
collusive
collywobbles
Colne
cologne
Colombia (country)
colon
colonel (= military
  officer → kernel)

colonial
colonialism
colonialist
colonially
colonise
　colonises
　colonised
　colonising
colonist
colonize
　colonizes
　colonized
　colonizing
colonnade
　colonnaded
colonoscopy
colony
　colonies
coloration
coloratura
colossal
colossally
colosseum
colossus
　colossuses *or*
　colossi
colostrum
colour
　colours
　coloured
　colouring
coloured
colourfast
colourful
colourfully
colourise
　colourises
　colourised
　colourising
colourize
　colourizes
　colourized
　colourizing
colourless
colourlessly
colt
coltish
coltishly
coltishness
coltsfoot
columbine
column
columnar
columnist

coma
comas
Comanche
comatose
comb
　combs
　combed
　combing
combat
　combats
　combatted
　combatting
combatable
combatant
combative
combatively
comber
combinable
combination
combinative
combine
　combines
　combined
　combining
combo
　combos
combustibility
combustible
combustion
come
　comes
　came
　coming
comeback
comedian
comedienne
comedown
comedy
　comedies
comeing = coming
comeliness
comely
comer
comestible
comet
comeuppance
comfier
comfiest
comfit
comfort
　comforts
　comforted
　comforting
comfortable

comfortably
comforter
comforting
comfortingly
comfortless
comfy
　comfier
　comfiest
comic
comical
comically
coming
comission =
　commission
comitee = committee
comity
　comities
comma
　commas
command
　commands
　commanded
　commanding
commandant
commandeer
commander
commandership
commanding
commandingly
commandment
commando
　commandos *or*
　commandoes
commedia dell'arte
comme il faut
commemorate
　commemorates
　commemorated
　commemorating
commemoration
commemorative
commemoratively
commence
　commences
　commenced
　commencing
commencement
commend
　commends
　commended
　commending
commendable
commendably
commendation

commendatory
commensurate
comment
　comments
　commented
　commenting
commentary
　commentaries
commentate
　commentates
　commentated
　commentating
commentator
commerce
commercial
commercialisation
commercialise
　commercialises
　commercialised
　commercialising
commercialism
commercialization
commercialize
　commercializes
　commercialized
　commercializing
commercially
commie
　commies
commis chef
commiserate
　commiserates
　commiserated
　commiserating
commiseration
commissar
commissariat
commissary
　commissaries
commission
　commissions
　commissioned
　commissioning
commissionaire
commissioner
commissionership
commit
　commits
　committed
　committing
comitee = committee
comited = committed
commitment
committal

committed
committee
committeeman
  committeemen
committeewoman
  committeewomen
committment =
  commitment
commode
commodious
commodiously
commodiousness
commodity
  commodities
commodore
common
commonality
commoner
commonly
commonness
commonplace
commons
common sense
commonsensical
commonweal
commonwealth
Commonwealth
commotion
communal
communally
commune
  communes
  communed
  communing
communicable
communicably
communicant
communicate
  communicates
  communicated
  communicating
communication
communicative
communicatively
communicator
communion
communiqué
communism
communist
community
  communities
commutability
commutable
commutableness

commutation
commutative
commutator
commute
  commutes
  commuted
  commuting
commuter
compact
  compacts
  compacted
  compacting
compaction
compactly
compactness
compadre
companion
companionability
companionable
companionableness
companionably
companionless
companionship
companionway
company
  companies
comparable
comparability
comparably
comparative
comparatively
compare
  compares
  compared
  comparing
comparison
comparitive =
  comparative
compartment
compartmental
compartmentalisation
compartmentalise
  compartmentalises
  compartmentalised
  compartmentalising
compartmentalization
compartmentalize
  compartmentalizes
  compartmentalized
  compartmentalizing
compass
compassion
compassionate
compassionately

compatable =
  compatible
compatibility
compatible
compatibly
compatriot
compeer
compel
  compels
  compelled
  compelling
compelling
compellingly
compendious
compendiously
compendiousness
compendium
  compendiums or
  compendia
compensate
  compensates
  compensated
  compensating
compensation
compensatory
compere
  comperes
  compered
  compering
competant =
  competent
compete
  competes
  competed
  competing
competence
competency
competent
  competently
competition
competitive
competitively
competitiveness
competitor
compilation
compile
  compiles
  compiled
  compiling
compiler
complacency
complacent
complacently
complain

complains
complained
complaining
complainant
complainer
complaining
complainingly
complaint
complaisance
complaisant
complaisantly
complement (= make
  something complete
  → compliment)
  complements
  complemented
  complementing
complementary
complementation
complete
  completes
  completed
  completing
completely
completeness
completion
completive
complex
  complexes
complexion
complexioned
complexity
  complexities
compliance
compliant
compliantly
complicate
  complicates
  complicated
  complicating
complicated
complication
complicity
complied
complies
compliment (= make
  flattering remark
  → complement)
  compliments
  complimented
  complimenting
complimentary
compline
comply

complies
complied
complying
component
componential
comport
comports
comported
comporting
comportment
compose
composes
composed
composing
composed
composedly
composer
composite
composition
compositor
compos mentis
compost
composts
composted
composting
composure
compote
compound
compounds
compounded
compounding
comprehend
comprehends
comprehended
comprehending
comprehensible
comprehension
comprehensive
comprehensively
compress
compresses
compressed
compressing
compressibility
compressible
compression
compressor
comprisal
comprise
comprises
comprised
comprising
compromise
compromises

compromised
compromising
comptroller
compulsion
compulsive
compulsively
compulsiveness
compulsorily
compulsoriness
compulsory
compunction
computation
compute
computes
computed
computing
computer
computerisation
computerise
computerises
computerised
computerising
computerization
computerize
computerizes
computerized
computerizing
comrade
comradely
comradeship
coms
con
cons
conned
conning
concatenate
concatenates
concatenated
concatenating
concatenation
concave
concavity
concavities
concavo-concave
concavo-convex
conceal
conceals
concealed
concealing
concealable
concealer
concealment
concede
concedes

conceded
conceding
conceed = concede
conceit
conceited
conceitedly
conceitedness
conceivability
conceivable
conceivably
conceive
conceives
conceived
conceiving
concensus = consensus
concentrate
concentrates
concentrated
concentrating
concentration
concentrative
concentric
concentrically
concept
conception
conceptual
conceptualisation
conceptualise
conceptualises
conceptualised
conceptualising
conceptualization
conceptualize
conceptualizes
conceptualized
conceptualizing
conceptually
concern
concerns
concerned
concerning
concerned
concernedly
concerning
concernment
concert
concerted
concertedly
concertgoer
concertina
concertinas
concertmaster
concerto
concertos

concession
concessionaire
concessionary
concessive
conch
conches
conchie
conchies
conchologist
conchology
concierge
concieve = conceive
conciliate
conciliates
conciliated
conciliating
conciliation
conciliator
conciliatory
concise
concisely
conciseness
concision
conclave
conclude
concludes
concluded
concluding
conclusion
conclusive
conclusively
concoct
concocts
concocted
concocting
concoction
concomitant
concomitantly
concord
concordance
concordant
concordantly
concordat
Concorde
concourse
concrete
concretes
concreted
concreting
concretise
concretises
concretised
concretising
concretize

concretizes
concretized
concretizing
concubinage
concubine
concupiscence
concupiscent
concur
concurs
concurred
concurring
concurrence
concurrent
concurrently
concuss
concusses
concussed
concussing
concussion
condem = condemn
condemn
condemns
condemned
condemning
condemnable
condemnably
condemnation
condemnatory
condemning
condemningly
condensation
condense
condenses
condensed
condensing
condenser
condescend
condescends
condescended
condescending
condescending
condescension
condign
condignly
condiment
condition
conditions
conditioned
conditioning
conditional
conditionally
conditioned
conditioner
conditioning

condolatory
condole
condoles
condoled
condoling
condolence
condom
condominium
condonable
condone
condones
condoned
condoning
condor
conduce
conduces
conduced
conducing
conducive
conduciveness
conduct
conducts
conducted
conducting
conduction
conductive
conductivity
conductor
conductress
conductresses
conduit
cone
cones
coned
coning
conection = connection
coney
coneys
confabulate
confabulates
confabulated
confabulating
confabulation
confection
confectioner
confectionery
confederacy
confederate
confederates
confederated
confederating
confederation
confederative
confer

confers
conferred
conferring
confered = conferred
conference
conferment
confess
confesses
confessed
confessing
confessed
confessedly
confession
confessional
confessor
confetti
confidant (= person
  with whom one
  shares secrets
  → confident)
confidante
confide
confides
confided
confiding
confidence
confident (= certain
  about something
  → confidant)
confidential
confidently
confiding
confidingly
confidingness
configuration
confinable
confine
confines
confined
confining
confinement
confiner
confirm
confirms
confirmed
confirming
confirmation
confirmatory
confirmed
confiscate
confiscates
confiscated
confiscating
confiscation

confiscatory
confit
conflagration
conflate
conflates
conflated
conflating
conflation
conflict
conflicts
conflicted
conflicting
conflicting
conflictingly
confluence
conform
conforms
conformed
conforming
conformance
conformation
conformist
conformity
confound
confounds
confounded
confounding
confounded
confoundedly
confraternity
confraternities
confrère
confront
confronts
confronted
confronting
confrontation
confrontational
Confucian
Confucianism
confusability
confusable
confuse
confuses
confused
confusing
confused
confusedly
confusedness
confusing
confusingly
confusion
confutable
confutation

confute
  confutes
  confuted
  confuting
congé
congeal
  congeals
  congealed
  congealing
congenial
congeniality
congenially
congenital
congenitally
conger
congested
congestion
conglomerate
conglomeration
congratulate
  congratulates
  congratulated
  congratulating
congratulation
congratulations
congratulative
congratulatory
congregate
  congregates
  congregated
  congregating
congregation
congregational
Congregationalism
congress
  congresses
Congress
congressional
Congressman
  Congressmen
Congresswoman
  Congresswomen
congruence
congruent
congruity
congruous
conic
conical
conifer
coniferous
conjectural
conjecturally
conjecture
  conjectures

conjectured
conjecturing
conjoin
  conjoins
  conjoined
  conjoining
conjoint
conjointly
conjugal
conjugate
  conjugates
  conjugated
  conjugating
conjugation
conjunction
conjunctive
conjunctivitis
conjuncture
conjure
  conjures
  conjured
  conjuring
conjurer
conjuror
conk
  conks
  conked
  conking
conker (= horse
  chestnut → conquer)
conman
  conmen
connect
  connects
  connected
  connecting
connecter
Connecticut
connection
connective
connector
conned
Connemara
connexion
conning
conniption
connivance
connive
  connives
  connived
  conniving
  connivingly
connoiseur =
  connoisseur

connoisseur
connotation
connotative
connote
  connotes
  connoted
  connoting
connotive
connubial
conquer (= defeat
  → conker)
  conquers
  conquered
  conquering
conquest
conquistador
consanguine
consanguinity
conscience
conscientious
conscientiously
conscientiousness
conscious
consciously
consciousness
conscript
  conscripts
  conscripted
  conscripting
conscription
consecrate
  consecrates
  consecrated
  consecrating
consecration
consecutive
consecutively
consensual
consensus
consent
  consents
  consented
  consenting
consequence
consequences
consequent
consequential
consequently
consern = concern
consession =
  concession
conservancy
conservation
conservationist

conservatism
conservative
conservativeness
conservatoire
conservator
conservatorial
conservatory
  conservatories
conserve
  conserves
  conserved
  conserving
consider
  considers
  considered
  considering
considerable
considerably
considerate
considerately
considerateness
consideration
considered
considering
consience = conscience
consign
  consigns
  consigned
  consigning
consignee
consigner
consignment
consignor
consious = conscious
consist
  consists
  consisted
  consisting
consistant = consistent
consistency
  consistencies
consistent
consistently
consistory
consolable
consolation
consolatory
console
  consoles
  consoled
  consoling
consolidate
  consolidates
  consolidated

consolidating
consolidation
consolingly
consols
consommé
consonance
consonant
consort
  consorts
  consorted
  consorting
consortium
  consortia *or*
  consortiums
conspectus
  conspectuses
conspicuous
conspicuously
conspicuousness
conspiracy
  conspiracies
conspirator
conspiratorial
conspiratorially
conspire
  conspires
  conspired
  conspiring
constable
constabulary
  constabularies
constancy
constant
Constantinople
constellation
consternation
constipate
  constipates
  constipated
  constipating
constipation
constituency
  constituencies
constituent
constitute
  constitutes
  constituted
  constituting
constitution
constitutional
constitutionalism
constitutionality
constitutionally
constrain

constrains
constrained
constraining
constrained
constrainedly
constraint
constrict
  constricts
  constricted
  constricting
constriction
constrictive
constrictor
construct
  constructs
  constructed
  constructing
constructer
construction
constructional
constructive
constructively
constructiveness
constructor
construe
  construes
  construed
  construing
consubstantiation
consul
consular
consulate
consulship
consult
  consults
  consulted
  consulting
consultancy
  consultancies
consultant
consultation
consultative
consulting
consumable
consumate =
  consummate
consume
  consumes
  consumed
  consuming
consumer
consumerism
consuming
consumingly

consummate
  consummates
  consummated
  consummating
consummately
consummation
consumption
consumptive
consumptively
contact
  contacts
  contacted
  contacting
contactable
contagion
contagious
contagiously
contagiousness
contain
  contains
  contained
  containing
container
containerisation
containerise
  containerises
  containerised
  containerising
containerization
containerize
  containerizes
  containerized
  containerizing
containment
contaminant
contaminate
  contaminates
  contaminated
  contaminating
contamination
contango
  contagos
contd
contemplate
  contemplates
  contemplated
  contemplating
contemplation
contemplative
contemporaneity
contemporaneous
contemporaneously
contemporarily
contemporary

contempory =
  contemporary
contempt
contemptibility
contemptible
contemptibly
contemptuous
contemptuously
contend
  contends
  contended
  contending
contender
content
  contents
  contented
  contenting
contented
contentedly
contention
contentious
contentiously
contentiousness
contently
contentment
contest
  contests
  contested
  contesting
contestable
contestant
contester
context
contextual
contextualisation
contextualise
  contextualises
  contextualised
  contextualising
contextualization
contextualize
  contextualizes
  contextualized
  contextualizing
contextually
Contiboard®
contiguity
contiguous
contiguously
continent
continental
contingency
  contingencies
contingent

contingently
continual
continually
continuance
continuation
continue
  continues
  continued
  continuing
continuingly
continuity
continuo
  continuos
~~continuos~~ = continuous
continuous
continuously
continuousness
continuum
  continuums *or*
  continua
contort
  contorts
  contorted
  contorting
contortion
contortionist
contour
contra-
contraband
contrabass
  contrabasses
contrabassist
contraception
contraceptive
contract
  contracts
  contracted
  contracting
contractible
contractile
contraction
contractionary
contractor
contractual
contractually
contradict
  contradicts
  contradicted
  contradicting
contradiction
contradictory
contradistinction
contraflow
contrail

contraindication
contralto
  contraltos
contraption
contrapuntal
contrarily
contrariness
contrariwise
contrary
contrast
  contrasts
  contrasted
  contrasting
contrastive
contravene
  contravenes
  contravened
  contravening
contravention
~~contraversial~~ =
  controversial
contretemps
contribute
  contributes
  contributed
  contributing
contribution
contributive
contributor
contributory
contrite
contritely
contrition
contrivance
contrive
  contrives
  contrived
  contriving
control
  controls
  controlled
  controlling
~~controll~~ = control
controllability
controllable
controllably
controller
controversial
controversially
controversy
  controversies
contumacious
contumacy
contumelious

contumely
contusion
conundrum
  conundrums
conurbation
convalesce
  convalesces
  convalesced
  convalescing
convalescence
convalescent
convection
convector
convene
  convenes
  convened
  convening
convener
~~conveniant~~ =
  convenient
convenience
convenient
conveniently
convenor
convent
conventicle
convention
conventional
conventionalism
conventionality
  conventionalities
conventionally
converge
  converges
  converged
  converging
convergence
convergent
conversant
conversation
conversational
conversationalist
conversationally
conversazione
  conversaziones *or*
  conversazioni
converse
  converses
  conversed
  conversing
conversely
conversion
convert
  converts

converted
converting
converter
convertibility
convertible
convertor
convex
convexly
convey
  conveys
  conveyed
  conveying
conveyance
conveyancer
conveyancing
conveyer
conveyor
convict
  convicts
  convicted
  convicting
conviction
convince
  convinces
  convinced
  convincing
convivial
conviviality
convivially
convocation
convoke
  convokes
  convoked
  convoking
convoluted
convolution
convolvulus
  convolvuluses
convoy
convulse
  convulses
  convulsed
  convulsing
convulsion
convulsive
convulsively
cony
  conies
coo
  coos
  cooed
  cooing
cooee
cooey

cook
  cooks
  cooked
  cooking
cooker
cookery
cookhouse
cookie
  cookies
cool
  cools
  cooled
  cooling
  cooler
  coolest
coolant
cooler
coolie
  coolies
coolish
coolly
coolness
coomb
coon
coop
  coops
  cooped
  cooping
co-op
cooper
cooperate
  cooperates
  cooperated
  cooperating
co-operate
  co-operates
  co-operated
  co-operating
cooperation
co-operation
cooperative
co-operative
cooperatively
co-operatively
cooperativeness
co-operativeness
co-opt
  co-opts
  co-opted
  co-opting
coordinate
  coordinates
  coordinated
  coordinating

coordinately
coordinates
coordination
coordinator
coot
cop
  cops
  copped
  copping
cope
  copes
  coped
  coping
copied
copier
copies
copilot
coping
copious
copiously
copped
copper
copperhead
copperplate
coppice
  coppices
  coppiced
  coppicing
  copping
copra
copse
Coptic
copula
copulate
  copulates
  copulated
  copulating
copulation
copy
  copies
  copied
  copying
copybook
copycat
copying
copyist
copyright
  copyrights
  copyrighted
  copyrighting
copywrite = copyright
copywriter
coq au vin
coquetry

  coquetries
coquette
coquettish
coquettishly
coquettishness
coracle
coral (= stonelike
  substance → corral,
  choral)
cor anglais
  cors anglais
corbel
cord (= string or rope
  → chord)
cordage
corded
cordial
cordiality
cordially
cordite
cordless
cordon
cordon bleu
cordon sanitaire
cords
corduroy
  corduroys
core (= make central
  hole → corps)
  cores
  cored
  coring
coreligionist
correspondence =
  correspondence
corespondent (=
  person cited in a
  divorce case
  → correspondent)
corgi
  corgis
coriander
Corinthian
cork (= stop up a
  bottle → caulk)
  corks
  corked
  corking
corkage
corked
corker
corkscrew
corm
cormorant

corn
cornball
corncob
corncockle
corncrake
cornea
  corneas
corned
cornelian
corner
  corners
  cornered
  cornering
cornerstone
cornet
cornetist
cornfield
cornflakes
cornflour
cornflower
cornice
corniche
cornier
corniest
cornily
corniness
Cornish
cornucopia
corny
  cornier
  corniest
corollary
  corollaries
corona
  coronas or
  coronae
coronary
  coronaries
coronation
coroner
coronet
corperation =
  corporation
corpora
corporal
corporate
corporately
corporation
corporeal
corporeally
corps (= group of
  soldiers → core)
corpse
corpulence

corpulent
corpus
  corpora *or*
  corpuses
corpuscle
corral (= area for
  animals → coral,
  choral)
correct
  corrects
  corrected
  correcting
correction
correctional
correctitude
corrective
correctively
correctly
correctness
correlate
  correlates
  correlated
  correlating
correlation
correlative
correspond
correspondence
correspondent (=
  person one writes to
  → corespondent)
corridor
corrigendum
  corrigenda
corroborate
  corroborates
  corroborated
  corroborating
corroboration
corroborative
corroborator
corrode
  corrodes
  corroded
  corroding
corrosion
corrosive
corrosively
corrosiveness
corrugated
corrugation
corrupt
  corrupts
  corrupted
  corrupting

corruptibility
corruptible
corruption
corruptly
corruptness
corsage
corsair
corselet
corset
corsetry
cortege
cortège
cortex
  cortices
corticosteroid
cortisone
corundum
coruscate
  coruscates
  coruscated
  coruscating
coruscation
corvette
cos
cosh
  coshes
  coshed
  coshing
cosier
cosiest
cosignatory
  cosignatories
cosily
cosine
cosiness
cosmetic
cosmetically
cosmetician
cosmic
cosmically
cosmogony
cosmology
cosmonaut
cosmopolitan
cosmos
Cossack
cosset
  cossets
  cossetted
  cossetting
cost
  costs
  cost
  costing

costa
Costa Rica
co-star
  co-stars
  co-starred
  co-starring
costermonger
costing
costive
costly
costume
costumier
cosy
  cosier
  cosiest
cot
cotangent
cotangential
Côte D'Ivoire
coterie
  coteries
coterminous
coterminously
cotillion
Cotswolds
cottage
cottager
cottaging
cotton
  cottons
  cottoned
  cottoning
cottonwood
couch
  couches
  couched
  couching
couchette
cougar
cough
  coughs
  coughed
  coughing
couldn't
couldst
council (= elected
  body → counsel)
councillor
councilman
  councilmen
councilwoman
  councilwomen
counsel (= give
  advice → council)

counsels
counselled
counselling
counsellor
count
  counts
  counted
  counting
countable
countdown
countenance
counter
counteract
  counteracts
  counteracted
  counteracting
counterattack
  counterattacks
  counterattacked
  counterattacking
counterattraction
counterbalance
  counterbalances
  counterbalanced
  counterbalancing
counterblast
counterclaim
counterclockwise
counterespionage
counterfeit
  counterfeits
  counterfeited
  counterfeiting
counterfeiter
~~counterfit~~ = counterfeit
counterfoil
countermand
  countermands
  countermanded
  countermanding
countermeasure
counteroffensive
counterpane
counterpart
counterpoint
counterpoise
counterproductive
countersign
  countersigns
  countersigned
  countersigning
countersignature
countervailing
countess

countesses
countless
countrified
country
　countries
countryman
　countrymen
countryside
countrywoman
　countrywomen
county
　counties
coup
coup de grâce
coup d'état
　coups d'état
coupé
couple
　couples
　coupled
　coupling
coupledom
coupler
couplet
coupling
coupon
courage
courageous
courageously
courageousness
~~couragous~~ =
　courageous
courgette
courier
　couriers
　couriered
　couriering
course (= path
　→ coarse)
court
　courts
　courted
　courting
court-bouillon
courteous
courteously
courteousness
courtesan
courtesy
courthouse
courtier
courtly
court-martial
　court-martials or

courts-martial
court-martialled
court-martialling
courtroom
courtship
courtyard
couscous
cousin
couture
couturier
cove
coven
covenant
Coventry
cover
　covers
　covered
　covering
coverage
covering
coverlet
covert
covet
　covets
　coveted
　coveting
covetous
covetously
cow
coward
cowardice
cowardly
cowbell
cowboy
cowcatcher
cower
　cowers
　cowered
　cowering
cowgirl
cowherd
cowhide
cowl
cowlick
cowling
cowman
　cowmen
cowpat
cowpox
cowpuncher
cowrie
cowry
cowslip
cox

coxes
coxcomb
coxswain
coy
coyly
coyness
coyote
coypu
　coypus or
　coypu
cozen
　cozens
　cozened
　cozening
cr try chr
crab
　crabs
　crabbed
　crabbing
crabbed
crabby
　crabbier
　crabbiest
crabs
crabstick
crabwise
crack
　cracks
　cracked
　cracking
crackbrained
crackdown
cracker
crackers
cracking
crackle
　crackles
　crackled
　crackling
crackling
crackpot
crackup
cradle
　cradles
　cradled
　cradling
cradlesnatcher
craft
　crafts
　crafted
　crafting
craftier
craftiest
craftily

craftiness
craftsman
　craftsmen
craftswoman
　craftswomen
crafty
　craftier
　craftiest
crag
craggy
cram
　crams
　crammed
　cramming
crammer
cramp
　cramps
　cramped
　cramping
crampon
cranberry
　cranberries
crane
　cranes
　craned
　craning
cranesbill
cranial
craniology
craniosacral
cranium
　craniums or
　crania
crank
　cranks
　cranked
　cranking
crankier
crankiest
crankiness
crankshaft
cranky
　crankier
　crankiest
cranny
　crannies
crap
　craps
　crapped
　crapping
crape
craps
crash
　crashes

crashed
crashing
crass
crassly
crassness
crate
  crates
  crated
  crating
crater
cravat
crave
  craves
  craved
  craving
craven
craving
crawfish
  crawfishes *or*
  crawfish
crawl
  crawls
  crawled
  crawling
crawler
Crawley
crayfish
  crayfish *or*
  crayfishes
crayon
  crayons
  crayoned
  crayoning
craze
crazed
crazily
craziness
crazy
  crazier
  craziest
creak
  creaks
  creaked
  creaking
cream
  creams
  creamed
  creaming
creamer
creamery
  creameries
creamy
  creamier
  creamiest

crease
  creases
  creased
  creasing
create
  creates
  created
  creating
creation
creationism
creationist
creative
creatively
creativeness
creator
creature
crèche
credence
credentials
credibility
credible
credibly
credit
  credits
  credited
  crediting
creditable
creditably
creditor
  credits
creditworthy
credo
  credos
credulity
credulous
credulously
credulousness
Cree
creed
creek
creel
creep
  creeps
  crept
  creeping
creeper
creeps
creepy
  creepier
  creepiest
creepy-crawly
cremate
  cremates
  cremated

cremating
cremation
crematorium
  crematoriums *or*
  crematoria
crème
crenellated
creole
creosote
  creosotes
  creosoted
  creosoting
crêpe
crêpes suzettes
crept
crepuscular
crescendo
  crescendos
crescent
cress
crest
crested
crestfallen
cretin
cretinism
cretinous
cretonne
crevasse
crevice
crew
  crews (= sail a ship
    → cruise)
  crewed
  crewing
Crewe (town)
crib
  cribs
  cribbed
  cribbing
cribbage
Criccieth
crick
  cricks
  cricked
  cricking
cricket
cricketer
cricketing
cried
crier
cries
crikey
crime
criminal

criminalise
  criminalises
  criminalised
  criminalising
criminality
criminalize
  criminalizes
  criminalized
  criminalizing
criminally
criminologist
criminology
crimp
  crimps
  crimped
  crimping
Crimplene®
crimson
cringe
  cringes
  cringed
  cringing
crinkle
  crinkles
  crinkled
  crinkling
crinkly
crinoline
cripes
cripple
  cripples
  crippled
  crippling
crisis
  crises
crisp
  crisps
  crisped
  crisping
crispy
crisscross
  crisscrosses
  crisscrossed
  crisscrossing
criterion
  criteria *or*
  criterions
critic
critical
critically
criticise
  criticises
  criticised
  criticising

criticism
criticize
  criticizes
  criticized
  criticizing
critique
criti̶si̶s̶m̶ = criticism
croak
  croaks
  croaked
  croaking
Croatia
Croatian
crochet
  crochets
  crocheted
  crocheting
crock
crockery
crocodile
crocodilian
crocus
  crocuses
croft
crofter
crofting
croissant
Cromer
cromlech
crone
cr̶o̶n̶i̶c̶ = chronic
crony
  cronies
crook
  crooks
  crooked
  crooking
crooked
crookedly
crookedness
croon
  croons
  crooned
  crooning
crop
  crops
  cropped
  cropping
cropper
croquet
croquette
crosier
cross
  crosses

crossed
crossing
cross-
crossbar
crossbench
crossbencher
crossbill
crossbones
crossbow
crossbred
crossbreed
crosscheck
  crosschecks
  crosschecked
  crosschecking
crossed
crosseyed
crossfire
crossing
crosslegged
crossover
crosspatch
  crosspatches
crosspiece
crossroads
crosswind
crosswise
crotch
  crotches
crotchet
crotchety
crouch
  crouches
  crouched
  crouching
croup
croupier
crouton
crow
  crows
  crowed
  crowing
crowbar
crowd
  crowds
  crowded
  crowding
crowed
crowing
crown
  crowns
  crowned
  crowning
crozier

crucial
crucially
crucible
cr̶u̶c̶i̶f̶i̶c̶t̶i̶o̶n̶ =
  crucifixion
crucifix
  crucifixes
crucifixion
cruciform
crucify
  crucifies
  crucified
  crucifying
crud
crude
crudely
crudity
  crudities
cruel
cruelly
cruelty
cruet
cruise (= sea voyage
  → crews)
  cruises
  cruised
  cruising
cruiser
cruller
crumb
crumble
  crumbles
  crumbled
  crumbling
crumbly
crummy
  crummier
  crummiest
crumpet
crumple
  crumples
  crumpled
  crumpling
crunch
  crunches
  crunched
  crunching
crusade
  crusades
  crusaded
  crusading
crusader
cruse
crush

crushes
crushed
crushing
crust
crustacean
crustaceous
crustily
crustiness
crusty
  crustier
  crustiest
crutch
  crutches
crux
cry
  cries
  cried
  crying
crybaby
  crybabies
cryogenic
cryogenics
cryonic
cryonics
crypt
cryptic
cryptically
cryptographer
cryptographic
cryptography
crystal
crystalline
crystallisation
crystallise
  crystallises
  crystallised
  crystallising
crystallization
crystallize
  crystallizes
  crystallized
  crystallizing
cub
Cuba
Cuban
cubbing
cubbyhole
cube
  cubes
  cubed
  cubing
cubic
cubicle
cubiform

cubism
cubist
cubit
cuckold
  cockolds
  cockolded
  cockolding
cuckoo
  cuckoos
cucumber
cucurbit
cud
cuddle
  cuddles
  cuddled
  cuddling
cuddly
cudgel
  cudgels
  cudgelled
  cudgelling
cue (= signal to
speak; billiard stick
  → queue)
  cues
  cued
  cueing
cuff
  cuffs
  cuffed
  cuffing
cuirass
cuisine
cul-de-sac
  cul-de-sacs or
  culs-de-sac
culinary
cull
  culls
  culled
  culling
culminate
  culminates
  culminated
  culminating
culmination
culottes
culpa
culpability
culpable
culpably
culprit
culs-de-sac
cult

cultivable
cultivar
cultivate
  cultivates
  cultivated
  cultivating
cultivation
cultivator
cultural
culture
cultured
culvert
cum
cumbersome
cumin
cum laude
cummerbund
cumquat
cumulative
cumulatively
cumulus
cuneiform
cunnilingus
cunning
cunningly
cunt
cup
  cups
  cupped
  cupping
Cupar
cupbearer
cupboard
cupcake
cupful
Cupid
cupidity
cupola
cuppa
cupped
cupping
cupric
cur
curable
curably
curacy
  curacies
curate
curative
curator
curatorship
curb (= control
  → kerb)
  curbs

curbed
curbing
curd
curdle
  curdles
  curdled
  curdling
cure
  cures
  cured
  curing
curé
~~curency~~ = currency
curettage
curfew
curia
  curiae
~~curiculum~~ = curriculum
curio
  curios
curiosity
  curiosities
curious
~~curiousity~~ = curiosity
curiously
curl
  curls
  curled
  curling
curler
curlew
curlicue
curling
curly
  curlier
  curliest
curmudgeon
curmudgeonly
currant (= dried grape
  → current)
currency
  currencies
current (= flow of
water or electricity;
happening now
  → currant)
curricular
curriculum
  curricula or
  curriculums
curry
  curries
  curried
  currying

curse
  curses
  cursed
  cursing
cursed
cursedly
cursive
cursor
cursorily
cursory
curt
curtail
  curtails
  curtailed
  curtailing
curtailment
curtain
  curtains
  curtained
  curtaining
~~curtesy~~ = courtesy
curtly
curtsey
  curtseys
  curtseyed
  curtseying
curtsy
  curtsies
  curtsied
  curtsying
curvaceous
curvaceously
curvature
curve
  curves
  curved
  curving
cushion
  cushions
  cushioned
  cushioning
cushy
  cushier
  cushiest
cusp
cuss
  cusses
  cussed
  cussedly
  cussedness
custard
custodial
custodian
custodianship

custody
custom
customarily
customary
customer
customise
  customises
  customised
  customising
customize
  customizes
  customized
  customizing
customs
cut
  cuts
  cut
  cutting
cutaway
cutback
cute
  cuter
  cutest
cutely

cuteness
cuticle
cutie
  cuties
cutlass
  cutlasses
cutler
cutlery
cutlet
cutoff
cutout
cutpurse
cutter
cutthroat
cutting
cuttingly
cuttlefish
  cuttlefish
CV
cwt
cyan
cyanide
cybernetic
cybernetically

cybernetics
cyclamate
cyclamen
  cyclamen
cycle
  cycles
  cycled
  cycling
cyclic
cyclical
cyclically
cyclist
cyclone
cyclops
cyclotron
cygnet (= young swan
  → signet)
cylinder
cylindrical
cylindrically
cymbal
cymbalist
cymbalo
  cymbalos

cynic
cynical
cynically
cynicism
cynosure
cypher
cypress
  cypresses
Cypriot
Cyprus
Cyrillic
cyst
cystic
cystic fibrosis
cystitis
cytologist
cytology
czar
Czech
Czechoslovakia
Czechoslovakian

D

dab
  dabs
  dabbed
  dabbing
dabble
  dabbles
  dabbled
  dabbling
dabchick
dachshund
~~dachsund~~ = dachshund
Dacron®
dactyl
dad
daddy
  daddies
daddy-longlegs
dado
  dadoes
daemon
daemonic
daemonically
daffodil
daft
  dafter
  daftest
  daftly
dagger
dago
  dagoes *or*
  dagos
dahlia
  dahlias
daily
  dailies
daintily
dainty
  daintier
  daintiest
daiquiri
  daiquiris
dairy
  dairies
dairymaid
dairyman
  dairymen

dais
  daises
daisy
  daisies
daisywheel
dale
Dales
dalliance
dally
  dallies
  dallied
  dallying
Dalmatian
dam
  dams
  dammed
  damming
damage
  damages
  damaged
  damaging
damascene
Damascus
damask
dame
dammit
damn
  damns
  damned
  damning
damnable
damnably
damnation
damned
damnedest
damning
damoiselle
damp
  damps
  damped
  damping
dampcourse
dampen
  dampens
  dampened
  dampening

damper
damsel
damselfly
  damselflies
damson
dance
  dances
  danced
  dancing
D and C
dandelion
dander
dandified
dandle
  dandles
  dandled
  dandling
dandruff
dandy
  dandies
Dane
danger
dangerous
dangerously
dangle
  dangles
  dangled
  dangling
Danish
dank
dankness
danse macabre
Danube
daphnia
  daphnias
dapper
dapple
dare
  dares
  dared
  daring
daredevil
daren't
daresay
daring
daringly

Darjeeling
dark
  darker
  darkest
darken
  darkens
  darkened
  darkening
darkey
  darkeys
darkie
  darkies
darkly
darkness
darkroom
darky
  darkies
darling
darn
  darns
  darned
  darning
dart
  darts
  darted
  darting
dartboard
darts
Darwinian
Darwinism
dash
  dashes
  dashed
  dashing
dashboard
dashing
dashingly
dastardly
data
database
date
  dates
  dated
  dating
dateless
dateline

dating
dative
daub
  daubs
  daubed
  daubing
daughter
daughterly
daunt
  daunts
  daunted
  daunting
dauntless
dauntlessly
dauphin
davenport
davit
dawdle
  dawdles
  dawdled
  dawdling
dawn
  dawns
  dawned
  dawning
day
dayboy
daybreak
daycare
daycentre
daydream
  daydreams
  daydreamed or
  daydreamt
  daydreaming
daydreamer
daygirl
Day-Glo™
daylight
daylights
daytime
daze
  dazes
  dazed
  dazing
dazedly
dazzle
  dazzles
  dazzled
  dazzling
D-day
DDT
deacon
deaconess

deaconesses
deaconry
  deaconries
deactivate
  deactivates
  deactivated
  deactivating
deactivation
dead
deadbeat
deaden
  deadens
  deadened
  deadening
deadhead
  deadheads
  deadheaded
  deadheading
deadlier
deadliest
deadline
deadlock
deadlocked
deadly
  deadlier
  deadliest
deadpan
deaf
deafen
  deafens
  deafened
  deafening
deafness
deal
  deals
  dealt
  dealing
dealer
dealings
dealt
dean
deanery
  deaneries
dear (= well-loved;
  expensive → deer)
  dearer
  dearest
dearie
  dearies
dearness
dearth
deary
  dearies
death

deathblow
deathless
deathlessly
deathly
deathtrap
deathwatch
debacle
debar
  debars
  debarred
  debarring
debase
  debases
  debased
  debasing
debasement
debatable
debate
  debates
  debated
  debating
debater
debauch
  debauches
  debauched
  debauching
debauchedly
debauchee
debauchery
debenture
debilitate
  debilitates
  debilitated
  debilitating
debilitation
debilitative
debility
  debilities
debit
  debits
  debited
  debiting
debonair
debouch
  debouches
  debouched
  debouching
debrief
  debriefs
  debriefed
  debriefing
debris
debt
debtor

debug
  debugs
  debugged
  debugging
debunk
  debunks
  debunked
  debunking
debunker
debut
debutante
decade
decadence
decadent
decadently
decaffeinated
decalitre
decamp
  decamps
  decamped
  decamping
decant
  decants
  decanted
  decanting
decanter
decapitate
  decapitates
  decapitated
  decapitating
decapitation
decathlete
decathlon
decay
  decays
  decayed
  decaying
decease
deceased
deceit
deceitful
deceitfully
deceitfulness
deceivable
deceive
  deceives
  deceived
  deceiving
deceiver
deceivingly
decelerate
  decelerates
  decelerated
  decelerating

deceleration
December
decencies
decency
decennial
decent (= acceptable
  → descent)
decently
decentralisation
decentralise
  decentralises
  decentralised
  decentralising
decentralization
decentralize
  decentralizes
  decentralized
  decentralizing
deception
deceptive
deceptively
deceptiveness
decibel
decide
  decides
  decided
  deciding
decided
decidedly
deciduous
decieve = deceive
decilitre
decimal
decimalise
  decimalises
  decimalised
  decimalising
decimalize
  decimalizes
  decimalized
  decimalizing
decimate
  decimates
  decimated
  decimating
decimation
decimetre
decipher
  deciphers
  deciphered
  deciphering
decipherable
decision
decisive

decisively
decisiveness
deck
  decks
  decked
  decking
deckle
declaim
  declaims
  declaimed
  declaiming
declaimer
declamation
declamatory
declarable
declaration
declarative
declare
  declares
  declared
  declaring
declassification
declassify
  declassifies
  declassified
  declassifying
declension
declination
decline
  declines
  declined
  declining
declivity
declivities
declutch
  declutches
  declutched
  declutching
decoction
decode
  decodes
  decoded
  decoding
décolletage
décolleté
decolonisation
decolonise
  decolonises
  decolonised
  decolonising
decolonization
decolonize
  decolonizes
  decolonized

decolonizing
decompose
  decomposes
  decomposed
  decomposing
decomposition
decompression
decongestant
deconsecrate
  deconsecrates
  deconsecrated
  deconsecrating
deconsecration
decontaminate
  decontaminates
  decontaminated
  decontaminating
decontamination
decontrol
  decontrols
  decontrolled
  decontrolling
decor
decorate
  decorates
  decorated
  decorating
decoration
decorative
decoratively
decorator
decorous
decorously
decorum
decoupage
decoy
  decoys
  decoyed
  decoying
decrease
  decreases
  decreased
  decreasing
decreasingly
decree
  decrees
  decreed
  decreeing
decree absolute
  decrees absolute
decree nisi
  decrees nisi
decrepit
decrepitude

decrescendo
decriminalise
  decriminalises
  decriminalised
  decriminalising
decriminalize
  decriminalizes
  decriminalized
  decriminalizing
decry
  decries
  decried
  decrying
dedicate
  dedicates
  dedicated
  dedicating
dedicated
dedicatedly
dedication
deduce
  deduces
  deduced
  deducing
deducible
deduct
  deducts
  deducted
  deducting
deductible
deductive
deductively
deed
deejay
  deejays
deem
  deems
  deemed
  deeming
deep
  deeper
  deepest
deepen
  deepens
  deepened
  deepening
deeply
deep-rooted
deep-seated
deer (= animal
  → dear)
  deer
deerskin
deface

defaces
defaced
defacing
defacement
de facto
defamation
defamatory
defame
  defames
  defamed
  defaming
default
  defaults
  defaulted
  defaulting
defeasance
defeat
  defeats
  defated
  defeating
defeatism
defeatist
defecate
  defecates
  defecated
  defecating
defect
  defects
  defected
  defecting
defection
defective
defectively
defectiveness
defector
defence
defenceless
defencelessly
defencelessness
defend
  defends
  defended
  defending
defendable
defendant
defendent = defendant
defender
defensible
defensibly
defensive
defensively
defensiveness
defer
  defers

deferred
deferring
deferable
deference
deferential
deferentially
deferment
deferrable
defiance
defiant
defiantly
defibrillation
defibrillator
deficiency
  deficiencies
deficient
deficiently
deficit
defile
  defiles
  defiled
  defiling
defilement
defiler
definable
definate = definite
definately = definitely
define
  defines
  defined
  defining
definite
definitely
definitly = definitely
definition
definitive
definitively
deflate
  deflates
  deflated
  deflating
deflation
deflationary
deflect
  deflects
  deflected
  deflecting
deflection
deflector
deflower
  deflowers
  deflowered
  deflowering
defoliant

defoliate
  defoliates
  defoliated
  defoliating
defoliation
deforest
  deforests
  deforested
  deforesting
deforestation
deform
  deforms
  deformed
  deforming
deformation
deformity
  deformities
defraud
  defrauds
  defrauded
  defrauding
defraudment
defray
  defrays
  defrayed
  defraying
defrock
  defrocks
  defrocked
  defrocking
defrost
  defrosts
  defrosted
  defrosting
defroster
deft
  deftly
  deftness
defunct
defuse
  defuses
  defused
  defusing
defy
  defies
  defied
  defying
Degas, Edgar
degeneracy
degenerate
  degenerates
  degenerated
  degenerating
degeneration

degenerative
degradability
degradable
degradation
degrade
  degrades
  degraded
  degrading
degradingly
degrease
degrees
degree
  degrees
dehumanisation
dehumanise
  dehumanises
  dehumanised
  dehumanising
dehumanization
dehumanize
  dehumanizes
  dehumanized
  dehumanizing
dehumidifier
dehydrate
  dehydrates
  dehydrated
  dehydrating
dehydration
dehydrogenate
de-ice
  de-ices
  de-iced
  de-icing
de-icer
deification
deify
  deifies
  deified
  deifying
deign
  deigns
  deigned
  deigning
Deirdre
deism
deity
  deities
déjà vu
dejected
dejectedly
dejection
de jure
dekko

delay
  delays
  delayed
  delaying
delectability
delectable
delectably
delectation
delegate
  delegates
  delegated
  delegating
delegation
delete
  deletes
  deleted
  deleting
deleterious
deletion
Delhi
deliberate
  deliberates
  deliberated
  deliberating
deliberately
deliberateness
deliberation
deliberative
delicacy
  delicacies
delicate
delicately
delicatessen
delicious
deliciously
deliciousness
delight
  delights
  delighted
  delighting
delightedly
delightful
delightfully
delightfulness
delimit
  delimits
  delimited
  delimiting
delimitation
delinquency
delinquent
deliquescence
deliquescent
delirious

deliriously
delirium
  deliriums
delirium tremens
deliver
  delivers
  delivered
  delivering
deliverance
deliverer
delivery
  deliveries
deliveryman
  deliverymen
dell
Delphic
delphinium
delta
  deltas
delude
  deludes
  deluded
  deluding
deluge
  deluges
  deluged
  deluging
delusion
delusional
delusive
delusively
delusory
deluxe
delve
  delves
  delved
  delving
demagogic
demagogue
demagoguery
demand
  demands
  demanded
  demanding
demandingly
demarcate
  demarcates
  demarcated
  demarcating
demarcation
demean
  demeans
  demeaned
  demeaning

demeanour
demented
dementedly
dementia
demerara
demerit
demigod
demijohn
demilitarisation
demilitarise
  demilitarises
  demilitarised
  demilitarising
demilitarization
demilitarize
  demilitarizes
  demilitarized
  demilitarizing
demimonde
demise
demist
  demists
  demisted
  demisting
demister
demo
  demos
demob
  demobs
  demobbed
  demobbing
demobilisation
demobilise
  demobilises
  demobilised
  demobilising
demobilization
demobilize
  demobilizes
  demobilized
  demobilizing
democracy
  democracies
democrat
democratic
  democratically
democratisation
democratise
  democratises
  democratised
  democratising
democratization
democratize
  democratizes

  democratized
  democratizing
démodé
demographer
demographic
demography
demolish
  demolishes
  demolished
  demolishing
demolition
demon
demoniac
  demoniacal
demonic
demonically
  demonstrability
demonstrable
demonstrably
demonstrate
  demonstrates
  demonstrated
  demonstrating
demonstration
demonstrative
demonstratively
demonstrativeness
demonstrator
demoralisation
demoralise
  demoralises
  demoralised
  demoralising
demoralization
demoralize
  demoralizes
  demoralized
  demoralizing
demos
demote
  demotes
  demoted
  demoting
demotion
demotic
demur
  demurs
  demurred
  demurring
demure
demurely
demureness
demystification
demystify

demystifies
demystified
demystifying
den
denationalisation
denationalise
  denationalises
  denationalised
  denationalising
denationalization
denationalize
  denationalizes
  denationalized
  denationalizing
deniable
deniably
denial
denier
denigrate
  denigrates
  denigrated
  denigrating
denigration
denim
  denims
Denis
denizen
denomination
Denmark
denominational
denominator
denotation
denotative
denotatively
denote
  denotes
  denoted
  denoting
denouement
denounce
  denounces
  denounced
  denouncing
denouncer
dense
densely
denseness
density
  densities
dent
  dents
  dented
  denting
dental

dentifrice
dentine
dentist
dentistry
dentition
denture
denude
  denudes
  denuded
  denuding
denunciation
denunciatory
deny
  denies
  denied
  denying
deodar
deodorant
deodorise
  deodorises
  deodorised
  deodorising
deodorize
  deodorizes
  deodorized
  deodorizing
deoxygenate
  deoxygenates
  deoxygenated
  deoxygenating
deoxygenation
deoxyribonucleic
depart
  departs
  departed
  departing
department
departmental
departmentalise
  departmentalises
  departmentalised
  departmentalising
departmentalize
  departmentalizes
  departmentalized
  departmentalizing
departure
depend
  depends
  depended
  depending
dependability
dependable
dependably

dependant
dependence
dependency
  dependencies
dependent
depict
  depicts
  depicted
  depicting
depiction
depilatory
deplete
  depletes
  depleted
  depleting
depletion
deplorable
deplorably
deplore
  deplores
  deplored
  deploring
deploy
  deploys
  deployed
  deploying
deployment
depoliticise
  depoliticises
  depoliticised
  depoliticising
depoliticize
  depoliticizes
  depoliticized
  depoliticizing
depopulate
  depopulates
  depopulated
  depopulating
depopulation
deport
  deports
  deported
  deporting
deportation
deportee
deportment
depose
  deposes
  deposed
  deposing
deposit
  deposits
  deposited

depositing
deposition
depositor
depository
  depositories
depot
depravation
deprave
  depraves
  depraved
  depraving
depravity
deprecate
  deprecates
  deprecated
  deprecating
deprecatory
depreciate
  depreciates
  depreciated
  depreciating
depreciation
depredation
depress
  depresses
  depressed
  depressing
depressant
depressing
depressingly
depression
depressive
depressurisation
depressurise
  depressurises
  depressurised
  depressurising
depressurization
depressurize
  depressurizes
  depressurized
  depressurizing
deprivation
deprive
  deprives
  deprived
  depriving
depth
deputation
depute
  deputes
  deputed
  deputing
deputise

deputises
deputised
deputising
deputize
deputizes
deputized
deputizing
deputy
deputies
derail
derails
derailed
derailing
derailment
deranged
derangement
derby
derbies
deregulate
deregulates
deregulated
deregulating
deregulation
deregulatory
derelict
dereliction
deride
derides
derided
deriding
de-rigueur = de rigueur
de rigueur
derision
derisive
derisively
derisory
derivable
derivation
derivative
derivatively
derive
derives
derived
deriving
dermatitis
dermatological
dermatologist
dermatology
derogate
derogates
derogated
derogating
derogatory
derrick

derring-do
derv
dervish
dervishes
desalinate
desalinates
desalinated
desalinating
desalination
descale
descales
descaled
descaling
descant
descend
descends
descended
descending
descendant
descent (= going
down → decent)
describe
describes
described
describing
description
descriptive
descriptively
descriptiveness
descry
descries
descried
descrying
desease = disease
desecrate
desecrates
desecrated
desecrating
desecration
desegregate
desegregates
desegregated
desegregating
desegregation
deselect
deselects
deselected
deselecting
desensitisation
desensitise
desensitises
desensitised
desensitising
desensitization

desensitize
desensitizes
desensitized
desensitizing
desert (= leave; area
of arid land
→ dessert)
deserts
deserted
deserting
deserter
desertification
desertion
deserve
deserves
deserved
deserving
deservedly
deserving
deservingly
deshabille
desiccant
desiccate
dessicates
dessicated
dessicating
desideratum
desiderata
design
designs
designed
designing
designate
designates
designated
designating
designedly
designer
designing
desirability
desirable
desirably
desire
desires
desired
desiring
desirous
desirously
desist
desists
desisted
desisting
desk
deskill

deskills
deskilled
deskilling
desktop
desolate
desolated
desolation
despair
despairs
despaired
despairing
despairingly
desparate = desperate
despatch
despatches
despatched
despatching
desperado
desperadoes or
desperados
desperate
desperately
desperation
desperatly =
desperately
despicable
despicably
despise
despises
despised
despising
despite
despoil
despoils
despoiled or
despoilt
despoiling
despondency
despondent
despondently
despot
despotic
despotically
despotism
dessert (= sweet food
→ desert)
dessertspoon
dessicated = desiccated
destabilisation
destabilise
destabilises
destabilised
destabilising
destabilization

destabilize
  destabilizes
  destabilized
  destabilizing
destination
destined
destiny
  destinies
destitute
destitution
destroy
  destroys
  destroyed
  destroying
destroyer
destructibility
destructible
destruction
destructive
destructively
destructiveness
desultorily
desultory
detach
  detaches
  detached
  detaching
detachable
detached
detachment
detail
  details
  detailed
  detailing
detain
  detains
  detained
  detaining
detainee
detatch = detach
detect
  detects
  detected
  detecting
detectable
detection
detective
detector
détente
detention
deter
  deters
  deterred
  deterring

detergent
deteriorate
  deteriorates
  deteriorated
  deteriorating
deterioration
determinant
determination
determine
  determines
  determined
  determining
determined
determinedly
determiner
determinism
determinist
deterministic
deterrence
deterrent
detest
  detests
  detested
  detesting
detestable
detestably
detestation
detonate
  detonates
  detonated
  detonating
detonation
detonator
detour
detract
  detracts
  detracted
  detracting
detraction
detractor
detriment
detrimental
detritus
de trop
deuce
deuced
deus ex machina
devaluation
devalue
  devalues
  devalued
  devaluing
devastate
  devastates

devastated
  devastating
devastation
develop
  develops
  developed
  developing
develope = develop
developement =
  development
developer
development
developmental
deviance
deviant
deviate
  deviates
  deviated
  deviating
deviation
deviationist
device
devide = divide
devil
devilish
devilishly
devilled
devilment
devilry
devious
deviously
deviousness
devise
  devises
  devised
  devising
devoid
devolution
devolve
  devolves
  devolved
  devolving
devote
  devotes
  devoted
  devoting
devotedly
devotedness
devotee
devotion
devotional
devour
  devours
  devoured

devouring
devout
devoutly
devoutness
dew (= moisture on
  ground → due)
dewdrop
dewy
  dewier
  dewiest
dewy-eyed
dexter
dexterity
dexterous
dexterously
dextrose
dextrous
dextrously
Dhaka
diabetes
diabetic
diabolical
diabolically
diacritic
diadem
diaeresis
  diaereses
diagnose
  diagnoses
  diagnosed
  diagnosing
diagnosis
  diagnoses
diagnostic
diagnostician
diagnostics
diagonal
diagonally
diagram
diagrammatic
diagrammatically
dial
  dials
  dialled
  dialling
dialect
dialectic
dialectical
dialectics
dialogue
dialyse
  dialyses
  dialysed
  dialysing

dialyser
dialysis
diamanté
diameter
diametric
diametrically
diamond
diaphanous
diaphram = diaphragm
diaphragm
diarist
diarrea = diarrhoea
diarrhoea
diary
  diaries
Diaspora
diatonic
diatribe
dibber
dibble
  dibbles
  dibbled
  dibbling
dibs
dice
  dices
  diced
  dicing
dicey
  dicier
  diciest
dichotomy
  dichotomies
dicier
diciest
dicision = decision
dick
dickens
Dickens, Charles
Dickensian
dickhead
dicky
  dickies
dicta
Dictaphone™
dictate
  dictates
  dictated
  dictating
dictation
dictator
dictatorial
dictatorially
dictatorship

diction
dictionary
  dictionaries
dictum
  dicta
did
didactic
didactically
didacticism
diddle
  diddles
  diddled
  diddling
didgeridoo
didn't
didst
die (= become dead
  → dye)
  dies
  died
  dying
dieback
die-casting
diegn = deign
diehard
dieing = dying
dieresis
  diereses
diesel
diet
  diets
  dieted
  dieting
dietary
dieter
dietetic
dietetics
dietician
dietitian
diferent = different
differ
  differs
  differed
  differing
difference
different
differential
differentiate
  differentiates
  differentiated
  differentiating
differentiation
differently
difficult

difficulty
  difficulties
diffidence
diffident
diffidently
diffract
  diffracts
  diffracted
  diffracting
diffraction
diffrent = different
diffuse
  diffuses
  diffused
  diffusing
diffusely
diffuseness
diffuser
diffusion
diffusor
dig
  digs
  dug
  digging
digest
  digests
  digested
  digesting
digestibility
digestible
digestif
digestion
digestive
digger
digit
digital
digitalis
digitalise
  digitalises
  digitalised
  digitalising
digitalize
  digitalizes
  digitalized
  digitalizing
digitise
  digitises
  digitised
  digitising
digitize
  digitizes
  digitized
  digitizing
dignified

dignify
  dignifies
  dignified
  dignifying
dignitary
dignity
digraph
digress
  digresses
  digressed
  digressing
digression
digs
dike (= wall to keep
  back water → dyke)
diktat
dilapidated
dilapidation
dilate
  dilates
  dilated
  dilating
dilation
dilatory
dildo
  dildos
dilema = dilemma
dilemma
  dilemmas
dilettante
diligence
diligent
diligently
dill
dilute
  dilutes
  diluted
  diluting
dilution
dim
  dims
  dimmed
  dimming
  dimmer
  dimmest
dime
dimension
dimensional
dimensionality
diminish
  diminishes
  diminished
  diminishing
diminuendo

diminuendos
diminution
diminutive
diminutively
dimity
dimmed
dimmer
dimmest
dimming
dimple
dim sum
dimwit
dimwitted
din
   dins
   dinned
   dinning
dine
   dines
   dined
   dining
diner
ding-dong
dinghy
   dinghies
dingle
dingo
   dingoes
dingy
   dingier
   dingiest
dingily
dinginess
dinky
dinned
dinner
dinning
dinosaur
dint
diocesan
diocese
Dionysian
Dionysus
dioxide
dioxin
dip
   dips
   dipped
   dipping
diphtheria
diphthong
diplodocus
   diplodocuses
diploid

diploma
diplomacy
diplomat
diplomatic
diplomatically
diplomatist
dipped
dipper
dipping
dippy
dipsomania
dipsomaniac
dipstick
diptheria = diphtheria
dipthong = diphthong
diptych
   diptychs
dire
direct
   directs
   directed
   directing
direction
directional
directionality
directive
directly
directness
director
directorate
directorship
directory
   directories
direful
dirge
dirigible
dirndl
dirt
   dirties
   dirtied
   dirtying
   dirtier
   dirtiest
disability
   disabilities
disable
   disables
   disabled
   disabling
disabled
disablement
disabuse
   disabuses
   disabused

disabusing
disadvantage
disadvantaged
disadvantageous
disadvantageously
disaffected
disaffiliate
   disaffiliates
   disaffiliated
   disaffiliating
disafforest
   disafforests
   disafforested
   disafforesting
disafforestation
disagree
   disagrees
   disagreed
   disagreeing
disagreeable
disagreeably
disagreement
disallow
   disallows
   disallowed
   disallowing
disallusion = disillusion
disambiguate
   disambiguates
   disambiguated
   disambiguating
disapear = disappear
disapointed =
   disappointed
disappear
   disappears
   disappeared
   disappearing
disappoint
   disappoints
   disappointed
   disappointing
disappointedly
disappointingly
disappointment
disapproval
disapprove
   disapproves
   disapproved
   disapproving
disapprovingly
disarm
   disarms
   disarmed

disarming
disarmament
disarming
disarmingly
disarray
disassociate
   disassociates
   disassociated
   disassociating
disaster
disasterous =
   disastrous
disastrous
disastrously
disatisfied =
   dissatisfied
disavow
   disavows
   disavowed
   disavowing
disband
   disbands
   disbanded
   disbanding
disbandment
disbar
   disbars
   disbarred
   disbarring
disbarment
disbelief
disbelieve
   disbelieves
   disbelieved
   disbelieving
disburse
   disburses
   disbursed
   disbursing
disbursement
disc
discard
   discards
   discarded
   discarding
discern
   discerns
   discerned
   discerning
discernible
discernibly
discerning
discerningly
discernment

discharge
　discharges
　discharged
　discharging
disciple
discipleship
disciplinarian
disciplinary
discipline
　disciplines
　disciplined
　disciplining
disclaim
　disclaims
　disclaimed
　disclaiming
disclaimer
disclose
　discloses
　disclosed
　disclosing
disclosure
disco
　discos
discoloration
discolour
　discolours
　discoloured
　discolouring
discomfit (= make
　uneasy or confused
　→ discomfort)
　discomfits
　discomfited
　discomfiting
discomfiture
discomfort (= lack of
　comfort → discomfit)
discommode
　discommodes
　discommoded
　discommoding
discompose
　discomposes
　discomposed
　discomposing
discomposure
disconcert
　disconcerts
　disconcerted
　disconcerting
disconcertingly
disconnect
　disconnects

disconnected
　disconnecting
disconnectedly
disconsolate
disconsolately
discontent
discontented
discontinue
　discontinues
　discontinued
　discontinuing
discontinuity
　discontinuities
discord
discordant
discordantly
discotheque
discount
　discounts
　discounted
　discounting
discountenance
discourage
　discourages
　discouraged
　discouraging
discouragement
discouragingly
discourse
　discourses
　discoursed
　discoursing
discourteous
discourteously
discourteousness
discourtesy
　discourtesies
discover
　discovers
　discovered
　discovering
discoverer
discovery
　discoveries
discredit
　discredits
　discredited
　discrediting
discreditable
discreditably
discreet (= careful
　and sensitive
　→ discrete)
　discreetly

discreetness
discrepancy
　discrepancies
discrete (= distinct,
　apart → discreet)
discretely
discreteness
discretion
discretionary
discriminate
　discriminates
　discriminated
　discriminating
discriminatingly
discrimination
discriminatory
~~discription~~ =
　description
discursive
discursively
discursiveness
discus (= object for
　throwing → discuss)
　discuses or disci
discuss (= talk about
　→ discus)
　discusses
　discussed
　discussing
discussion
disdain
　disdains
　disdained
　disdaining
disdainful
disdainfully
disease
diseased
disembark
　disembarks
　disembarked
　disembarking
disembarkation
disembodied
disembowel
　disembowels
　disembowelled
　disembowelling
disenchanted
disenfranchise
　disenfranchises
　disenfranchised
　disenfranchising
disenfranchisement

disengage
　disengages
　disengaged
　disengaging
disentangle
　disentangles
　disentangled
　disentangling
disequilibrium
disestablish
　disestablishes
　disestablished
　disestablishing
disestablishment
disfavour
disfigure
　disfigures
　disfigured
　disfiguring
disfigurement
disforest
　disforests
　disforested
　disforesting
disforestation
disfranchise
　disfranchises
　disfranchised
　disfranchising
disfranchisement
disgorge
　disgorges
　disgorged
　disgorging
disgrace
　disgraces
　disgraced
　disgracing
disgraceful
disgracefully
disgruntled
disguise
　disguises
　disguised
　disguising
disgust
　disgusts
　disgusted
　disgusting
disgustedly
disgusting
disgustingly
dish
　dishes

dished
dishing
dishabille
disharmonious
disharmony
dishcloth
dishearten
  disheartens
  disheartened
  disheartening
dishearteningly
dished
dishevelled
dishier
dishiest
dishing
dishonest
dishonestly
dishonesty
dishonour
  dishonours
  dishonoured
  dishonouring
dishonourable
dishonourableness
dishonourably
dishpan
dishwasher
dishwater
dishy
  dishier
  dishiest
disign = design
disillusion
  disillusions
  disillusioned
  disillusioning
disillusionment
disim try disem
disin try disen
disincentive
disinclination
disinclined
disinfect
  disinfects
  disinfected
  disinfecting
disinfectant
disinformation
disingenuous
disingenuously
disintegrate
  disintegrates
  disintegrated

disintegrating
disintegration
disinter
  disinters
  disinterred
  disinterring
disinterested
disinterestedly
disipline = discipline
disjointed
disjointedly
disk
diskette
dislikable
dislike
  dislikes
  disliked
  disliking
dislikeable
dislocate
  dislocates
  dislocated
  dislocating
dislocation
dislodge
  dislodges
  dislodged
  dislodging
disloyal
disloyally
disloyalty
dismal
dismally
dismantle
  dismantles
  dismantled
  dismantling
dismay
dismember
  dismembers
  dismembered
  dismembering
dismiss
  dismisses
  dismissed
  dismissing
dismissal
dismissive
dismount
  dismounts
  dismounted
  dismounting
disobedience
disobedient

disobediently
disobey
  disobeys
  disobeyed
  disobeying
disobliging
disobligingly
disolve = dissolve
disorder
  disorders
  disordered
  disordering
disorderliness
disorderly
disorganisation
disorganise
  disorganises
  disorganised
  disorganising
disorganization
disorganize
  disorganizes
  disorganized
  disorganizing
disorient
  disorients
  disoriented
  disorienting
disorientate
  disorientates
  disorientated
  disorientating
disorientation
disown
  disowns
  disowned
  disowning
dispair = despair
disparagement
disparaging
disparagingly
disparate
disparately
disparity
  disparities
dispassionate
dispassionately
dispatch
  dispatches
  dispatched
  dispatching
dispel
  dispels
  dispelled

dispelling
dispensable
dispensary
  dispensaries
dispensation
dispense
  dispenses
  dispensed
  dispensing
dispenser
dispersal
dispersant
disperse
  disperses
  dispersed
  dispersing
dispersion
dispirited
dispiritedly
dispiriting
displace
  displaces
  displaced
  displacing
displacement
display
  displays
  displayed
  displaying
displease
  displeases
  displeased
  displeasing
displeasure
disposable
disposal
dispose
  disposes
  disposed
  disposing
disposition
dispossess
  dispossesses
  dispossessed
  dispossessing
dispossession
disproof
disproportion
disproportionate
disproportionately
disprove
  disproves
  disproved
  disproving

disputably
disputation
disputatious
dispute
　disputes
　disputed
　disputing
disqualification
disqualify
　disqualifies
　disqualified
　disqualifying
disquiet
　disquiets
　disquieted
　disquieting
disquieting
disquietingly
disquietude
disregard
　disregards
　disregarded
　disregarding
disrepair
disreputable
disreputably
disrepute
disrespect
disrobe
　disrobes
　disrobed
　disrobing
disrupt
　disrupts
　disrupted
　disrupting
disruption
disruptive
disruptively
dissapear = disappear
dissapointed =
　disappointed
dissatisfy
　dissatisfies
　dissatisfied
　dissatisfying
dissect
　dissects
　dissected
　dissecting
dissection
dissemble
　dissembles

dissembled
dissembling
disseminate
　disseminates
　disseminated
　disseminating
dissemination
dissension
dissent
　dissents
　dissented
　dissenting
dissenter
dissertation
disservice
dissidence
dissident
dissimilar
dissimilarity
dissimilarly
dissimulate
　dissimulates
　dissimulated
　dissimulating
dissimulation
dissipate
　dissipates
　dissipated
　dissipating
dissipation
dissociate
　dissociates
　dissociated
　dissociating
dissociation
dissolute
dissolutely
dissolution
dissolve
　dissolves
　dissolved
　dissolving
dissonance
dissonant
dissuade
　dissuades
　dissuaded
　dissuading
dissuasion
distaff
distance
　distances
　distanced
　distancing

distant
distantly
distaste
distasteful
distastefully
distastefulness
distemper
distend
　distends
　distended
　distending
distension
distil
　distils
　distilled
　distilling
distillation
distiller
distillery
　distilleries
distinct
distinction
distinctive
distinctively
distinctly
distinctness
distinguish
　distinguishes
　distinguished
　distinguishing
distinguishable
distinguished
distort
　distorts
　distorted
　distorting
distortion
distract
　distracts
　distracted
　distracting
distractedly
distraction
distraught
distress
　distresses
　distressed
　distressing
distressing
distressingly
distribute
　distributes
　distributed
　distributing

distribution
distributive
distributively
distributor
district
distroy = destroy
distrust
　distrusts
　distrusted
　distrusting
distrustful
distrustfully
disturb
　disturbs
　disturbed
　disturbing
disturbance
disturbed
disturbing
disturbingly
disunite
　disunites
　disunited
　disuniting
disunity
disuse
disused
disyllabic
ditch
　ditches
　ditched
　ditching
dither
　dithers
　dithered
　dithering
ditto
　dittos
ditty
　ditties
diuretic
diurnal
divan
dive
　dives
　dived
　diving
diver
diverge
　diverges
　diverged
　diverging
divergence
divergent

divergently
divers
diverse
diversely
diversification
diversify
　diversifies
　diversified
　diversifying
diversion
diversionary
diversity
divert
　diverts
　diverted
　diverting
divest
　divests
　divested
　divesting
divestiture
divestment
divide
　divides
　divided
　dividing
dividend
divider
divination
divine
　divines
　divined
　divining
divinely
diviner
diving
divinity
divisible
division
divisive
divisively
divisor
divorce
　divorces
　divorced
　divorcing
divorcé (= man)
divorcée (= woman)
divulge
　divulges
　divulged
　divulging
divulgence
Diwali

dizzy
　dizzier
　dizziest
djinn
DNA
do
　does
　did
　done
　doing
doc
docile
docility
dock
　docks
　docked
　docking
docker
docket
　dockets
　docketed
　docketing
dockland
dockyard
doctor
　doctors
　doctored
　doctoring
doctoral
doctorate
doctrinaire
doctrinal
doctrine
docudrama
document
　documents
　documented
　documenting
documentary
　documentaries
documentation
dodder
　dodders
　doddered
　doddering
doddery
dodge
　dodges
　dodged
　dodging
dodgem
dodger
dodgy
　dodgier

dodgiest
dodo
　dodos *or*
　dodoes
doe (= female deer
　→ dough)
doer (= someone who
　does things → dour)
does
doesn't
does'nt = doesn't
doff
　doffs
　doffed
　doffing
dog
　dogs
　dogged
　dogging
doge
dogfight
dogfish
　dogfish *or*
　dogfishes
dogged
doggedly
doggedness
doggerel
doggie
dogging
doggo
doggy
　doggies
dogleg
dogma
dogmatic
dogmatically
dogmatism
dogmatist
do-gooder
dogsbody
　dogsbodies
dogtrot
dogwood
doh
doily
　doilies
doing
doings
Dolby™
doldrums
dole
　doles
　doled

doling
doleful
dolefully
dolefulness
doll
　dolls
　dolled
　dolling
dollar
dollop
dolly
　dollies
dolmen
doloroso
dolorous
dolorously
dolphin
dolphinarium
　dolphinariums
dolt
domain
dome
domed
domesday
domestic
domestically
domesticate
　domesticates
　domesticated
　domesticating
domestication
domesticity
domicile
domiciled
domiciliary
dominance
dominant
dominate
　dominates
　dominated
　dominating
domination
domineering
Dominican
Dominican Republic
dominion
domino
　dominoes
don
　dons
　donned
　donning
Don
Doña

donate
  donates
  donated
  donating
donation
done
Donegal
Don Juan
donkey
  donkeys
donned
donning
donnish
donor
don't
doodah
doodle
  doodles
  doddled
  doodling
doodlebug
doom
doomed
door
doorframe
doorjamb
doorman
  doormen
doormat
~~doormouse~~ = dormouse
doorpost
doorstep
doorstop
doorway
dope
  dopes
  doped
  doping
dopey
  dopier
  dopiest
dopy
  dopier
  dopiest
Doric
dormant
dormer
dormitory
  dormitories
Dormobile™
dormouse
  dormice
dorsal
dosage
dose

doses
dosed
dosing
dosh
do-si-do
doss
  dosses
  dossed
  dossing
dosser
dosshouse
dossier
dost
dot
  dots
  dotted
  dotting
dot.com
dotage
dotard
dote
  dotes
  doted
  doting
doth
  dotted
  dotting
dotty
  dottier
  dottiest
double
  doubles
  doubled
  doubling
double-barrelled
double-breasted
double-decker
double-dutch
double-edged
double-jointed
doublet
doubloon
doubly
doubt
  doubts
  doubted
  doubting
doubtful
doubtfully
doubtless
douche
dough (= uncooked
  bread; money → doe)
doughnut
doughty

doughy
Douglas
dour (= gloomy
  → doer)
dourly
douse
  douses
  doused
  dousing
dove
dovecote
Dover
dovetail
  dovetails
  dovetailed
  dovetailing
dowager
dowdily
dowdy
dowel
dowelling
down
  downs
  downed
  downing
downbeat
downer
downfall
downgrade
  downgrades
  downgraded
  downgrading
downhearted
downhill
download
  downloads
  downloaded
  downloading
downpour
downright
downs
downside
downstage
downstairs
downstream
downtime
downtown
downtrodden
downturn
downward
downwards
downwind
downy
dowry
  dowries

dowse
  dowses
  dowsed
  dowsing
doyen
doyenne
doyly
  doylies
doz.
dozed
dozen
dozily
doziness
dozing
dozy
  dozier
  doziest
DPhil
DPP
Dr
drab
  drabs
drachma
  drachmae *or*
  drachmas
draconian
draft (= sketch out
  → draught)
  drafts
  drafted
  drafting
draftdodger
drag
  drags
  dragged
  dragging
draggy
dragnet
dragoman
  dragomans
dragon
dragonfly
  dragonflies
dragoon
  dragoons
  drogooned
  dragooning
dragster
drain
  drains
  drained
  draining
drainage
drainer
drainpipe

drake
dram
drama
dramatic
dramatically
dramatics
dramatisation
dramatise
  dramatises
  dramatised
  dramatising
dramatis personae
dramatist
dramatization
dramatize
  dramatizes
  dramatized
  dramatizing
drank
drape
  drapes
  draped
  draping
draper
drapery
  draperies
drastic
drastically
drat
dratted
draught (= current of
  air → draft)
draughtboard
draughts
draughtsman
  draughtsmen
draughtswoman
  draughtswomen
draughty
  draughtier
  draughtiest
draw
  draws
  drew
  drawn
  drawing
drawback
drawbridge
drawer
drawl
  drawls
  drawled
  drawling
drawn
drawstring

dray
dread
  dreads
  dreaded
  dreading
dreadful
dreadfully
dreadfulness
dreadlocks
dreadnought
dream
  dreams
  dreamed *or*
  dreamt
  dreaming
dreamboat
dreamer
dreamier
dreamiest
dreamland
dreamt
dreamy
  dreamier
  dreamiest
drear
dreary
  drearier
  dreariest
dredge
  dredges
  dredged
  dredging
dredger
dregs
drench
  drenches
  drenched
  drenching
dress
  dresses
  dressed
  dressing
dressage
dresser
dressmaker
dressy
  dressier
  dressiest
drew
dribble
  dribbles
  dribbled
  dribbling
dried
drier

dries
driest
drift
  drifts
  drifted
  drifting
drifter
driftwood
drill
  drills
  drilled
  drilling
drily
drink
  drinks
  drank
  drunk
  drinking
drinker
drip
  drips
  dripped
  dripping
drip-dry
  dripped
  dripping
drippy
drive
  drives
  drove
  driven
  driving
drivel
  drivels
  drivelled
  drivelling
driven
driver
driveway
driving
drizzle
  drizzles
  drizzled
  drizzling
Drogheda
droll
drollery
drolly
dromedary
  dromedaries
drone
  drones
  droned
  droning
drool

drools
drooled
drooling
droop
  droops
  drooped
  drooping
drop
  drops
  dropped
  dropping
drop-kick
droplet
dropout
dropper
dropping
  droppings
dropsy
dross
drought
drove
drover
droves
drown
  drowns
  drowned
  drowning
drowse
  drowses
  drowsed
  drowsing
drowsy
  drowsier
  drowsiest
drubbing
drudge
  drudges
  drudged
  drudging
drudgery
drug
  drugs
  drugged
  drugging
druggie
  druggies
drugstore
druid
druidic
druidical
drum
  drums
  drummed
  drumming
drumbeat

drummer
drumstick
drunk
drunkard
drunken
dry
  dries
  dried
  drying
  drier
  driest
dryad
dry-clean
dryer
dryly
dual (= consisting of
  two parts → duel)
dualism
dualistic
duality
dub
  dubs
  dubbed
  dubbing
dubbin
dubious
dubiously
dubiousness
Dublin
ducal
ducat
duchess
  duchesses
duchy
  duchies
duck
  ducks
  ducked
  ducking
duckling
duckweed
ducky
duct
ductile
ductility
dud
dude
due (= owed or
  owing; expected
  → dew)
duel (= fight → dual)
  duels
  duelled

duelling
~~duely~~ = duly
duenna
dues
duet
duff
duffel
duffer
dug
dugout
duke
dukedom
dulcet
dulcimer
dull
  dulls
  dulled
  dulling
dullard
duly
dumb
dumbbell
dumbfound
  dumbfounds
  dumbfounded
  dumbfounding
dumbly
dumbwaiter
Dumfries
dummy
  dummies
dump
  dumps
  dumped
  dumping
dumper
dumpier
dumpiest
dumpling
dumps
dumpy
  dumpier
  dumpiest
dun
dunce
Dundalk
dunderhead
dune
dung
dungarees
dungeon
dunk
  dunks

dunked
dunking
dunno
duo
  duos
duodecimal
duodenal
duodenum
  duodena or
  duodenums
duos
dupe
  dupes
  duped
  duping
duplex
duplicate
  duplicates
  duplicated
  duplicating
duplication
duplicator
duplicitous
duplicity
durability
durable
duration
duress
Durex™
Durham
during
durst
dusk
duskiness
dusky
dust
  dusts
  dusted
  dusting
dustbin
duster
dustier
dustiest
dustman
  dustmen
dustpan
dustsheet
dusty
  dustier
  dustiest
Dutch
Dutchman
  Dutchmen

dutiable
dutiful
dutifully
duty
  duties
duvet
dwarf
  dwarfs or
  dwarves
  dwarfs
  dwarfed
  dwarfing
dwell
  dwells
  dwelt or
  dwelled
  dwelling
dwelling
dwelt
dwindle
  dwindles
  dwindled
  dwindling
dye (= colour
  → die)
  dyes
  dyed
  dyeing
Dyfed
dying
dyke (= lesbian
  → dike)
dynamic
dynamically
dynamics
dynamism
dynamite
  dynamites
  dynamited
  dynamiting
dynamo
  dynamos
dynastic
dynasty
  dynasties
dysentery
~~dysentry~~ = dysentery
dyslexia
dyslexic
dysmenorrhoea
dyspepsia
dyspeptic
dystrophy

E

each
eager
eagerly
eagerness
eagle
eaglet
Ealing
ear
earache
eardrops
eardrum
eared
earful
earl
earldom
earliness
early
  earlier
  earliest
earmark
  earmarks
  earmarked
  earmarking
earmuff
earn (= deserve
  → urn)
  earns
  earned
  earning
earnest
earnings
earphone
earpiece
earplug
earring
earshot
earth
earthed
earthbound
earthen
earthenware
earthier
earthiest
earthliness
earthling
earthly

earthlier
earthliest
earthquake
earthshaking
earthward
earthwards
earthwork
earthworm
earthy
  earthier
  earthiest
earwax
earwig
earwigging
ease
  eases
  eased
  easing
easel
easement
easier
easiest
easily
easiness
east
eastbound
Easter
easterly
  easterlies
eastern
easternmost
easting
eastward
eastwards
easy
  easier
  easiest
easyer = easier
easyly = easily
eat
  eats
  ate (= took food
    → eight)
  eaten
  eating
eatable

eatables
eaten
eater
eatery
  eateries
eats
eaves
eau-de-Cologne
eavesdrop
  eavesdrops
  eavesdropped
  eavesdropping
eavesdropper
ebb
  ebbs
  ebbed
  ebbing
Ebbw Vale
E-boat
ebony
  ebonies
ebullience
ebulliency
ebullient
ebulliently
eccentric
eccentrically
eccentricity
  eccentricities
Eccles
ecclesiastic
ecclesiastical
ecclesiasticism
ECG
echelon
echidna
  echidnas or
  echidnae
echo
  echoes
  echoed
  echoing
echt
eclair
eclampsia
eclat

eclectic
eclectically
eclecticism
eclipse
  eclipses
  eclipsed
  eclipsing
ecological
ecologically
ecologist
ecology
e-commerce
econometric
econometrics
economic
economical
economically
economics
economise
  economises
  economised
  economising
economiser
economist
economize
  economizes
  economized
  economizing
economizer
economy
  economies
ecospecies
ecospecific
ecosphere
ecosystem
ecru
ecs try ex
ecstasy
  ecstasies
ecstatic
ecstatically
ectomorph
ectopia
ectopic
ectoplasm
Ecuador

ecumenical
ecumenicism
eczema
eczematous
Edam (cheese)
eddy
  eddies
  eddied
  eddying
edelweiss
edge
  edges
  edged
edgily
edginess
  edging
edgeways
edgy
  edgier
  edgiest
edible
edibles
edict
edification
edifice
edify
  edifies
  edified
  edifying
Edinburgh
edit
  edits
  edited
  editing
edition
editor
editorial
editorially
editorialise
  editorialises
  editorialised
  editorialising
editorialize
  editorializes
  editorialized
  editorializing
educable
educate
  educates
  educated
  educating
education
educational
educationalist

educationally
educative
educator
Edwardian
EEC
eel
e'en
e'er (= ever → air,
  ere, heir)
eerie (= spooky
  → eyrie)
  eerier
  eeriest
eeriness
eery = eerie
ef try af
eff
efface
  effaces
  effaced
  effacing
effaceable
effacement
effacer
effect (= result; bring
  about → affect)
  effects
  effected
  effecting
effecter
effective
effectively
effector
effects
effectual
effectuality
effeminacy
effeminate
effendi
  effendis
effervesce
  effervesces
  effervesced
  effervescing
effervescent
effervescently
effete
efficacious
efficacy
efficiency
  efficiencies
efficient
efficiently
effigy

effigies
effluence
effluent
effluvial
effluvium
  effluviums or
  effluvia
effort
effortless
effortlessly
effrontery
  effronteries
effusion
effusive
effusively
eficient = efficient
egalitarian
egalitarianism
egest
  egests
  egested
  egesting
egestion
egg
  eggs
  egged
  egging
egghead
eggnog
eggplant
eggshell
eglantine
ego
  egos
egocentric
egocentrically
egocentricity
egocentrism
egoism
egoist
egomania
egomaniacal
egos
egotism
egotist
egregious
egress
egression
egret
egs try ex or exh
Egypt
Egyptian
Egyptology
Egyptologist

eh
eider
eiderdown
eigenfrequency
eigenfunction
eigentone
eigenvalue
eight (= number
  → ate)
eighteen
eighteenth
eightfold
eighth
eightieth
eighty
  eighties
eigth = eighth
Einstein
einsteinium
Eire
eisteddfod
  eisteddfods or
  eisteddfodau
either
Eleanor
Eliot, George
Eliot, T.S.
ejaculate
  ejaculates
  ejaculated
  ejaculating
ejaculation
eject
  ejects
  ejected
  ejecting
ejection
ejective
ejector
eke
  ekes
  eked
  eking
elaborate
  elaborates
  elaborated
  elaborating
elaboration
élan
eland
elapse
  elapses
  elapsed
  elapsing

elastic
elastically
elasticate
elasticates
elasticated
elasticating
elastication
elasticise
elasticises
elasticised
elasticising
elasticity
elasticize
elasticizes
elasticized
elasticizing
elastomer
elate
elates
elated
elating
elation
elbow
elbows
elbowed
elbowing
elbowroom
elder
elderberry
elderberries
elderliness
elderly
eldest
elect
elects
elected
electing
electable
election
electioneering
elective
electivity
elector
electoral
electorally
electorate
electric
electrical
electrically
electrician
electricity
electrifiable
electrification
electrifier

electrify
electrifies
electrified
electrifying
electrocardiogram
electrocardiograph
electrocardiography
electrocute
electrocutes
electrocuted
electrocuting
electrocution
electrode
electroencephalogram
electroencephalograph
electrolysis
electrolyte
electromagnet
electromagnetic
electromagnetically
electromagnetics
electromagnetism
electron
electronic
electronically
electronics
electroplate
electroplates
electroplated
electroplating
electroplater
electrostatic
elegance
elegant
elegantly
elegiac
elegiacally
elegible = eligible
elegise
elegises
elegised
elegising
elegize
elegizes
elegized
elegizing
elegy
elegies
element
elemental
elementally
elementary
elephant
elephantiasis

elephantine
elevate
elevates
elevated
elevating
elevation
elevator
eleven
elevenses
eleventh
elf
elves
elfin
elfish
elicit
elicits
elicited
eliciting
eligible
eliminate
eliminates
eliminated
eliminating
elimination
eliminator
eliminatory
elision
elite
elitism
elitist
elixir
Elizabethan
elk
elk or
elks
ell
ellipse
ellipsis
ellipsoid
ellipsoidal
elliptic
elliptical
elliptically
elm
elocution
elongate
elongates
elongated
elongating
elongation
elope
elopes
eloped
eloping

elopement
eloper
eloquence
eloquent
El Salvador
else
elsewhere
elucidate
elucidates
elucidated
elucidating
elucidation
elude
eludes
eluded
eluding
elusive
elusively
elusory
elver
elves
elvish
emaciated
emaciation
e-mail
emanate
emanates
emanated
emanating
emanation
emancipate
emancipates
emancipated
emancipating
emancipation
emancipative
emancipator
emancipatory
emasculate
emasculates
emasculated
emasculating
emasculation
embalm
embalms
embalmed
embalming
embalmer
embalmment
embankment
embarass = embarrass
embargo
embargoes
embargoed

embargoing
embark
  embarks
  embarked
  embarking
embarras = embarrass
embarrass
  embarrasses
  embarrassed
  embarrassing
embarrassingly
embarrassment
embassy
  embassies
embattled
embed
  embeds
  embedded
  embedding
embellish
  embellishes
  embellished
  embellishing
embellisher
embellishment
ember
embezzle
  embezzles
  embezzled
  embezzling
embezzlement
embezzler
embittered
embitterment
emblazon
  emblazons
  emblazoned
  emblazoning
emblem
embodiment
embody
  embodies
  embodied
  embodying
embolden
embolism
embonpoint
emboss
  embosses
  embossed
  embossing
embosser
embouchure
embrace

embraces
embraced
embracing
embracer
embrasure
embrasured
embrocation
embroider
  embroiders
  embroidered
  embroidering
embroiderer
embroidery
  embroideries
embroil
  embroils
  embroiled
  embroiling
embryo
  embryos
embryology
embryonic
emcee
emend (= correct a
  text → amend)
  emends
  emended
  emending
emendation
emerald
emerge
  emerges
  emerged
  emerging
emergence
emergency
  emergencies
emergent
emeritus
emersion
emery
emesis
emetic
emetically
emigrant
emigrate
  emigrates
  emigrated
  emigrating
emigré
emigration
eminence
eminency
  eminencies

eminent
emir
emirate
emissary
  emissaries
emission
emissive
emissivity
emit
  emits
  emitted
  emitting
emitter
Emmenthal
emollience
emollient
emolument
emote
emotion
emotional
emotionally
emotionless
emotionlessly
emotive
emotively
empathic
empathically
empathise
  empathises
  empathised
  empathising
empathize
  empathizes
  empathized
  empathizing
empathy
emperor
emphasis
  emphases
emphasise
  emphasises
  emphasised
  emphasising
emphasize
  emphasizes
  emphasized
  emphasizing
emphatic
emphatically
emphysema
empire
empiric
empirical
empirically

empiricism
empiricist
employ
  employs
  employed
  employing
employability
employable
employee
employer
employment
emporium
  emporiums or
  emporia
empower
  empowers
  empowered
  empowering
empowerment
empress
emptiable
emptily
emptiness
empty
  empties
  emptied
  emptying
empty
  emptier
  emptiest
emu
  emus or
  emu
emulate
  emulates
  emulated
  emulating
emulation
emulsifiable
emulsification
emulsifier
emulsify
  emulsifies
  emulsified
  emulsifying
emulsion
enable
  enables
  enabled
  enabling
enablement
enabler
enact
  enacts

enacted
enacting
enactment
enactor
enamel
  enamels
  enamelled
  enamelling
enameller
enamellist
enamelwork
enamoured
encampment
encapsulate
  encapsulates
  encapsulated
  encapsulating
encapsulation
encase
  encases
  encased
  encasing
enceinte
encephalic
encephalin
encephalitic
encephalitis
encephalogram
encephalograph
encephalographic
encephalographically
encephalography
encephaloma
  encephalomas or
  encephalomata
encephalomyelitic
encephalomyelitis
encephalon
  encephala
encephalopathy
encephalous
enchant
  enchants
  enchanted
  enchanting
enchanter
enchantingly
enchantment
enchantress
enchilada
encipher
  enciphers
  enciphered
  enciphering

encipherer
encipherment
encircle
  encircles
  encircled
  encircling
encirclement
encircling
enclave
enclitic
enclosable
enclose
  encloses
  enclosed
  enclosing
encloser
enclosure
encode
  encodes
  encoded
  encoding
encodement
encoder
encomium
  encomiums or
  encomia
encompass
  encompasses
  encompassed
  encompassing
encompassment
encore
encounter
  encounters
  encountered
  encountering
encounterer
encourage
  encourages
  encouraged
  encouraging
encouragement
encouraging
encouragingly
encroach
  encroaches
  encroached
  encroaching
encroacher
encroachment
encrust
  encrusts
  encrusted
  encrusting

encumbrance
encyclical
encyclopaedia
encyclopaedic
encyclopaedically
encyclopedia
encyclopedic
encyclopedically
end
  ends
  ended
  ending
endanger
  endangers
  endangered
  endangering
endangerment
endbrain
endear
  endears
  endeared
  endearing
endearingly
endearment
endeavour
  endeavours
  endeavoured
  endeavouring
endeavourer
endemic
endemical
endemically
endgame
ending
endive
endless
endlessly
endmost
endocardium
  endocardia
endocarp
endocranium
  endocrania
endocrine
endocrinologic
endocrinology
endocrinous
endometriosis
endometrium
  endometria
endomorph
endoplasm
endorphin
endorsable

endorse
endorses
endorsed
endorsing
endorsee
endorsement
endorser
endorsor
endoscope
endoscopic
endoscopist
endoscopy
endoskeleton
endosperm
endospore
endosporous
endothelium
  endothelia
endothermic
endow
  endows
  endowed
  endowing
endower
endowment
endpaper
endplate
endplay
endurability
endurable
endurably
endurance
endure
  endures
  endured
  enduring
endways
enema
  enemas
enemy
  enemies
energetic
energid
energise
  energises
  energised
  energising
energize
  energizes
  energized
  energizing
energy
  energies
enervate

enervates
enervated
enervating
enfeeble
enfeebles
enfeebled
enfeebling
enfeeblement
enfeebler
enfold
enfolds
enfolded
enfolding
enforcable =
enforceable
enforce
enforces
enforced
enforcing
enforceability
enforceable
enforceably
enforcement
enforcer
enfranchise
enfranchises
enfranchised
enfranchising
enfranchisement
enfranchiser
engage
engages
engaged
engaging
engagement
engager
engender
engenders
engendered
engendering
engine
engineer
engineering
English
engorge
engorges
engorged
engorging
engorgement
engrave
engraves
engraved
engraving
• engraver

engraving
engross
engrosses
engrossed
engrossing
engrossment
engulf
engulfs
engulfed
engulfing
enhance
enhances
enhanced
enhancing
enhancement
enhancer
enharmonic
enigma
enigmatic
enjoin
enjoins
enjoined
enjoining
enjoy
enjoys
enjoyed
enjoying
enjoyable
enjoyably
enjoyer
enjoyment
enlarge
enlarges
enlarged
enlarging
enlargeable
enlargement
enlarger
enlighten
enlightens
enlightened
enlightening
enlightenment
enlist
enlists
enlisted
enlisting
enlister
enlistment
enliven
enlivens
enlivened
enlivening
enlivener

enlivenment
enmesh
enmeshes
enmeshed
enmeshing
enmeshment
Enniskillen
enmity
enmities
ennoble
ennobles
ennobled
ennobling
ennoblement
ennobler
ennobling
ennui
enormity
enormities
enormous
enormously
enough
enquire
enquires
enquired
enquiring
enquirer
enquiry
enquiries
enrage
enrages
enraged
enraging
enragement
enrapture
enraptures
enraptured
enrapturing
enrich
enriches
enriched
enriching
enricher
enrichment
enrobe
enrobes
enrobed
enrobing
enrober
enrol
enrols
enrolled
enrolling
enrolment

ensconce
ensconces
ensconced
ensconcing
ensemble
ensign
enslave
enslaves
enslaved
enslaving
enslavement
enslaver
ensnare
ensnares
ensnared
ensnaring
ensnarement
ensnarer
ensue
ensues
ensued
ensuing
ensuing
ensure
ensures
ensured
ensuring
entail
entails
entailed
entailing
entailment
entangle
entangles
entangled
entangling
entanglement
entangler
entente
enter
enters
entered
entering
enteric
enteritis
enterprise
enterprising
entertain
entertains
entertained
entertaining
entertainer
entertaining
entertainingly

entertainment
enthral
  enthrals
  enthralled
  enthralling
enthuse
  enthuses
  enthused
  enthusing
enthusiasm
enthusiast
enthusiastic
enthusiastically
entice
  entices
  enticed
  enticing
enticement
enticer
enticing
enticingly
entire
entirely
entirety
  entireties
entitle
  entitles
  entitled
  entitling
entitlement
entity
  entities
entoderm
entomb
  entombs
  entombed
  entombing
entombment
entomological
entomology
entourage
entozoic
entozoon
entrails
entrance
  entrances
  entranced
  entrancing
entrancing
entrancingly
entrancement
entrant
entrap
  entraps

entrapped
entrapping
entrapment
entrapper
entreat
  entreats
  entreated
  entreating
entreatment
entreaty
  entreaties
entrechat
entrecôte
entrée
entrench
  entrenches
  entrenched
  entrenching
entrencher
entrenchment
entrepôt
entrepreneur
entropy
  entropies
entrust
  entrusts
  entrusted
  entrusting
entry
  entries
entwine
  entwines
  entwined
  entwining
enumerable
enumerate
  enumerates
  enumerated
  enumerating
enumeration
enumerative
enumerator
enunciable
enunciate
  enunciates
  enunciated
  enunciating
enunciation
enunciator
enuresis
enuretic
envelop (= to wrap)
  envelops
  enveloped

enveloping
envelope (=
  stationery)
envelopment
enviable
enviably
envious
enviroment =
  environment
environment
environmental
environmentalism
environmentalist
environmentally
environs
envisage
  envisages
  envisaged
  envisaging
envisagement
envision
  envisions
  envisioned
  envisioning
envoy
envy
  envies
  envied
  envying
enzyme
eolith
Eolithic
Eozoic
EP
epaulet
epaulette
ephedrine
ephemera
  ephemeras or
  ephemerae
ephemeral
ephemerally
ephemerality
epic
epically
epicanthus
  epicanthi
epicardium
  epicardia
epicarp
epicene
epicentre
epicure
epicurean

epidemic
epidemiological
epidemiology
epidermis
epididymis
  epididymides
epidural
epiglottis
epigram
epigraph
epilepsy
epileptic
epilogue
epiphany
  epiphanies
episcopacy
episcopal
episcopalian
episiotomy
  episiotomies
episode
episodic
episodically
epistemological
epistemologically
epistemologist
epistemology
epistle
epitaph
epithelium
  epithelia or
  epitheliums
epithet
epitome
epitomise
  epitomises
  epitomised
  epitomising
epitomize
  epitomizes
  epitomized
  epitomizing
epitomy = epitome
epizoic
epizoite
epizoon
epizootic
epoch
epochal
eponym
eponymous
eponymy
epoxy
  epoxies

epsilon
equable
equal
  equals
  equalled
  equalling
equalise
  equalises
  equalised
  equalising
equaliser
equality
  equalities
equalize
  equalizes
  equalized
  equalizing
equalizer
equalled
equally
equals
equanimity
equanimous
equatability
equatable
equate
  equates
  equated
  equating
equation
equator
equatorial
equerry
  equerries
equestrian
equestrianism
equiangular
equidistant
equilateral
equilibrium
  equilibriums or
  equilibria
equine
equinoctial
equinox
equip
  equips
  equipped
  equipping
equipage
equiped = equipped
equipment
equipoise
equipper

equitable
equity
  equities
equivalence
equivalency
equivalent
equivocal
equivocally
equivocate
  equivocates
  equivocated
  equivocating
equivocation
equivocator
equivocatory
era
eradicable
eradicably
eradicate
  eradicates
  eradicated
  eradicating
eradication
eradicator
erasable
erase
  erases
  erased
  erasing
eraser
erasure
erbium
ere (= before → air, e'er, heir)
erect
  erects
  erected
  erecting
erectable
erecter
erectile
erectility
erection
erector
erelong
erewhile
erg
ergo
ergonomic
ergonomics
ergonomist
ericaceous
Eritrea
ermine

erode
  erodes
  eroded
  eroding
erogenous
erosion
erosive
erotic
erotica
erotically
eroticism
err (= do wrong → ere)
  errs
  erred
  erring
errand
errant
errata
erratic
erratically
erratum
  errata
erroneous
error
ersatz
Erse
erstwhile
erudite
eruditely
erudition
erupt
  erupts
  erupted
  erupting
eruptible
eruption
eruptive
eruptivity
erysipelas
erythrocyte
erythrocytic
erythromycin
escalate
  escalates
  escalated
  escalating
escalator
escalope
escapable
escapade
escape
  escapes
  escaped

escaping
escapee
escaper
escapism
escapist
escapologist
escargot
escarpment
eschatological
eschatology
escort
  escorts
  escorted
  escorting
escudo
  escudos
esential = essential
Eskimo
  Eskimo or
  Eskimos
esoteric
ESP
espadrille
espalier
España
especial
especially
especialy = especially
Esperanto
espionage
esplanade
espousal
espouse
  espouses
  espoused
  espousing
espresso
  espressos
esprit
espy
  espies
  espied
  espying
esquire
essay
essayist
essence
essential
essentially
establish
  establishes
  established
  establishing
establisher

establishment	eucalyptuses *or*	evaluating	Everest
estate	eucalypti	evaluation	evergreen
esteem	Eucharist	evaluative	everlasting
esteemed	eugenic	evaluator	evermore
ester	eugenically	evanescent	every
estimable	eugenicist	evangelical	everybody
estimate	eugenics	evangelically	everyday
estimates	eugenist	evangelisation	everyone
estimated	eulogise	evangelise	everything
estimating	eulogises	evangelises	everywhere
estimation	eulogised	evangelised	Evesham
estimator	eulogising	evangelising	evict
Estonia	eulogize	evangeliser	evicts
estuary	eulogizes	evangelism	evicted
estuaries	eulogized	evangelist	evicting
eta	eulogizing	evangelistic	eviction
etc.	eulogy	evangelistically	evictor
etcetera	eulogies	evangelization	evidence
etch	eunuch	evangelize	evident
etches	euphemism	evangelizes	evidential
etched	euphonic	evangelized	evidently
etching	euphonically	evangelizing	evil
eternal	euphonium	evangelizer	evildoer
eternally	euphony	evaporability	evilly
eternity	euphonies	evaporable	evince
eternities	euphoria	evaporate	evinces
ethane	euphoric	evaporates	evinced
ethanol	Eurasian	evaporated	evincing
ether	eureka	evaporating	evincible
ethereal	eurhythmic	evaporation	eviscerate
ethereally	eurocrat	evaporative	eviscerates
etheric	eurocurrency	evaporator	eviscerated
ethic	eurodeposit	evapotranspiration	eviscerating
ethical	eurodollar	evasion	evisceration
ethics	euromarket	evasive	eviscerator
Ethiopia	Europe	evasively	evocative
Ethiopian	European	eve	evocatively
ethnic	europium	even	evoke
ethnicity	euthanasia	evening	evokes
ethnocentrism	evacuate	evenings	evoked
ethnographic	evacuates	evenly	evoking
ethnography	evacuated	evens	evoker
ethnologist	evacuating	evensong	evolution
ethnology	evacuation	event	evolutionary
ethnomethodology	evacuee	eventer	evolutionist
ethos	evadable	eventful	evolve
ethyl	evade	eventfully	evolves
ethylene	evades	eventide	evolved
etiquette	evaded	eventing	evolving
Etruscan	evading	eventual	evolvement
etymological	evader	eventuality	ewe (= sheep → yew,
etymology	evaluate	eventualities	you)
etymologies	evaluates	eventually	ewer
eucalyptus	evaluated	ever	ex

exacerbate
  exacerbates
  exacerbated
  exacerbating
exacerbation
exact
  exacts
  exacted
  exacting
exactable
exacter
exacting
exactingly
exactitude
exactly
exactor
exagerate =
  exaggerate
exaggerate
  exaggerates
  exaggerated
  exaggerating
exaggeration
exaggerator
exalt (= raise
  → exult)
  exalts
  exalted
  exalting
exaltation
exalted
exam
examinable
examination
examine
  examines
  examined
  examining
examinee
examiner
example
exasperate
  exasperates
  exasperated
  exasperating
exasperating
exasperatingly
exasperation
exaust = exhaust
excavate
  excavates
  excavating
excavator
excede = exceed

exceed
  exceeds
  exceeded
  exceeding
exceedable
exceeder
exceeding
exceedingly
excel
  excels
  excelled
  excelling
excellence
Excellency
  Excellencies
except (= apart from;
  to leave out
  → accept)
  excepts
  excepted
  excepting
exception
exceptionable
exceptionably
exceptional
exceptionally
excerpt
excess
excessive
exchange
  exchanges
  exchanged
  exchanging
exchangeability
exchangeable
exchangeably
exchequer
excipient
excisable
excise
  excises
  excised
  excising
excision
excitability
excitable
excitably
excitation
excite
  excites
  excited
excitedly
  exciting
excitement

exclaim
  exclaims
  exclaimed
  exclaiming
exclaimer
exclamation
exclamatory
excludable
exclude
  excludes
  excluded
  excluding
excluder
exclusion
exclusionary
exclusionism
exclusionist
exclusive
exclusivity
excommunicate
  excommunicates
  excommunicated
  excommunicating
excrement
excrescence
excrescent
excreta
excretal
excrete
  excretes
  excreted
  excreting
excreter
excretion
excretive
excretory
excruciating
exculpable
exculpatory
excursion
excursive
excusable
excusably
excuse
  excuses
  excused
  excusing
exeat
execrable
execute
  executes
  executed
  executing
execution

executioner
executive
executor
executory
executrix
  executrices or
  executrixes
exegesis
  exegeses
exellent = excellent
exemplar
exemplarily
exemplariness
exemplary
exemplifiable
exemplification
exemplifier
exemplify
  exemplifies
  exemplified
  exemplifying
exempt
  exempts
  exempted
  exempting
exemption
exept = except
exercise (= do
  activity → exorcise)
  exercises
  exercised
  exercising
exerciser
exercize = exercise
exerpt = excerpt
exert
  exerts
  exerted
  exerting
exertion
exeunt
exfoliation
exhalable
exhalant
exhale
  exhales
  exhaled
  exhaling
exhaust
  exhausts
  exhausted
  exhausting
exhaustibility
exhaustible

exhaustibly
exhausting
exhaustingly
exhaustion
exhaustive
exhaustively
exhibit
  exhibits
  exhibited
  exhibiting
exhibition
exhibitioner
exhibitionism
exhibitionist
exhibitor
exhilarate
  exhilarates
  exhilarated
  exhilarating
exhilaration
exhilerating =
  exhilarating
exhileration =
  exhilaration
exhort
  exhorts
  exhorted
  exhorting
exhortation
exhortative
exhortatory
exhumation
exhume
  exhumes
  exhumed
  exhuming
exhumer
exibition = exhibition
exigency
exigent
exiguous
exile
exist
  exists
  existed
  existing
existance = existence
existence
existent
existential
existentialism
existing
exit
  exits

exited
exiting
exocarp
exocrine
exoderm
exodus
exogenous
exonerate
  exonerates
  exonerated
  exonerating
exoneration
exonerative
exonerator
exorbitance
exorbitant
exorcise (= get rid of
  spirits → exercise)
  exorcises
  exorcised
  exorcising
exorcize (= get rid of
  spirits → exercise)
  exorcizes
  exorcized
  exorcizing
exoskeleton
exosmic
exosmosis
exosmotic
exosphere
exospore
exoteric
exotic
exotica
exotically
exoticism
expand
  expands
  expanded
  expanding
expandable
expander
expanse
expansibility
expansible
expansile
expansion
expansionary
expansionism
expansionist
expansionistic
expansive
expansivity

expat
expatriate
expatriation
expect
  expects
  expected
  expecting
expectancy
expectant
expectantly
expectation
expectative
expecting
expectorant
expediency
expedient
expedite
  expedites
  expedited
  expediting
expediter
expedition
expeditionary
expeditious
expeditor
expel
  expels
  expelled
  expelling
expellant
expellent
expence = expense
expend
  expends
  expended
  expending
expendable
expender
expenditure
expense
expensive
expensively
experiance =
  experience
experience
  experiences
  experienced
  experiencing
experiential
experientially
experiment
  experiments
  experimented
  experimenting

experimental
experimentalist
experimentally
experimentation
experimenter
expert
expertise
expiate
  expiates
  expiated
  expiating
expiation
expiatory
expiration
expiratory
expire
  expires
  expired
  expiring
expirer
expiry
  expiries
explain
  explains
  explained
  explaining
explainable
explainer
explanation
explanatorily
explanatory
expletive
explicable
explicably
explicate
  explicates
  explicated
  explicating
explication
explicative
explicatory
explicit
explicitly
explode
  explodes
  exploded
  exploding
exploder
exploit
  exploits
  exploited
  exploiting
exploitable
exploitative

exploitive
exploration
explorative
exploratory
explore
  explores
  explored
  exploring
explorer
explosion
explosive
expo
  expos
exponent
exponential
exponentially
export
  exports
  exported
  exporting
exportable
exportation
exporter
exposable
exposal
expose
  exposes
  exposed
  exposing
exposé
exposer
exposition
expositor
expostulate
  expostulates
  expostulated
  expostulating
expostulation
exposure
expound
  expounds
  expounded
  expounding
expounder
express
  expresses
  expressed
  expressing
expresser
expressible
expression
expressionism
expressionist
expressionistic

expressionless
expressive
expressively
expressly
expropriate
  expropriates
  expropriated
  expropriating
expropriation
expropriator
expulsion
expulsive
expunction
expunge
  expunges
  expunged
  expunging
expurgate
  expurgates
  expurgated
  expurgating
expurgatorial
expurgatory
exquisite
extant
~~extasy~~ = ecstasy
extemporaneous
extempore
extemporisation
extemporise
  extemporises
  extemporised
  extemporising
extemporiser
extemporization
extemporize
  extemporizes
  extemporized
  extemporizing
extemporizer
extend
  extends
  extended
  extending
extendability
extendable
extended
extender
extendibility
extendible
extensibility
extensible
extensibleness
extension

extensive
extensively
extensor
extent
extenuating
extenuation
exterior
exterminable
exterminate
  exterminates
  exterminated
  exterminating
extermination
exterminator
external
externalisation
externalise
  externalised
  externalising
externalization
externalize
  externalizes
  externalized
  externalizing
externally
exteroceptor
exterritorial
extinct
extinction
extinguish
  extinguishes
  extinguished
  extinguishing
extinguishable
extinguisher
extinguishment
extol
  extols
  extolled
  extolling
extort
  extorts
  extorted
  extorting
extortion
extortionate
extortionately
extortioner
extortionist
extra
extracellular
extract
  extracts
  extracted

extracting
extractability
extractable
extraction
extractions
extractive
extractor
extracurricular
extraditable
extradite
  extradites
  extradited
  extraditing
extradition
extramarital
extramural
extraneous
extranuclear
extraordinarily
extraordinariness
extraordinary
extraordinarily
extrapolate
  extrapolates
  extrapolated
  extrapolating
extrapolation
extrasensory
extraterrestrial
extraterritorial
extravagance
extravagant
extravagantly
extravaganza
extravehicular
extraversion
extremal
extreme
extremely
~~extremly~~ = extremely
extremism
extremist
extremity
  extremities
extricate
  extricates
  extricated
  extricating
extrinsic
extrinsically
~~extrordinary~~ =
  extraordinary
extroversion
extrovert

extroverted
extrude
  extrudes
  extruded
  extruding
extrusible
extrusion
extrusive
exuberance
exuberant
exude
  exudes

exuded
exuding
exult (= rejoice
  → exalt)
  exults
  exulted
  exulting
exultant
exultation
exultingly
eye
  eyes

eyed
eyeing *or*
  eying
eyeball
eyebrow
eyed (= looked at
  → I'd)
eyeful
eyelash
eyelet
eyelevel
eyelid

eyeliner
eyes
eyesight
eyesore
eyestrain
eyetooth
eyewitness
eying
eyrie (= eagle's nest
  → eerie)
  eyries

F

fab
Fabian
fable
fabled
fabric
fabricate
  fabricates
  fabricated
  fabricating
fabulous
façade
face
  faces
  faced
  facing
faceless
facet
  faceted
facetious
facetiously
facetiousness
facia
facial
facile
facilitate
facilitation
facilitative
facilitator
facility
facism = fascism
facsimile
fact
faction
factious
factitious
factitiously
factitiousness
factive
factoid
factor
factorage
factorial
factoring
factorise
  factorises
  factorised

factorising
factorize
  factorizes
  factorized
  factorizing
factory
  factories
factotum
factual
faculty
fad
fade
  fades
  faded
  fading
fadeless
faecal
faeces
faerie
Faeroese
faery
fag
  fags
  fagged
  fagging
faggot
fah
Fahrenheit
fail
  fails
  failed
  failing
failure
fain (= would like
  → feign)
faint (= lose
  consciousness
  → feint)
  faints
  fainted
  fainting
fair (= funfair → fare)
fairer
fairest
fairground
fairies

fairing
fairish
fairly
fairway
fairy
  fairies
fairyland
fairytale
faith
faithful
faithfully
faithfulness
faithless
fake
  fakes
  faked
  faking
fakir
falafel
falcon
falconer
falconry
falderal
fall
  falls
  fell
  fallen
  falling
fallacious
fallaciously
fallaciousness
fallacy
  fallacies
fallible
falling
fallow
Falmouth
false
falsehood
falsetto
falsies
falsification
falsify
  falsifies
  falsified
  falsifying

falsity
Falstaffian
falter
  falters
  faltered
  faltering
fame
familial
familiar
familiarisation
familiarise
  familiarises
  familiarised
  familiarising
familiariser
familiarity
familiarization
familiarize
  familiarizes
  familiarized
  familiarizing
familiarly
familiarness
familier = familiar
family
  families
famine
famous
fan
  fans
  fanned
  fanning
fanatic
fanatical
fanatically
fanaticism
fancied
fancier
fanciful
fancy
  fancies
  fancied
  fancying
fandango
  fandangos
fanfare

fang
fanlight
fanned
fanning
fanny
fantail
fantasia
fantasise
  fantasises
  fantasised
  fantasising
fantasize
  fantasizes
  fantasized
  fantasizing
fantastic
fantastically
fantasy
fanzine
faqir
far
farad
faraday
faradic
faradise
  faradises
  faradised
  faradising
faradism
faradize
  faradizes
  faradized
  faradizing
faraway
farce
farcemeat
farcical
fare (= get on → fair)
  fares
  fared
  faring
~~Farenheit~~ = Fahrenheit
farewell
farina
farinaceous
farinose
farm
  farms
  farmed
  farming
farmer
farmhouse
farmland
farmstead

farmyard
Faroese
farraginous
farrago
farrier
farriery
farrow
  farrows
  farrowed
  farrowing
Farsi
farther
farthermost
farthest
farthing
farthingale
fascia
fascicle
fascinate
  fascinates
  fascinated
  fascinating
fascinator
fascism
Fascism
fascist
Fascist
fashion
  fashions
  fashioned
  fashioning
fashionable
~~fashon~~ = fashion
~~fasinate~~ = fascinate
fast
  fasts
  fasted
  fasting
fastback
fasten
  fastens
  fastened
  fastening
fast-food
fastforward
fastidious
fastidiously
fastidiousness
fastness
fat
  fatter
  fattest
fatal
fatalism

fatality
  fatalities
fatally
fate
fated
fateful
father
  fathers
  fathered
  fathering
fatherhood
father-in-law
fatherland
fatherless
fatherly
fathers-in-law
fathom
  fathoms
  fathomed
  fathoming
fathomless
fatigue
  fatigues
  fatigued
  fatiguing
fatted
fatten
  fattens
  fattened
  fattening
fatter
fattest
fatty
  fattier
  fattiest
fatuity
fatuous
fatwa
fatwah
faucal
fauces
faucet
Faulkner, William
fault
faultless
faulty
  faultier
  faultiest
faun (= an imaginary
  creature → fawn)
fauna
favour
  favours
  favoured

favouring
favourable
favourite
favouritism
fawn
  fawns
  fawned
  fawning
fawn (= baby deer;
  colour; flatter
  → faun)
fax
  faxes
  faxed
  faxing
faze
  fazes
  fazed
  fazing
fealty
fear
  fears
  feared
  fearing
fearful
fearfully
fearfulness
fearsome
~~feasable~~ = feasible
feasible
feast
feat (= a deed
  → feet)
feather
  feathers
  feathered
  feathering
featherbed
  featherbeds
  featherbedded
  featherbedding
featherbrain
featherweight
feature
featureless
febrifacient
febrific
febrifugal
febrifuge
febrile
febrility
February
~~Febuary~~ = February
feckless

fecula
feculent
fecund
fecundity
fed
federal
federalise
  federalises
  federalised
  federalising
federalism
Federalist
federalize
  federalizes
  federalized
  federalizing
federate
federation
fedora
fee
feeble
feed
  feeds
  fed
  feeding
feedback
feeder
feel
  feels
  felt
  feeling
feeler
feeling
feet (= plural of foot
  → feat)
feign (= pretend
  → fain)
  feigns
  feigned
  feigning
~~feind~~ = fiend
feint (= make a mock
  attack or movement
  → faint)
  feints
  feinted
  feinting
felafel
feldspar
feldspathic
feldspathoid
felicitate
  felicitates
  felicitated

felicitating
felicitation
felicitous
felicitously
felicitousness
felicity
  felicities
feline
felinity
fell
fellatio
feller
felloe
fellow
fellowship
felon
felonious
feloniously
feloniousness
felony
felspar
felspathic
felt
felting
felucca
felwort
female
feminine
femininity
feminise
  feminises
  feminised
  feminising
feminism
feminize
  feminizes
  feminized
  feminizing
femoral
femur
fen
fence
  fences
  fenced
  fencing
fencer
fend
  fends
  fended
  fending
fender
fenestration
feng shui
fennec

fennel
fenny
fenugreek
feoff
fer try fur
feral
Fermanagh
ferment
  ferments
  fermented
  fermenting
fermentation
fermenter
fern
fernery
ferocious
ferociously
ferociousness
ferocity
ferrate
ferreous
ferret
  ferrets
  ferreted
  ferreting
ferri-
ferric
ferriferous
ferrite
ferroelectric
ferroelectricity
ferrotype
ferrous
ferruginous
ferrule
ferry
  ferries
  ferried
  ferrying
fertile
fertilisation
fertilise
  fertilises
  fertilised
  fertilising
fertiliser
fertility
fertilization
fertilize
  fertilizes
  fertilized
  fertilizing
fertilizer
ferula

ferulaceous
ferule
fervency
fervent
fervour
fescue
fess
fesse
fester
  festers
  festered
  festering
festination
festival
festive
festivity
festoon
  festoons
  festooned
  festooning
festschrift
feta
fetch
  fetches
  fetched
  fetching
fete
  fetes
  feted
  feting
fête
  fêtes
  fêted
  fêting
fetid
fetish
fetishism
fetlock
fetor
fetter
  fetters
  fettered
  fettering
fettle
fettucini
fettucine
feu
feud
feudal
feudalism
feudality
feudatory
feudist
feuilleton

fever
feverfew
feverish
few
fey
fez
  fezzes
fiancé (= man)
fiancée (= woman)
fiasco
  fiascoes
  fiascos
fiat
fib
  fibs
  fibbed
  fibbing
fibre
fibreboard
fibreglass
fibriform
fibril
fibrillation
fibrilliform
fibrillose
fibrin
fibrinogen
fibrinogenic
fibrinogenous
fibrinolysis
fibrinolytic
fibrinous
fibroid
fibroma
fibromatous
fibrosis
fibrositis
fibrotic
fibrous
fibula
fiche
fichu
fickle
ficticious = fictitious
fictile
fiction
fictionalise
  fictionalises
  fictionalised
  fictionalising
fictionalize
  fictionalizes
  fictionalized
  fictionalizing

fictitious
fictitiously
fictitiousness
fictive
ficus
fiddle
  fiddles
  fiddled
  fiddling
fiddle-de-dee
fiddlededee
fiddledeedee
fiddler
fiddlesticks
fiddly
  fiddlier
  fiddliest
fidelity
fidget
  fidgets
  fidgeted
  fidgeting
fiducial
fiducially
fiduciarily
fiduciary
fie
fief
fiefdom
field
  fields
  fielded
  fielding
fielder
fieldfare
fieldmouse
fieldwork
fiend
fiendish
fierce
fiery
  fierier
  fieriest
fiesta
  fiestas
fife
fifteen
fifteenth
fifth
fifthly
fiftieth
fifty
fifty-fifty
fig

fight
  fights
  fought
  fighting
fighter
figment
figuline
figural
figurate
figuration
figurative
figure
  figures
  figured
  figuring
figurehead
figurine
figwort
Fiji
Fijian
filagree = filigree
filament
filamentary
filbert
filch
  filches
  filched
  filching
file
  files
  filed
  filing
filial
filibeg
filibuster
  filibusters
  filibustered
  filibustering
filibusterer
filicide
filiform
filigree
filings
Filipino
  Filipinos
fill
  fills
  filled
  filling
filllagree = filigree
filler
fillet
  fillets
  filleted

filleting
filling
fillip
filly
  fillies
film
  films
  filmed
  filming
filmy
  filmier
  filmiest
filo
Filofax®
  Filofaxes®
filose
filter
  filters
  filtered
  filtering
filterable
filth
filthy
  filthier
  filthiest
filtrate
  filtrates
  filtrated
  filtrating
filtration
filum
fimbriate
fin
finable
finagle
  finagles
  finagled
  finagling
finagler
final
finale
finalise
  finalises
  finalised
  finalising
finalism
finalist
finality
finalize
  finalizes
  finalized
  finalizing
finally
finals

finance
  finances
  financed
  financing
financial
financially
finch
  finches
find
  finds
  found
  finding
finder
fine
  fines
  fined
  fining
fineable
fine-drawn
finely
fineness
finery
finesse
finger
  fingers
  fingered
  fingering
fingernail
fingerprint
fingertip
finical
finicky
fining
finis
finish
  finishes
  finished
  finishing
finisher
finite
Finland
Finn
finned
finner
Finnish
finnish = finish
finny
fino
  finos
fiord
fioritura
fir
fire
  fires

fired
firing
firearm
firebird
firebomb
firebreak
firebrick
firecracker
firedamp
firedog
firefighter
firefly
  fireflies
fireguard
firelock
fireman
  firemen
fireplace
fireproof
fireside
firestone
fireweed
firework
fireworks
firing
firkin
firm
  firms
  firmed
  firming
firmament
firmamental
firmware
firn
firry
  firrier
  firriest
first
firstly
first-rate
firth
fiscal
fish
  fish or
  fishes
  fished
  fishing
fisher
fisherman
  fishermen
fishery
  fisheries
fishmonger
fishnet

fishtail
fishwife
  fishwives
fishy
  fishier
  fishiest
fissile
fissility
fission
fissionable
fissiparous
fissure
fist
fistful
  fistfuls
fisticuffs
fistula
  fistulas or
  fistulae
fistulous
fit
  fits
  fitted
  fitting
fitch
fitter
fittest
fitful
fitfully
fitly
fitment
fitness
fitter
five
fivefold
fiver
fives
fix
  fixes
  fixed
  fixing
fixate
  fixates
  fixated
  fixating
fixation
fixative
fixedly
fixer
fixings
fixity
fixture
fizz
  fizzes

fizzed
fizzing
fizzle
  fizzles
  fizzled
  fizzling
fjord
flab
flabbergast
  flabbergasts
  flabbergasted
  flabbergasting
flabby
  flabbier
  flabbiest
flabellate
flaccid
flaccidity
flacid = flaccid
flack
flacon
flag
  flags
  flagged
  flagging
flagellant
flagellate
  flagellates
  flagellated
  flagellating
flagellum
  flagella or
  flagellums
flageolet
flagging
flagitious
flagitiously
flagitiousness
flagon
flagpole
flagrant
flagship
flagstone
flail
  flails
  flailed
  flailing
flair (= style → flare)
flak
flake
  flakes
  flaked
  flaking
flaky

flakier
flakiest
flambé
flambeau
flambée
flamboyance
flamboyancy
flamboyant
flamboyantly
flame
flames
flamed
flaming
flamenco
flamencos
flameproof
flamingo
flamingos *or*
flamingoes
flammable
flan
flange
flanges
flanged
flanging
flank
flanks
flanked
flanking
flanker
flannel
flannelette
flap
flaps
flapped
flapping
flapjack
flapper
flare (= flame → flair)
flares
flared
flaring
flash
flashes
flashed
flashing
flashback
flasher
flashlight
flashy
flashier
flashiest
flask
flat

flatter
flattest
flatboat
flatfish
flatiron
flatlet
flatmate
flatted
flatten
flattens
flattened
flattening
flatter
flatters
flattered
flattering
flattery
flattest
flattish
flatulence
flatulent
flatus
flatworm
flaunt
flaunts
flaunted
flaunting
flautist
flavescent
flavin
flavine
flavone
flavonoid
flavour
flavours
flavoured
flavouring
flaw
flaws
flawed
flawing
flax
flaxen
flay
flays
flayed
flaying
flea (= insect → flee)
fleabite
fleam
fleapit
flèche
fleck
flecks

flecked
flecking
flection
fled
fledged
fledgeling
fledgling
flee (= run away from
   → flea)
flees
fled
fleeing
fleece
fleeces
fleeced
fleecing
fleecy
fleecier
fleeciest
fleet
fleeting
Fleming
Flemish
flesh
flesher
fleshly
fleshlier
fleshliest
fleshpots
fleshy
fleshier
fleshiest
fleur-de-lis
fleurs-de-lis
fleur-de-lys
fleurs-de-lys
flew (to fly → flu, flue)
flex
flexes
flexed
flexing
flexable = flexible
flexible
flexile
flexion
flexitime
flexor
flexuous
flexure
flibbertigibbet
flick
flicks
flicked
flicking

flicker
flickers
flickered
flickering
flier
flies
flight
flightless
flighty
flightier
flightiest
flimflam
flimsy
flimsier
flimsiest
flinch
flinches
flinched
flinching
fling
flings
flung
flinging
flint
flintlock
flinty
flintier
flintiest
flip
flips
flipped
flipping
flipflop
flippant
flipper
flipping
flirt
flirts
flirted
flirting
flirtation
flirtatious
flirtatiously
flirtatiousness
flit
flits
flitted
flitting
flitch
flitches
float
floats
floated
floating

floatage
floatation
floater
floaty
  floatier
  floatiest
flocci
floccose
flocculate
floccule
flocculent
flocculus
  flocculi
floccus
  flocci
flock
  flocks
  flocking
  flocked
floe
floes
flog
  flogs
  flogged
  flogging
flood
  floods
  flooded
  flooding
floodgate
floodlight
floor
  floors
  floored
  flooring
floorage
floosie
floozie
floozy
flop
  flops
  flopped
  flopping
floppy
  floppier
  floppiest
floral
floreated
Florentine
florescence
floret
floriated
floribunda
floriculture

florid
floridity
floriferous
florigen
florin
florist
floristic
floristics
floss
flossy
  flossier
  flossiest
flotage
flotation
flotilla
  flotillas
flotsam
flounce
  flounces
  flounced
  flouncing
flounder
  flounders
  floundered
  floundering
flour (= powder made
  from grain → flower)
~~flourescent~~ =
  fluorescent
~~flouride~~ = fluoride
flourish
  flourishes
  flourished
  flourishing
flout
  flouts
  flouted
  flouting
flow
  flows
  flowed
  flowing
flower (= to bloom
  → flour)
  flowers
  flowered
  flowering
flowerage
floweret
flowerless
flowery
  flowerier
  floweriest
flowmeter

flown
flu (= illness → flue,
  flew)
fluctuant
fluctuate
  fluctuates
  fluctuated
  fluctuating
fluctuation
flue (= chimney
  → flu)
fluency
fluent
fluff
  fluffs
  fluffed
  fluffing
fluffy
  fluffier
  fluffiest
flugelhorn
fluid
fluidic
fluidics
fluidise
  fluidises
  fluidised
  fluidising
fluidity
fluidize
  fluidizes
  fluidised
  fluidizing
fluke
flukey
  flukier
  flukiest
fluky
  flukier
  flukiest
flume
flummox
  flummoxes
  flummoxed
  flummoxing
flung
flunk
  flunks
  flunked
  flunking
flunkey
  flunkeys
flunky
  flunkies

fluor-
fluoresce
fluorescence
fluorescent
fluoric
fluoridate
  fluoridates
  fluoridated
  fluoridating
fluoridation
fluoride
fluorinate
  fluorinates
  fluorinated
  fluorinating
fluorine
fluoro-
fluorocarbon
fluorometer
flurry
  flurries
  flurried
  flurrying
flush
  flushes
  flushed
  flushing
fluster
  flusters
  flustered
  flustering
flute
  flutes
  fluted
  fluting
flutist
flutter
  flutters
  fluttered
  fluttering
fluvial
flux
fly
  flies
  flew
  flown
  flying
flyblown
flyer
flying
flyleaf
  flyleaves
flyover
flyweight

flywheel
foal
  foals
  foaled
  foaling
foam
  foams
  foamed
  foaming
foamy
  foamier
  foamiest
fob
  fobs
  fobbed
  fobbing
focal
fo´c´sle
fo´c´s´le
focus
  foci *or*
  focusses
focus
  focuses *or*
  focusses
  focused *or*
  focussed
  focusing *or*
  focussing
fodder
foe
foetal
foetid
foetus
  foetuses
fog
  fogs
  fogged
  fogging
fogey
  fogies *or*
  fogeys
foggy
  foggier
  foggiest
fogy
  fogies
föhn
foible
foil
  foils
  foiled
  foiling
foist

foists
foisted
foisting
fol try fal
folacin
fold
  folds
  folded
  folding
foldaway
folder
folderol
folia
foliaceous
foliage
foliar
foliate
  foliates
  foliated
  foliating
foliation
folio
  folios
foliolate
foliose
folium
  folia
folk
Folkestone
folklore
folksy
  folksier
  folksiest
follicle
follicular
folliculated
follow
  follows
  followed
  following
follower
folly
  follies
foment
  foments
  fomented
  fomenting
fomentation
fomenter
fond
fondant
fondle
  fondles
  fondled

fondling
fondue
font
fontanelle
food
foodie
foodstuff
fool
  fools
  fooled
  fooling
foolery
foolhardy
  foolhardier
  foolhardiest
foolish
foolproof
foolscap
foot
  feet
foot
  foots
  footed
  footing
footage
football
foothill
foothold
footie
footing
footle
  footles
  footled
  footling
footlights
footling
footloose
footman
  footmen
footnote
footpath
footprint
footsie
footsore
footstep
footstool
footwear
footwork
footy
fop
foppery
  fopperies
for try four
for

forage
  forages
  foraged
  foraging
foramen
  foramina *or*
  foramens
foray
  forays
  forayed
  foraying
forbade
forbear (= restrain
  → forebear)
  forbears
  forbore
  forbearing
forbearance
forbid
  forbids
  forbade
  forbidding
forbidden
forbidder
forbidding
~~forboding~~ = foreboding
forbore
forborne
force
  forces
  forced
  forcing
forcedly
forceful
forcefully
forcefulness
forcemeat
forceps
forcible
forcibly
ford
  fords
  forded
  fording
fore (= front → four)
forearm
  forearms
  forearmed
  forearming
forebear (= ancestor
  → forbear)
foreboding
forebodingly
forebrain

forecast
  forecasts
  forecast
  forecasting
forecastle
foreclose
  forecloses
  foreclosed
  foreclosing
foreclosure
forefather
forefend
forefinger
forefront
foregather
  foregathers
  foregathered
  foregathering
forego (= go before
  → forgo)
  foregoes
  forewent
  foregone
  foregoing
foregoer
foreground
forehead
foreign
foreigner
foreignness
foreknowledge
foreleg
forelock
foreman
  foremen
foremast
foremost
forenamed
forenoon
forensic
forensically
forensics
foreordain
foreordination
forepaw
foreplay
forequarters
forerunner
foresaid
foresail
foresee
  foresees
  foresaw
  foreseeing

foreseeable
foreseer
foreshadow
  foreshadows
  foreshadowed
  foreshadowing
foreshore
foreshorten
  foreshortens
  foreshortened
  foreshortening
foresight
foreskin
forest
forestall
  forestalls
  forestalled
  forestalling
forestaller
forestalment
forester
forestry
foretaste
  foretastes
  foretasted
  foretasting
foretell
  foretells
  foretold
  foretelling
foreteller
forethought
forever
forevermore
forewarn
  forewarns
  forewarned
  forewarning
forewarner
forewent
forewing
forewoman
  forewomen
foreword
forfeit
  forfeits
  forteited
  forfeiting
forfeiture
forfend
forfex
  forfices
forficate
forfiet = forfeit

forgather
  forgathers
  forgathered
  forgathering
forgave
forge
  forges
  forged
  forging
forgery
  forgeries
forget
  forgets
  forgot
  forgotten
  forgetting
forgetful
forgetfully
forgetfulness
forgettable
forgetter
forging
forgivable
forgivably
forgive
  forgives
  forgave
  forgiven
  forgiving
forgiveness
forgiver
forgiving
forgivingly
forgivingness
forgo (= go without
  → forego)
  forgoes
  forwent
  forgone
  forgoing
forgot
forgotten
forhead = forehead
foriegn = foreign
fork
  forks
  forked
  forking
forlorn
forlornly
forlornness
form
  forms
  formed

forming
formal
formaldehyde
formalin
formalise
  formalises
  formalised
  formalising
formalism
formality
formalize
  formalizes
  formalized
  formalizing
format
formation
formational
formative
forme
former
formerly
formic
Formica®
formicary
formication
formidable
formless
formula
  formulas or
  formulae
formulaic
formularise
  formularises
  formularised
  formularising
formularize
  formularizes
  formularized
  formularizing
formulary
formulate
  formulates
  formulated
  formulating
formulism
formyl
fornicate
  fornicates
  fornicated
  fornicating
fornication
forsake
  forsakes
  forsook

forsaken
forsaking
forsaker
forseeable =
  foreseeable
forsooth
forswear
  forswears
  forswore
  forsworn
  forswearing
forswearer
forsythia
fort
forte (= talent
  → forty)
forth (= forward
  → fourth)
forthcoming
forthright
forthwith
fortieth
fortification
fortify
  fortifies
  fortified
  fortifying
fortissimo
fortitude
fortnight
Fortran℗
fortress
  fortresses
fortuitism
fortuitist
fortuitous
fortuitously
fortuitousness
fortuity
fortunate
fortunatly = fortunately
fortune
forty (= number
  → forte)
forum
  fora or
  forums
forward
  forwards
  forwarded
  forwarding
  forwards
forwent
fossa

fosse
fossil
fossiliferous
fossilise
  fossilises
  fossilised
  fossilising
fossilize
  fossilizes
  fossilized
  fossilizing
foster
  fosters
  fostered
  fostering
fosterage
foudroyant
fought
foul (= horrible
  → fowl)
fouler
foulest
foully
foulness
found
  founds
  founded
  founding
foundation
founder (starter)
founder (= sink)
  founders
  foundered
  foundering
foundling
foundry
  foundries
fount
fountain
fountainhead
four (= number
  → fore)
fourfold
fourposter
fourscore
foursome
fourteen
fourteenth
fourth (= number
  → forth)
fourthly
fourty = forty
fovea
  foveae

foveolar
foveolate
fowl (= hen → foul)
fowling
fox
  foxes
fox
  foxes
  foxed
  foxing
foxglove
foxhound
foxhunting
foxtrot
  foxtrots
  foxtrotted
  foxtrotting
foxy
  foxier
  foxiest
foyer
fracas
fractal
fraction
fractional
fractionary
fractionate
  fractionates
  fractionated
  fractionating
fractionise
  fractionises
  fractionised
  fractionising
fractionize
  fractionizes
  fractionized
  fractionizing
fractious
fracture
  fractures
  fractured
  fracturing
fraenum
  fraena
fragile
fragility
fragment
fragmentary
fragmentation
fragrance
fragrant
frail
frailty

frame
  frames
  framed
  framing
franc (= money
  → frank)
France
Frances (female)
franchise
Francis (male)
Franciscan
francium
Francophile
Francophobe
Francophone
frangible
frangipane
frangipani
Franglais
frank (= honest
  → franc)
frankfurter
frankincense
frankly
frantic
frantically
franticly = frantically
frappé
fraternal
fraternalism
fraternally
fraternise
  fraternises
  fraternised
  fraternising
fraternity
  fraternities
fraternize
  fraternizes
  fraternized
  fraternizing
fratricide
fraud
fraudulence
fraudulent
fraught
fraxinella
fray
  frays
  frayed
  fraying
frazzle
  frazzles
  frazzled

frazzling
freak
  freaks
  freaked
  freaking
freakish
freaky
  freakier
  freakiest
freckle
  freckles
  freckled
  freckling
free
  freer
  freest
free
  frees
  freed
  freeing
freebie
freebooter
freed
freedom
Freephone™
freehold
freeholder
freeing
freelance
  freelances
  freelanced
  freelancing
freeloader
freeman
  freemen
freemartin
freemason
freemasonry
Freepost™
free-range
freesheet
freesia
  freesias
freeway
freewheel
  freewheels
  freewheeled
  freewheeling
freeze (= become ice
  → frieze)
  freezes
  froze
  frozen
  freezing

freezer
freight
freightage
freighter
freind = friend
freize = frieze
fremitus
  fremitus
French
frenetic
frenetically
freneticness
frenzied
frenzy
Freon™
frequence
frequency
  frequencies
frequent
frequentation
frequentative
frequenter
fresco
  frescoes or
  frescos
fresh
freshen
  freshens
  freshened
  freshening
fresher
freshet
fresnel
fret
  frets
  fretting
  fretted
fretful
fretwork
Freudian
Freud, Sigmund
friable
friar
friary
fricassee
  fricassees
  fricasseeing
  fricasseed
fricative
friction
Friday
fridge
fried
frieght = freight

friend
friendliness
friendly
frier
fries
Friesian
frieze (= decoration
  → freeze)
frig
  frigs
  frigged
  frigging
frigate
fright
frighten
  frightens
  frightened
  frightening
frightful
frightfully
frigid
frigidity
frigorific
frill
  frills
  frilled
  frilling
fringe
  fringes
  fringed
  fringing
frippery
  fripperies
Frisbee™
Frisian
frisk
  frisks
  frisked
  frisking
frisky
  friskier
  friskiest
frisson
frit
  frits
  fritted
  fritting
fritillary
  fritillaries
fritter
  fritters
  frittered
  frittering
frivolity

frivolous
frizz
  frizzes
  frizzed
  frizzing
frizzle
  frizzles
  frizzled
  frizzling
frizzy
  frizzier
  frizziest
fro
frock
  frocks
  frocked
  frocking
froe
frog
  frogs
  frogged
  frogging
frogman
  frogmen
frogmarch
  frogmarches
  frogmarched
  frogmarching
frolic
  frolics
  frolicked
  frolicking
frolicsome
from
frond
frondescence
frondescent
front
frontage
frontal
frontier
frontispiece
frontlet
frontrunner
frontwards
frost
  frosts
  frosted
  frosting
frostbite
frostbitten
frosty
  frostier
  frostiest

froth
  froths
  frothed
  frothing
frottage
froufrou
frown
  frowns
  frowned
  frowning
frowsty
  frowstier
  frowstiest
frowsy
  frowsier
  frowsiest
frowzy
  frowzier
  frowziest
froze
frozen
fructan
fructiferous
fructification
fructify
  fructifies
  fructified
  fructifying
fructose
fructuous
frugal
frugality
frugivorous
fruit
  fruits
  fruited
  fruiting
fruitage
fruitarian
fruitarianism
fruiter
fruiterer
fruitful
fruition
fruitless
fruity
  fruitier
  fruitiest
frumentaceous
frump
frumpy
  frumpier
  frumpiest
frustrate

frustrates
frustrated
frustrating
frustration
frustule
frustum
frutescence
frutescent
fry
  fries
  fried
  frying
fryer
fucivorous
fuck
  fucks
  fucked
  fucking
fucker
fucoid
fucous
fucus
  fucuses
fuddle
  fuddles
  fuddled
  fuddling
fuddy-duddy
fudge
  fudges
  fudged
  fudging
fuel
  fuels
  fuelled
  fuelling
fug
fugacious
fugaciously
fugaciousness
fugacity
fugal
fugitive
fugue
fulcrum
fulfil
  fulfils
  fulfilled
  fulfilling
fulfiller
fulfilment
fulgent
fuliginous
full

fulls
fulled
fulling
fullback
fuller
~~fullfill~~ = fulfil
full-time
fully
fulmar
fulminant
fulminate
  fulminates
  fulminated
  fulminating
fulsome
fulvous
fumarole
fumarolic
fumble
  fumbles
  fumbled
  fumbling
fume
  fumes
  fumed
  fuming
fumet
fumigant
fumigate
  fumigates
  fumigated
  fumigating
fun
funambulism
funambulist
function
functional
functionalism
functionary
  functionaries
fund
  funds
  funded
  funding
fundament
fundamental
fundamentalism
~~fundemental~~ =
  fundamental
fundus
  fundi
funebrial
funeral
funerary

funereal
funereally
funfair
fungal
fungi
fungible
fungic
fungicide
fungiform
fungoid
fungus
  fungi or
  funguses
funicle
funicular
funiculate
funiculus
funk
funky
  funkier
  funkiest
funnel
funny
  funnier
  funniest
fur
  furs
  furred
  furring
furbelow
furbish
  furbishes
  furbished
  furbishing
furcation
Furies (= fates)
furious
  furiously
furl
  furls
  furled
  furling
furlong
furnace
furnish
  furnishes
  furnished
  furnishing
furnishings
furniture
furore
furrier
furriery
furrow

furrows
furrowed
furrowing
furry
  furrier
  furriest
further
furtherance
furthermore
furthermost
furthest
furtive
fury
  furies
furze

~~fuschia~~ = fuchsia
fuse
  fuses
  fused
  fusing
fusee
fuselage
fusible
fusiform
fusile
fusilier
fusillade
fusion
fuss
  fusses

fussed
fussing
fussy
  fussier
  fussiest
fustian
fusty
  fustier
  fustiest
futile
futility
futon
futtock
future
futurism

futuristic
futurity
futurology
fuzee
fuzz
  fuzzes
  fuzzed
  fuzzing
fuzzy
  fuzzier
  fuzziest
f-word

G

gab
  gabs
  gabbed
  gabbing
gabardine
gabble
  gabbles
  gabbled
  gabbling
gabby
  gabbier
  gabbiest
gable
gabled
Gabon
gad
  gads
  gadded
  gadding
gadfly
  gadflies
gadget
gadgetry
gadroon
gadzooks
Gael
Gaelic
gaff (= blow the gaff
  → gaffe)
gaffe (= blunder
  → gaff)
gaffer
gaffsail
gag
  gags
  gagged
  gagging
gaga
gage (= pledge
  → gauge)
gage = gauge
gagger
gaggle
Gaia
gaiety
gaily

gain
  gains
  gained
  gaining
gainer
gainful
gainfully
gainly
  gainlier
  gainliest
gains
gainsay
  gainsays
  gainsaid
  gainsaying
gait (= walk
  → gate)
gaiter
gal
gala
  galas
galactic
galactose
galah
Galahad
galantine
Galatea
Galashiels
Galatians
galaxy
  galaxies
galbanum
gale
galena
Galilee
gall
  galls
  galled
  galling
gallant
gallantry
  gallantries
galleon
gallery
  galleries
galley

galleys
gallfly
  gallflies
galliard
gallic
Gallic
Gallicism
gallimaufry
galling
gallium
gallivant
  gallivants
  gallivanted
  gallivanting
gallon
gallonage
gallop
  gallops
  galloped
  galloping
Galloway
gallows
galoot
galore
galoshes
galtonia
galumph
  galumphs
  galumphed
  galumphing
galvanic
galvanise
  galvanises
  galvanised
  galvanising
galvanism
galvanize
  galvanizes
  galvanized
  galvanizing
galvanometer
galvanotropic
galvanotropism
Galway
gam
gambado

gambadoes or
  gambados
Gambia
gambit
gamble (= take a risk
  → gambol)
  gambles
  gambled
  gambling
gamboge
gambogian
gambol (= frolic
  → gamble)
  gambols
  gambolled
  gambolling
game
  games
  gamed
  gaming
gamekeeper
gamelan
gamely
gameness
gamesmanship
gamesome
gamester
gamete
gametic
gametogenesis
gametocyte
gametophyte
gamey
  gamier
  gamiest
gamic
gamin
gamine
gaming
gamma
gammon
gammy
gamp
gamut
gamy
  gamier

gamiest
gander
Gandhi
Gandhian
~~gane~~ = gain
gang
　gangs
　ganged
　ganging
ganger
gangling
ganglion
gangrene
gangrenous
gangster
gangue
gangway
ganister
ganja
gannet
gannister
gantlet
gantline
gantry
　gantries
Ganymede
gaol
　gaols
　gaoled
　gaoling
gap
gape
　gapes
　gaped
　gaping
gaper
garage
　garages
　garaged
　garaging
~~garantee~~ = guarantee
garb
　garbs
　garbed
　garbing
garbage
garble
　garbles
　garbled
　garbling
garboard
garçon
gardai
garden

gardens
gardened
gardening
gardener
gardenia
~~gardian~~ = guardian
garfish
gargantuan
garget
gargle
　gargles
　gargled
　gargling
gargoyle
garibaldi
garish
garland
garlic
　garlicky
　garlickier
　garlickiest
garment
garner
　garners
　garnered
　garnering
garnet
garnierite
garnish
　garnishes
　garnished
　garnishing
garnishee
garnishment
garniture
garotte
　garottes
　garotted
　garotting
garotter
garpike
garret
garrison
　garrisons
　garissoned
　garissoning
garron
garrotte
　garrottes
　garrotted
　garrotting
garrotter
garrulity
garrulous

garter
garth
gas
　gasses
　gassed
　gassing
gas
　gases *or*
　gasses
gasconade
gaselier
gaseous
gash
　gashes
　gashed
　gashing
gasiform
gasify
　gasifies
　gasified
　gasifying
gasket
gaskin
gasolene
gasoline
gasometer
gasp
　gasps
　gasped
　gasping
gasper
gassed
gasser
gasses
gassing
gassy
　gassier
　gassiest
gasteropod
gastrectomy
gastric
gastritic
gastritis
gastroenterology
gastroenterostomy
gastronome
gastronomic
gastronomy
gastropod
gastropodan
gastropodous
gastroscope
gastroscopy
gat

gate (= barrier
　→ gait)
gates
gated
gating
gateau
　gateaus *or*
　gateaux
gatepost
gateway
gather
　gathers
　gathered
　gathering
gauche
gaucho
　gauchos
gaudy
　gaudier
　gaudiest
gauffer
　gauffers
　gauffered
　gauffering
gauge
　gauges
　gauged
　gauging
gauger
Gauguin, Paul
gauleiter
Gaullism
gault
gaunt
gauntlet
gauntry
　gauntries
gaup
　gaups
　gauped
　gauping
~~gaurd~~ = guard
gauss
gaussmeter
gauze
gauzy
　gauzier
　gauziest
gave
gavel
gavotte
　gavottes
　gavotted
　gavotting

gawk
  gawks
  gawked
  gawking
gawky
  gawkier
  gawkiest
gawp
  gawps
  gawped
  gawping
gay
  gayer
  gayest
gaze
  gazes
  gazed
  gazing
gazebo
  gazebos *or*
  gazeboes
gazelle
gazette
  gazettes
  gazetted
  gazetting
gazetteer
gazpacho
gazump
  gazumps
  gazumped
  gazumping
gazumper
GCHQ
GCSE
geanticlinal
geanticline
gear
  gears
  geared
  gearing
gearing
gearshift
gecko
  geckoes *or*
  geckos
gee
  gees
  geed
  geeing
gee-gee
geek
geese
geisha

geisha *or*
  geishas
gel
  gels
  gelled
  gelling
gelatin
gelatine
gelatinisation
gelatinise
  gelatinises
  gelatinised
  gelatinising
gelatinization
gelatinize
  gelatinizes
  gelatinized
  gelatinizing
gelatinoid
gelatinous
gelation
geld
  gelds
  gelded
  gelding
gelding
gelid
gelidity
gelignite
gelled
gelling
gelsemium
gem
  gems
  gemmed
  gemming
gemfish
  gemfish *or*
  gemfishes
geminate
  geminates
  geminated
  geminating
gemination
Gemini
gemma
gemmate
gemmation
gemmiferous
gemmiparous
gemmological
gemmologist
gemmology
gemological

gemologist
gemology
gemsbok
gen
  gens
  genned
  genning
gendarme
gendarmerie
gender
gene
genealogical
genealogy
~~geneology~~ = genealogy
genera
generable
general
generalisation
generalise
  generalises
  generalised
  generalising
generalist
generality
generalization
generalize
  generalizes
  generalized
  generalizing
generally
generate
  generates
  generated
  generating
generation
generative
generator
generic
generically
generosity
generous
genesis
genet
genetic
genetically
geneticist
genetics
genial
geniality
genic
genicular
geniculate
geniculation
genie

genies
genii
genital
genitalia
genitals
genitival
genitive
genitor
genius
  geniuses
genom
genome
genotype
genre
gent
genteel
genteelly
genteelness
gentian
gentile
gentilesse
gentility
gentle
gentleman
  gentlemen
gentleness
gentlewoman
  gentlewomen
gentrification
gentrify
  gentrifies
  gentrified
  gentrifying
gentry
  gentries
gents
genuflect
genuine
genus
  genera *or*
  genuses
geocentric
geochronology
geode
geodesic
geodesy
geodetic
geodic
geodynamics
Geoffrey
geognostic
geognosy
geographer
geographical

geographically
geography
geoid
geological
geologically
geologist
geology
geomagnetic
geomagnetism
geometric
geometrical
geometrically
geometry
geophagist
geophagous
geophagy
geophysics
geophyte
geophytic
geopolitical
geopolitics
geoponic
geoponics
Geordie
George
georgette
Georgia
Georgian
geoscience
geosphere
geostatic
geostatics
geostrophic
geotaxis
geotectonic
geothermal
geotropic
geotropism
geranium
  geraniums
gerbil
gerfalcon
geriatric
geriatrician
geriatrics
germ
German
germane
germanely
germaneness
Germanic
germanium
Germanophile
Germanophobe

Germany
germicide
germinal
germinant
germinate
  germinates
  germinated
  germinating
gerontic
gerontocracy
gerontocratic
gerontological
gerontology
gerrymander
  gerrymanders
  gerrymandered
  gerrymandering
gerund
gerundial
gerundival
gerundive
gesso
Gestalt
Gestapo
gestate
  gestates
  gestated
  gestating
gestation
gestative
gesticulate
  gesticulates
  gesticulated
  gesticulating
gesticulation
gesticulator
gesticulatory
gesture
  gestures
  gestured
  gesturing
get
  gets
  got
  getting
get-at-able
getter
geum
gewgaw
geyser
G-force
Ghana
~~Ghandi~~ = Gandhi
ghastly

ghastlier
ghastliest
ghee
gherkin
ghetto
  ghettos or
  ghettoes
ghillie
ghost
  ghosts
  ghosted
  ghosting
ghostly
  ghostlier
  ghostliest
ghostwrite
ghoul
GHQ
gi try gui
GI
giant
giantess
giantism
giardiasis
gib
  gibs
  gibbed
  gibbing
gibber
  gibbers
  gibbered
  gibbering
gibberish
gibbet
gibbon
gibbosity
gibbous
gibe
  gibes
  gibed
  gibing
giblets
giddy
  giddier
  giddiest
gift
  gifts
  gifted
  gifting
giftwrap
gig
  gigs
  gigged
  gigging

gigahertz
gigantic
gigantically
giganticness
giggle
  giggles
  giggled
  giggling
GIGO
gigolo
  gigolos
gigot
gigue
gilbert
Gilbertian
gild
  gilds
  gilded or gilt
  gilding
gilet
gill
gilled
gillie
gilliflower
gillion
gillyflower
gilt (= gold paint
  → guilt)
gimbals
gimcrack
gimlet
gimlet-eyed
gimmick
gin
  gins
  ginned
  ginning
ginger
gingerbread
gingerly
gingery
  gingerier
  gingeriest
gingham
gingiva
gingival
gingivitis
ginkgo
ginned
ginning
ginormous
ginseng
Gioconda
gip

gips
gipped
gipping
gipsy
giraffe
girandole
girasol
gird
girds
girded *or*
girt
girding
girder
girdle
girdles
girdled
girdling
girl
girlfriend
girlhood
girlish
giro
giros
giron
girosol
girt
girth
gismo
gismos
gist
git
~~giutar~~ = guitar
give
gives
gave
given
giving
giveaway
gizmo
gizzard
glabella
glabellar
glabrescent
glabrous
glacé
glacial
glaciate
glaciates
glaciated
glaciating
glacier
glad
gladder
gladdest

gladden
gladdens
gladdened
gladdening
glade
gladiator
gladiatorial
gladiolus
gladioli *or*
gladioluses
gladsome
Glamorgan
glamorise
glamorises
glamorising
glamorised
glamorous
glamorize
glamorizes
glamorized
glamorizing
glamour
glance
glances
glanced
glancing
gland
glanders
glandular
glandule
glans
glandes
glare
glares
glared
glaring
Glasgow
glass
glasses
glassful
glassfuls
glassware
glassy
glassier
glassiest
Glaswegian
glaucoma
glaucomatous
glaucous
glaze
glazes
glazed
glazing
glazier

gleam
gleams
gleamed
gleaming
glean
gleans
gleaned
gleaning
glebe
glee
gleeful
gleet
glen
Glenrothes
gley
glib
glibly
glide
glides
glided
gliding
glider
glimmer
glimmers
glimmered
glimmering
glimpse
glint
glints
glinted
glinting
glissade
glissades
glissaded
glissading
glissando
glisten
glistens
glistened
glistering
glister
glitch
glitter
glitters
glittered
glittering
glitterati
glitz
glitzy
glitzier
glitziest
gloaming
gloat
gloats

gloated
gloating
glob
global
globalisation
globalization
globate
globe
globetrotter
globin
globoid
globose
globosity
globular
globularity
globule
globulin
globus
glockenspiel
gloom
gloomy
gloomier
gloomiest
glorification
glorify
glorifies
glorified
glorifying
gloriole
glorious
glory
glories
gloried
glorying
gloss
glosses
glossed
glossing
glossarial
glossary
glossaries
glossitis
glossolalia
glossy
glossier
glossiest
glottal
glottic
glottis
Gloucester
glove
gloves
gloved
gloving

glover
glow
  glows
  glowed
  glowing
glower
  glowers
  glowered
  glowering
gloxinia
glucose
glucosic
glucoside
glue
  glues
  glued
  gluing
glum
  glummer
  glummest
glut
  gluts
  glutted
  glutting
glutaeal
glutamate
glutamine
gluten
gluteus
  glutei
glutinosity
glutinous
glutton
gluttony
glyceric
glyceride
glycerin
glycerine
glycerol
glyceryl
glycine
glycogen
glycol
glycolic
glycose
glycoside
glycosidic
glyph
glyptal
glyptic
glyptics
G-man
GMT
gnarled

gnash
  gnashes
  gnashed
  gnashing
gnat
gnathic
gnathite
gnaw
  gnaws
  gnawed
  gnawed *or*
  gnawn
  gnawing
gneiss
gnocchi
gnome
gnomic
gnomon
gnomonic
gnosis
gnostic
Gnosticism
gnotobiotics
gnu
  gnus
go
  goes
  went
  gone
  going
goa
goad
  goads
  goaded
  goading
goal
goalie
goalkeeper
goat
goatee
goatherd
goatish
goatskin
gob
  gobs
  gobbed
  gobbing
gobbet
gobble
  gobbles
  gobbled
  gobbling
gobbledegook
gobbledygook

gobbler
goblet
goblin
gobo
  goboes *or*
  gobos
gobsmacked
gobstopper
goby
  gobies
go-by
god
God
Godalming
godchild
goddamn
goddaughter
goddess
  goddesses
godet
godetia
godfather
God-fearing
godforsaken
godless
godlike
godly
godmother
godparent
godsend
godson
goer
goes
gofer
goffer
go-getter
goggle
  goggles
  goggled
  goggling
go-go
going
going-over
  goings-over
goitre
go-kart
gold
goldcrest
gold-digger
golden
goldenrod
goldfinch
  goldfinches
goldfish

goldfish *or*
  goldfishes
goldilocks
goldsmith
golf
  golfs
  golfed
  golfing
golfer
Golgotha
Goliath
golliwog
golly
goloshes
gonad
gonadic
gonadotrophin
gondola
  gondolas
gondolier
Gondwanaland
gone
goner
gong
goniometer
gonococcus
  gonococci
gonocyte
gonopod
gonorrhoea
gonosome
goo
goober
good
  better
  best
goodbye
  goodbyes
good-humoured
goodies
good-looking
goodly
good-natured
goodness
goods
good-sized
good-tempered
goodwill
goody
goody-goody
gooey
  gooier
  gooiest
goof

goofy
  goofier
  goofiest
googly
  googlies
googol
gook
gooly
  goolies
goon
goosander
goose
  geese
goose
  gooses
  goosed
  goosing
gooseberry
  gooseberries
goosefoot
goosegrass
goosestep
gopher
Gorbachev, Mikhail
Gordian knot
gore
  gores
  gored
  goring
gorge
gorgeous
  gorgeously
gorgon
Gorgonzola (cheese)
gorilla (= animal
  → guerrilla)
gormand
gormandise
  gormandises
  gormandised
  gormandising
gormandize
  gormandizes
  gormandized
  gormandizing
gormless
gorrilla = gorilla
gorse
gory
  gorier
  goriest
gosh
goshawk
gosling

gospel
gospeller
gossamer
gossip
  gossips
  gossiped
  gossiping
gossipmonger
got
Gothic
Götterdämmerung
gouache
gouge
  gouges
  gouged
  gouging
gouger
goujon
goulash
gourd
gourmand
gourmandise
  gourmandises
  gourmandised
  gourmandising
gourmandize
  gourmandizes
  gourmandized
  gourmandizing
gourmet
gout
govenor = governor
goverment =
  government
govern
  governs
  governed
  governing
governance
governess
government
governmental
governor
gown
  gowns
  gowned
  gowning
goy
  goyim *or*
  goys
grab
  grabs
  grabbed
  grabbing

graben
grace
  graces
  graced
  gracing
graceful
graceless
gracious
gradable
gradation
grade
  grades
  graded
  grading
grader
gradient
gradual
gradualism
graduand
graduate
  graduates
  graduated
  graduating
graduation
Graeme
graffitist
graffito
  graffiti
grafitti = graffiti
graft
  grafts
  grafted
  grafting
Graham
grail
grain
graining
grainy
  grainier
  grainiest
gram
grama
graminaceous
gramineous
graminicolous
graminivorous
grammar
grammarian
grammatical
grammatically
grammaticalness
gramme
grammer = grammar
gramophone

gramophonic
grampus
  grampuses
gran
granadilla
granary
  granaries
grand
  grander
  grandest
grandam
granddaughter =
  granddaughter
grandaunt
grandchild
granddad
granddaughter
grandee
grandeur
grandfather
grandfatherly
grandiloquence
grandiloquent
grandiloquently
grandiose
grandiosity
grandma
grandmaster
grandmother
grandmotherly
grandnephew
grandniece
grandpa
grandparent
grandsire
grandson
grandstand
granduncle
grange
granite
granitic
granitite
granivore
granivorous
grannie
granny
  grannies
grant
  grants
  granted
  granting
grantee
grantor
granular

granularity
granulate
  granulates
  granulated
  granulating
granulation
granule
granulite
granulitic
granulomatous
grape
grapefruit
  grapefruits
grapeshot
grapevine
graph
graphic
graphically
graphics
graphite
graphitic
graphologist
graphology
grapnel
grappa
grapple
  grapples
  grappled
  grappling
grasp
  grasps
  grasped
  grasping
grass
  grasses
  grassed
  grassing
grasshopper
grassland
grassy
  grassier
  grassiest
grate (= shred into
  small pieces;
  fireplace → great)
  grates
  grated
  grating
grateful
  gratefully
grater
gratification
gratify
  gratifies

gratified
gratifying
gratin
gratis
gratitude
gratuitous
gratuitously
gratuitousness
gratuity
  gratuities
gratulate
  gratulates
  gratulated
  gratulation
gravadlax
grave
gravel
gravelly
graven
gravestone
graveyard
gravid
gravidity
gravitate
  gravitates
  gravitated
  gravitating
gravitation
gravitational
gravity
gravlax
gravure
gravy
  gravies
graylag
graze
  grazes
  grazed
  grazing
grazier
grease
  greases
  greased
  greasing
greasepaint
greaser
greasewood
greasy
  greasier
  greasiest
great (= very large;
  good → grate)
  greater
  greatest

greataunt
greatcoat
~~greatful~~ = grateful
great-hearted
greatnephew
greatniece
greatuncle
grebe
Grecian
Greco-Roman
Greece
greed
greedy
  greedier
  greediest
greegree
Greek
green
greenback
Greene, Graham
greenery
greenfield
greenfinch
  greenfinches
greenfly
  greenflies
greengage
greengrocer
greenhorn
greenhouse
greening
greenroom
greenshank
Greenwich
greenwood
greet
  greets
  greeted
  greeting
greetings card
gregarious
gregariously
gregariousness
Gregorian
greisen
~~greive~~ = grieve
gremlin
grenade
grenadier
grew
grey
  greyer
  greyest
greyhound

greylag
greywacke
gricer
griddle
gridiron
gridlock
grief
Grieg, Edvard
grievance
grieve
  grieves
  grieved
  grieving
grievous
griffin
grigri
grill (= cook
  → grille)
  grills
  grilled
  grilling
grille (= screen
  → grill)
grilse
grim
  grimmer
  grimmest
grimace
  grimaces
  grimaced
  grimacing
grimacer
grimalkin
grime
Grimsby
grin
  grins
  grinned
  grinning
grind
  grinds
  ground
  grinding
grinder
grindstone
gringo
  gringos
grip
  grips
  gripped
  gripping
gripe
  gripes
  griped

griping
grippe
grisaille
gris-gris
grisly (= horrible
   → grizzly)
   grislier
   grisliest
grison
grist
gristle
grit
   grits
   gritted
   gritting
gritter
gritty
   grittier
   grittiest
grizzle
   grizzles
   grizzled
   grizzling
grizzly (= bear
   → grisly)
   grizzlier
   grizzliest
groan
   groans
   groaned
   groaning
groat
grocer
groceries
grocery
grog
groggy
   groggier
   groggiest
groin
groom
   grooms
   groomed
   grooming
groomsman
   groomsmen
groove
   grooves
   grooved
   grooving
groovy
   groovier
   grooviest
grope

gropes
groped
groping
groper
grosbeak
grosgrain
gross
   grosses
   grossed
   grossing
grot
grotesque
   grotesquely
   grotesqueness
grotto
   grottoes *or*
   grottos
grotty
   grottier
   grottiest
grouch
   grouches
   grouched
   grouching
grouchy
   grouchier
   grouchiest
ground
   grounds
   grounded
   grounding
groundage
grounding
groundless
groundnut
groundsel
groundsheet
groundsman
   groundsmen
groundwork
group
   groups
   grouped
   grouping
grouper
groupie
grouse
   grouse
grouse
   grouses
   groused
   grousing
grout
   grouts

grouted
grouting
grove
grovel
   grovels
   grovelled
   grovelling
grow
   grows
   grew
   grown
   growing
grower
growl
   growls
   growled
   growling
growler
grown-up
   grown-ups
growth
groyne
grub
   grubs
   grubbed
   grubbing
grubby
   grubbier
   grubbiest
grudge
   grudges
   grudged
   grudging
gruel
gruelling
gruesome
gruff
   gruffly
grumble
   grumbles
   grumbled
   grumbling
grummet
grump
grumpy
   grumpier
   grumpiest
grunt
   grunts
   grunted
   grunting
grunter
Gruyère (cheese)
gryphon

grysbok
G-string
G-suit
guacamole
Guadalajara
~~guage~~ = gauge
guanaco
   guanacos
guano
guar
guarantee
   guarantees
   guaranteed
   guaranteeing
guarantor
guaranty
   guaranties
guard
   guards
   guarded
   guarding
guardee
guardian
Guatemala
guava
guayule
gubbins
gubernatorial
gudgeon
guelder-rose
guerilla
guerrilla (= terrorist
   → gorilla)
guerrillaism
guess
   guesses
   guessed
   guessing
guesstimate
guesswork
guest
guffaw
   guffaws
   guffawed
   guaffawing
guidance
guide
   guides
   guided
   guiding
guidebook
guideline
~~guidence~~ = guidance
guild (= association

→ gild)
guilder
Guildford
guildhall
guile
guileless
guillemot
guillotine
　guillotines
　guillotined
　guillotining
guilt (= blame → gilt)
guiltless
guilty
　guiltier
　guiltiest
guimpe
guinea
Guinea
guipure
Guisborough
guise
guitar
guitarist
Gujarati
gulf
gull
gullet
gullible
gully
　gullies
gulp
　gulps
　gulped
　gulping
gum
　gums
　gummed
　gumming
gumboots
gumbotil
gummite

gummy
　gummier
　gummiest
gumption
gumshield
gumshoe
gumtree
gun
　guns
　gunned
　gunning
gunboat
gunfight
gunfire
gunge
gungey
　gungier
　gungiest
gunk
gunman
　gunmen
gunmetal
gunnel
gunner
gunnery
　gunneries
gunpoint
gunpowder
gunrunning
gun-shy
gunslinger
gunsmith
gunwale
guppy
　guppies
gurgitation
gurgle
　gurgles
　gurgled
　gurgling
gurjun
Gurkha

Gurkhali
gurnard
guru
　gurus
gush
　gushes
　gushed
　gushing
gusher
gushy
　gushier
　gushiest
gusset
gust
　gusts
　gusted
　gusting
gustation
gustatory
gusto
gusty
　gustier
　gustiest
gut
gutless
guts
gutsy
　gutsier
　gutsiest
gutta-percha
gutted
gutter
gutteral = guttural
guttering
guttersnipe
guttural
guv
guy
guyot
guzzle
　guzzles
　guzzled

guzzling
Gwent
Gwynedd
gybe
　gybes
　gybed
　gybing
gym
gymkhana
　gymkhanas
gymnasium
　gymnasia or
　gymnasiums
gymnast
gymnastic
gymnastically
gymnastics
gymslip
gynaecological
gynaecology
gynandrous
gynandry
gynodioecious
gynomonoecious
gyp
　gyps
　gypped
　gypping
gypsum
gypsy
gyral
gyrate
　gyrates
　gyrated
　gyrating
gyration
gyrator
gyratory
gyrfalcon
gyrocompass
gyroscope
gyroscopic

H

haberdasher
haberdashery
habiliment
habilitate
habilitation
habit
habitable
habitant
habitat
habitation
habitual
habitually
habitualness
habituate
  habituates
  habituated
  habituating
habituation
habitué
hack
  hacks
  hacked
  hacking
hacker
hackles
hackney
hackneyed
hacksaw
had
hadal
haddock
Hades
Haiti
hadj
  hadjes
hadji
hadjis
hadron
hadrosaur
hadst
haem
haemal
haematic
haematite
haematoid
haematology

haematoma
  haematomas *or*
  haematomata
haematuria
haemodialysis
haemoglobin
haemolysis
haemolytic
haemophile
haemophilia
haemophiliac
haemophilic
haemopoiesis
~~haemorrage~~ =
  haemorrhage
haemorrhage
  haemorrhages
haemorrhage
  haemorrhages
  haemorrhaged
  haemorrhaging
haemostasis
hafnium
haft
hag
hagfish
  hagfish *or*
  hagfishes
Haggadah
haggard
haggis
  haggis
haggle
  haggles
  haggled
  haggling
hagiarchy
hagiocracy
hagiographer
hagiographic
hagiography
hagiolatry
hagiologic
hagiology
hah
ha-ha

hahnium
haiku
hail (= rain heavily
  → hale)
  hails
  hailed
  hailing
hailstone
hair (= on the head
  → hare)
~~hair-brained~~ =
  harebrained
hairdo
  hairdos
hairdresser
hairless
hairpiece
hair-raising
hair's-breadth
hairsplitting
hairstyle
hairy
  hairier
  hairiest
Haitian
hajj
  hajjes
hake
halal
halation
halberd
halcyon
halcyonic
hale
  hales
  haled
  haling
haler
half (= segment
  → halve)
half-a-crown
half-baked
half-brother
half-caste
half-cock
half-cocked

half-hearted
half-hour
half-inch
half-length
half-marathon
half-mast
half-nelson
halfpenny
halfpennyworth
half-price
half-sister
half-size
half-timbered
half-truth
half-volley
halfway
halfwit
halibut
halide
halite
halitosis
hall
halleluiah
Halley (comet)
hallelujah
halliard
hallmark
hallo
  hallos
halloo
  halloos
  hallooed
  hallooing
hallow
  hallows
  hallowed
  hallowing
Halloween
Hallowe'en
hallucinate
  hallucinates
  hallucinated
  hallucinating
hallucination
hallucinator
hallucinatory

hallucinogen
hallucinogenic
hallux
hallway
halma
halo
  haloes or
  halos
halogen
haloid
halophyte
halophytic
halothane
halt
  halts
  halted
  halting
halter
halva
halvah
halve (= divide in two
  → half)
  halves
  halved
  halving
halves
halyard
ham
  hams
  hammed
  hamming
hamadryad
hamburger
hame
ham-fisted
ham-handed
Hamitic
hamlet
hammer
  hammers
  hammered
  hammering
hammertoe
hamming
hammock
hamper
  hampers
  hampered
  hampering
hamster
hamstring
  hamstrings
  hamstrung
  hamstringing

hand
  hands
  handed
  handing
handbarrow
handbrake
handbreadth
handcart
handcraft
handcrafted
handcuff
handedness
Handel, George
  Frederick
handful
  handfuls
handicap
  handicaps
  handicapped
  handicapping
handicraft
handier
handiest
handily
handiwork
handkerchief
handle
  handles
  handled
  handling
handlebars
handler
handmaid
handmade
handsaw
hand's-breadth
handshake
handshaking
handsome
hand-to-hand
hand-to-mouth
handwriting
handwritten
handy
  handier
  handiest
handyman
hang
  hangs
  hanged or
  hung
  hanging
hangar (= for planes
  → hanger)

hanged (= killed by
  rope → hung)
hanger (= for clothes
  → hangar)
hanger-on
  hangers-on
hangman
hangnail
hangover
  hangovers
hang-up
  hang-ups
hank
hanker
  hankers
  hankered
  hankering
~~hankerchief~~ =
  handkerchief
hankie
  hankies
hanky
  hankies
hanky-panky
Hanoi
Hanover
Hanoverian
Hansard
Hanseatic
hansom
Hanukkah
~~hapen~~ = happen
ha'penny
haphazard
haphazardly
haphazardness
hapless
haploid
haply
ha'p'orth
happen
  happens
  happened
  happening
happenstance
happy
  happier
  happiest
happy-go-lucky
~~happyness~~ = happiness
haptic
hara-kiri
harangue
  harangues

harangued
haranguing
haranguer
Harare
harass
  harasses
  harassed
  harassing
harbinger
harbour
  harbours
  harboured
  harbouring
harbourage
hard
hardbitten
hardboard
hardboiled
harden
  hardens
  hardened
  hardening
hardener
hardhitting
hardihood
hardily
hardiness
hardly
hardness
hardpressed
hardship
hardware
hardwood
hardworking
hardy
  hardier
  hardiest
hare (= animal
  → hair)
harebell
harebrained
harelip
harem
hare's-foot
haricot
hari-kari
hark
harken
  harkens
  harkened
  harkening
harl
  harls
  harled

harling
Harlech
harlequin
harlequinade
harlot
harm
　harms
　harmed
　harming
harmattan
harmful
　harmfully
harmless
harmonic
harmonica
harmonically
harmonics
harmonious
harmoniously
harmonisation
harmonise
　harmonises
　harmonised
　harmonising
harmoniser
harmonist
harmonium
harmonization
harmonize
　harmonizes
　harmonized
　harmonizing
harmonizer
harmony
　harmonies
harmotome
harness
　harnesses
　harnessed
　harnessing
harp
　harps
　harped
　harping
harpoon
　harpoons
　harpooned
　harpooning
harpooner
harpsichord
harpy
　harpies
harrass = harass
harridan

harrier
harrow
　harrows
　harrowed
　harrowing
harrumph
　harrumphs
　harrumphed
　harrumphing
harry
　harries
　harried
　harrying
harsh
　harsher
　harshest
hart try heart
hart (= deer → heart)
hartebeest
hartshorn
harum-scarum
harvest
　harvests
　harvested
　harvesting
harvester
Harwich
has
has-been
hash
　hashes
　hashed
　hashing
hashish
Haslemere
haslet
hasn't
hasp
hassle
　hassles
　hassled
　hassling
hassock
hast
hastate
haste
hasten
　hastens
　hastened
　hastening
hasty
　hastier
　hastiest
hat

hatch
　hatches
　hatched
　hatching
hatchback
hatchery
　hatcheries
hatchet
hatchment
hatchway
hate
　hates
　hated
　hating
hateful
hath
hatred
hatted
hatter
hauberk
haughty
　haughtier
　haughtiest
haul
　hauls
　hauled
　hauling
haulage
haulier
haulm
haunch
　haunches
　haunched
haunt
　haunts
　haunted
　haunting
haustellum
haustorium
hauteur
have
　has
　had
　having
have
haves
haven
have-not
haven't
haver
　havers
　havered
　havering
haversack

haversine
havildar
havoc
haw
　haws
　hawed
　hawing
Hawaii
Hawaiian
haw-haw
hawk
　hawks
　hawked
　hawking
hawker
hawk-eyed
hawkweed
hawse
　hawses
　hawsed
　hawsing
hawser
hawthorn
hay
haybox
haycock
Haydn, Franz Josef
hayfork
haymaking
haymaker
hayseed
haystack
haywire
hazard
　hazards
　hazarded
　hazarding
hazardous
haze
hazel
hazelhen
hazelnut
hazy
　hazier
　haziest
H-bomb
he
head
　heads
　headed
　heading
headache
headband
headboard

head-butt
  head-butts
  head-butted
  head-butting
headcase
headdress
header
headfirst
headgear
headhunting
heading
headland
headless
headlight
headline
headlock
headlong
headman
  headmen
headmaster
headmistress
  headmistresses
headmost
headphones
headpiece
headquarters
headrace
headrest
headroom
headscarf
headset
headship
headstone
headstrong
headwaters
headway
headwind
heady
  headier
  headiest
heal (= make better
  → heel)
  heals
  healed
  healing
heal-all
health
healthful
healthy
  healthier
  healthiest
heap
  heaps
  heaped

heaping
hear (= listen
  → here)
  hears
  heard
  hearing
hearken
  hearkens
  hearkened
  hearkening
hearsay
hearse
heart (= body organ
  → hart)
heartache
heartbeat
heartbreaking
heartbroken
heartburn
hearten
  heartens
  heartened
  heartening
heartfelt
hearth
hearthstone
heartier
heartiest
heartily
heartland
heartless
heartrending
heartsease
heart's-ease
heartstrings
heart-throb
heart-to-heart
hearty
  heartier
  heartiest
heat
  heats
  heated
  heating
heater
heath
heathberry
  heathberries
heathen
heathendom
heathenish
heather
heathfowl
heating

heatstroke
heave
  heaves
  heaved
  heaving
heave-ho
heaven
heavenly
heaven-sent
heavenward
heavenwards
heavily
heavy
  heavier
  heaviest
heavy-duty
heavy-footed
heavy-handed
heavy-hearted
heavyweight
Hebraic
Hebraism
Hebraist
Hebrew
heck
heckle
  heckles
  heckled
  heckling
hectare
hectic
hectolitre
hectometre
hector
  hectors
  hectored
  hectoring
Hecuba
he'd (= he had
  → heed)
hedge
  hedges
  hedged
  hedging
hedgehog
hedgerow
hedonic
hedonics
hedonism
heebie-jeebies
heed (= attend
  → he'd)
  heeds
  heeded

heeding
heedless
heehaw
heel (= part of shoe
  → heal)
heels
heeled
heeling
heelpiece
heeltap
hefty
heftier
heftiest
hegemonic
hegemony
Hegira
hegumen
heh
he-he
heifer
heigh-ho
height
heighten
  heightens
  heightened
  heightening
~~heighth~~ = height
heinous
heir (= inheritor
  → air)
~~heirarchy~~ = hierarchy
heirdom
heiress
  heiresses
heirloom
heirship
Hejira
held
helenium
helianthemum
helianthus
helical
helices
helicline
helicograph
helicoid
helicopter
heliocentric
heliocentricism
heliocentricity
heliograph
heliographer
heliographic
heliolatry

heliophyte
heliosphere
heliostat
heliotactic
heliotaxis
heliotrope
heliotropic
heliotropism
helipad
heliport
helium
helix
　helices *or*
　helixes
hell
he'll
Hellas
hellbent
hellcat
hellebore
Hellenic
Hellenism
Hellenist
Hellenistic
hellfire
hellhole
hellhound
hellish
hello
　hellos
helluva
helm
helminth
helminthiasis
helminthic
helminthoid
helmsman
help
　helps
　helped
　helping
helpful
helping
helpless
helpline
helpmate
helpmeet
helter-skelter
Helvetian
Helvetic
Helvetii
hem
　hems
　hemmed

hemming
hemal
he-man
Hemel Hempstead
hemichordate
hemicycle
hemicyclic
hemihedral
hemihydrate
hemimorphic
Hemingway, Ernest
hemiola
hemiolic
hemiplegia
hemipteran
hemipteron
hemipterous
hemisphere
hemispheric
hemispheroid
hemistich
hemitrope
hemizygous
hemline
hemlock
hemmed
hemmer
hemming
hemo- (see haemo)
hemp
hen
henbane
henbit
hence
henceforth
henchman
　henchmen
hencoop
hendecagon
hendecagonal
hendecahedron
hendecasyllabic
hendecasyllable
hendiadys
henequen
henequin
heniquen
henge
henna
hennery
　henneries
henotheism
henpeck
　henpecks

henpecked
henpecking
henry
　henries *or*
　henrys
hep
heparin
hepatic
hepatica
hepatitis
Hepplewhite
heptad
heptagon
heptagonal
heptahedron
heptamerous
heptameter
heptane
heptangular
heptarchal
heptarchic
heptarchy
Heptateuch
heptathlete
heptathlon
heptavalent
heptose
her
herald
　heralds
　heralded
　heralding
heraldic
heraldically
heraldry
herb
　herbs
　herbed
　herbing
herbaceous
herbage
herbal
herbalist
herbarial
herbarium
herbicide
herbivore
herbivorous
herbivorousness
herby
　herbier
　herbiest
herculean
Hercules

Hercynian
herd
　herds
　herded
　herding
herder
herdsman
　herdsmen
here (= in this place
　→ hear)
hereabouts
hereafter
hereat
hereby
hereditability
hereditable
hereditarily
hereditariness
hereditary
hereditist
heredity
herein
hereinafter
hereinbefore
hereinto
hereof
hereon
heresy
　heresies
heretic
heretical
heretically
hereto
heretofore
hereunder
hereunto
hereupon
herewith
heritable
heritage
heritor
heritress
hermaphrodite
hermaphroditic
hermaphroditical
hermaphroditism
hermeneutic
hermeneutics
hermetic
hermetically
hermit
hermitage
hermitic
hermitical

hermitically
hernia
hero
  heroes
heroic
heroically
heroicalness
heroicness
heroics
heroin (= drug)
heroine (= hero)
heroism
heron
heronry
  heronries
hero-worship
herpes
herpetic
herpetologic
herpetology
herring
herringbone
hers
herself
hertz
Herzegovina
he's
hesitant
hesitate
  hesitates
  hesitated
  hesitating
hesperidin
hesperidium
hessian
hetero-
heterocercal
heterochromatic
heterochromosome
heterochromous
heteroclite
heterocyclic
heterodactyl
heterodont
heterodox
heterodyne
heteroecious
heterogamete
heterogametic
heterogamy
heterogeneity
heterogeneous
heterogenous
heterogony

heterogynous
heterokaryon
heterologous
heteromerous
heteromorphic
heteronomous
heteronym
heteronymous
heterophony
heterophyllous
heterophyte
heteroploid
heteropterous
heterosexism
heterosexual
heterosexuality
heterosporous
heterostyly
heterotaxis
heterotopic
heterotrophic
heterozygote
heterozygous
heuristic
heuristically
heuristics
~~heven~~ = heaven
hew (= cut down
  → hue)
  hews
  hewed or
  hewn
  hewing
hex
hexachord
hexad
hexadecimal
hexadic
hexaemeron
hexagon
hexagonal
hexagonally
hexagram
hexahedron
hexamerism
hexamerous
hexameter
hexametric
hexangular
hexapod
hexapodic
hexapody
hexastyle
Hexateuch

hexavalent
hexose
hexyl
hey
heyday
HGV
hi try high
hi
hiatal
hiatus
  hiatuses
hibachi
hibernaculum
hibernal
hibernate
  hibernates
  hibernated
  hibernating
hibiscus
hic
hiccough
  hiccoughs
  hiccoughed
  hiccoughing
hiccup
  hiccups
  hiccuped or
  hiccupped
  hiccuping or
  hiccupping
hick
hickey
hickory
  hickories
hid
hidden
hide
  hides
  hid
  hidden
  hiding
hide-and-seek
hideaway
hidebound
hideosity
hideous
hideousness
hide-out
hidey-hole
hie
  hies
  hied
  hieing or
  hying

~~hieght~~ = height
hierarch
  hierarchial
hierarchy
hieratic
hierocracy
hierocratic
hieroglyphic
hieroglyphics
hieroglyphist
hierogram
hifalutin
hi-fi
higgledy-piggledy
high
  higher
  highest
highball
highbrow
higher (= further up
  → hire)
higher-up
highfalutin
high-flier
high-flown
high-flyer
Highland
Highlander
highlife
highlight
highly
highness
Highness
  Highnesses
high-octane
high-powered
high-pressure
high-rise
highroad
high-spirited
high-stepper
hight
hightail
  hightails
  hightailed
  hightailing
high-tech
high-tension
high-up
highway
highwayman
  highwaymen
High Wycombe
hijack

hijacks
hijacked
hijacking
hijinks
hike
  hikes
  hiked
  hiking
hilarious
hilariously
hilariousness
hilarity
Hilary
hill
hillbilly
  hillbillies
hillock
hilt
hilum
  hila
him (= male → hymn)
hind
  hinder
  hindermost *or*
  hindmost
hindbrain
hinder
  hinders
  hindered
  hindering
~~hinderance~~ = hindrance
Hindi
hindquarter
hindrance
hindsight
Hindu
Hinduism
Hindustani
hinge
  hinges
  hinged
  hinging
hinny
hint
  hints
  hinted
  hinting
hinterland
hip
  hipper
  hippest
hipbone
hip-hop
hipped

hippie
hippo
  hippos
hippocampus
hippodrome
hippogriff
hippogryph
hippopotamus
  hippopotamuses *or*
  hippopotami
hippy
  hippies
hipsters
hiragana
hircine
hire (= rent → higher)
  hires
  hired
  hiring
hireling
hire-purchase
Hiroshima
hirsute
his
Hispanic
hispid
hispidity
hiss
  hisses
  hissed
  hissing
hist-
histamine
histogen
histogram
histoid
histological
histologist
histology
histolysis
histolytic
histone
historian
historiated
historic
historical
historically
historicalness
historicism
historicist
historicity
historiographer
historiographic
historiographical

historiography
history
histrionic
hit
  hits
  hit
  hitting
hitch
  hitches
  hitched
  hitching
hitchhike
  hitchhikes
  hitchhiked
  hitchhiking
hi-tech
hither
hithermost
hitherto
hitherward
Hitlerism
hitter
HIV
HIV-positive
hive
  hives
  hived
  hiving
HMG
HMS
HNC
HND
ho try who
hoar (= frost
  → whore)
hoard (= collect
  → horde)
  hoards
  hoarded
  hoarding
hoarfrost
hoarhound
hoarse
hoarsen
  hoarsens
  hoarsened
  hoarsening
hoary
  hoarier
  hoariest
hoatzin
hoax
  hoaxes
  hoaxed

hoaxing
hob
  hobs
  hobbed
  hobbing
hobbit
hobble
  hobbles
  hobbled
  hobbling
hobbledehoy
hobby
  hobbies
hobbyhorse
hobgoblin
hobnail
hobnob
  hobnobs
  hobnobbed
  hobnobbing
hobo
  hoboes *or*
  hobos
hock
hockey
hocus-pocus
hod
hodgepodge
hoe
  hoes
  hoed
  hoeing
hoedown
hog
  hogs
  hogged
  hogging
hogback
hogfish
  hogfish *or*
  hogfishes
hoggish
Hogmanay
hogshead
hogwash
hogweed
ho-ho
hoicks
hoiden
hoist
  hoists
  hoisted
  hoisting
hoity-toity

hokey-pokey
hokku
Holarctic
hold
  holds
  held
  holding
holdall
holder
hold-up
  hold-ups
hole
  holes
  holed
  holing
hole-and-corner
holiday
  holidays
  holidayed
  holidaying
holiday-maker
holier
holiest
holily
holiness
holism
holistic
holistically
holland
holler
  hollers
  hollered
  hollering
hollo
  hollos
  holloed
  holloing
hollow
  hollows
  hollowed
  hollowing
hollow
  hollower
  hollowest
hollow-eyed
hollowware
holly
hollyhock
holmic
holmium
holoblastic
holocaust
holocrine
holoenzyme

hologram
holograph
holographic
holography
holohedral
holophrastic
holophyte
holophytic
holoplankton
holothurian
holotype
holotypic
holozoic
hols
holster
holus-bolus
holy
  holier
  holiest
holystone
homage
hombre
homburg
home
  homes
  homed
  homing
homebred
homebrew
homecoming
homegrown
homeland
homely
  homelier
  homeliest
homemade
homeopath
homeopathic
homeopathy
homeostasis
homeostatic
homeotypic
Homer
Homeric
homesick
homespun
homestead
homeward
homey
  homier
  homiest
homicidal
homicide
homiletic

homiletics
homily
  homilies
homing
hominid
hominoid
homo
  homos
homocentric
homocercal
homochromatic
homochromatism
homochromous
homocyclic
homoeopathic
homoeopathy
homoeostasis
homoeostatic
homoeroticism
homogametic
homogamous
homogamy
homogeneity
homogeneous
homogenisation
homogenise
  homogenises
  homogenised
  homogenising
homogeniser
homogenization
homogenize
  homogenizes
  homogenized
  homogenizing
homogenizer
homogenous
homogeny
homogonous
homogony
homograft
homograph
homoiothermic
homologate
homologation
homologise
  homologises
  homologised
  homologising
homologiser
homologize
  homologizes
  homologized
  homologizing

homologizer
homologous
homolographic
homologue
homology
homolysis
homolytic
homomorphism
homonym
homonymous
homonymy
Homoousian
homophobia
homophone
homophonic
homophonous
homophony
homophyllic
homophyly
homoplastic
homopolar
homopolarity
homopterous
homosexual
homosexuality
homotaxis
homothallic
homozygote
homozygotic
homozygous
homuncular
homuncule
homunculus
homy
  homier
  homiest
honcho
  honchos
Honduras
hone
  hones
  honed
  honing
honest
honestly
honesty
honewort
honey
honeybee
honeycomb
honeydew
honey-eater
honeyed
honeymoon

honeysucker
honeysuckle
Hong Kong
honied
honk
  honks
  honked
  honking
honker
honky-tonk
Honolulu
honorarium
  honorariums *or*
  honoraria
honorary
honorific
honour
  honours
  honoured
  honouring
honourable
hooch
hood
  hoods
  hooded
  hooding
hoodlum
hoodoo
  hoodoos
hoodwink
  hoodwinks
  hoodwinked
  hoodwinking
hooey
hoof
  hoofs *or*
  hooves
hoofed
hoo-ha
hook
  hookd
  hooked
  hooking
hooka
hookah
hooker
hookey
hook-up
  hook-ups
hookworm
hooky
hooley
  hooleys *or*
  hoolies

hoolie
hooligan
hoop
hooper
hoopla
hoopoe
hooray
  hoorays
  hoorayed
  hooraying
hoot
  hoots
  hooted
  hooting
hootch
hooter
Hoover™
hooves
hop
  hops
  hopped
  hopping
hope
  hopes
  hoped
  hoping
hopeful
hopefully
~~hopeing~~ = hoping
hopeless
hoplologist
hoplology
hopper
hopsack
hopscotch
horal
horary
horde (= crowd
  → hoard)
hordein
horehound
horizon
horizontal
horizontally
hormonal
hormonally
hormone
horn
  horns
  horned
  horning
hornbeam
hornbill
hornblende

hornet
hornpipe
horntail
hornwort
hornwrack
horny
  hornier
  horniest
horologic
horologion
horologist
Horologium
horology
horoscope
horoscopic
horoscopy
horrendous
horrendously
horrible
horribly
horrid
  horrider
  horriddest
horridly
horridness
horrific
horrifically
horrify
  horrifies
  horrified
  horrifying
horripilation
horror
horrorstruck
horse
  horses
  horsed
  horsing
horseback
horsebox
horsefly
  horseflies
horsehair
horseman
  horsemen
horsemanship
horseplay
horsepower
horseradish
horseshoe
horseweed
horsewhip
  horsewhips
  horsewhipped

horsewhipping
horsewoman
  horsewomen
horsey
horst
horsy
  horsier
  horsiest
hortation
hortatory
horticultural
horticulture
hosanna
hose
  hoses
  hosed
  hosing
hosier
hosiery
hospice
hospitable
hospital
hospitalisation
hospitalise
  hospitalises
  hospitalised
  hospitalising
hospitality
hospitalization
hospitalize
  hospitalizes
  hospitalized
  hospitalizing
hospitaller
host
  hosts
  hosted
  hosting
hostage
hostel
hosteller
hostelling
hostelry
hostess
hostile
hostility
  hostilities
hostler
hot
  hotter
  hottest
hotbed
hotblooded
hotchpotch

hotel
hotelier
hotfoot
  hotfoots
  hotfooted
  hotfooting
hothead
hotheaded
hothouse
hotplate
hotpot
hotshot
Hottentot
hotter
hottest
hottish
hotwire
  hotwires
  hotwired
  hotwiring
houdah
hough
houmous
houmus
hound
  hounds
  hounded
  hounding
hour
hourglass
houri
  houris
hourly
house
  houses
  housed
  housing
houseboat
housebound
houseboy
housebreaking
housecoat
housefather
housefly
  houseflies
household
householder
househusband
housekeep
  housekeeps
  housekept
  housekeeping
housekeeper
housekeeping

housemaid
houseman
  housemen
housemaster
housemistress
houseroom
houses
housetop
housewarming
housewife
housewifely
housewifery
housework
housey-housey
housing
hove
  hoves
  hoved
  hoving
hovel
hover
  hovers
  hovered
  hovering
hovercraft
hoverport
how
howbeit
howdah
how-do-you-do
howdy
however
howitzer
howl
  howls
  howled
  howling
howler
howsoever
hoy
hoyden
hub
hubble-bubble
hubbub
hubby
  hubbies
hubcap
Hubble (telescope)
hubris
hubristic
huck
huckaback
huckleberry
huckster

huddle
  huddles
  huddled
  huddling
hudibrastic
hue (= colour → hew)
huff
huffish
hug
  hugs
  hugged
  hugging
huge
hugely
hugeness
huggermugger
Hugh
Huguenot
huh
hula
hula-hoop
hulk
  hulks
  hulked
  hulking
hull
  hulls
  hulled
  hulling
hullaballoo
hullabaloo
hullo
  hullos
hum
  hums
  hummed
  humming
human
humane
humanely
humaneness
humanise
  humanises
  humanised
  humanising
humanism
humanitarian
humanitarianism
humanitarianist
humanity
humanize
  humanizes
  humanized
  humanizing

humankind
humanly
humanoid
humble
  humbler
  humblest
humbug
humdinger
humdrum
humectant
humeral
humerus
humic
humid
humidification
humidifier
humidify
  humidifies
  humidified
  humidifying
humidistat
humidity
humidor
humify
  humifies
  humified
  humifying
humiliate
  humiliates
  humiliated
  humiliating
humiliatingly
humiliation
humiliative
humiliator
humiliatory
humility
huminist = humanist
hummed
humming
hummingbird
hummock
hummus
humongous
humoral
humoresque
humorist
humorous
humour
humourous = humorous
humoursome
hump
humpback
humph

humpy
  humpier
  humpiest
humungous
humungously
humus
Hun
hunch
  hunches
  hunched
  hunching
hunchback
hundred
hundredth
hundredweight
hung (= suspended,
  put up → hanged)
Hungary
Hungarian
hunger
  hungers
  hungered
  hungering
hungry
  hungrier
  hungriest
hunk
hunker
  hunkers
  hunkered
  hunkering
hunky-dory
hunt
  hunts
  hunted
  hunting
hunter
huntress
  huntresses
huntsman
  huntsmen
hurdle
  hurdles
  hurdled
  hurdling
hurdy-gurdy
hurl
  hurls
  hurled
  hurling
hurley
hurly-burly
  hurly-burlies
hurrah

hurrahs
hurrahed
hurrahing
hurricane
hurry
  hurries
  hurried
  hurrying
hurt
  hurts
  hurt
  hurting
hurter
hurtful
hurtle
  hurtles
  hurtled
  hurtling
husband
husbandry
hush
  hushes
  hushed
  hushing
hushaby
hush-hush
husk
  husks
  husked
  husking
husky
  huskier
  huskiest
husky
  huskies
huss
hussar
hussy
  hussies
hustings
hustle
  hustles
  hustled
  hustling
hut
hutch
hutzpah
hyacinth
hyacinthine
hyaena
hyaline
hyalite
hyaloid
hyaloplasm

hybrid
hybridise
  hybridises
  hybridised
  hybridising
hybridity
hybridize
  hybridizes
  hybridized
  hybridizing
hybris
hybristic
hydathode
hydatid
hydra
hydracid
hydrangea
  hydrangeas
hydrant
hydranth
hydrargyria
hydrargyric
hydrastine
hydrastinine
hydrastis
hydrate
  hydrates
  hydrated
  hydrating
hydration
hydraulic
hydraulically
hydraulics
hydrazide
hydrazine
hydric
hydride
hydrilla
hydro
  hydros
hydrocarbon
hydrocele
hydrocephalic
hydrocephalus
hydrochloride
hydrocortisone
hydrodynamic
hydrodynamics
hydroelectric
hydroelectricity
hydrofoil
hydrogel
hydrogen
hydrogenate

hydrogenates
hydrogenated
hydrogenating
hydrogenise
hydrogenises
hydrogenised
hydrogenising
hydrogenize
hydrogenizes
hydrogenized
hydrogenizing
hydrogenolysis
hydrogenous
hydrograph
hydrographer
hydrographic
hydrography
hydroid
~~hydrolic~~ = hydraulic
hydrologic
hydrologist
hydrology
hydrolyse
hydrolyses
hydrolysed
hydrolysing
hydrolysis
hydrolyte
hydrolytic
hydromancy
hydrometeor
hydrometer
hydrometric
hydrometry
hydropathic
hydropathist
hydropathy
hydrophane
hydrophanous
hydrophilic
hydrophilous
hydrophily
hydrophobia
hydrophobic
hydrophyte
hydrophytic
hydroplane
hydroponics
hydropower
hydroscope
hydroscopic
hydrosome
hydrosphere
hydrostat

hydrostatic	hyoscyamine	hypersonic	hypocrite
hydrostatics	hypaesthesia	hyperspace	hypocycloid
hydrosulphide	hypalgesia	hyperspatial	hypodermic
hydrosulphite	hypallage	hypersthene	hypodermis
hydrotaxis	hype	hypersthenic	hypoglycaemia
hydrothermal	hypes	hypertension	hypognathism
hydrotropic	hyped	hypertensive	hypognathous
hydrotropism	hyping	hypertext	hypogynous
hydrous	hyper	hyperthermia	hypogyny
hydroxide	hyperacidity	hyperthyroidism	hypomania
hydroxy	hyperactive	hypertonic	hypomanic
hydroxyl	hyperaemia	hypertrophic	hyponym
hydroxylamine	hyperaesthesia	hypertrophy	hyponymy
hydrozoan	hyperbaric	hyperventilate	hypophysial
hyena	hyperbaton	hyperventilates	hypophysis
hyenic	hyperbola	hyperventilated	hypopituitarism
~~hygeine~~ = hygiene	hyperbole	hyperventilating	hypoplasia
hygiene	hyperbolic	hyperventilation	hypoplastic
hygienic	hyperbolise	hypha	hypoploid
hygienically	hyperbolises	hyphae	hypopnoea
hygienics	hyperbolised	hyphen	hyposensitise
hygienist	hyperbolising	hyphenate	hyposensitises
hygrograph	hyperbolism	hyphenates	hyposensitised
hygrometer	hyperbolize	hyphenated	hyposensitising
hygrometric	hyperbolizes	hyphenating	hyposensitize
hygrometry	hyperbolized	hypnagogic	hyposensitizes
hygrophile	hyperbolizing	hypnogenesis	hyposensitized
hygrophilous	hyperboloid	hypnogenetic	hyposensitizing
hygrophyte	Hyperborean	hypnoid	hypostasis
hygrophytic	hypercapnia	hypnologic	hypostasisation
hygroscope	hypercritical	hypnologist	hypostasise
hygroscopic	hypergamy	hypnology	hypostasises
hygrostat	hyperglycaemia	hypnosis	hypostasised
hying	hypericum	hypnotherapy	hypostasising
hyla	hyperinflation	hypnotic	hypostasization
hylomorphism	Hyperion	hypnotically	hypostasize
hylophagous	hyperkinesia	hypnotise	hypostasizes
hylotheism	hyperkinetic	hypnotises	hypostasized
hylozoism	hypermania	hypnotised	hypostasizing
hymen	hypermarket	hypnotising	hypostatic
hymeneal	hypermeter	hypnotism	hypostatisation
hymenopteran	hypermetric	hypnotist	hypostatise
hymenopterous	hypermnesia	hypnotize	hypostatises
hymn (= song → him)	hyperon	hypnotizes	hypostatised
hymnal	hyperphagia	hypnotized	hypostatising
hymnic	hyperphysical	hypnotizing	hypostatization
hymnist	hyperplane	hypoacidity	hypostatize
hymnodical	hyperplasia	hypoallergenic	hypostatizes
hymnody	hyperplastic	hypocentre	hypostatized
hymnologic	hyperploid	hypochondria	hypostatizing
hymnologist	hyperpnoea	hypochondriac	hyposthenia
hymnology	hyperpyretic	hypochondriasis	hyposthenic
hyoid	hyperpyrexia	hypochondrium	hypostyle
hyoscine	hypersensitive	hypocrisy	hypotactic

hypotension
hypotensive
hypotenuse
hypothalamic
hypothalamus
hypothermal
hypothermia
hypothesis
  hypotheses
hypothesise
  hypothesises
  hypothesised

hypothesising
hypothesiser
hypothesist
hypothesize
  hypothesizes
hypothesized
  hypothesizing
hypothesizer
hypothetical
hypothetically
hypothymia
hypothyroidism

hypotonic
hypoxia
hypoxic
hypsographic
hypsography
hypsometer
hypsometric
hypsometrist
hypsometry
hyracoid
hyrax
  hyraces *or*

hyraxes
hyson
hyssop
hysterectomy
hysteresis
hysteretic
hysteria
hysteric
hysterical
hysterically
hysterics
Hywel

I

Iain
iambic
Ian
iatrogenic
Iberian
ibex
  ibexes
ibid.
ibis
  ibis *or*
  ibises
ICA
ice
  ices
  iced
  icing
iceberg
icebound
icebox
icebreaker
icecap
ice-cream
iced
icefall
Iceland
Icelander
Icelandic
I Ching
ichthyic
ichthyoid
ichthyology
ichthyophagous
ichthyornis
ichthyosaur
ichthysaurus
  ichthysauri *or*
  ichthysauruses
ichthyosis
icicle
icier
iciest
icily
iciness
icing
icon
iconic

iconoclasm
iconoclast
iconographical
iconography
iconolatry
iconology
iconomatic
iconoscope
icterus
icy
  icier
  iciest
id
I'd
idea
ideal
idealisation
idealise
  idealises
  idealised
  idealising
idealism
idealization
idealize
  idealizes
  idealized
  idealizing
identical
identification
identify
  identifies
  identified
  identifying
Identikit™
identity
  identities
ideogram
ideologist
ideology
  ideologies
ides
idioblast
idiocy
  idiocies
idiol try ideol
idiolect

idiom
idiopathy
idiophone
~~idiosyncracy~~ =
  idiosyncrasy
idiosyncrasy
  idiosyncratic
  idiosyncratically
idiot
idiotic
idle
  idles
  idled
  idling
idler
idol (= something or
  someone worshipped
  → idle)
idolatry
idolise
  idolises
  idolised
  idiolising
idolize
  idiolizes
  idiolized
  idiolizing
idyll
idyllic
  idyllically
i.e.
if
iffy
  iffier
  iffiest
igloo
  igloos
igneous
ignescent
ignite
  ignites
  ignited
  igniting
igniter
ignitibility
ignitible

ignition
ignoble
ignobleness
ignominy
  ignominies
ignoramus
  ignoramuses
ignorance
ignorant
ignore
  ignores
  ignored
  ignoring
iguana
iguanid
iguanodon
ikebana
ikon
ileac
~~ilegal~~ = illegal
ileostomy
ileum (= part of the
  small intestine
  → ilium)
ilex
  ilexes
ilia
iliac
Iliad
ilium (= part of the
  hipbone → ileum)
ilk
Ilkley
ill
  worse
  worst
I'll
ill-advised
ill-assorted
ill-behaved
ill-bred
ill-considered
ill-defined
ill-disposed
illegal
illegalise

illegalises
illegalised
illegalising
illegalize
illegalizes
illegalized
illegalizing
illegally
illegible
illegibleness
illegitimate
ill-fated
ill-favoured
ill-founded
ill-gotten
illiberal
illiberalism
illicit (= not lawful
  → elicit)
illimitable
illimitableness
Illinois
illiquid
illiterate
illiterateness
ill-judged
ill-mannered
ill-natured
illness
  illnesses
illogic
illogical
illogicalness
ill-omened
ill-starred
ill-treat
  ill-treats
  ill-treated
  ill-treating
illuminance
illuminant
illuminate
  illuminates
  illuminated
  illuminating
illuminati
illuminating
illumination
illumine
  illumines
  illumined
  illumining
ill-use
  ill-uses

ill-used
ill-using
illusion (= false
  impression
  → allusion)
illusionism
illusionist
illusive (= unreal;
  deceptive → elusive)
illusively
illusiveness
illusory
illustrate
  illustrates
  illustrated
  illustrating
illustration
illustrious
illuviation
illuvium
I'm
image
imagery
  imageries
imaginal
imaginary
imagination
imaginative
imagine
  imagines
  imagined
  imagining
imaginery = imaginary
imagism
imago
  imagines *or*
  imagoes
imam
imbalance
imbecile
imbed
  imbeds
  imbedded
  imbedding
imbibe
  imbibes
  imbiibed
  imbibing
imbricate
imbroglio
  imbroglios
imbue
  imbues
  imbued

imbuing
imediately =
  immediately
imitate
imitates
imitated
imitating
imitation
imitative
immaculate
immaculateness
immanent (= existing;
  inherent → imminent)
immaterial
immaterialise
  immaterialises
  immaterialised
  immaterialising
immaterialism
immaterialize
  immaterializes
  immaterialized
  immaterializing
immature
immeasurable
immeasurableness
immediate
immediately
immediateness
immemorial
immense
immensity
  immensities
immerse
  immerses
  immersed
  immersing
immerser
immersion
immethodical
immigrant
immigrate
  immigrates
  immigrated
  immigrating
imminent (= about to
  happen → immanent)
immiscible
immobile
immobilisation
immobilise
  immobilises
  immobilised
  immobilising

immobiliser
immobilism
immobilize
  immobilizes
  immoblized
  immobilizing
immoderate
immoderateness
immodest
immolate
  immolates
  immolated
  immolating
immoral
immorality
immortal
immortalisation
immortalise
  immortalises
  immortalised
  immortalising
immortalize
  immortalizes
  immortalized
  immortalizing
immortelle
immotile
immovable
immovably
immovableness
immoveable
immoveably
immoveableness
immune
immunise
  immunises
  immunised
  immunising
immunity
immunize
  immunizes
  immunized
  immunizing
immunodeficiency
immunogen
immunogenic
immunoglobulin
immunological
immunology
immunosuppression
immunosuppressive
immunotherapeutic
immunotherapy
immure

immures
immured
immuring
immutable
immutably
immutableness
imp
impact
impacts
impacted
impacting
impactive
impair
impairs
impaired
impairing
impala
impala *or*
impalas
impale
impales
impaled
impaling
impalpable
imparity
imparities
impart
imparts
imparted
imparting
impartial
impartialness
impassable
impassableness
impasse
impassioned
impassive
impassivity
impatience
impatiens
impatient
impeach
impeaches
impeached
impeaching
impeachable
impeachment
impeccable
impeccably
impecuniosity
impecunious
impedance
impede
impedes

impeded
impeding
impediment
impedimenta
impedimentary
impel
impels
impelled
impelling
impeller
impend
impends
impended
impending
impenetrable
impenetrably
impenitent
impenitentness
imperative
imperatively
imperceptible
imperceptibly
imperceptive
imperceptively
imperfect
imperfectly
imperfection
imperial
imperialism
imperil
imperils
imperilled
imperilling
imperious
imperishable
imperishableness
impermanency
impermanent
impermeable
impermeableness
impermissible
impersonal
impersonally
impersonalisation
impersonalise
impersonalises
impersonalised
impersonalising
impersonalize
impersonalizes
impersonalized
impersonalizing
impersonate
impersonates

impersonated
impersonating
impersonation
impersonator
impertinence
impertinent
impertinently
imperturbable
imperturbation
impervious
imperviously
imperviousness
impetigo
impetuosity
impetuous
impetuously
impetuousness
impetus
impiety
impinge
impinges
impinged
impinging
impingement
impinger
impious
impish
implacability
implacable
implacableness
implacably
implant
implants
implanted
implanting
implantation
implanter
implausibility
implausible
implausibleness
implausibly
implement
implements
implemented
implementing
implicate
implicates
implicated
implicating
implication
implicit
implicitly
implicitness
implicity

implied
implode
implodes
imploded
imploding
imploratory
implore
implores
implored
imploring
implorer
imploringly
implosion
implosive
imply
implies
implied
implying
impolite
impolitic
impoliticness
imponderability
imponderable
imponderableness
imponderably
import
imports
imported
importing
importance
important
importantly
importation
impotent = important
importer
importunacy
importunate
importunately
importunateness
importune
importunes
importuned
importuning
importuner
imposable
impose
imposes
imposed
imposing
imposer
imposing
imposingly
imposingness
imposition

impossibility
　impossibilities
impossible
impossibleness
impossibly
impostor
imposture
impotent
impound
　impounds
　impounded
　impounding
impoundage
impounder
impoverish
　impoverishes
　impoverished
　impoverishing
impoverishment
impracticability
impracticable
　impracticabilities
impracticableness
impracticably
impractical
impracticality
　impracticalities
impractically
impracticalness
imprecate
　imprecates
　imprecated
　imprecating
imprecation
imprecise
imprecision
impregnability
impregnable
impregnableness
impregnably
impregnate
　impregnates
　impregnated
　impregnating
impregnator
impresario
　impresarios
impress
　impresses
　impressed
　impressing
impresser
impressible
impression

impressionability
impressionable
impressionableness
impressionism
impressionist
impressionistic
impressive
impressively
impressiveness
imprimatur
imprint
　imprints
　imprinted
　imprinting
imprinter
imprinting
imprison
　imprisons
　imprisoned
　imprisoning
imprisonment
improbability
　improbabilities
improbable
improbableness
improbably
impromptu
improper
improperly
improperness
impropriety
　improprieties
improve
　improves
　improved
　improving
improvement
improver
improvidence
improvident
improvidently
improvingly
improvisation
improvise
　improvises
　improvised
　improvising
imprudence
imprudent
imprudently
impudence
impudent
impugn
　impugns

impugned
impugning
impugner
impugnment
impulse
impulsive
impulsively
impulsiveness
impunity
impure
impurely
impureness
impurity
imputability
imputable
imputableness
impute
　imputes
　imputed
　imputing
imputer
in
inability
inaccessible
inaccuracy
inaccurate
inaccurately
inaccurateness
inaction
inactivate
　inactivates
　inactivated
　inactivating
inactivation
inactive
inactively
inactiveness
inadequacy
　inadequacies
inadequate
inadequately
inadmissible
inadvertence
inadvertent
inadvisable
inalienability
inalienable
inalienableness
inalienably
inalterability
inalterable
inalterableness
inalterably
inamorata

inamoratas
inamorato
　inamoratos
inane
inanely
inanimate
inanimately
inanimateness
inanition
inanity
　inanities
inapplicability
inapplicable
inapplicableness
inapplicably
inapposite
inappositely
inappositeness
inappreciable
inappreciably
inappreciative
inappreciatively
inappropriate
inappropriately
inapt
inaptitude
inaptly
inaptness
inarticulate
inarticulately
inarticulateness
inartistic
inartistically
inattentive
inattentively
inaudibility
inaudible
inaudibleness
inaudibly
inaugural
inaugurate
　inaugurates
　inaugurated
　inaugurating
inauguration
inaugurator
inauguratory
inauspicious
inborn
inbred
inbuilt
incalculability
incalculable
incalculableness

incalculably
incandesce
  incandesces
  incandesced
  incandescing
incandescence
incandescent
incantation
incapability
incapable
incapableness
incapably
incapacitate
  incapacitates
  incapacitated
  incapacitating
incapacity
incarcerate
  incarcerates
  incarcerated
  incarcerating
incarceration
incarcerator
incarnate
incarnation
incaution
incautious
incautiously
incautiousness
incendiary
incendiary
  incendiaries
incense
incentive
inception
incessancy
incessant
incessantly
  incessantness
incest
incestuous
incestuously
incestuousness
inch
  inches
  inched
  inching
inchoate
inchoateness
inchoative
incidence
incident
incidental
incidentally

incidently =
  incidentally
incinerate
  incinerates
  incinerated
  incinerating
incineration
incinerator
incipience
incipiency
incipient
incipiently
incise
incision
incisive
incisively
incisiveness
incisor
incite
  incites
  incited
  inciting
incitement
inciter
incivility
  incivilities
inclemency
inclement
inclemently
inclementness
inclination
incline
  inclines
  inclined
  inclining
include
  includes
  included
  including
inclusion
inclusive
inclusiveness
incognito
incoherent
incoherence
incombustible
income
incomer
incoming
incommensurate
incommode
  incommodes
  incommoded
  incommoding

incommodious
incommunicable
incommunicado
incommunicative
incommutable
incomparability
incomparable
incomparableness
incomparably
incompatible
incompatibly
incompetence
incompetency
incompetent
incompetently
incomplete
incomprehensible
incomprehensibly
incomprehension
inconceivable
inconceivably
inconclusive
incongruence
incongruently
incongruity
incongruous
incongruously
incongruousness
inconsequential
inconsiderable
inconsiderate
inconsistency
inconsistent
inconsolable
inconsolably
inconspicuous
inconstancy
inconstant
inconstantly
incontestable
incontinence
incontinency
incontinent
incontinently
incontrovertible
incontrovertibly
inconvenience
incorporate
  incorporates
  incorporated
  incorporating
incorporation
incorporator
incorporeal

incorrect
incorrigibility
incorrigible
incorrigibleness
incorrigibly
incorruptible
increase
  increases
  increased
  increasing
increaser
incredable = incredible
incredibility
incredible
incredibleness
incredibly
incredulity
incredulous
incredulously
incredulousness
increment
incremental
increscent
incriminate
  incriminates
  incriminated
  incriminating
incrimination
incriminator
incriminatory
in-crowd
incubate
  incubates
  incubated
  incubating
incubator
incubus
  incubi *or*
  incubuses
inculcate
  inculcates
  inculcated
  inculcating
incumbency
incumbent
incunabula
incur
  incurs
  incurred
  incurring
incurability
incurable
incurableness
incurably

incurrence
incursion
incursive
incurvate
incurvature
incus
indebted
indebtedness
indecency
indecent
indecipherable
　indecipherably
indecisive
indeclinable
indecorously
indecorousness
indecorum
indeed
indefatigable
　indefatigably
indefensible
indefensibly
indefinable
indefinably
indefinite
indefinitely
indefiniteness
indehiscent
indelibility
indelible
indelibleness
indelibly
indelicacy
indelicate
indelicately
indelicateness
indemnification
indemnifier
indemnify
　indemnifies
　indemnified
　indemnifying
indemnity
indent
　indents
　indented
　indenting
indentation
indenture
independant =
　independent
independence
independency
independent

indepth
indescribable
　indescribably
indespensable =
　indispensable
indestructible
indeterminable
indestructable =
　indestructible
indeterminate
index
　index or
　indices
indexation
India
Indian
indicate
　indicates
　indicated
　indicating
indication
indicative
indicator
indices
indict
　indicts
　indicted
　indicting
indictable
indicter
indictment
indictor
indifference
indifferent
indifferently
indigenous
indigent
indigestible
indigestion
indignant
indignantly
indignation
indignity
　indignities
indigo
indirect
indiscipline
indiscreet (= tactless
　→ indiscrete)
indiscrete (= not
　divisible
　→ indiscreet)
indiscretion
indiscriminate

indispensable
indispensably
indispensible =
　indispensable
indisposed
indisposition
indisputable
indisputably
indissoluble
indistinct
indistinctive
indistinguishable
indistinguishably
indium
individual
individualise
　individualises
　individualised
　individualising
individualism
individualist
individuality
individualize
　individualizes
　individualized
　individualizing
individuate
　individuates
　individuated
　individuating
individuation
indivisible
indoctrinate
　indoctrinates
　indoctrinated
　indoctrinating
indoctrination
indoctrinator
indolent
indomitability
indomitable
indomitableness
indomitably
Indonesia
Indonesian
indoor
indoors
indorsable
indorse
indorsee
indorsement
indorser
indorsor
indrawn

indubitability
indubitable
indubitableness
indubitably
induce
　induces
　induced
　inducing
inducement
inducer
inducible
induct
　inducts
　inducted
　inducting
inductance
induction
inductive
inductor
indulge
　indulges
　indulged
　indulging
indulgence
indulgent
indulgently
indulger
indusium
industrial
industrialisation
industrialise
　industrialises
　industrialised
　industrialising
industrialism
industrialist
industrialization
industrialize
　industrializes
　industrialized
　industrializing
industrially
industrious
industriously
industriousness
industry
　industries
inebriant
inebriate
inebriation
inebriety
inedibility
inedible
ineducability

ineducable
ineffability
ineffable
ineffableness
ineffably
ineffective
ineffectual
inefficacious
inefficacy
inefficiency
inefficient
inelegance
inelegancy
inelegant
inelegantly
ineligibility
ineligible
ineligibleness
ineligibly
ineloquence
ineloquent
ineloquently
ineluctable
ineluctably
inept
ineptitude
ineptly
ineptness
inequable
inequality
  inequalities
inequitable
inequitableness
inequitably
inequity
ineradicable
ineradicably
inert
inertia
inertly
inertness
inescapable
inescapably
inescutcheon
inessential
inessive
inestimability
inestimable
inestimableness
inestimably
inevitability
inevitable
inevitableness
inevitably

inexact
inexcusable
inexcusably
inexhaustible
inexorability
inexorable
inexorableness
inexorably
inexpensive
inexperience
inexpert
inexpertly
inexpertness
inexpiable
inexplicable
inexplicably
inexplicit
inexpressible
inexpressibly
inexpressive
inexpungible
inextinguishable
inextirpable
inextricable
inextricably
infallibility
infallible
infallibleness
infallibly
infamous
infamy
infancy
  infancies
infant
infanticidal
infanticide
infantile
infantry
  infantries
infantryman
  infantrymen
infarct
infarcted
infarction
infatuate
  infatuates
  infatuated
  infatuating
infatuation
infeasibility
infeasible
infeasibleness
infect
  infects

infected
  infecting
infecter
infection
infectious
infectiously
infectiousness
infective
infector
infecund
infecundity
infelicitous
  infelicities
infelicity
infen try infan
infer
  infers
  inferred
  inferring
inference
inferential
inferior
inferiority
inferiorly
infernal
infernally
inferno
  infernos
inferrer
infertile
infertility
infest
  infests
  infested
  infesting
infester
infidel
infidelity
  infidelities
infielder
infighting
infill
  infills
  infilled
  infilling
infiltrate
  infiltrates
  infiltrated
  infiltrating
infinite
infinitesimal
infinitive
infinity
infirm

infirmary
  infirmaries
infirmity
  infirmities
infirmness
inflame
  inflames
  inflamed
  inflaming
inflammability
inflammable
inflammableness
inflammably
inflammation
inflammatorily
inflammatory
inflatable
inflate
  inflates
  inflated
  inflating
inflation
inflationary
inflationism
inflationist
inflect
  inflects
  inflected
  inflecting
inflection
inflectional
inflective
inflexed
inflexibility
inflexibleness
inflexibly
inflexionless
inflict
  inflicts
  inflicted
  infliction
inflicter
infliction
inflictor
inflight
inflorescence
inflow
influence
~~influencial~~ = influential
influential
influenza
influx
inform
  informs

informed
informing
informal
informality
informally
informant
informatics
information
informative
informatively
informativeness
informed
informedly
informer
infotainment
infract
  infracts
  infracted
  infraction
infraction
infractor
infrangibility
infrangible
infrangibleness
infrared
infrasonic
infrasound
infrastructure
infrequence
infrequency
infrequent
infrequently
infringe
  infringes
  infringed
  infringing
infringement
infringer
infundibular
infuriate
  infuriates
  infuriated
  infuriating
infuriating
infuriatingly
infuse
  infuses
  infused
  infusing
infuser
infusion
ingenious
ingeniously
ingeniousness

ingénue
ingenuity
ingenuous
ingenuously
ingenuousness
ingest
  ingests
  ingested
  ingesting
ingestible
ingestion
ingestive
ingle
inglenook
inglorious
ingloriously
ingloriousness
ingoing
ingot
ingrain
  ingrains
  ingrained
  ingraining
ingrate
ingratiate
  ingratiates
  ingratiated
  ingratiating
ingratiating
ingratiatingly
ingratitude
ingrediant = ingredient
ingredient
ingress
ingrowing
ingrown
inguinal
inhabit
  inhabits
  inhabited
  inhabiting
inhabitability
inhabitable
inhabitance
inhabitancy
inhabitant
inhabitation
inhalant
inhalation
inhale
  inhales
  inhaled
  inhaling
inhaler

inhere
  inheres
  inhered
  inhering
inherence
inherent
inherently
inherit
  inherits
  inherited
  inheriting
inheritability
inheritable
inheritableness
inheritance
inheritor
inhibit
  inhibits
  inhibited
  inhibiting
inhibition
inhibitive
inhospitable
inhospitableness
inhospitably
inhospitality
inhuman
inhumane
inhumanity
inhumanly
inhumanness
inimical
inimicality
inimically
inimicalness
inimitability
inimitable
inimitableness
inimitably
iniquitous
iniquity
  iniquities
initial
  initials
  initialled
  initialling
  initially
initiate
  initiates
  initiated
  initiating
initiation
initiative
initiator

initiatory
inject
  injects
  injected
  injecting
injection
injector
injudicious
injunction
injure
  injures
  injured
  injuring
injurious
injury
  injuries
injust = unjust
injustice
ink
inkling
inky
inkier
inkiest
inlaid
inland
in-law
  in-laws
inlay
  inlays
  inlaid
  inlaying
inlet
inlist = enlist
inlying
inmate
inmost
inn
innacurate = inaccurate
innards
innate
innately
innateness
inner
innermost
innings
innkeeper
innocence
innocent
innoculation =
  inoculation
innocuous
innocuously
innocuousness
innovate

innovates
innovated
innovating
innovation
innoxious
innoxiously
innoxiousness
innuendo
  innuendoes
Innuit
innumerability
innumerable
innumerableness
innumerably
innumeracy
innumerate
inoculate
  inoculates
  inoculated
  inoculation
inoffensive
inofficious
inoperability
inoperable
inoperableness
inoperably
inoperative
inoperativeness
inopportune
inopportunely
inopportuneness
inordinate
inordinately
inordinateness
inorganic
inpatient
input
  inputs
  input
  inputting
inquest
inquietude
inquire
  inquires
  inquired
  inquiring
inquirer
inquiring
inquiringly
inquiry
  inquiries
inquisition
inquisitive
inquisitively

inquisitiveness
inquisitor
inquisitorial
inroad
inrush
insalubrious
insalubrity
insane
insanely
insaneness
insanitariness
insanitary
insanity
insatiability
insatiable
insatiableness
insatiably
inscribe
  inscribes
  inscribed
  inscribing
inscriber
inscription
inscrutability
inscrutable
inscrutableness
inscrutably
inse *try* insu
insect
insectarium
  insectaria *or*
  insectariums
insecticidal
insecticide
insectivore
insectivorous
insecure
inseminate
  inseminates
  inseminated
  inseminating
insemination
inseminator
insensate
insensately
insensateness
insensibility
insensible
insensibleness
insensibly
insensitive
insensitively
insensitiveness
insensitivity

insentience
insentient
inseparability
inseparable
inseparableness
inseparably
insert
  inserts
  inserted
  inserting
inserter
insertion
inset
inshore
inside
insider
insidious
insidiously
insidiousness
insight
insignia
insignificant
insincere
insincerity
insinuate
  insinuates
  insinuated
  insinuating
insinuation
insinuator
insipid
insipidly
insipidness
insist
  insists
  insisted
  insisting
insistence
insistency
insistent
insistently
insister
insobriety
insofar
insole
insolent
insolubility
insoluble
insolubleness
insolubly
insolvability
insolvable
insolvency
insolvent

insomnia
insomniac
insomuch
insouciance
insouciant
insouciantly
inspect
  inspects
  inspected
  inspecting
inspection
inspector
inspectorate
inspiration
inspirational
inspire
  inspires
  inspired
  inspiring
inspirer
inst.
instability
instable
instalation =
  installation
install
installant
installation
installer
instalment
instance
instancy
instantaneity
instantaneous
instantly
instate
  instates
  instated
  instating
instatement
instead
instep
instigate
  instigates
  instigated
  instigating
instil
  instils
  instilled
  instilling
instiller
instilment
instinct
instinctive

instinctively
institute
  institutes
  instituted
  instituting
institution
institutional
institutionalise
  institutionalises
  institutionalised
  institutionalising
institutionalism
institutionalize
  institutionalizes
  institutionalized
  institutionalizing
instruct
  instructs
  instructed
  instructing
instructible
instruction
instructional
instructive
instructively
instructiveness
instructor
instrument
instrumental
instrumentalism
instrumentalist
instrumentation
insubordinate
insubstantial
insufferable
insufferableness
insufferably
insufficiency
insufficient
insufflate
  insufflates
  insufflated
  insufflating
insular
insularity
insulate
  insulates
  insulated
  insulating
insulation
insulator
insulin
insult
  insults

insulted
insulting
insulter
insuperability
insuperable
insuperableness
insuperably
insupportable
insuppressible
insurability
insurable
insurance
insure
  insures
  insured
  insuring
insurer
insurgence
insurgency
insurgent
insurmountable
insurrection
intact
intactness
intaglio
  intaglios
intake
intangibility
intangible
intangibleness
intangibly
intarsia
integer
integral
integrand
integrant
integrate
  integrates
  integrated
  integrating
integration
integrator
integrity
integument
integumental
integumentary
~~intelectual~~ =
  intellectual
~~inteligence~~ =
  intelligence
intellect
intellectual
intellectualise
  intellectualises

intellectualised
intellectualising
intellectualism
intellectualize
  intellectualizes
  intellectualized
  intellectualizing
intelligence
intelligent
intelligently
intelligentsia
intelligibility
intelligible
intelligibleness
intelligibly
intemperance
intemperate
intemperately
intemperateness
intend
  intends
  intended
  intending
intense
intensely
intenseness
intensification
intensifier
intensify
  intensifies
  intensified
  intensifying
intensity
intensive
intensively
intensiveness
intent
intention
intentional
intentionally
intently
intentness
inter
  inters
  interred
  interring
interact
  interacts
  interacted
  interacting
interaction
interactive
intercede
  intercedes

interceded
interceding
intercept
  intercepts
  intercepted
  intercepting
interceptor
intercession
interchange
  interchanges
  interchanged
  interchanging
intercity
intercom
intercourse
interdict
  interdicts
  interdicted
  interdicting
interdiction
interdisciplinary
interest
  interests
  intrested
  interesting
interface
interfacing
~~interferance~~ =
  interference
interfere
  interferes
  interfered
  interfering
interference
interim
interior
interject
  interjects
  interjected
  interjection
interlace
interlay
  interlays
  interlaid
  interlaying
interleave
  interleaves
  interleaved
  interleaving
interlock
  interlocks
  interlocked
  interlocking
interlocution

interlocutor
interlocutory
interloper
interlude
intermarry
  intermarries
  intermarried
  intermarrying
intermediary
intermediate
  intermediates
  intermediated
  intermediating
intermezzo
interminability
interminable
interminableness
interminably
intermission
intermittent
intern
internal
internalisation
internalise
  internalises
  internalised
  internalising
internalization
internalize
  internalizes
  internalized
  internalizing
internally
internalness
international
internationalise
  internationalises
  internationalised
  internationalising
internationalism
internationalist
internationalize
  internationalizes
  internationalized
  internationalizing
internee
Internet
internuncio
  internuncios
interplay
Interpol
interpolate
  interpolates
  interpolated

interpolating
interpolater
interpolation
interpolative
interpolator
interpose
interposition
interpratation = interpretation
interpret
  interprets
  interpreted
  interpreting
interpretability
interpretable
interpretableness
interpretably
interpretation
interpretational
interpretatively
interpreter
interpretive
interregnum
interrelate
  interrelates
  interrelated
  interrelating
interrogate
  interrogates
  interrogated
  interrogating
interrogatingly
interrogation
interrogational
interrogative
interrogator
interrogatory
interrupt
  interrupts
  interrupted
  interrupting
interrupter
interruption
interruptor
intersect
  intersects
  intersected
  intersecting
intersection
interspace
  interspaces
  interspaced
  interspacing
intersperse

intersperses
interspersed
interspersing
interspersedly
interstate
interstice
interstitial
intertidal
intertwine
  intertwines
  intertwined
  intertwining
intertwist
  intertwists
  intertwisted
  intertwisting
interupt = interrupt
intervene
  intervenes
  intervened
  intervening
intervention
interventionist
interview
interweave
  interweaves
  interweaved
  interweaving
intestacy
intestate
intestinal
intestine
intimacy
  intimacies
intimate
intimation
intimidate
  intimidates
  intimidated
  intimidating
intimidating
intimidation
intimidator
into
intolerability
intolerable
intolerableness
intolerably
intolerance
intolerant
intolerantly
intolerent = intolerant
intonation
intone

intones
intoned
intoning
intoner
intorsion
intoxicant
intoxicate
  intoxicates
  intoxicated
  intoxicating
intoxicating
intoxicatingly
intoxication
intoxicative
intractability
intractable
intractableness
intractably
intrados
  intrados *or*
  intradoses
intramuscular
intransigence
intransigency
intransigent
intransigently
intransitive
intransitively
intransitiveness
intransitivity
intrauterine
intravasation
intravenous
intrepid
intrepidly
intrepidness
intrest = interest
intricate
intriguer
intriguing
intriguingly
intrinsic
intrinsically
intro
introduce
  introduces
  introduced
  introducing
introduction
introductory
introit
introspection
introspective
introversion

introvert
introverted
intrude
intruder
intrusion
intrusive
intrusiveness
intubate
intuit
  intuits
  intuited
  intuiting
intuition
intuitive
intuitiveness
intumescence
intussuscept
  intussuscepts
  intussuscepted
  intussuscepting
intussusception
inuendo = innuendo
Inuit
inulin
inundate
  inundates
  inundated
  inundating
inundatory
inurbane
inurbanity
inure
inurement
invadable
invade
  invades
  invaded
  invading
invader
invalid
invalidate
  invalidates
  invalidated
  invalidating
invalidation
invalidism
invalidity
invalidness
invaluable
invaluableness
invaluably
invariability
invariable
invariableness

invariably
invariance
invariancy
invariant
invasion
invasive
invective
invectiveness
inveigh
  inveighs
  inveighed
  inveighing
inveigher
inveigle
inveiglement
inveigler
invent
invention
inventive
inventively
inventiveness
inventor
inventory
  inventories
Inverness
inverse
inversely
inversion
inversive
invert
  inverts
  inverted
  inverting
invertebrate
invertible
invest
  invests
  invested
  investing
investigable
investigate
  investigates
  investigated
  investigating
investigation
investigational
investigator
investigatory
investitive
investiture
investment
investor
inveteracy
inveterate

inveterately
inveterateness
inviability
inviable
inviableness
inviably
invidious
invidiously
invidiousness
invigilate
  invigilates
  invigilated
  invigilating
invigilation
invigilator
invigorate
  invigorates
  invigorated
  invigorating
invigoratingly
invigoration
invincibility
invincible
invincibleness
invincibly
inviolability
inviolable
inviolableness
inviolably
inviolacy
inviolate
inviolateness
invisibility
invisible
invisibleness
invitation
invite
  invites
  invited
  inviting
inviter
invitingly
invitingness
invoke
  invokes
  invoked
  invoking
invoker
involuntarily
involuntariness
involuntary
involute
involution
involve

involves
involved
involving
involvement
involver
invulnerability
invulnerable
invulnerableness
invulnerably
inward
inwardly
inwards
iodate
iodide
iodise
  iodises
  iodised
  iodising
iodism
iodize
  iodizes
  iodized
  iodizing
iodous
ion
Ionesco, Eugene
Ionian
Ionic
ionisation
ionise
  ionises
  ionised
  ionising
ionosphere
ionotropy
iota
IOU
Iowa
ipecacuanha
IQ
Iran
Iranian
Iraq
Iraqi
irascibility
irascible
irascibleness
irascibly
irate
irately
irational = irrational
ire
Ireland
irenic

irenically
irenics
iridescent
iridium
iridology
iris
  irises
Irish
Irishman
irk
  irks
  irked
  irking
irksome
iron
  irons
  ironed
  ironing
ironic
ironically
ironing
ironmonger
ironware
ironwork
irony
irradiance
irradiant
irradiate
  irradiates
  irradiated
  irradiating
irradiation
irrational
irrationality
irrationally
irrationalness
irreclaimable
irreconcilability
irreconcilable
irreconcilableness
irreconcilably
irrecoverable
irredeemable
irredeemably
irreducible
irrefragability
irrefragable
irrefragableness
irrefragably
irrefrangible
irrefutability
irrefutable
irrefutableness
irrefutably

irregular
irregularity
  irregularities
irregularly
irrelative
irrelatively
irrelevance
irrelevancy
irrelevant
irrelevantly
~~irrelevent~~ = irrelevant
irreligious
irremediable
irremovable
irreparability
irreparable
irreparableness
irreparably
irreplaceable
irrepressible
irrepressibly
irreproachable
irreproachably
~~irresistable~~ =
  irresistible
irresistible
irresistibly
irresolute
irresolutely
irresoluteness
irresolution
irresolvable
irrespective
irresponsible
irresponsibly
irretrievable
irretrievably
~~irrevelant~~ = irrelevant
irreverence
irreverent
irreverential
irreverently
irreversible
irrevocability
irrevocable
irrevocableness
irrevocably
irrigate
  irrigates
  irrigated
  irrigation
irritable
irritant
irritate

irriates
irritated
irriating
irritation
irrupt (= enter
  abruptly → erupt)
irruption
irruptive
is
isatin
ischaemia
ischaemic
ischium
Islam
Islamic
island
islander
Islay
isle (= small island
  → aisle)
islet
isn't
isobar
isobaric
isobath
isochromatic
isochronal
isoclinal
isocline
isocracy
isocratic
isogamete
isogametic
isogamous
isogamy
isogenic
isogenous
isogeny
isogon
isogonic
isogram
isolate
  isolates
  isolated
  isolating
isolation
isolationism
isomer
isomerism
isomerous
isometric
isometrics
isonomy
isopod

isoprene
isosceles
isothere
isothermal
isotone
isotonic
isotope
isotopic
isotopy
isotron
isotropic
isotropy
Israel
Israeli
~~Isreal~~ = Israel
issue
  issues
  issued
  issuing
Istanbul
isthmian
isthmus
it
Italian
italic
italicisation
italicise
  italicises
  italicised
  italicising
italicization
italicize
  italicizes
  italicized
  italicizing
Italy
itch
  itches
  itched
  itching
item
itemise
  itemises
  itemised
  itemising
itemize
  itemizes
  itemized
  itemizing
iterate
  iterises
  interised
  interising
iterative

itinerancy
itinerant
itinerary
it'll

its (= of it (its cover)
→ its)
it's (= it is → its)
itself

itsy-bitsy
I've
ivied
ivory

ivories
ivy
ivies

J

jab
  jabs
  jabbed
  jabbing
jabber
  jabbers
  jabbered
  jabbering
jabberwocky
  jabberwockies
jabot
jacaranda
  jacarandas
jack
  jacks
  jacked
  jacking
jackal
jackanapes
jackass
  jackasses
jackdaw
jacket
  jackets
  jacketed
  jacketing
jack-in-the-box
  jack-in-the-boxes
jackknife
  jackknives
  jackknifes
  jackknifed
  jackknifing
jackpot
jacks-in-the-box
Jacobean
Jacqueline
jactitation
Jacuzzi™
jade
  jades
  jaded
  jading
jag
  jags
  jagged

jagging
jaggery
jaggy
  jaggier
  jaggiest
jaguar
jail
  jails
  jailed
  jailing
jailbird
jailer
jailor
Jakarta
jalopy
  jalopies
jam (= sweet spread;
  stick → jamb)
  jams
  jammed
  jamming
Jamaica
jamb (= door-post
  → jam)
jambalaya
  jambalayas
jamboree
jammy
  jammier
  jammiest
jangle
  jangles
  jangled
  jangling
January
japan
  japans
  japanned
  japanning
Japan
Japanese
jape
  japes
  japed
  japing
japonica

jar
  jars
  jarred
  jarring
jardinière
jargon
jasmine
jasper
jaundice
  jaundices
  jaundiced
  jaundicing
jaunt
  jaunts
  jaunted
  jaunting
jaunty
  jauntier
  jauntiest
Javanese
javelin
jaw
  jaws
  jawed
  jawing
jawbone
jay
jaywalk
  jaywalks
  jaywalked
  jaywalking
jazz
jazzy
  jazzes
  jazzed
  jazzing
  jazzier
  jazziest
JCB™
jealous
jealousy
  jealousies
Jeanette
jeans
Jedburgh
Jeep™

jeepers
jeer
  jeers
  jeered
  jeering
Jeffrey
Jehovah
jejune
jell
  jells
  jelled
  jelling
jelly
  jellies
  jelled
  jellying
jellybean
jellyfish
  jellyfish or
  jellyfishes
jelous = jealous
jemmy
  jemmies
jennet
Jennifer
jeopardise
  jeopardises
  jeopardised
  jeopardising
jeopardize
  jeopardizes
  jeopardized
  jeopardizing
jeopardy
jerboa
jeremiad
jerk
  jerks
  jerked
  jerking
jerkin
jerky
  jerkier
  jerkiest
jeroboam
jerry-built

142

jersey
Jerusalem
jessamine
jest
  jests
  jested
  jesting
jester
Jesuit
jet
  jets
  jetted
  jetting
jetsam
jettison
  jettisons
  jettisoned
  jettisoning
jetty
  jetties
Jew
jewel
jeweller
jewellery
Jewish
Jewry
jew's-harp
jezebel
jib
  jibs
  jibbed
  jibbing
jibe
  jibes
  jibed
  jibing
jiffy
  jiffies
Jiffybag™
jig
  jigs
  jigged
  jigging
jigger
jiggery-pokery
jiggle
  jiggles
  jiggled
  jiggling
jigsaw
jilt
  jilts
  jilted
  jilting

jingle
  jingles
  jingled
  jingling
jingoism
jingoistic
jingoistically
jinnee
  jinn
jinni
  jinn
jitter
  jitters
  jittered
  jittering
jitterbug
  jitterbugs
  jitterbugged
  jitterbugging
jiujitsu
jiujutsu
jive
  jives
  jived
  jiving
job
  jobs
  jobbed
  jobbing
jobber
jobbing
Jobcentre
jobless
joblessness
jockey
  jockeys
  jockeyed
  jockeying
jockstrap
jocose
jocosely
jocoseness
jocosity
jocular
jocularity
jocund
jocundity
jodhpurs
jog
  jogs
  jogged
  jogging
jogger
joggle

joggles
joggled
joggling
Johannesburg
John
johnny
  johnnies
Johnsonian
join
  joins
  joined
  joining
joiner
joinery
joint
  joints
  jointed
  jointing
jointer
jointure
joist
  joists
  joisted
  joisting
jojoba
joke
  jokes
  joked
  joking
joker
jollification
jollify
  jollifies
  jollified
  jollifying
jollity
  jollities
jolly
  jollies
  jollied
  jollying
jolt
Jonathan
jonquil
Jordan
jorum
Joseph
jostle
  jostles
  jostled
  jostling
jot
  jots
  jotted

jotting
joule
journal
journalese
journalism
journalist
journalistic
journel = journal
journey
  jouneys
  journeyed
  journeying
journeyman
joust
  jousts
  jousted
  jousting
jovial
jowl
jowled
joy
  joys
  joyed
  joying
Joyce
Joycean
joyful
joyless
joyous
joyride
  joyrides
  joyrode
  joyriding
joystick
jubilant
jubilation
jubilee
Judaic
judder
  judders
  juddered
  juddering
judge
  judges
  judged
  judging
judgement
judgemental
judgment
judgmental
judicature
judicial
judicially
judiciary

judicious
judiciously
judiciousness
judo
jug
  jugs
  jugged
  jugging
jugful
  jugfuls
juggernaut
juggins
juggle
  juggles
  juggled
  juggling
juggler
jugular
juice
juicy
  juicier
  juiciest
jujitsu
jujube
jujutsu

jukebox
julep
julienne
July
jumble
  jumbles
  jumbled
  jumbling
jumbo
  jumbos
jump
  jumps
  jumped
  jumping
jumper
jumpy
  jumpier
  jumpiest
junction
juncture
June
Jungian
jungle
junior
juniper

junk
  junks
  junked
  junking
junket
junkie
  junkies
junky
  junkies
Junoesque
junta
junto
Jupiter
Jurassic
jurisdiction
jurisprudence
jurisprudent
jurisprudential
jurist
juror
jury
  juries
jussive
just
justice

justiciary
justiciary
justifiable
justification
justificatory
justify
  justifies
  justified
  justifying
jut
  juts
  jutted
  jutting
jute
juvenescence
juvenescent
juvenile
juvenilia
juvenility
juxtapose
  juxtaposes
  juxtaposed
  juxtaposing

K

Kabul
Kafka, Franz
kaftan
kagoul
kagoule
~~kahki~~ = khaki
kail
kailyard
kala-azar
kale
kaleidoscope
kaleidoscopic
kaleidoscopically
kalends
kaleyard
~~kaliedoscope~~ =
  kaleidoscope
kalif
Kamasutra
kamikaze
kanga
kangaroo
  kangaroos
kangha
Kantian
kaolin
kaoline
kaolinite
kaon
kapok
kaput
karaoke
karate
karma
karri
kart
karting
kasbah
Kathmandu
katydid
kauri
kayak
kayo
  kayoes *or*
  kayos
  kayoed

kayoing
Kazakhstan
kebab
ked
kedge
kedgeree
keef
keel
  keels
  keeled
  keeling
keelhaul
  keelhauls
  keelhauled
  keelhauling
keelson
keen
  keens
  keened
  keening
keep
  keeps
  kept
  keeping
keeper
keeping
keepsake
keeshond
kef
keg
Keighley
Keith
kelim
keloid
kelp
kelpie
kelvin
kemp
kempt
ken
Kendal
kendo
kennel
  kennels
  kennelled
  kennelling

kenosis
kenotic
Kenya
kepi
  kepis
kept
keratin
keratoid
keratose
keratosis
kerb
kerbstone
kerchief
kerfuffle
kermes
kernel
kerogen
kerosene
kerosine
kesh
kestrel
ketch
ketchup
ketone
ketonic
kettle
kettledrum
key (= opener of
  locks → quay)
  keys
  keyed
  keying
keyboard
  keyboards
  keyboarded
  keyboarding
keyhole
keynote
keystone
khaki
khalif
khanga
Khartoum
kiang
kibble
  kibbles

kibbled
kibbling
kibbutz
kibbutzim
kibosh
kick
kickshaw
kid
  kids
  kidded
  kidding
kiddie
  kiddies
kiddy
  kiddies
kidnap
  kidnaps
  kidnapped
  kidnapping
kidney
kidology
kief
kif
kilim
Kilimanjaro
kill
  kills
  killed
  killing
killick
killjoy
kiln
kilo
  kilos
kilobyte
kilocalorie
kilocycle
kilogram
kilogramme
kilohertz
kilometre
kilometric
kilos
kiloton
kilovolt
kilowatt

kilt
  kilts
  kilted
  kilting
kilter
kimberlite
kimono
  kimonos
kimonoed
kin
kinaesthesia
kinaesthetic
kinase
kind
kindergarten
kindle
  kindles
  kindled
  kindling
kindling
kindly
  kindlier
  kindliest
kindness
  kindnesses
kindred
kinematics
kinesics
kinesiology
kinesis
kinetic
kinetically
kinetics
king
kingdom
kingfisher
kingly
kingpin
kingsize
kingsized
Kingussie
kink
  kinks
  kinked
  kinking
kinky
  kinkier
  kiniest
kino
kinsfolk
kinship
kinsman
  kinsmen
kinswoman

kinswomen
kiosk
kip
  kips
  kipped
  kipping
kippa
kipper
kir
Kircudbright
kirigami
Kirkby Lonsdale
kirmess
kirpan
Kirsch
Kirundi
kish
kismet
kiss
  kisses
  kissed
  kissing
kissagram
kit
  kits
  kitted
  kitting
kitbag
kitchen
kitchenette
kite
kith
kitsch
kitten
kittenish
kittiwake
kitty
  kitties
kiwis
klaxon
Kleenex®
kleptomania
klystron
knack
knacker
  knackers
  knackered
  knackering
knapsack
knapweed
Knaresborough
knave (= rogue
  → nave)
knavery

knead (= press with
  hands → kneed)
  kneads
  kneaded
  kneading
knee
  knees
  kneed (= hit with
    knee → knead)
  kneeing
kneecap
  kneecaps
  kneecapped
  kneecapping
knee-deep
knee-high
kneel
  kneels
  kneeled or
    knelt
  kneeling
knee-length
knees-up
knell
  knells
  knelled
  knelling
knew
knickerbockers
knickers
knick-knack
knife
  knives
  knifes
  knifed
  knifing
knight (= person of
  rank → night)
knighthood
knightly (= of a
  knight → night)
knit (= make from
  wool → nit)
  knits
  knitted
  knitting
knitwear
knives
knob
knobbly
  knobblier
  knobbliest
knock
  knocks

knocked
knocking
knocker
knock-knee
knockout
knoll
knot (= tangle in
  string, etc. → not)
  knots
  knotted
  knotting
knotty (= tangled
  → naughty)
  knottier
  knottiest
know (= have
  knowledge of → no)
  knows
  knew (= had
    knowledge of
    → new)
  known
  knowning
know-all
know-how
knowledgable
knowledge
knowledgeable
knuckle
knuckle-duster
KO
  KO's
  KO'ed
  KO'ing
koala
kofta
kohl
konimeter
koniology
kookaburra
koppa
Koran
Korea
Korean
korma
kosher
koumis
koumiss
koumyss
kowtow
  kowtows
  kowtowed
  kowtowing
kraal

kremlin
krill
kris
krypton
Kuala Lumpur

kudos
kumiss
kümmel
kumquat
Kurdish

kurfuffle
kurtosis
Kuwait
kwashiorkor
kyphosis

kyphotic
Kyrgystan

L

label
labelloid
labellum
  labella
labia
labial
labiate
labile
lability
labium
  labia
laboratory
  laboratories
laborious
laboriously
laboriousness
labour
  labours
  laboured
  labouring
labourer
Labourite
Labrador
labradorite
labratory = laboratory
labroid
laburnum
  laburnums
labyrinth
labyrinthine
labyrinthitis
laccolith
lace
  laces
  laced
  lacing
lacerate
  lacerates
  lacerated
  lacerating
lace-up
  lace-ups
lachrymal
lachrymose
lachrymosity
lacing

lack
  lacks
  lacked
  lacking
lackadaisical
lackey
  lackeys
lacklustre
laconic
laconically
laconism
lacquer
lacrosse
lactam
lactase
lactate
  lactates
  lactated
  lactating
lactation
lacteal
lactic
lactiferous
lactone
lactonic
lactose
lacuna
  lacunae
lacunal
lacunary
lacustrine
lacy
  lacier
  laciest
lad
ladder
laddie
lade
ladel = ladle
laden
la-di-da
ladies
ladies-in-waiting
ladle
  ladles
  ladled

  ladling
lady
  ladies
lady-in-waiting
  ladies-in-waiting
ladylike
lag
  lags
  lagged
  lagging
lager
laggard
  laggardly
lagging
lagomorph
lagoon
lah
lahar
lah-di-dah
laic
laicise
  laicises
  laicised
  laicising
laicize
  laicizes
  laicized
  laicizing
laid (= put down
  → lade)
lain (= placed
  horizontally → lane)
lair (= den
  → layer)
laird
laity
lake
lam (= thrash → lamb)
  lams
  lammed
  lamming
lama (= Tibetan
  priest → llama)
Lamaism
lamb
  lambs

lambed
lambing
lambada
lambast
  lambasts
  lambasted
  lambasting
lambda
lambdoid
lambent
lambert
lambkin
lame
  lames
  lamed
  laming
lamella
  lamellae *or*
  lamellas
lamellar
lamellate
lamellicorn
lamelliform
lamellose
lamellosity
lament
  laments
  lamented
  lamenting
lamentable
lamentation
lamenter
lamina
  laminae *or*
  laminas
laminaria
laminate
  laminates
  laminated
  laminating
lamination
laminose
Lammas
lamp
lampoon
  lampoons

lampooned
lampooning
lampooner
lampoonist
lamppost
lamprey
lanate
Lancashire
lance
  lances
  lanced
  lancing
lanceolate
lancer
lancers
lancet
lanceted
lancinate
land
  lands
  landed
  landing
landau
  landaus
landfall
landfill
landform
landing
landlady
  landladies
landlocked
landlord
landlubber
landmark
landmass
landowner
landrace
landscape
landscapist
landside
landslide
landslip
landsman
landward
landwards
lane (= path → lain)
langouste
langoustine
langrage
language
languid
languish
  languishes
  languished

languishing
languor
languorous
laniary
laniferous
lank
lanky
  lankier
  lankiest
lanner
lanneret
lanolated
lanolin
lanose
lanosity
lantern
lanthanum
lanuginose
lanuginous
lanuginousness
lanugo
  lanugos
lanyard
laodicean
Laos
lap
  laps
  lapped
  lapping
laparoscopy
laparotomy
lapchart
lapdog
lapel
lapelled
lapidarian
lapidary
  lapidaries
lapillus
lapis lazuli
lappet
lapse
  lapses
  lapsed
  lapsing
lapsus
laptop
lapwing
laquer = lacquer
larceny
  larcenies
larch
  larches
lard

lards
larded
larding
larder
large
largehearted
largely
largen
  largens
  largened
  largening
largescale
largess
largesse
largish
largo
lariat
lark
  larks
  larked
  larking
larkspur
larva
  larvae
laryngeal
larynges
laryngitic
laryngitis
laryngologic
laryngological
laryngologically
laryngoscope
laryngotomy
larynx
  larynges
lasagna
lasagne
lascivious
lasciviously
lasciviousness
laser
lash
  lashes
  lashed
  lashing
lass
  lasses
lassitude
lasso
  lassoes or
  lassos
lassoer
last
  lasts

lasted
lasting
lastly
latch
  latches
  latched
  latching
latchet
latchkey
late
latecomer
lately
latency
latent
later
lateral
laterally (= sideways
  → latterly)
laterality
laterigrade
laterite
lateritic
latest
latex
lath
lathe
lather
  lathers
  lathered
  lathering
laticiferous
Latin
Latinate
Latino
latish
latitude
latitudinarian
latria
latrine
latter
latter-day
latterly (= lately
  → laterally)
lattermost
lattice
Latvia
Latvian
laud
  lauds
  lauded
  lauding
laudable
laudanum
laudation

laudatory
laugh
 laughs
 laughed
 laughing
laughable
laughter
launch
 launches
 launched
 launching
launcher
launder
 launders
 laundered
 laundering
laundress
launderette
laundrette
laundry
 laundries
laundryman
lauraceous
laureate
laurel
Laurentian
lava
lavabo
 lavaboes *or*
 lavabos
lavage
lava-lava
lavatorial
lavatory
 lavatories
lavender
laver
lavish
 lavishes
 lavished
 lavishing
law
law-and-order
lawbreaker
lawful
lawless
lawmaker
lawn
Lawrence
lawrencium
Lawrentian
lawsuit
lawyer
lax

laxative
laxity
laxness
lay (= put down
 → lies)
 lays
 laid
 laying
layabout
lay-by
 lay-bys
layer (= coating
 → lair)
 layers
 layered
 layering
layette
layman
 laymen
lay-off
 lay-offs
layout
lays
laze
 lazes
 lazed
 lazing
lazuli
lazy
 lazier
 laziest
lazybones
lbw
LCD
L-driver
lea
LEA
leach
 leaches
 leached
 leaching
lead (= metal → led)
 leads
 led (= guided
 → lead)
 leading
leaden
leader
leadership
leading
leaf
 leaves
leaflet
leafy

leafier
leafiest
league
leak (= drip → leek)
 leaks
 leaked
 leaking
leakage
leaky
 leakier
 leakiest
Leamington
lean
 leans
 leaned *or*
 leant
 leaning
lean-to
 lean-tos
leap
leap
 leaps
 leaped
 leaping
leapfrog
 leapfrogs
 leapfrogged
 leapfrogging
learn
 learns
 learned *or*
 learnt
 learning
learned (=
 knowledgeable)
lease
 leases
 leased
 leasing
leasehold
leaseholder
leash
 leashes
 leashed
 leashing
least
leastways
leather
 leathers
 leathered
 leathering
leathery
 leatherier
 leatheriest

leave
 leaves
left
leaving
leaved
leaven
leavings
Lebanon
lecher
lecherous
 lecherously
lechery
lecithin
lectern
lector
lecture
 lectures
 lectured
 lecturing
lecturer
lectureship
led (= guided → lead)
ledger
lee
leeboard
leech
 leeches
Leeds (city)
leek (= vegetable
 → leak)
leer
 leers
 leered
 leering
lees
leeward
leeway
left
~~leftenant~~ = lieutenant
left-handed
left-hander
lefties
leftist
leftover
 leftovers
leftward
leftwards
left-wing
lefty
 lefties
leg
 legs
 legged
 legging

legacy
  legacies
legal
legalese
legalise
  legalises
  legalised
  legalising
legality
legalize
  legalizes
  legalized
  legalizing
legally
legate
legatee
legation
legationary
legend
legendary
legerdemain
legged
legging
leggings
leggy
  leggier
  leggiest
leghorn
legible
  legibly
legion
legionnaire
legislate
  legislates
  legislated
  legislating
legislation
legislative
legislatively
legislator
legislatorial
legislature
legit
legitimacy
legitimate
  legitimates
  legitimated
  legitimating
legitimately
legitimateness
legitimisation
legitimatise
  legitimises
  legitimised

legitimising
legitimatization
legitimatize
  legitimatizes
  legitimatized
  legitimatizing
legless
legman
  legmen
Lego®
legpull
legroom
legume
legumin
leguminous
legwarmer
legwork
lei
Leicester
Leicestershire
leisure
leisured
leisurely
leitmotif
leitmotiv
lek
lemma
lemming
lemniscate
lemniscus
  lemnisci
lemon
lemonade
lemony
  lemonier
  lemoniest
lemur
lend
  lends
  lended
  lending
length
lengthen
  lengthens
  lengthened
  lengthening
lengthways
lengthy
  lengthier
  lengthiest
lenient
Leninism
lenitive
lenity

lens
lent
Lent (= before
  Easter)
lenth = length
lentic
lenticel
lenticle
lenticular
lentil
lentissimo
lentivirus
lento
lentoid
Leo
Leominster
Leonardo da Vinci
leone
Leonid
leonine
leopard
leotard
leper
lepidopteran
  lepidoptera or
  lepidopterans
lepidopterist
lepidopteron
lepidote
leporid
leporine
leprechaun
leprose
leprosy
leprous
lepton
leptophyllous
leptosomatic
leptosome
leptospirosis
lesbian
lesbianism
lese-majesty
lesion
Lesley (female)
Leslie (male)
less
lessee
lessen (= grow less
  → lesson)
lesser (= not so great
  → lessor)
lesson (= instruction
  → lessen)

lessor (= one who
  leases → lesser)
lest
let
  lets
  let
  letting
letch
lethal
  lethally
lethargic
lethargically
lethargy
let-out
  let-outs
let's (= let us, as in
  let's go → lets)
letter
lettered
letterbox
letterhead
lettering
letting
lettuce
let-up
  let-ups
leucocyte
leucocytic
leukaemia
leukocyte
Levant
levee
level
  levels
  levelled
  levelling
levelheaded
leveller
lever
  levers
  levered
  levering
leverage
leveret
leviathan
levied
levies
levitate
  levitates
  levitated
  levitating
levity
levy
  levies

levied
levying
lewd
Lewes (town)
Lewis (island; name)
lexeme
lexical
lexicographic
lexicographically
lexicographer
lexicography
lexicon
lexis
liabilities
liability
liable
liaise
　liaises
　liaised
　liaising
liaison
liana
lianoid
liar (= teller of lies
　→ lyre)
liason = liaison
libary = library
libation
libel
　libels
　libelled
　libelling
libellant
libellee
libellous
liberal
Liberal
liberalise
　liberalises
　liberalised
　liberalising
liberalism
liberality
liberalize
　liberalizes
　liberalized
　liberalizing
liberate
　liberates
　liberated
　liberating
liberation
Liberia
libertarian

libertine
liberty
　liberties
libidinal
libidinous
libidinousness
libido
Libra
librarian
librarianship
library
　libraries
　libraries
libray = library
librettist
libretto
　libretti or
　librettos
Libya
Libyan
lice
licence (= official
　permission → license
license (= to give
　official permission
　→ licence)
　licenses
　licensed
　licensing
licensee
licentiate
licentious
licentiously
licentiousness
lichee
lichen
Lichfield
licit
lick
　licks
　licked
　licking
lid
　lidded
lido
　lidos
lie (= be in a horizontal
　position → lay)
　lies
　lay
　lain
　lying
lie (= tell untruths)
　lies

lied
　lying
lieder
liege
liesure = leisure
lieu
lieutenancy
lieutenant
life
　lives
lifeboat
lifeguard
lifeless
lifelike
lifelong
lifer
lifesize
lifesized
lifestyle
lifetime
lift
　lifts
　lifted
　lifting
liftoff
ligament
ligamentous
ligase
ligature
ligger
light
　lights
　lighted or
　lit
　lighting
lighten (= grow
　lighter)
　lightens
　lightened
　lightening
lightening
lighter
lighterage
lightheaded
lighthearted
lighthouse
lightness
lightning (= flash)
lightweight
ligneous
lignicolous
ligniform
lignify
　lignifies

lignified
lignifying
lignin
lignite
lignitic
lignivorous
likable
like
　likes
　liked
　liking
likeable
likelihood
likely
likelyhood = likelihood
liken
　likens
　likened
　likening
likeness
　likenesses
likewise
liking
lilac
liliaceous
lilies
Lilliputian
Lilo℗
　Lilos
lilt
　lilts
　lilted
　lilting
lily
　lilies
lily-livered
limaciform
limacine
Limassol
limb
limbed
limber
　limbers
　limbered
　limbering
limbo
lime
limeade
limekiln
limelight
limerick
limestone
limicoline
limicolous

limit
  limits
   limited
   limiting
limitation
limiter
limitrophe
limivorous
limn
  limns
   limned
   limning
limnetic
limnological
limnologist
limnology
limnophilous
limo
  limos
Limoges
limousine
limp
  limps
   limped
   limping
limpet
limpid
limpidity
Limpopo
limulus
limy
  limier
   limiest
linage
linchpin
Lincoln
linctus
  lictuses
linden
line
  lines
   lined
   lining
lineage
lineal
lineament
lineamental
linear
linearity
lineate
lineation
linen
liner
linesman

line-up
ling
linger
  lingers
   lingered
   lingering
lingerie
lingo
  lingoes
lingual
linguini
linguist
linguistic
linguistically
linguistics
lingulate
liniment
lining
link
  links
   linked
   linking
linkage
linker
linkup
Linnaean
Linnean
linnet
lino
linocut
linoleate
linoleum
linseed
lint
lintel
linum
lion
lioness
lionhearted
lionise
  lionises
   lionised
   lionising
lionize
  lionizes
   lionized
   lionizing
lip
lipaemia
lipase
lipid
lipide
lipogenesis
lipoid

lipoma
lipomatous
liposome
liposuction
lipped
lip-synch
lipuria
liquefacient
liquefaction
liquefy
  liquefies
   liquefied
   liquefying
liquer = liqueur
liquesce
  liquesces
   liquesced
   liquescing
liquescence
liquescency
liquescent
liqueur
liquid
liquidate
  liquidates
   liquidated
   liquidating
liquidation
liquidator
liquidise
  liquidises
   liquidised
   liquidising
liquidiser
liquidity
liquidize
  liquidizes
   liquidized
   liquidizing
liquidizer
liquor
liquorice
Liskeard
lisle
lisp
  lisps
   lisped
   lisping
lissom
lissome
list
  lists
   listed
   listing

listen
  listens
   listened
   listening
listeria
listeriosis
listless
lit
litany
  litanies
litchi
literacy
literal (= word for
  word → littoral)
literally
literary
literate
literati
literatim
literation
literature
lithe
lithesome
lithic
lithification
lithium
litho
lithograph
lithographer
lithographic
lithography
lithoid
lithologic
lithologist
lithology
lithophyte
lithophytic
lithosphere
Lithuania
Lithuanian
litigant
litigate
  litigates
   litigated
   litigating
litigation
litigious
litmus
litotes
litrature = literature
litre
litter
  litters
   littered

littering
littérature = literature
little
littler
littlest
littoral (= of the
  shore → literal)
liturgical
liturgically
liturgics
liturgy
  liturgies
livable
live
  lives
  lived
  living
liveable
live-in
livelihood
livelong
lively
  livelier
  liveliest
livelyhood = livelihood
liven
  livens
  livened
  livening
liver
liveried
liverish
Liverpudlian
liverwort
liverwurst
livery
  liveries
livestock
livid
lividity
living
lizard
Ljubljana
llama (= animal
  → lama)
Llanelli
Llangollen
llano
  llanos
Lloyd's
lo
loach
  loach or
  loaches

load (= place goods
  on → lode)
  loads
  loaded
  loading
loader
loadstar
loadstone
loaf
  loafs or
  loaves
  loafed
  loafing
loafer
loam
loan (= lend → lone)
  loans
  loaned
  loaning
loath
loathe
  loathes
  loathed
  loathing
loathesome =
  loathsome
loathing
loathly
  loathlier
  loathliest
loathsome
loaves
lob
  lobs
  lobbed
  lobbing
lobar
lobate
lobby
  lobbies
lobbyist
lobe
lobectomy
lobelia
lobotomised
lobotomized
lobotomy
  lobotomies
lobster
lobular
lobule
lobworm
local
locale

localise
  localises
  localised
  localising
localism
locality
  localities
localize
  localizes
  localized
  localizing
locally
locatable
locate
  locates
  located
  locating
locater
location
locative
loch
lochia
loci
lock
  locks
  locked
  locking
locker
locket
lockjaw
lockout
locksmith
lockup
loco
locomotion
locomotive
locomotor
locular
locule
  locules or
  loculi
locum
locus
  loci
locust
locution
locutionary
lode (= metal → load)
lodestar
lodestone
lodge
  lodges
  lodged
  lodging

lodgement
lodger
lodgings
lodgment
loess
loessal
loessial
loft
  lofts
  lofted
  lofting
lofter
lofty
  loftier
  loftiest
log
  logs
  logged
  logging
logagraphia
loganberry
logarithm
logarithmic
logbook
loge
logger
loggerheads
loggia
logia
logical
logically
logician
logicism
logistically
logistician
logistics
loglog
logo
  logos
logogram
logogrammatic
logographer
logography
logogriph
logomachist
logomachy
logorrhoea
logotype
loin
loincloth
loiter
  loiters
  loitered
  loitering

Loki
loll
  lolls
  lolled
  lolling
Lollard
lollipop
lollop
  lollops
  lolloped
  lolloping
lolly
  lollies
Lomond, Loch
London
lone (= alone → loan)
lonely
  lonelier
  loneliest
~~lonelyness~~ = loneliness
loner
lonesome
long
  longs
  longed
  longing
longboat
longbow
long-drawn-out
longevity
longevous
longing
longish
longitude
longitudinal
longitudinally
longlegged
longlived
longship
longsighted
longsuffering
longueur
longways
longwinded
loo
loofa
loofah
look
  looks
  looked
  looking
lookalike
looker
lookin

lookout
loom
  looms
  loomed
  looming
loon
loony
  loonier
  looniest
loop
  loops
  looped
  looping
loophole
loopy
  loopier
  loopiest
loose (= undo → lose)
  looses
  loosed
  loosing
looseleaf
loosen
  loosens
  loosened
  loosening
loosestrife
loot (= booty → lute)
lop
  lops
  lopped
  lopping
lope
  lopes
  loped
  loping
lopsided
loquacious
loquaciously
loquaciousness
loquacity
loquat
loran
lord
lordly
  lordlier
  lordliest
lordosis
lordotic
lordship
lore
lorgnette
loris
lorry

lorries
lose (= mislay → lose)
loses
lost
losing
loser
loss
lossmaker
lossy
lost
lot
loth
Lothario
lotic
lotion
lots
lottery
  lotteries
lotto
lotus
louche
loud
louden
  loudens
  loudened
  loudening
loudhailer
loudish
loudmouth
loudmouthed
loudspeaker
lough (= lake)
Loughborough
Louis
lounge
  lounges
  lounged
  lounging
lounger
loupe
lour
  lours
  loured
  louring
louse
  lice
lousewort
lousy
  lousier
  lousiest
lout
loutish
louvre
louvred

lovable
lovage
lovat
love
  loves
  loved
  loving
lovebird
lovebite
love-in-a-mist
~~loveing~~ = loving
loveless
lovelorn
lovely
  lovelier
  loveliest
lovemaking
lover
lovesick
lovey-dovey
loving
low
  lows
  lowed
  lowing
lowbrow
lowdown
lower
  lowers
  lowered
  lowering
lowermost
Lowestoft
low-key
low-keyed
lowland
lowly
  lowlier
  lowliest
low-necked
low-rise
low-tech
lox
loyal
loyalist
loyally
loyalty
  loyalties
lozenge
LP
  LPs
L-plate
LSD
Ltd

lubber
lubricant
lubricate
  lubricates
  lubricated
  lubricating
lubricator
lubricious
lubriciously
lubricity
luce
lucent
lucerne
lucid
lucidity
lucidly
Lucifer
~~lucious~~ = luscious
luck
luckily
luckless
lucky
  luckier
  luckiest
lucrative
lucre
Luddite
ludicrous
ludo
luff
luffa
lug
  lugs
  lugged
  lugging
luge
Luger
luggage
lugger
lugsail
lugubrious
lugubriously
lugubriousness
lugworm
lukewarm
lull
  lulls
  lulled
  lulling
lullaby
  lullabies
lulu
lumbago
lumbar (= of the

lower back → lumber)
lumber (= move
  clumsily → lumbar)
  lumbers
  lumbered
  lumbering
lumberjack
lumberjacket
lumen
  lumens or
  lumina
luminance
luminary
  luminaries
luminesce
  luminesces
  luminesced
  luminescing
luminescence
luminescent
luminosity
luminous
lummox
lump
lumpectomy
lumpen
lumpfish
lumpy
  lumpier
  lumpiest
lunacy
  lunacies
lunar
lunate
lunatic
lunatically
lunch
  lunches
  lunched
  lunching
luncheon
lune
lunette
lung
lunge
  lunges
  lunged
  lunging
lungfish
lungworm
lungwort
lunula
  lunulae
lunular

lunulate
lupin
lupine
lupus
lurch
  lurches
  lurched
  lurching
lurcher
lure
  lures
  lured
  luring
Lurex™
lurid
lurk
  lurks
  lurked
  lurking
luscious
lusciously
lush
lust
  lusts
  lusted
  lusting
lustful
lustfully
lustral
lustrate
  lustrates
  lustrated
  lustrating
lustration
lustrative
lustre
lustreware
lusty
  lustier
  lustiest
lute (= musical
  instrument → loot)
luteal
lutein
lutenist
luteolin
Lutheran
lux
  lux
Luxembourg
luxuriance
luxuriant
luxuriantly
luxuriate

luxuriates
luxuriated
luxuriating
luxuriation
luxurious
luxuriously
luxuriousness
luxury
  luxuries
lyase
lycanthrope
lycanthropic
lycanthropy
lychee
Lycra™
lye
lying
Lyme Regis
Lymington
lymph
lymphangial
lymphatic
lymphoblast
lymphocyte
lymphocytic
lymphoid
lymphoma
  lymphomas or
  lymphomata
lyncean
lynch
lynx
  lynx or
  lynxes
lyre (= musical
  instrument → liar)
lyrebird
lyric
lyrical
lyrically
lyricism
lyricist
lyrist
lyse
  lyses
  lysed
  lysing
lysin
lysine
lysis
lysosome
Lytham
lythraceous
lytic

M

ma
ma'am
mac (= mackintosh
→ Mach)
macabre
macadam
macadamia
macaque
macaroni
macaroon
macaw
mace
Macedonia
macerate
  macerates
  macerated
  macerating
Mach (= Mach
  number → mac)
machete
Machiavellian
machinable
machination
machine
  machines
  machined
  machining
machineable
machinery
machinist
machismo
Machynlleth
macho
macintosh
mackeral = mackerel
mackerel
mackintosh
macramé
macrobiotics
macrocosm
macroeconomics
macroscopic
mad
  madder
  maddest
Madagascar

madam
madame
madcap
madden
  maddens
  maddened
  maddening
madder
maddest
madding
Madeira
made (=
  manufactured
  → maid)
mademoiselle
  mesdemoiselles
madrigal
maelstrom
Maesteg
maestro
  maestri or
  maestros
Mafia
mafioso
  mafiosi or
  mafiosos
magazine
mage
magenta
maggot
maggoty
magi
magic
magician
magisterial
magistracy
magistral
magistrate
maglev
magma
magmatic
magnanimity
magnanimous
magnate
magnesia
magnesium

magnet
magnetic
magnetically
magnetise
  magnetises
  magnetised
  magnetising
magnetism
magnetite
magnetize
  magnetizes
  magnetized
  magnetizing
magneto
magneton
magnetron
magnificant =
  magnificent
magnification
magnificence
magnificent
magnifier
magnify
  magnifies
  magnified
  magnifying
magniloquence
magniloquent
magnitude
magnolia
magnox
magnum
magpie
magus
  magi
maharaja
maharajah
maharanee
maharani
maharishi
mahjong
mah-jongg
mahogany
Mahometan
mahout
maid (= girl → made)

maiden
maidenhair
maidenhead
maidenhood
maidservant
mail (= post → male)
  mails
  mailed
  mailing
mailcoach
mailshot
maim
  maims
  maimed
  maiming
main (= most
  important → mane)
mainbrace
mainframe
mainland
mainline
mainsail
mainstay
mainstream
maintain
  maintains
  maintained
  maintaining
maintainable
maintenance
maintenence =
  maintenance
maisonette
maize (= corn
  → maze)
majestic
majestically
majesty
  majesties
major
  majors
  majored
  majoring
major-domo
  major-domos
majorette

majority
　majorities
make
　makes
　made
　making
makeover
maker (=
　manufacturer)
Maker (= God)
makes
makeshift
makeweight
making
mako
　makos
malachite
maladjusted
maladjustment
maladroit
malady
　maladies
malaise
malapropism
malapropos
malaria
malarial
malarkey
malarky
malate
Malawi
Malaysia
malcontent
male (= masculine
　gender → mail)
maleate
malediction
malefactor
maleficence
maleficent
malevolence
malevolent
malformation
malformed
malfunction
malice
malicious
malign
　maligns
　maligned
　maligning
malignancy
malignant
malignity

malinger
malingers
malingered
malingering
malingerer
mall
mallard
malleable
mallet
mallow
Malmesbury
malmsey
malnourished
malnutrition
malodorous
malpractice
malpractitioner
malt (= grain
　→ moult)
maltase
Malthusian
maltier
maltiest
malting
maltose
maltreat
　maltreats
　maltreated
　maltreating
maltreatment
malty
　maltier
　maltiest
mam
mama
mamba
mambo
　mambos
mamma
mammal
mammalian
mammalogy
mammary
mammography
mammon
Mammon
mammoth
man
　men
　mans
　manned
　manning
manacle
　manacles

manacled
manacling
managable =
　manageable
manage
　manages
　managed
　managing
manageable
management
manager
manageress
managerial
managment =
　management
Manchester
mandala
mandarin
mandate
mandatorily
mandatory
mandible
mandolin
mandoline
mandrake
mandrel
mandril
mandrill
mane (= long hair
　→ main)
maned
manful
manganate
manganese
manganite
mange
mangelwurzel
manger
mangetout
mangey
　mangier
　mangiest
mangily
manginess
mangle
　mangles
　mangled
　mangling
mango
　mangoes or
　mangos
mangoldwurzel
mangosteen
mangrove

mangy
　mangier
　mangiest
manhandle
　manhandles
　manhandled
　manhandling
Manhattan
manhole
manhood
manhunt
mania
maniac
maniacal
manic
manicotti
manicure
manicurist
manifest
manifestation
manifesto
manifold
manikin
Manila (city)
manilla
manipulate
　manipulates
　manipulated
　manipulating
manipulation
manipulative
manipulator
manipulatory
mankind
manky
　mankier
　mankiest
manlike
manna (=food
　→ manner, manor)
manned
manning
mannequin
manner (= way
　→ manna,
　manor)
mannered
mannerism
mannerless
mannikin
mannish
manoeuvrability
manoeuvrable
manoeuvre

manoeuvres
manoeuvred
manoeuvring
manoeuvrer
manor (= house
→ manna; manner)
manorial
~~manoeuvre~~ = manoeuvre
manpower
manse
mansion
manslaughter
mantel (= frame
→ mantle)
mantelpiece
mantis
  mantes *or*
  mantises
mantle (= cloak
→ mantel)
mantra
manual
manufacture
  manufactures
  manufactured
  manufacturing
manufacturer
manure
manuscript
Manx
Manxman
  Manxmen
many
many-sided
manzanilla
Maoism
Maori
  Maori *or*
  Maoris
map
  maps
  mapped
  mapping
maple
maquis
mar
  mars
  marred
  marring
marabou
marabout
maraca
maraschino
marathon

maraud
  marauds
  marauded
  marauding
marauder
marble
marbling
march (= walk)
  marches
  marched
  marching
March (= month)
marcher
marchioness
mardy
mare
margarine
margarita
margarite
margay
marge
margin
marginal
marginalise
  marginalises
  marginalised
  marginalising
marginality
marginalize
  marginalizes
  marginalized
  marginalizing
marguerite
mariachi
~~mariage~~ = marriage
mariculture
marigold
marihuana
marijuana
marina
marinade
  marinades
  marinaded
  marinading
marinate
  marinates
  marinated
  marinating
marine
mariner
marionette
marital
maritime
marjoram

mark (= spot, symbol
etc. → marque)
  marks
  marked
  marking
markdown
marker
market
marketable
marketing
marketplace
marking
marksman
  marksmen
marl
marlin
marline
marmalade
marmoreal
marmoset
marmot
maroon
  maroons
  marooned
  marooning
marque (= product
brand → mark)
marquee
marquess
marquetry
  marquetries
marquis
  marquis *or*
  marquises
marquise
~~marrage~~ = marriage
Marrakesh
marred
marriage
marriageable
marring
marrow
marry
  marries
  married
  marrying
Marseilles
marsh
marshal (= officer;
organize → martial)
  marshals
  marshalled
  marshalling
marshland

marshmallow
marshwort
marshy
  marshier
  marshiest
marsupial
mart
marten
martial (= military
→ marshal)
Martian
martin
martinet
martini
  martinis
martyr
martyrdom
marvel
  marvels
  marvelled
  marvelling
Marvell, Andrew
marvellous
Marxism
Marxist
marzipan
mascara
mascot
masculine
maser
mash
  mashes
  mashed
  mashing
mask (= disguise
→ masque)
  masks
  masked
  masking
masochism
mason
masonic
masonry
masque (=
entertainment
→ mask)
masquerade
mass (= large
amount)
  masses
  massed
  massing
Mass (= church
service)

Massachusetts
massacre
  massacres
  massacred
  massacring
massacrer
massage
  massages
  massaged
  massaging
masseur
masseuse
massif (= mountains)
massive (= huge)
mast
mastectomy
  mastectomies
master
  masters
  mastered
  mastering
masterful
masterpiece
mastery
masticate
  masticates
  masticated
  masticating
mastiff
mastitis
mastodon
masturbate
  masturbates
  masturbated
  masturbating
masturbatory
mat
  mats
  matted
  matting
matador
match
  matches
  matched
  matching
matchbox
matchmaker
matchstick
mate
  mates
  mated
  mating
mater
materfamilias

material
materialisation
materialise
  materialises
  materialised
  materialising
materialism
materialist
materialistic
materialistically
materialization
materialize
  materializes
  materialized
  materializing
matériel
maternal
maternalism
maternalistic
maternally
maternity
matey
  matier
  matiest
mathematical
mathematics
~~mathmatics~~ =
  mathematics
maths
matily
matiness or
mateyness
matin
matinée
matins
~~matress~~ = mattress
matriarch
matriarchy
  matriarchies
matric
matrices
matricide
matriculate
  matriculates
  matriculated
  matriculating
matriculation
matriculator
matrilineal
matrimonial
matrimony
matrix
  matrices or
  matrixes

matron
matronage
matronymic
matt
matte
matter
  matters
  mattered
  mattering
matting
mattins
mattress
maturation
mature
  matures
  matured
  maturing
maturity
maty
  matier
  matiest
maudlin
maul
  mauls
  mauled
  mauling
Mauritania
Mauritius
mausoleum
  mausolea or
  mausoleums
mauve
maven
maverick
maw (= mouth
  → more, moor,
  Moor)
mawkish
maxim
maxima
maximal
maximin
maximise
  maximises
  maximised
  maximising
maximize
  maximizes
  maximized
  maximizing
maximum
may (= might)
May (= month)
maybe

mayfly
  mayflies
mayhem
mayn't
~~mayonaise~~ =
  mayonnaise
mayonnaise
mayor
mayoralty
mayoress
maypole
maze (= paths
  → maize)
mazourka
mazuma
mazurka
me
mead
meadow
meagre
meal
mealworm
mean (= average;
  stingy; intend → mien)
  means
  meant
  meaning
meander
  meanders
  meandered
  meandering
meandrous
meanie
meaning
meaningful
meaningless
meantime
meanwhile
meany
  meanies
measles
measly
measurable
measure
  measures
  measured
  measuring
measurement
meat (= beef, etc.
  → meet, mete)
meatball
meaty
  meatier
  meatiest

meca try mecha
Meccano™
mechanic
mechanical
mechanics
mechanise
 mechanises
 mechanised
 mechanising
mechanism
mechanistic
mechanize
 mechanizes
 mechanized
 mechanizing
medal (= award
 → meddle)
medallion
medallist
meddle (= interfere
 → medal)
 meddles
 meddled
 meddling
meddler (= someone
 who meddles
 → medlar)
meddlesome
medecine = medicine
medeival = medieval
media
mediacy
mediaeval
mediaevalism
mediaevalist
medial
median
mediate
 mediates
 mediated
 mediating
mediation
medic
medical
medicament
medicate
 medicates
 medicated
 medicating
medication
medicinal
medicine
medick (= plant)
medico

medicos
medieval
medievalism
medievalist
mediocre
mediocrity
meditate
 meditates
 meditated
 meditating
meditation
Meditteranean =
 Mediterranean
medium
 media or
 mediums
medlar (= tree
 → meddler)
medley
medusa (= jellyfish)
Medusa (= in Greek
 myth)
meek
meerkat
meerschaum
meet (= join → meat,
 mete)
 meets
 met
 meeting
mega-
megabit
megabyte
megacycle
megadeath
megaflop
megahertz
megalith
megalomania
megalomaniacal
megalosaur
megaphone
megascopic
megastar
megaton
megavolt
megawatt
megohm
meiosis
meiotic
Meirionnydd
melamine
melancholia
melancholic

melancholically
melancholiness
melancholy
melange or
mélange
melanin
melanoma
melatonin
Melbourne
meld
 melds
 melded
 melding
melee or
mélée
mellifluous
mellow
 mellows
 mellowed
 mellowing
melodeon
melodic
melodically
melodion
melodious
melodist
melodrama
melodramatic
melody
 melodies
melon
melt
 melts
 melted
 melting
meltdown
Melton Mowbray
member
membership
membrane
membranous
memento
 mementoes or
 mementos
memo
 memos
memoir
memoirs
memorabilia
memorable
memorandum
 memoranda or
 memorandums
memorial

memorise
 memorises
 memorised
 memorising
memorize
 memorizes
 memorized
 memorizing
memory
 memories
memos
memsahib
men
menace
 menaces
 menaced
 menacing
ménage
menagerie
menarche
mend
 mends
 mended
 mending
mendacious
mendacity
mendelevium
mendicant
menhir
menial
meningeal
meningitis
menopause
menorah
menorrhoea
menses
menstrual
menstruate
 menstruates
 menstruated
 menstruating
menstruation
mensurable
mensuration
mensurative
menswear
mental
mentalism
mentality
 mentalities
menthol
mentholated
mention
 mentions

mentioned
mentioning
mentor
mentorial
mentoring
menu
  menus
meow
  meows
  meowed
  meowing
mercantile
mercantilism
Mercator (projection)
mercenary
  mercenaries
mercer
merchandise
  merchandises
  merchandised
  merchandising
merchant
merchantable
mercies
merciful
merciless
mercurial
mercury
mercy
  mercies
mere
meretricious
merge
  merges
  merged
  merging
merger
meridian
meridional
meringue
Merioneth
merit
  merits
  merited
  meriting
meritocracy
  meritocracies
meritocratic
meritorious
merlin
mermaid
merman
  mermen
meroblastic

merocrine
merriment
merry
  merrier
  merriest
merrymaking
Merthyr Tydfil
mesa
mésalliance
mesarch
mescal
mescalin
mescaline
mesdames
mesdemoiselles
mesh
  meshes
  meshed
  meshing
mesmeric
mesmerise
  mesmerises
  mesmerised
  mesmerising
mesmerism
mesmerize
  mesmerizes
  mesmerized
  mesmerizing
Mesolithic
Mesozoic
mesquit
mesquite
mess
  messes
  messed
  messing
message
messanger =
  messenger
messenger
messianic
messianism
messieurs
messily
messiness
messmate
Messrs
messy
  messier
  messiest
met
metabolic
metabolisable

metabolise
  metabolises
  metabolised
  metabolising
metabolizable
metabolize
  metabolizes
  metabolized
  metabolizing
metal (= iron, etc.
  → mettle)
metallic
metallically
metallurgist
metallurgy
metalwork
metamorphic
metamorphism
metamorphose
  metamorphoses
  metamorphosed
  metamorphosing
metamorphosis
metaphor
metaphoric
metaphysical
metaphysics
metastasis
metastatic
metathesis
metazoan
mete (= distribute
  → meat, meet)
  metes
  meted
  meting
meteor
meteoric
meteorite
meteoritic
meteoroid
meteorological
meteorology
meter (= parking, etc.
  → metre)
  meters
  metered
  metering
methadone
methane
methanol
method
methodical
Methodism

Methodist
methodological
methodology
  methodologies
meths
methyl
meticulous
métier
metonym
metonymical
metonymy
  metonymies
metre (= measure
  → meter)
metric
metrical
metro
  metros
metrological
metrologist
metrology
metronome
metronomic
metronymic
metropolis
metropolitan
mettle (= courage
  → metal)
mettled
mew
  mews (= sound like
    a cat → muse, Muse)
  mewed
  mewing
mewl
  mewls
  mewled
  mewling
mews (= building
  → muse, Muse)
Mexico
mezuzah
  mezuzahs *or*
  mezuzoth
mezzanine
mezzo
  mezzos
mezzotint
miaou
  miaous
  miaoued
  miaouing
miaow
  miaows

miaowed
miaowing
miasma
miasmal
mica
mice
Michael
Michelangelo
mickey
micra
microbe
microbiological
microbiology
microchemistry
microchip
microcircuit
microcomputer
microcosm
microeconomics
microfauna
microfiche
microfilm
microlight
micrometer
micron
microorganism
microphone
microprocessor
microscope
microscopic
microsecond
microsurgery
microtechnology
microwave
  microwaves
  microwaved
  microwaving
micturate
  micturates
  micturated
  micturating
micturition
midair
midday
middle
middlebrow
middleman
  middlemen
Middlesbrough
middleweight
middling
midfield
midge
midget

midnight
mid-off
mid-on
midpoint
midrash
  midrashim
midriff
midst
midsummer
midterm
midway
midweek
midwife
  midwives
midwifery
midwinter
mien (= manner
  → mean)
miff
  miffs
  miffed
  miffing
might (= may;
  strength → mite)
mightily
mightiness
mighty
  mightier
  mightiest
migrain = migraine
migraine
migrant
migrate
  migrates
  migrated
  migrating
migration
migrator
migratory
mikado
  mikados
milady
mild
mildew
mile
mileage
mileometer
milepost
miler
milestone
milieu
militant
militaria
militarise

militarises
militarised
militarising
militarism
militarize
  militarizes
  militarized
  militarizing
military
militate
  militates
  militated
  militating
militia
milk
  milks
  milked
  milking
milkily
milkiness
milky
  milkier
  milkiest
mill
  mills
  milled
  milling
millefleurs
millenary (= to do
  with a thousand
  → millinery)
millenium = millennium
millennial
millennium
millepede
miller
millet
milliampere
milliard
millibar
millieme
milligram
milligramme
millilitre
millimetre
millimicron
milliner
millinery (= hats
  → millenary)
million
millionaire
millionth
millipede
millisecond

millpond
millstone
millstream
millwheel
milo
milometer
milquetoast
mime
  mimes
  mimed
  miming
Mimeograph®
mimesis
mimetic
mimetically
mimic
  mimics
  mimicked
  mimicking
mimicry
miminy-piminy
mimosa
mina (= bird → miner,
  minor)
minaret
mince
  minces
  minced
  mincing
mincemeat
mind (= care about
  → mined)
  minds
  minded
  minding
minder
mindful
mindless
mine
  mines
  mined (= dug out
    → mind)
  mining
minefield
minelayer
miner (= coalminer
  → mynah, minor)
mineral
mineralogical
mineralogy
minestrone
minesweeper
mingle
  mingles

mingled
mingling
mingy
  mingier
  mingiest
mini
  minis
miniature
miniaturise
  miniaturises
  miniaturised
  miniaturising
miniaturist
miniaturize
  miniaturizes
  miniaturized
  miniaturizing
minibus
minicab
minicomputer
minim
minimal
minimalism
minimax
minimise
  minimises
  minimised
  minimising
minimize
  minimizes
  minimized
  minimizing
minimum
minion
minipill
~~miniture~~ = miniature
~~miniscule~~ = minuscule
miniseries
miniskirt
minister
  ministers
  ministered
  ministering
ministerial
ministerialist
ministration
ministry
  ministries
mink
minneola
minnow
Minoan
minor (= not major
  → miner, mynah)

minority
minster
minstrel
mint
  mints
  minted
  minting
mintage
minuend
minuet
minus
minuscular
minuscule
minute
  minutes
  minuted
  minuting
minutiae
minx
Miocene
miosis
miotic
miracle
miraculous
mirage
mire
mirk
mirkily
mirkiness
mirky
  mirkier
  mirkiest
mirror
  mirrors
  mirrored
  mirroring
mirth
misadventure
misanthrope
misanthropic
misanthropy
misapprehend
  misapprehends
  misapprehended
  misapprehending
misapprehension
misbehave
  misbehaves
  misbehaved
  misbehaving
misbehaviour
misbelief
miscalculate
  miscalculates

miscalculated
miscalculating
miscarriage
miscarry
  miscarries
  miscarried
  miscarrying
~~miscelaneous~~ =
  miscellaneous
miscegenation
miscellanea
miscellaneous
miscellanist
miscellany
  miscellanies
mischance
~~mischeif~~ = mischief
mischief
~~mischievous~~ =
  mischievous
mischievous
miscible (= capable
  of mixing
  → missable)
misconceive
  misconceives
  misconceived
  misconceiving
misconception
misconduct
misconstrue
  misconstrues
  misconstrued
  misconstruing
miscount
  miscounts
  miscounted
  miscounting
miscreant
misdeed
misdemeanour
miser
miserable
misère
misericord
misericorde
misery
  miseries
misfire
  misfires
  misfired
  misfiring
misfit
  misfits

misfitted
misfitting
misfortune
misgiving
misguided
mishandle
mishandles
mishandled
mishandling
mishap
mishear
mishears
misheard
mishearing
mishit
mishits
mishit
mishitting
mishmash
misinform
misinforms
misinformed
misinforming
misinformation
misinterpret
misinterprets
misinterpreted
misinterpreting
misjudge
misjudges
misjudged
misjudging
mislay
mislays
mislaid
mislaying
mislead
misleads
misled
misleading
mismatch
misnomer
miso
misogamist
misogamy
misogynist
misogynous
misogyny
~~mispelling~~ =
  misspelling
misplace
  misplaces
  misplaced
  misplacing

misprint
mispronounce
  mispronounces
  mispronounced
  mispronouncing
mispronunciation
misquote
  misquotes
  misquoted
  misquoting
misread
  misreads
  misread
  misreading
misrepresent
  misrepresents
  misrepresented
  misrepresenting
misrule
  misrules
  misruled
  misruling
miss
  misses
  missed (= failed to
  hit → mist)
  missing
missable (= can be
  missed → miscible)
missal
misshapen
  misshapenly
missile
missing
mission
missionary
  missionaries
missis
Mississippi
missive
misspell
  misspells
  misspelled or
  misspelt
  misspelling
misspend
  misspends
  misspent
  misspending
misstate
  misstates
  misstated
  misstating
misstep

missus
mist (= fog
  → missed)
  mists
  misted
  misting
mistakable
mistakably
mistake
  mistakes
  mistook
  mistaken
  mistaking
mistakeable
mistakeably
mister
mistier
mistiest
mistily
mistiness
mistime
  mistimes
  mistimed
  mistiming
mistletoe
mistral
mistreat
  mistreats
  mistreated
  mistreating
mistress
mistrial
mistrust
  mistrusts
  mistrusted
  mistrusting
misty
  mistier
  mistiest
misunderstand
  misunderstands
  misunderstood
  misunderstanding
misuse
  misuses
  misused
  misusing
mite (= small creature,
  etc. → might)
mither
mitigate
  mitigates
  mitigated
  mitigating

mitochondria
mitosis
mitotic
mitotically
mitre
mitt
mitten
mitzvah
  mitzvahs or
  mitzvoth
mix
  mixes
  mixed
  mixing
mixer
mixture
m'lud
mnemonic
mnemonically
mnemonics
mo
moan (= complain
  → mown)
  moans
  moaned
  moaning
moat (= round a ditch
  → mote)
mob
  mobs
  mobbed
  mobbing
mobcap
mobile
mobilise
  mobilises
  mobilised
  mobilising
mobility
mobilize
  mobilizes
  mobilized
  mobilizing
~~mocassin~~ = moccasin
moccasin
mocha (= coffee
  → mocker)
mock
  mocks
  mocked
  mocking
mocker (= person
  who mocks → mocha)
mockers

mockery
  mockeries
mockingbird
mod
modal
modality
  modalities
mode (= fashion
  → mowed)
model
  models
  modelled
  modelling
modem
moderate
  moderates
  moderated
  moderating
moderation
moderator
modern
modernise
  modernises
  modernised
  modernising
modernism
modernity
modernize
  modernizes
  modernized
  modernizing
modest
modesty
modicum
modification
modifier
modify
  modifies
  modified
  modifying
modish
modular
modulate
  modulates
  modulated
  modulating
modulation
module
modulus
  moduli
mogul
mohair
Mohammedan
Mohammedanism

mohel
Mohican
moiety
  moieties
moire *or*
  moiré
moist
moisten
  moistens
  moistened
  moistening
moisture
moisturise
  moisturises
  moisturised
  moisturising
moisturize
  moisturizes
  moisturized
  moisturizing
molal
molar
molarity
molasses
Moldova
mole
molecular
molecularity
molecule
molehill
moleskin
moleskins
molest
  molests
  molested
  molesting
molestation
molester
Molière
moll
mollify
  mollifies
  mollified
  mollifying
mollusc
  molluscs
mollycoddle
  mollycoddles
  mollycoddled
  mollycoddling
molten
moment
momentarily
momentariness

momentary
momentous
momentum
  momenta *or*
  momentums
momma
monarch
monarchic
monarchical
monarchy
  monarchies
monasterial
monastery
  monasteries
monastic
monastically
monasticism
~~monastry~~ = monastery
Monday
Monet, Claude
monetarism
monetary
money
  moneys *or*
  monies
moneybags
moneychanger
moneyed
moneylender
monger
mongol (= person
  with Down's
  syndrome)
Mongol (= of or from
  Mongolia)
Mongolia
mongolism
mongoloid (= having
  Down's syndrome)
Mongoloid (= racial
  group)
mongoose
  mongooses
mongrel
monicker
monied
monies
moniker
monitor
  monitors
  monitored
  monitoring
monk
monkery

monkey
  monkeys
  monkeyed
  monkeying
monkfish
monkhood
monochrome
monocle
monocotyledon
monogamist
monogamous
monogamy
monogram
monograph
monolingual
monolith
monolithic
monologue
monomania
monomaniacal
monomer
monoplane
  monopolies
monopolisation
monopolise
  monopolises
  monopolised
  monopolising
monopolization
monopolize
  monopolizes
  monopolized
  monopolizing
monopoly
  monopolies
monorail
monoski
monosodium
monosyllabic
monosyllable
monotheism
monotone
monotonous
monotony
  monotonies
monounsaturated
monsieur
  messieurs
Monsignor
  Monsignori *or*
  Monsignors
monsoon
monster
monstrosity

monstrous
montage
montbretia
month
Montreal
monument
monumental
moo
  moos
  mooed (= sound
    like a cow → mood)
  mooing
mooch
  mooches
  mooched
  mooching
mood (= state of mind
  → mooed)
moodily
moodiness
moody
  moodier
  moodiest
moon
  moons
  mooned
  mooning
moonbeam
Moonie
moonlight
  moonlights
  moonlighted
  moonlighting
moonlit
moonquake
moonrise
moonscape
moonshine
moonshot
moonstone
moonstruck
moor (waste ground;
  tie up a boat → maw,
  more, Moor)
  moors
  moored
  mooring
Moor (= a North
  African Muslim
  → maw, moor, more)
moorage
moorcock
moorfowl
moorhen

moorings
Moorish (= to do with
  the Moors
  → moreish)
moorland
moose (= animal
  → mousse)
  moose
moot
mop
  mops
  mopped
  mopping
mope
  mopes
  moped
  moping
moped
moraine
morainic
moral (= behaviour)
morale (= optimism)
moralise
  moralises
  moralised
  moralising
moralism
moralist
morality
  moralities
moralize
  moralizes
  moralized
  moralizing
morass
moratorium
  moratoria or
  moratoriums
moratory
moray
Moray (in Scotland)
morbid
morbidity
mordant
more (= opposite of
  less → maw, moor,
  Moor)
moregage = mortgage
moreish (= making
  you want more
  → Moorish)
morel
morello
  morellos

moreover
mores
morgage = mortgage
morgue
moribund
morish (= making you
  want more
  → Moorish)
Mormon
morn (= morning
  → mourn)
mornay
morning (= before
  noon → mourning)
Morocco
moron
moronic
moronically
moronity
morose
morph
morpheme
morphemic
morphine
morphology
morrow
morsel
mortal
mortality
  mortalities
mortar
mortarboard
mortgage
  mortgages
  mortgaged
  mortgaging
mortgagee
mortgagor
mortice
mortician
mortification
mortify
  mortifies
  mortified
  mortifying
mortise
mortuary
  mortuaries
mosaic (= pattern)
Mosaic (= to do with
  Moses)
mosasaur
Moscow
Moselle

Moslem
mosque
mosquito
  mosquitoes or
  mosquitos
moss
most
MOT
mote (= small speck
  → moat)
motel
moter = motor
motet
moth
mothball
mother
  mothers
  mothered
  mothering
motherboard
motherhood
motherland
motherliness
motherly
motif
motile
motility
motion
  motions
  motioned
  motioning
motionless
motivate
  motivates
  motivated
  motivating
motivation
motive
motivity
motley
motocross
motoneuron
motor
  motors
  motored
  motoring
motorbicycle
motorbike
motorboat
motorcade
motorcar
motorcoach
motorcycle
motorise

motorises
motorised
motorising
motorist
motorize
  motorizes
  motorized
  motorizing
motorway
motte
mottle
  mottles
  mottled
  mottling
motto
  mottoes or
  mottos
mouillé
mould
mouldboard
mouldily
mouldiness
moulding
mouldy
  mouldier
  mouldiest
moulin
moult (= lose hair
  → malt)
  moults
  moulted
  moulting
mound
mount
  mounts
  mounted
  mounting
mountain
mountaineer
mountainous
mountebank
mounting
mourn (= grieve
  → morn)
  mourns
  mourned
  mourning
mourner
mournful
mourning (= grieving
  → morning)
mouse
  mice
mouser

mousetail
mousetrap
mousey
  mousier
  mousiest
mousily
mousiness
moussaka
mousse (= cream
  → moose)
mousseline
moustache
moustached
mousy
  mousier
  mousiest
mouth
  mouths
  mouthed
  mouthing
mouthful
mouthpart
mouthpiece
mouthwash
mouthwatering
mouthy
  mouthier
  mouthiest
movable
move
  moves
  moved
  moving
moveable
movement
mover
movie
mow (= cut grass
  → mo)
  mows
  mowed (= cut
    grass → mode)
  mowing
mown (= grass
  → moan)
Mozambique
Mozart, Wolfgang
  Amadeus
mozzarella
mu
much
mucid
mucidity
mucigen

mucilage
mucilaginous
mucin
muck
  mucks
  mucked
  mucking
mucky
  muckier
  muckiest
mucoid
mucoprotein
mucosa
mucosal
mucosity
mucous (= of or like
  mucus)
mucro
  mucrones
mucronate
mucus (= slimy fluid
  → mucous)
mud
muddily
muddiness
muddle
  muddles
  muddled
  muddling
muddleheaded
muddler
muddy
  muddier
  muddiest
mudguard
mudlark
mudpack
mudslinging
muesli
muezzin
muff
muffin
muffle
  muffles
  muffled
  muffling
muffler
mufti
mug
  mugs
  mugged
  mugging
mugful
mugger

muggily
mugginess
muggins
muggy
  muggier
  muggiest
Muhammadan
Muhammedan
mujaheddin
mujahedeen
mujahideen
mukluk
mulatto
  mulattoes or
  mulattos
mulberry
  mulberries
mulch
  mulches
  mulched
  mulching
mule
muleteer
mulish
mull
  mulls
  mulled
  mulling
mulla
mullah
mullet
mulligatawny
mullion
mullite
multiangular
multicoloured
multicultural
multiculturalism
multidisciplinary
multiethnic
multifaceted
multifactorial
multifarious
multilateral
multilingual
multimillionaire
multinational
multinomial
multinuclear
multipartite
multiparty
multipath
multiped
multiple

multiplet
multiplex
multiplicand
multiplication
multiplicative
multiplicity
  multiplicities
multiplier
multiply
  multiplies
  multiplied
  multiplying
multiprocessor
multiprogramming
multipurpose
multiracial
multistorey
multitude
multitudinous
mum
mumble
  mumbles
  mumbled
  mumbling
mummer
mummery
  mummeries
mummify
  mummifies
  mummified
  mummifying
mummy
  mummies
mumps
munch
  munches
  munched
  munching
Munch, Edvard
mundane
municipal
municipality
  municipalities
munificence
munificent
muniment
muniments
munition
munitioner
munitions
muntjac
muntjak
muon
mural

murder
  murders
  murdered
  murdering
murderous
murk
murkily
murkiness
murky
  murkier
  murkiest
~~murmer~~ = murmur
murmur
  murmurs
  murmured
  murmuring
murrain
muscadel
muscadelle
muscat
muscatel
muscle (= body part
  → mussel)
  muscles
  muscled
  muscling
muscovado
muscovite (= a
  mineral)
Muscovite (= of or
  from Moscow)
muscular
muscularity
musculature
musculocutaneous
muse (= think about
  → mews, Muse)
  muses
  mused
  musing
Muse (= goddess
  → mews, muse)
museology
museum
mush
  mushes
  mushed
  mushing
mushily

mushiness
mushroom
mushy
  mushier
  mushiest
music
musical
musically
musicassette
musician
musicianship
musicological
musicology
musk
musket
musketeer
muskiness
muskmelon
muskrat
  muskrat *or*
  muskrats
musky
  muskier
  muskiest
~~musle~~ = muscle
Muslim
muslin
musquash
muss
  musses
  mussed (= messed
  up → must)
  mussing
mussel (= shellfish
  → muscle)
must (= has to
  → mussed)
mustache
mustached
mustachio
mustachioed
mustang
mustard
muster
mustily
mustiness
musty
  mustier
  mustiest

mutable
mutagen
mutagenic
mutant
mutate
  mutates
  mutated
  mutating
mutation
mutational
mutative
mute
  mutes
  muted
  muting
mutilate
  mutilates
  mutilated
  mutilating
mutineer
mutinous
mutiny
  mutinies
  mutinied
  mutinying
mutism
mutt
mutter
  mutters
  muttered
  muttering
mutton
mutual
mutualism
mutuality
muu-muu
Muzak℠
muzhik
muzzily
muzziness
muzzle
  muzzles
  muzzled
  muzzling
muzzy
  muzzier
  muzziest
mwah-mwah
my

myalgia
myalgic
myasthenia
myasthenic
mycelial
mycelium
  mycelia
myceloid
Mycenaean
mycology
mycosis
myelin
myelinated
myelitis
myeloblast
myeloblastic
myeloid
myeloma
myna (= bird
  → miner, minor)
mynah (= bird
  → miner, minor)
myoma
  myomas *or*
  myomata
myopia
myopic
myopically
myriad
myrrh
myrtle
myself
mysterious
mystery
  mysteries
mystic
mystical
mysticism
mystify
  mystifies
  mystified
  mystifying
mystique
myth
mythical
mythological
mythology
  mythologies
myxomatosis

N

na try kna
naan
nab
  nabs
  nabbed
  nabbing
nabob
nacre
nadir
naff
nag
  nags
  nagged
  nagging
naiad
naïf
nail
  nails
  nailed
  nailing
nailbrush
nailfile
Nairobi
naive or naïve
naively
naivety
naked
namby-pamby
name
  names
  named
  naming
nameless
namely
nameplate
namesake
nametape
Namibia
nan
nana
nancy
  nancies
nanny
  nannies
nanometre
nanosecond

nap
  naps
  napped
  napping
napalm
nape
napery
naphtha
napkin
Napoleonic
napping
nappy
  nappies
narcissism
narcissus
narcotic
nark
narrate
  narrates
  narrated
  narrating
narration
narrative
narrator
narrow
narwal
narwhal
nary
NASA
nasal
nasalise
  nasalises
  nasalised
  nasalising
nasality
nasalize
  nasalizes
  nazalized
  nasalizing
nascent
nash = gnash
nasogastric
nasopharyngeal
nasopharynx
nasturtium
nastily

nastiness
nasty
  nastier
  nastiest
natal
natality
nation
nationalisation
nationalise
  nationalises
  nationalised
  nationalising
nationality
  nationalities
nationalization
nationalize
  nationalizes
  nationalized
  nationalizing
nationwide
native
Nativity
Nato
NATO
natter
  natters
  nattered
  nattering
nattily
nattiness
natty
  nattier
  nattiest
natural
naturalisation
naturalise
  naturalises
  naturalised
  naturalising
naturalist
naturalization
naturalize
  naturalizes
  naturalized
  naturalizing
naturally

nature
naturism
naturopath
naturopathic
naturopathy
naught (= nothing
  → nought)
naughtily
naughtiness
naughty
  naughtier
  naughtiest
nausea
nauseate
  nauseates
  nauseated
  nauseating
nauseous
nautical
naval (= to do with a
  navy → navel)
nave (= in a church
  → knave)
navel (= tummy
  button → naval)
navigable
navigate
  navigates
  navigated
  navigating
navigation
navigator
navvy
  navvies
navy
  navies
nawab
nay (= no → née,
  neigh)
Nazi
ne try kne
Neagh, Lough
Neanderthal
neap
near
  nears

neared
nearing
nearby
nearly
nearside
neat
neaten
  neatens
  neatened
  neatening
Neath
nebula
  nebulae *or*
  nebulas
nebulous
neccesary = necessary
neccessary = necessary
necessarily
necessary
necessitate
  necessitates
  necessitated
  necessitating
necessitous
necessity
  necessities
neck
  necks
  necked
  necking
neckband
neckerchief
necklace
neckline
necktie
necrology
necromancy
necrophilia
necrophobia
nectar
nectarine
nee *or*
née (= born → nay,
  neigh)
need
  needs
  needed
  needing
needful
neediness
needle
  needles
  needled
  needling

needlecord
needlecraft
needlepoint
needlework
needs
needy
  needier
  neediest
ne´er
nefarious
negate
  negates
  negated
  negating
negation
negative
negator
neglect
  neglects
  neglected
  neglecting
neglectful
negligee *or*
  negligée
negligence
negligent
negligible
negligibly
negotiable
negotiate
  negotiates
  negotiated
  negotiating
negotiation
negotiator
Negro
neice = niece
neigh (= make horse
  noise → nay, née)
  neighs
  neighed
  neighing
neighbour
neighbourhood
neighbourly
neither
nematode
Neolithic
neologism
neon
neonate
Nepal
nephew
nephrectomy

nephrectomies
nephritic
nephritis
nephrosis
nepotism
nerd
nerve
  nerves
  nerved
  nerving
nerveracking
nervewracking
nervily
nerviness
nervous
nervously
nervy
  nervier
  nerviest
nest
  nests
  nested
  nesting
nestle
  nestles
  nestled
  nestling
net (= catch fish, etc.
  → nett)
  nets
  netted
  netting
netball
nether
Netherlands
nethermost
nett (= nett profit
  → net)
  netting
nettle
network
networking
neural
neuralgia
neuralgic
neurasthenia
neurasthenic
neurological
neurologist
neurology
neuromuscular
neuron
neurosis
  neuroses

neurosurgery
neurotic
neurotically
neuroticism
neurovascular
neuter
  neuters
  neutered
  neutering
neutral
neutralise
  neutralises
  neutralised
  neutralising
neutrality
neutralize
  neutralizes
  neutralized
  neutralizing
neutrino
  neutrinos
neutron
never
nevermore
nevertheless
new (= opposite of
  old → knew)
Newark
newborn
newcomer
newfangled
newly
newlywed
news
newsagent
newsflash
newsier
newsiest
newsletter
newspaper
newspeak
newsprint
newsreader
newsreel
newsroom
newsstand
newsworthy
newsy
  newsier
  newsiest
newt
newton
New Zealand
next

nexus
  nexuses
NHS
ni try kni
niacin
Niagara
~~niave~~ = naive
nib
nibble
  nibbles
  nibbled
  nibbling
NICAM
Nicaragua
nice (= good
  → gneiss)
nicety
  niceties
niche
nick
  nicks
  nicked
  nicking
nickel
nickelodeon
~~nickle~~ = nickel
nick-nack
nickname
nicotine
niece
~~nieghbour~~ = neighbour
~~niether~~ = neither
niff
niftily
niftiness
nifty
  niftier
  niftiest
nigella
Niger
Nigeria
niggardly
nigger
niggle
  niggles
  niggled
  niggling
nigh
night (= opposite of
  day → knight)
nightcap
nightclothes
nightclub
nightdress

nightfall
nightgown
nighthawk
nightie
nightingale
nightjar
nightlife
nightlong
nightly
nightmare
nightshade
nightshirt
nightspot
nighttime
nightwear
nighty
  nighties
nihilism
nil
nimble
nimbostratus
  nimbostrati
nimbus
  nimbi or
  nimbuses
NIMBY
niminy-piminy
nincompoop
nine
ninefold
ninepins
nineteen
nineteenth
~~nineth~~ = ninth
ninetieth
ninety
  nineties
ninny
  ninnies
ninth
ninthly
~~ninty~~ = ninety
nip
  nips
  nipped
  nipping
nipper
nippily
nipple
nippy
  nippier
  nippiest
nirvana
nisi

nit (= louse egg
  → knit)
nitrate
nitration
nitric
nitride
nitrite
nitrogen
nitroglycerine
nitrous
nitty-gritty
nitwit
no try kno
no (= opposite of yes
  → know)
  noes or
  nos (= negatives
    → nose, knows)
nobble
  nobbles
  nobbled
  nobbling
nobility
  nobilities
noble
nobleman
  noblemen
noblesse
noblewoman
  noblewomen
nobody
  nobodies
nocturnal
nocturnally
nocturne
nod
  nods
  nodded
  nodding
nodal
nodality
noddle
noddy
node
nodule
Noel or
  Noël
noes (= negatives
  → knows, nos,
  nose)
nog
noggin
noir
noise

noiseless
noisily
noisiness
noisome
noisy
  noisier
  noisiest
nomad
nomadic
nomenclature
nominal
nominally
nominate
  nominates
  nominated
  nominating
nomination
nominative
nominee
nonagenarian
nonaggression
nonagon
nonagonal
nonaligned
nonappearance
nonce
nonchalant
noncommittal
nonconductor
nonconformist
noncontributory
noncooperation
noncooperative
nondescript
nondrip
none (= not any
  → nun)
nonentity
  nonentities
nonequivalence
nonessential
nonesuch
nonetheless
nonevent
nonferrous
nonfiction
nonflammable
nonintervention
noniron
nonjudgemental
nonjudgmental
nonmetal
nonpareil
nonparticipating

nonpartisan
nonplus
　nonplusses
　nonplussed
　nonplussing
nonproductive
nonproliferation
nonresident
nonreturnable
nonscheduled
nonsense
nonsensical
nonslip
nonsmoker
nonsmoking
nonstandard
nonstarter
nonstick
nonstop
non-U
nonunion
nonviolent
noodle
nook
nooky
noon
noonday
noontime
noose
nope
nor (= neither
　→ gnaw)
noradrenaline
Nordic
Norfolk
norm
normal
normalisation
normalise
　normalises
　normalised
　normalising
normality
normalization
normalize
　normalizes
　normalized
　normalizing
normally
Norman
normative
Norse
north
Northampton

northbound
northeast
northeasterly
northeastern
northeastward
northeastwards
northerly
northern
Northerner
northernmost
Northumberland
northward
northwards
northwest
northwesterly
northwestward
northwestwards
Norway
Norwegian
Norwich
nos (= negatives
　→ knows, nose)
nose (= investigate
　→ knows, noes, nos)
noses
nosed
nosing
nosebag
nosebleed
nosepiece
nosey
　nosier
　nosiest
nosh
nosily
nosiness
nostalgia
nostalgic
nostalgically
nostril
nostrum
nosy
　nosier
　nosiest
not (= negative
　→ knot)
notability
notable
notably
notarise
　notarises
　notarised
　notarising
notarize

notarizes
notarized
notarizing
notary
　notaries
notate
　notates
　notated
　notating
notation
notch
　notches
　notched
　notching
note
　notes
　noted
　noting
noteable = notable
notebook
notecase
notelet
notepaper
notes
noteworthily
noteworthiness
noteworthy
nothing
nothingness
noticable = noticeable
notice
　notices
　noticed
　noticing
noticeable
noticeably
notifiable
notification
notify
　notifies
　notified
　notifying
notion
notional
notionally
notions
notoriety
notorious
notwithstanding
nougat
nought (= zero
　→ naught)
noun
nourish

nourishes
nourished
nourishing
nourishment
nous
nouveau riche
　nouveaux riches
nova
　novae or
　novas
novel
novelette
novelise
　novelises
　novelised
　novelising
novelist
novelize
　novelizes
　novelized
　novelizing
novella
novelty
　novelties
November
novena
novice
noviciate
novitiate
now
nowadays
nowhere
nowt
noxious
nozzle
nu
nuance
nub
nubile
nuclear
nuclease
nucleate
nuclei
nuclein
nucleon
nucleoplasm
nucleoprotein
nucleosynthesis
nucleotide
nucleus
　nuclei or
　nucleuses
nude
nudge

nudges
nudged
nudging
nudism
nudity
nudities
nugatory
nugget
nuisance
nuke
nukes
nuked
nuking
null
nullify
nullifies
nullified
nullifying
nullity
nullities
numb
number
numbers
numbered
numbering

numberless
numberplate
numbskull
numerable
numeracy
numeral
numerary
numerate
numeration
numerator
numerical
numerological
numerology
numerous
numismatics
numismatist
numskull
nun (= in a convent
→ none)
Nuneaton
nunnery
nunneries
nuptial
nuptials
nur try neur

nurse
nurses
nursed
nursing
nursemaid
nursery
nurseries
nurture
nurtures
nurtured
nurturing
nut try neut
nut
nutcase
nutcracker
nuthatch
nuthouse
nutlet
nutmeg
nutrient
nutrition
nutritional
nutritionally
nutritionary
nutritionist

nutritious
nutritiously
nutritive
nutshell
nutter
nuttily
nuttiness
nutty
nuttier
nuttiest
nuzzle
nuzzles
nuzzled
nuzzling
nyala
nyala *or*
nyalas
nylon
nylons
nymph
nymphet
nympho
nymphos
nymphomania
nymphomaniacal

O

o try au
oak
OAP
oar (= on a boat
   → awe, or, ore)
   oars
   oared
   oaring
oarlock
oasis
   oases
oast
oat
oatcake
oath
oatmeal
obdurate
OBE
obedience
obedient
obeisance
obeisant
obelisk
obese
obesity
obey
   obeys
   obeyed
   obeying
obfuscate
   obfuscates
   obfuscated
   obfuscating
obituarist
obituary
   obituaries
object
   objects
   objected
   objecting
objection
objective
obligate
   obligates
   obligated
   obligating

obligation
obligatorily
obligatory
oblige
   obliges
   obliged
   obliging
oblique
obliterate
   obliterates
   obliterated
   obliterating
obliteration
oblivion
oblivious
oblong
obloquy
   obloquies
obnoxious
oboe
   oboes
obscene
obscenity
   obscenities
obscure
   obscures
   obscured
   obscuring
obscurity
   obscurities
obsequious
obsene = obscene
observable
observably
observance
observant
observation
observatory
   observatories
observe
   observes
   observed
   observing
observer
obsess
   obsesses

obsessed
obsessing
obsession
obsessive
obsessively
obsolescent
obsolete
obstacle
obstetric
obstetrically
obstetrician
obstetrics
obstinacy
   obstinacies
obstinate
obstreperous
obstreperously
obstruct
   obstructs
   obstructed
   obstructing
obstruction
obstructive
obstructively
obstructor
obtain
   obtains
   obtained
   obtaining
obtainable
obtrude
   obtrudes
   obtruded
   obtruding
obtruder
obtrusion
obtrusive
obtuse
obverse
obviate
   obviates
   obviated
   obviating
obvious
obviously
ocarina

ocasionally =
   occasionally
ocasion = occasion
occasion
occasional
occasionally
occident
occidental
occidentally
occlude
   occludes
   occluded
   occluding
occult
occultism
occupancy
   occupancies
occupant
occupation
occupational
occupier
occupy
   occupies
   occupied
   occupying
occur
   occurs
   occurred
   occurring
occurance = occurrence
occured = occurred
occurence = occurrence
occurrence
ocean
oceanic
oceanography
ocelot
och
ochre
o'clock
ocs try ox
octagon
octagonal
octagonally
octahedral
octahedron

175

octahedra _or_
  octahedrons
octal
octane
octangular
octave
octavo
octet
octette
octillion
octillionth
October
octogenarian
octopus
  octopi _or_
  octupuses
octuple
ocular
~~ocupation~~ = occupation
~~ocurred~~ = occurred
~~ocurrence~~ = occurrence
odd
oddball
oddity
  oddities
oddly
ode (= poem → owed)
odious
~~odissey~~ = odyssey
odium
odorous
odour
Odysseus
Oedipus
oenologist
oenology
o'er (= over → ower)
oesophageal
oesophagus
  oesophagi
oestrogen
oestrus
oeuvre
of
off
offal
offbeat
offcut
offence
offend
  offends
  offended
  offending
offender

offensive
offer
  offers
  offered
  offering
~~offerred~~ = offered
offertory
  offertories
offhand
office
officer
official
officially
officiate
  officiates
  officiated
  officiating
officiation
officiator
officious
officiously
offing
offish
offprint
offset
  offsets
  offset
  offsetting
offshoot
offshore
offside
offspring
offstage
oft
often
ogle
  ogles
  ogled
  ogling
ogre
ogress
oh (= exclamation
  → owe)
ohm
ohmage
ohmmeter
oho
oik
oil
  oils
  oiled
  oiling
oilcan
oilcloth

oilfield
oilfired
oilily
oiliness
oilskin
oily
  oilier
  oiliest
oink
ointment
O.K.
okapi
  okapi _or_
  okapis
okay
  okays
  okayed
  okaying
O'Keeffe, Georgia
Okehampton
okey-doke
Oklahoma
okra
old
olden
olde-worlde
oldfangled
oldie
oldster
olé
oleaginous
oleander
oleaster
olfaction
olfactory
  olfactories
oligarch
oligarchy
  oligarchies
Oligocene
oligopoly
  oligopolies
olive
Oliver
oloroso
Olympiad
Olympian
Olympic
Olympus
Oman
ombudsman
  ombudsmen
omega
omelet

omelette
omen
omicron
ominous
omission
omit
  omits
  omitted
  omitting
~~ommission~~ = omission
~~ommited~~ = omitted
~~ommitted~~ = omitted
omnibus
  omnibuses
omnipotence
omnipotent
omnipresent
omniscience
omniscient
omnisciently
omnivore
omnivorous
on
onanism
onanistic
once
oncogene
oncogenic
oncological
oncologist
oncology
oncoming
one (= number
  → won)
onerous
oneself
one-upmanship
ongoing
ongoingly
onion
onionskin
online
onlooker
only
onomatopoeia
onomatopoeic
onomatopoeically
onrush
onset
onshore
onside
onslaught
onstage
on to

onus
  onuses
onward
onwards
onyx
oodles
ooh
oompah
oomph
oops
ooze
  oozes
  oozed
  oozing
oozily
ooziness
oozy
  oozier
  ooziest
opacity
  opacities
opal
opaque
open
  opens
  opened
  opening
opener
opening
openly
opera
operable
operate
  operates
  operated
  operating
operater = operator
operatic
operatically
operation
operational
operationally
operative
operator
operetta
  operettas
ophthalmic
ophthalmological
ophthalmologist
ophthalmology
ophthalmoscope
opiate
opine
  opines

opined
  opining
opinion
opinionated
opinionatedly
opium
oponent = opponent
oportunity =
  opportunity
opossum
  opossum or
  opossums
oposite = opposite
opperation = operation
oppinion = opinion
opponent
opportune
opportunist
opportunistic
opportunistically
opportunity
  opportunities
oppose
  opposes
  opposed
  opposing
opposite
opposition
oppress
  oppresses
  oppressed
  oppressing
oppression
oppressive
oppressor
opprobrious
opprobrium
opression = oppression
opt
  opts
  opted
  opting
opthalmology =
  ophthalmology
optic
optical
optically
optician
optics
optimal
optimise
  optimises
  optimised
  optimising

optimism
optimist
optimistic
optimize
  optimizes
  optimized
  optimizing
optimum
  optima or
  optimums
option
optional
optionally
optometrist
optometry
optomist = optimist
optomistic = optimistic
opulent
opus
  opera or
  opuses
or (= either . . . or
  → awe, oar, ore)
oracle
oracy
oral
orally
orange
orangeade
orangery
  orangeries
orangewood
orang-utan
  orang-utans
orate
  orates
  orated
  orating
oration
orator
oratorio
  oratorios
oratory
orb
orbit
orbital
orbiter
orc
orchard
orchestra
  orchestras
orchestral
orchestrally
orchestrate

orchestrates
orchestrated
orchestrating
orchestration
orchid
ordain
  ordains
  ordained
  ordaining
ordeal
order
  orders
  ordered
  ordering
orderliness
orderly
  orderlies
ordinal
ordinance
ordinand
ordinarily
ordinary
ordinate
ordination
ordnance
ordure
ore (= metal → awe,
  oar, or)
oregano
organ
organdie
organic
organically
organisation
organise
  organises
  organised
  organising
organiser
organism
organist
organization
organize
  organizes
  organized
  organizing
organizer
orgasm
orgasmic
orgy
  orgies
oriel
orient
oriental

orientalism
orientalist
orientally
orientate
   orientates
   orientated
   orientating
orientation
orienteering
orifice
origami
origin
original
originality
originally
originate
   originates
   originated
   originating
origination
originator
oriole
Orion
Orkney
ormolu
ornament
ornamental
ornamentally
ornate
ornithological
ornithologically
ornithology
orotund
orphan
orphanage
orthodontist
orthodontics
orthodox
orthodoxy
orthogonal
orthography
   orthographies
orthopaedics
orthopaedist
orthoptic
orthoptics
orthoptist
oryx
   oryx or
   oryxes
oscillate
   oscillates
   oscillated
   oscillating

oscillation
oscillator
oscillatory
oscillogram
oscillograph
oscilloscope
osier
Oslo
osmiridium
osmium
osmosis
osmotic
osmotically
osprey
ossification
ossify
   ossifies
   ossified
   ossifying
ossuary
   ossuaries
ostensible
ostensibly
ostentation
ostentatious
osteoarthritic
osteoarthritis
osteomyelitis
osteopath
osteopathic
osteopathy
osteoporosis
ostler
Ostpolitik
ostracise
   ostracises
   ostracised
   ostracising
ostracize
   ostracizes
   ostracized
   ostracizing
ostrich
   ostrich or
   ostriches
Ostrogoth
Oswestry
otalgia
other
otherwise
otherworldly
otiose
otiosity
otitis

otolaryngology
otology
otter
ottoman (= seat or
   stool)
   ottomans
Ottoman (= of the
   Turkish empire)
ouch
ought
Ouija®
ounce
Oundle
our (= belonging to us
   → hour)
ourself
   ourselves
oust
   ousts
   ousted
   ousting
out (= not in → owt)
   outs
   outed
   outing
outback
outboard
outbreak
outbuilding
outburst
outcast
outclass
   outclasses
   outclassed
   outclassing
outcome
outcrop
outcry
   outcries
outdated
outdistance
   outdistances
   outdistanced
   outdistancing
outdo
   outdoes
   outdid
   outdone
   outdoing
outdoor
outdoors
outer
outermost
outface

outfaces
outfaced
outfacing
outfield
outfit
outfitter
outflank
   outflanks
   outflanked
   outflanking
outflow
outfoot
   outfoots
   outfooted
   outfooting
outgoing
outgoings
outgrow
   outgrows
   outgrew
   outgrown
   outgrowing
outgrowth
outgun
   outguns
   outgunned
   outgunning
outhouse
outing
outlandish
outlaw
   outlaws
   outlawed
   outlawing
outlay
   outlays
   outlaid
   outlaying
outlet
outlier
outline
   outlines
   outlined
   outlining
outlive
   outlives
   outlived
   outliving
outlook
outlying
outmanoeuvre
   outmanoeuvring
outmoded
outnumber

outnumbers
outnumbered
outnumbering
outpatient
outpost
outpour
outpouring
output
outrageous
outrageously
outragious =
   outrageous
outragous =
   outrageous
outré
outreach
outrider
outrigger
outright
outrun
   outruns
   outran
   outrun
   outrunning
outset
outside
outsider
outsize
outsized
outskirts
outspoken
outstanding
outstandingly
outstay
   outstays
   outstayed
   outstaying
outstretched
outstrip
   outstrips
   outstripped
   outstripping
outtake
outward
outwards
outweigh
   outweighs
   outweighed
   outweighing
outwit
   outwits
   outwitted
   outwitting
outwork

outworker
outworn
ouzo
ova
oval
ovally
ovalness
ovarian
ovary
   ovaries
ovation
oven
ovenware
over
overachieve
overachiever
overact
   overacts
   overacted
   overacting
overage
overall
overarm
overawe
   overawes
   overawed
   overawing
overbalance
   overbalances
   overbalanced
   overbalancing
overbearing
overbearingly
overboard
overcast
overcharge
   overcharges
   overcharged
   overcharging
overcoat
overcome
   overcomes
   overcame
   overcome
   overcoming
overcompensate
   overcompensates
   overcompensated
   overcompensating
overdo
   overdoes
   overdid
   overdone
   overdoing

overdose
overdraft
overdrive
overdue
overestimate
overflow
   overflows
   overflowed
   overflown
   overflowing
overgarment
overground
overgrow
   overgrows
   overgrew
   overgrown
   overgrowing
overhang
overhaul
   overhauls
   overhauled
   overhauling
overhead
overheads
overhear
   overhears
   overheard
   overhearing
overheat
   overheats
   overheated
   overheating
overide = override
overindulge
   overindulges
   overindulged
   overindulging
overkill
overlap
   overlaps
   overlapped
   overlapping
overleaf
overload
   overloads
   overloaded
   overloading
overlong
overlook
   overlooks
   overlooked
   overlooking
overly
overmuch

overnight
overpass
overpopulated
overpower
   overpowers
   overpowered
   overpowering
overpowering
overpoweringly
overqualified
overrated
overreact
   overreacts
   overreacted
   overreacting
overreaction
override
   overrides
   overrode
   overridden
   overriding
overrule
   overrules
   overruled
   overruling
overrun
   overruns
   overran
   overrun
   overrunning
overseas
oversee
   oversees
   oversaw
   overseen
   overseeing
overseer
oversensitive
oversensitively
oversensitivity
overshadow
   overshadows
   overshadowed
   overshadowing
oversight
oversimplify
   oversimplifies
   oversimplified
   oversimplifying
oversize
overskirt
oversleep
   oversleeps
   overslept

oversleeping
overspill
overstatement
overt
overtake
  overtakes
  overtook
  overtaken
  overtaking
overtime
overtone
overture
overturn
  overturns
  overturned
  overturning
overvalued
overview
overweening
overweight
overwhelming
overwhelmingly
overwrought

oviduct
ovine
oviparous
ovoid
ovulate
  ovulates
  ovulated
  ovulating
ovule
ovum
  ova
ow
owe (= owe money
  → oh)
  owes
  owed (= owed
    something → ode)
  owing
ower (= person who
  owes → o'er)
owl
owlet
owlish

owlishly
own
  owns
  owned
  owning
owner
ownership
owt (= anything
  → out)
ox
  oxen
oxbow
oxeye
oxhide
oxidant
oxidase
oxidation
oxide
oxidise
  oxidises
  oxidised
  oxidising
oxidiser

oxidize
  oxidizes
  oxidized
  oxidizing
oxidizer
oxlip
oxtail
oxtongue
oxyacetylene
oxygen
oxygenate
  oxygenates
  oxygenated
  oxygenating
oxygenator
oxyhaemoglobin
oxymoron
oyes
oyez
oyster
oystercatcher
ozone

P

pa
pace
  paces
  paced (= walked
   → paste)
  pacing
pacemaker
pacesetter
pachyderm
pacifism
pacifist
pacify
  pacifies
  pacified
  pacifying
pack
  packs
  packed (= full
   → pact)
  packing
package
  packages
  packaged
  packaging
packer
packet
packhorse
pact (= bargain
 → packed)
pad
  pads
  padded
  padding
paddle
  paddles
  paddled
  paddling
paddock
paddy
  paddies
padlock
padre
paean
paediatrician
paedophile
paedophilia

paella
pagan
page
  pages
  paged
  paging
pageant
pageantry
pageboy
~~pagent~~ = pageant
pagoda
paid
pail (= bucket
 → pale)
pain (= hurt → pane)
  pains
  pained
  paining
painful
painfully
painkiller
painstaking
paint
  paints
  painted
  painting
paintbox
paintbrush
painter
painting
paintwork
pair (= to couple, join
 → pare, pear)
  pairs
  paired
  pairing
paisley
Pakistan
pakora
pal
palace
Palaeocene
Palaeolithic
palatable
palatal
palate (= part of the

mouth → pallet,
 palette)
palatial
palatinate
palaver
palazzo
pale
  pales
  paled
  paling
paleface
Palestinian
palette (= paint tray
 → palate, pallet)
palimony
palindrome
palindromic
paling
palisade
palish
pall
  palls
  palled
  palling
pallbearer
pallet (= bed or
 platform → palate,
 palette)
palliative
pallid
pallor
pally
  pallier
  palliest
palm
  palms
  palmed
  palming
palmate
palmistry
palomino
  palominos
palpable
palpate
  palpates
  palpated

palpating
palpation
palpitate
  palpitates
  palpitated
  palpitating
palsy
  palsies
paltrily
paltriness
paltry (= insignificant
 → poultry)
  paltrier
  paltriest
~~pamflet~~ = pamphlet
pampas (= grass
 → pampers)
pamper
  pampers (=
   indulges
   → pampas)
  pampered
  pampering
pamphlet
pamphleteer
pan
  pans
  panned
  panning
panacea
panache
Panama
pancake
pancreas
pancreatic
panda (= animal
 → pander)
pandemic
pandemonium
pander (= gratify
 → panda)
  panders
  pandered
  pandering
pane (= glass in
 window, etc. → pain)

panel
panelling
panellist
panettone
　panettones *or*
　pannetoni
pang
pangolin
panic
　panics
　panicked
　panicking
panicky
panned
pannier
panning
panoply
　panoplies
panorama
panoramic
pans
pansy
　pansies
pant
　pants
　panted
　panting
pantaloons
pantechnicon
pantheism
pantheon
panther
panties
pantihose
pantile
panto
　pantos
pantograph
pantomime
pantry
　pantries
pants
pantyhose
panzer
pap
papa
papacy
　papacies
papal
paparazzo
　paparazzi
papaw
papaya
paper

papers
papered
papering
paperback
paperboy
paperclip
papergirl
paperweight
paperwork
papier-mâché
papillote
papist
papoose
pappoose
paprika
Papua New Guinea
papyrus
　papyri *or*
　papyruses
par
para
parable
parabola
parabolic
paracetamol
parachute
　parachutes
　parachuted
　parachuting
parade
　parades
　paraded
　parading
paradice = paradise
paradigm
paradigmatic
paradise
paradisiacal
paradox
paraffin
parafin = paraffin
paragliding
paragon
paragraph
Paraguay
parakeet
paralel = parallel
paralized = paralysed
parallax
parallel
　parallels
　paralleled
　paralleling
parallelogram

paralyse
　paralyses
　paralysed
　paralysing
paralysis
paralytic
paramedic
parameter
paramilitary
paramount
paramour
paranoia
paranoid
paranormal
parapet
paraphanalia =
　paraphernalia
paraphernalia
paraphrase
　paraphrases
　paraphrased
　paraphrasing
paraplegia
parasailing
parascending
parasite
parasitic
paraskiing
parasol
paratroops
parboil
　parboils
　parboiled
　parboiling
parcel
　parcels
　parcelled
　parcelling
parch
　parches
　parched
　parching
parchment
pardon
　pardons
　pardoned
　pardoning
pardoner
pare (= peel → pair,
　pear)
parent
　parents
　parented
　parenting

parentage
parental
parentally
parenteral
parenterally
parenthesis
　parentheses
parenthetic
parenting
parfait
pariah
parietal
paring
parish
parishioner
parity
　parities
park
　parks
　parked
　parking
parka
parkin
parkland
parky
　parkier
　parkiest
parlament/parlement/
　parliment =
　parliament
parlance
parley
parliament
parliamentarian
parliamentarianism
parliamentary
parlour
parlous
Parmesan
parochial
parochialism
parochially
parody
　parodies
parole
paroxysm
parquet
parquetry
parralel = parallel
parricide
parrot
　parrots
　parroted
　parroting

parry
  parries
  parried
  parrying
parse (= describe in
  grammar → pass)
  parses
  parsed
  parsing
parsec
Parsee
parsimonious
parsimony
parsley
parsnip
parson
parsonage
part
  parts
  parted
  parting
partake
  partakes
  partook
  partaken
  partaking
partial
partiality
partially
participant
participate
  participates
  participated
  participating
participation
participator
participatory
participial
participle
particlar = particular
particle
particoloured
particular
parting
partisan
partition
partly
partner
  partners
  partnered
  partnering
partnership
partook
partridge

parts
parturition
partway
party
  parties
parve
pascal
pasha
pass (= succeed, go
  by → parse)
  passes
  passed (= went by
    → past)
  passing
passable
passably
passage
passageway
passé
passenger
passer-by
  passers-by
passing
passion
passionate
passionflower
passive
passivity
Passover
passport
passtime = pastime
password
past (= long ago
  → passed)
pasta
paste (= glue, affix
  → paced)
  pastes
  pasted
  pasting
pastel
pasteurisation
pasteurise
  pasteurises
  pasteurised
  pasteurising
pasteurization
pasteurize
  pasteurizes
  pasteurized
  pasteurizing
pastiche
pastier
pasties

pastiest
pastil
pastille
pastime
pasting
pastis
pastitsio
pastor
pastoral
pastrami
pastry
  pastries
pasturage
pasture
pasturized =
  pasteurized
pasty
  pasties
  pastier
  pastiest
pat
  pats
  patted
  patting
patch
  patches
  patched
  patching
patchily
patchiness
patchouli
patchwork
patchy
  patchier
  patchiest
pate
pâté
patella
patent
patentee
patentor
pater
paterfamilias
  patresfamilias
paternal
paternalism
paternalist
paternalistic
paternalistically
paternity
paternoster
path
pathetic
pathetically

pathogen
pathogenic
pathological
pathologist
pathology
pathos
pathway
patience
patient
patina
patio
  patios
patisserie
patois
  patois
patresfamilias
patriarch
patriarchy
  patriarchies
patrician
patricide
patrilineal
patrimonial
patrimony
  patrimonies
patriot
patriotic
patriotism
patrol
  patrols
  patrolled
  patrolling
patron
patronage
patronise
  patronises
  patronised
  patronising
patronize
  patronizes
  patronized
  patronizing
patronymic
pats
patted
patten (= clog
  → pattern)
patter
  patters
  pattered
  pattering
pattern (= style or
  decoration → patten)
patty

patties
paucity
paunch
pauper
pause (= wait
  → paws)
  pauses
  paused
  pausing
pavane
pave
  paves
  paved
  paving
pavement
pavilion
~~pavillion~~ = pavilion
paw (= to touch,
 handle → pore, poor,
 pour)
  paws (= touches
  → pause)
  pawed
  pawing
pawn (= chess piece;
 leave with a
 pawnbroker → porn)
  pawns
  pawned
  pawning
pawnbroker
pawnshop
pawpaw
pax
pay
  pays
  paid
  paying
payable
payday
PAYE
~~payed~~ = paid
payee
payer
payload
paymaster
payment
payoff
payout
payphone
payroll
pays
pazazz
pazzazz

PE
pea (= vegetable
  → pee)
peace (= not war
  → piece)
~~peacable~~ = peaceable
peaceable
peaceful
peacekeeping
peacemaker
peacetime
peach
peachiness
peachy
  peachier
  peachiest
peacock
  peacock or
  peacocks
peafowl
  peafowl or
  peafowls
peak (= reach the top
  → peek, peke, pique)
  peaks
  peaked
  peaking
peaked
peal (= ring bells
  → peel)
  peals
  pealed
  pealing
peanut
pear (= fruit → pair,
 pare)
pearl (= precious gem
  → purl)
pearliness
pearlised
pearlized
pearly
  pearlier
  pearliest
pearmain
peasant
peasantry
pease
peasouper
peat
pebble
pecan
peccadillo
  peccadilloes or

peccadillos
peccary
  peccaries or
  peccary
peck
  pecks
  pecked
  pecking
pecker
peckish
pectase
pectin
pectoral
peculiar
peculiarity
  peculiarities
~~peculier~~ = peculiar
pecuniary
pedagogic
pedagogue
pedagogy
pedal (= to cycle
  → peddle)
  pedals
  pedalled
  pedalling
pedalo
  pedaloes or
  pedalos
pedant
pedantic
pedantically
pedantry
  pedantries
peddle (= sell
  → pedal)
peddler
pedestal
pedestrian
pedestrianisation
pedestrianization
pedicure
pedigree
pedlar
pedometer
pee (= urinate → pea)
  pees
  peed
  peeing
peek (= peep → peak,
 peke, pique)
peekaboo
peel (= remove skin
  → peal)

peels
peeled
peeling
peeler
peeling
peep
  peeps
  peeped
  peeping
peephole
peepshow
peer (= look;
  nobleman → pier)
peerage
peeress
pees
peeve
  peeves
  peeved
  peeving
peevish
peewit
~~peform~~ = perform
peg
  pegs
  pegged
  pegging
pegboard
~~peice~~ = piece
peignoir
~~peir~~ = pier
pejoration
pejorative
peke (= dog → peak,
 peek, pique)
Peking
Pekingese
pekoe
pel try pol
pelican
pellagra
pellet
pellmell
pelmet
pelt
  pelts
  pelted
  pelting
pelvic
pelvis
pemican
pemmican
pen
  pens

penned
penning
penal
penalise
  penalises
  penalised
  penalising
penalize
  penalizes
  penalized
  penalizing
penalty
  penalties
penance
pence
penchant
pencil
pendant (= necklace)
pendent (= hanging)
pending
pendulous
pendulum
Penelope
penetrate
  penetrates
  penetrated
  penetrating
penetration
penguin
penicillin
penile
peninsula
peninsular
penis
penitent
penitential
penitentiary
  penitentiaries
penknife
  penknives
pennant
penned
pennies
penniless
penning
pennon
penny
  pence or
  pennies
Pennicuik
Pennines
Pennsylvania
pennyworth
pens

pension
pensioner
pensive
pent
pentagon
pentagonal
pentagram
pentahedron
  pentahedra or
  pentahedrons
pentameter
pentathlon
penthouse
penultimate
penurious
penury
Penzance
peony
  peonies
people
pep
  peps
  pepped
  pepping
pepper
  peppers
  peppered
  peppering
peppercorn
peppermint
pepperoni
peppery
pepping
peptic
peptide
per try pur
per
peradventure
perambulation
perambulator
percale
perceivable
perceivably
perceive
  perceives
  perceived
  perceiving
percieve = perceive
percentage
percentile
perceptible
perceptibly
perception
perceptive

perceptual
perch
  perches
  perched
  perching
perchance
percipience
percipient
percolate
  percolates
  percolated
  percolating
percolator
percussion
percussionist
percussive
perdition
peregrine
peremptorily
peremptoriness
peremptory
perenial = perennial
perennial
perennially
perfect
perfection
perfectionist
perfidious
perfidy
  perfidies
perforate
  perforates
  perforated
  perforating
perforation
perforce
perform
  performs
  performed
  performing
performance
performer
perfume
perfumer
perfumery
perfunctorily
perfunctoriness
perfunctory
pergola
perhaps
pericardium
  pericardia
pericarp
peril

perilous
perimeter
perinatal
perineum
  perinea
period
periodic
periodical
periodically
periodontal
periodontics
peripatetic
peripheral
periphery
  peripheries
periscope
periscopic
perish
  perishes
  perished
  perishing
perishable
peristalsis
peritoneum
  peritonea or
  peritoneums
periwig
periwinkle
perjorative = pejorative
perjure
  perjures
  perjured
  perjuring
perjurious
perjury
  perjuries
perk
  perks
  perked
  perking
perkily
perkiness
perky
  perkier
  perkiest
perm
  perms
  permed
  perming
permafrost
permanant =
  permanent
permanence
permanent

permanganate
permeability
permeable
permeate
  permeates
  permeated
  permeating
~~permenent~~ =
  permanent
~~permissable~~ =
  permissible
permissible
permissibly
permission
permissive
permit
  permits
  permitted
  permitting
permutability
permutable
permutably
permutation
permute
  permutes
  permuted
  permuting
pernicious
pernickety
~~perogative~~ =
  prerogative
peroneal
peroration
peroxide
perpendicular
perpetrate
  perpetrates
  perpetrated
  perpetrating
perpetrator
perpetual
perpetually
perpetuate
  perpetuates
  perpetuated
  perpetuating
perpetuation
perpetuity
perplex
  perplexes
  perplexed
  perplexing
perquisite
~~perrenial~~ = perennial

persecute
  persecutes
  persecuted
  persecuting
persecution
perseverance
persevere
  perseveres
  persevered
  persevering
~~perseverence~~ =
  perseverance
persimmon
persist
  persists
  persisted
  persisting
~~persistant~~ = persistent
persistence
persistent
person
  people or
  persons
persona
  personae
personable
personage
personal
personalise
  personalises
  personalised
  personalising
personality
  personalities
personalize
  personalizes
  personalized
  personalizing
personally
~~personel~~ = personnel
~~personell~~ = personnel
personification
personify
  personifies
  personified
  personifying
personnel
persons
perspective
Perspex®
perspicacious
perspicacity
perspicuity
perspicuous

perspiration
perspire
  perspires
  perspired
  perspiring
persuade
  persuades
  persuaded
  persuading
persuader
persuasible
persuasion
persuasive
~~persue~~ = pursue
~~persuit~~ = pursuit
pert
pertain
  pertains
  pertained
  pertaining
pertinacious
pertinent
perturb
  perturbs
  perturbed
  perturbing
perturbable
perturbably
perturbation
perturbing
pertussis
Peru
peruke
perusal
peruse
  peruses
  perused
  perusing
pervade
  pervades
  pervaded
  pervading
pervasive
perverse
perversion
perversive
pervert
  perverts
  perverted
  perverting
perverted
pervertible
pervious
peseta

peskily
peskiness
pesky
  peskier
  peskiest
peso
  pesos
pessary
  pessaries
pessimism
pessimist
pest
pester
  pesters
  pestered
  pestering
pesticide
pestilence
pestilent
pestilential
pestle
pesto
pet
  pets
  petted
  petting
petal
petard
peter
  peters
  petered
  petering
Peterborough
petersham
pethidine
petiole
petit
petite
petition
  petitions
  petitioned
  petitioning
petitioner
petrel (= sea bird
  → petrol)
petrify
  petrifies
  petrified
  petrifying
petrochemical
petrochemistry
petrodollar
petrol (= for vehicles
  → petrel)

petroleum
pets
petted
petticoat
petting
pettily
pettiness
petty
  pettier
  pettiest
petulant
petunia
Pevensey
pew
pewee
pewit
pewter
peyote
pfennig
  pfennige *or*
  pfennigs
pH
phaeton
phagocyte
phalange
phalangeal
phalanx
  phalanges *or*
  phalanxes
phallic
phallus
  phalli *or*
  phalluses
phantasm
phantasmagoria
phantasmagoric
phantasmal
phantasmic
phantasmically
phantom
pharaoh
Pharisee
pharmaceutical
pharmacist
pharmacological
pharmacology
pharmacopoeia
pharmacuetical =
  pharmaceutical
pharmacy
  pharmacies
pharoah = pharaoh
pharynx
  pharynges *or*

pharynxes
phase
  phases
  phased
  phasing
PhD
pheasant
phenobarbitone
phenol
phenomena
phenomenal
phenomenon
  phenomena
phenotype
phenyl
pheromone
phew (= exclamation
  → few)
phi
phial
Philadelphia
philanderer
philanthropic
philanthropist
philanthropy
philatelic
philatelist
philately
philharmonic
Philipines = Philippines
Philippines
Phillipines =
  Philippines
Phillippines =
  Philippines
philologist
philology
philosopher
philosophical
philosophise
  philosophises
  philosophised
  philosophising
philosophize
  philosophizes
  philosophized
  philosophizing
philosophy
  philosophies
philtre (= love potion
  → filter)
phisical = physical
phiz
phizog

phlegm
phlegmatic
phlox
  phlox *or*
  phloxes
phobia
phobic
Phoebe
phoenix
phone
  phones
  phoned
  phoning
phonecard
phoneme
phonemic
phonetic
phonetically
phonetics
phoney
  phonier
  phoniest
phonics
phonily
phoniness
phonograph
phonology
phony
  phonier
  phoniest
phooey
phosphate
phosphor
phosphorescence
phosphorescent
phosphorous (adj.)
phosphorus (noun)
photo
  photos
photocell
photocopier
photocopy
  photocopies
  photocopied
  photocopying
photoes = photos
Photofit®
photogenic
photograph
photographer
photographic
photography
photogravure
photojournalism

photomontage
photon
photosensitive
Photostat®
photosynthesis
photosynthesise
  photosynthesises
  photosynthesised
  photosynthesising
photosynthesize
  photosynthesizes
  photosynthesized
  photosynthesizing
phototropic
phototropism
phrasal
phrase
  phrases
  phrased
  phrasing
phraseology
  phraseologies
phrenology
phut
phylactery
  phylacteries
phylum
  phyla
Phyllis
physic
physical
physician
physicist
physics
physiognomy
physiological
physiology
physiotherapy
physique
pi (= number or Greek
  letter → pie)
  pis
pianissimo
pianist
piano
  pianos
pianoforte
piazza
picaresque
piccalilli
piccolo
  piccolos
pick
  picks

picked
picking
pickaxe
picket
  pickets
  picketed
  picketing
pickier
pickiest
pickily
pickiness
pickings
pickle
  pickles
  pickled
  pickling
pickled
pickpocket
picky
  pickier
  pickiest
picnic
  picnics
  picnicked
  picnicking
picnicing = picnicking
pictogram
pictograph
pictorial
picture
  pictures
  pictured
  picturing
picturesque
piddling
pidgin (=language
  → pigeon)
pie (= food → pi)
  pies
piebald
piece (= part
  → peace)
  pieces
  pieced
  piecing
piecemeal
piecework
pied
pied-à-terre
  pieds-à-terre
pier (= seaside
  feature → peer)
pierce
  pierces

pierced
piercing
pies
piety
  pieties
piffle
piffling
pig
  pigs
  pigged
  pigging
pigeon (= bird
  → pidgin)
pigeonhole
  pigeonholes
  pigeonholed
  pigeonholing
piggish
piggy
  piggies
piggyback
piglet
pigment
pigmentation
pigmy
  pigmies
pigpen
pigskin
pigsty
  pigsties
pigswill
pike
pikelet
pikestaff
pilau
pilchard
pile
  piles
  piled
  piling
piles
pilfer
  pilfers
  pilfered
  pilfering
pilgrim
pilgrimage
pill
pillar
pillbox
pillion
pillock
pillory
  pillories

pilloried
pillorying
pillow
  pillows
  pillowed
  pillowing
pillowcase
pilot
  pilots
  piloted
  piloting
pilotage
pimento
  pimentos
pimiento
  pimientos
pimp
pimpernel
pimple
pin
  pins
  pinned
  pinning
pinacle = pinnacle
piña colada
pinafore
pinball
pince-nez
  pince-nez
pincers
pinch
  pinches
  pinched
  pinching
pincushion
pine
  pines
  pined
  pining
pineapple
ping
  pings
  pinged
  pinging
pinger
Ping-Pong®
pinion
pink
  pinks
  pinked
  pinking
pinkeye
pinnacle
pinned

pinning
pinny
  pinnies
pinochle
pinpoint
  pinpoints
  pinpointed
  pinpointing
pinprick
pins
pinstripe
pint
pinto
  pintos
pioneer
pious
pip
  pips
  pipped
  pipping
pipe
  pipes
  piped
  piping
pipefish
pipeline
piper
pipette
piping
pipistrelle
pipped
pippin
pipping
pips
pipsqueak
piquancy
piquant
pique (= vex, annoy
  → peak, peek)
  piques
  piqued
  piquing
piquet
piquing
piracy
  piracies
pirana
piranha
pirate
  pirates
  pirated
  pirating
piratic
piratical

pirouette
  pirouettes
  pirouetted
  pirouetting
Pisa
piscatorial
Pisces
pish
piss
  pisses
  pissed (= urinated
    → piste)
  pissing
pissed (= drunk
  → piste)
pistachio
  pistachios
piste (= ski slope
  → pissed)
pistil (= part of a
  flower)
pistol (= gun)
piston
pit
  pits
  pitted
  pitting
pitch
  pitches
  pitched
  pitching
pitcher
pitchfork
piteous
piteously
pitfall
pith
pithead
pithily
pithiness
pithy
  pithier
  pithiest
pitiable
pitied
pities
pitiful
pitifully
pitiless
piton
pits
pitta
pittance
pitterpatter

pituitary
  pituitaries
pity
  pities
  pitied
  pitying
pivot
  pivots
  pivoted
  pivoting
pivotal
pixel
pixie
  pixies
pixy
  pixies
pizazz
pizza
pizzazz
pizzeria
pizzicato
pizzle
placard
placate
  placates
  placated
  placating
placatory
place (= put
  → plaice)
  places
  placed
  placing
placebo
  placeboes or
  placebos
placement
placenta
  placentae or
  placentas
placid
placidity
placing
plagiarise
  plagiarises
  plagiarised
  plagiarising
plagiarism
plagiarize
  plagiarizes
  plagiarized
  plagiarizing
plague
  plagues

plagued
  plaguing
plaice (= fish
  → place)
  plaice or
  plaices
plaid
plain (= flat ground;
  simple → plane)
  plains
plaint
plaintiff
plait
plan
  plans
  planned
  planning
plane (= flat surface;
  aircraft → plain)
planet
planetarium
  planetaria or
  planetariums
planetary
plangent
plank
plankton
planned
planning
plant
  plants
  planted
  planting
plantain
plantation
planter
plaque
plasma
plaster
  plasters
  plastered
  plastering
plasterboard
plastic
Plasticine™
plasticiser
plasticity
plasticizer
plate
  plates
  plated
  plating
plateu = plateau
plateau

plateaus or
  plateaux
platelet
platform
platinum
platitude
Platonic
platoon
platter
platypus
plaudit
plausable = plausible
plausible
play
  plays
  played
  playing
playback
playboy
player
playful
playgoer
playground
playgroup
playhouse
playlet
playmate
playpen
playroom
playschool
plaything
playtime
playwright
playwrite = playwright
plaza
plc or PLC
plea
plead
  pleads
  pleaded
  plead or
  pled
  pleading
pleadings
pleasant
pleasantry
please
  pleases
  pleased
  pleasing
pleased
pleasent = pleasant
pleasurable
pleasure

pleat
  pleats
  pleated
  pleating
plebeian
plebian = plebeian
plebiscite
plectrum
  plectra or
  plectrums
pled
pledge
  pledges
  pledged
  pledging
Pleistocene
plenary
plenipotentiary
  plenipotentiaries
plenitude
plenteous
plenteously
plentiful
plentifully
plenty
plenum
  plena or
  plenums
plesant = pleasant
plethora
pleura
  pleurae
pleurisy
plexus
  plexus or
  plexuses
pliable
pliant
plié
plied
pliers
plies
plight
plimsoll
plink
plinth
Pliocene
PLO
plod
  plods
  plodded
  plodding
plonk
  plonks

plonked
plonking
plonker
plop
  plops
  plopped
  plopping
plosion
plosive
plot
  plots
  plotted
  plotting
plotter
plough
  ploughs
  ploughed
  ploughing
plover
ploy
pluck
  plucks
  plucked
  plucking
pluckily
pluckiness
plucky
  pluckier
  pluckiest
plug
  plugs
  plugged
  plugging
plughole
plum (= fruit)
plumage
plumb (= measure)
  plumbs
  plumbed
  plumbing
plumbago
plumbing
plume
plummet
  plummets
  plummeted
  plummeting
plummy
  plummier
  plummiest
plump
  plumps
  plumped
  plumping

plunder
  plunders
  plundered
  plundering
plunge
  plunges
  plunged
  plunging
plunger
plunk
  plunks
  plunked
  plunking
pluperfect
plural
pluralism
plus
plush
Pluto
plutocracy
plutocrat
plutocratic
plutonium
ply
  plies
  plied
  plying
ply
  plying
Plymouth
plywood
pm
p.m.
PM
PMS
PMT
pneumatic
pneumatically
pneumonia
pnuematic = pneumatic
pnuemonia =
    pneumonia
poach
  poaches
  poached
  poaching
poacher
pock
pocket
  pockets
  pocketed
  pocketing
pocketful
pocketknife

pocketknives
pockmark
pod
  pods
  podded
  podding
podge
podgily
podginess
podgy
  podgier
  podgiest
podiatry
podium
  podia or
  podiums
pods
poem
poesy
  poesies
poet
poetaster
poetic
poetically
poetry
po-faced
pogo
  pogoes
  pogoed
  pogoing
pogrom
poignant
poinsettia
point
  points
  pointed
  pointing
pointed
pointer
poise
poised
poisen = poison
poison
  poisons
  poisoned
  poisoning
poisoning
poisonous
poke
  pokes
  poked
  poking
poker
pokerwork

pokey
  pokier
  pokiest
pokily
pokiness
poky
  pokier
  pokiest
Poland
polar
polarisation
polarise
  polarises
  polarised
  polarising
polarity
  polarities
polarization
polarize
  polarizes
  polarized
  polarizing
Polaroid™
polder
pole (= stick → poll)
poleaxe
polecat
polemic
polemically
polemicist
polemics
polenta
police
  polices
  policed
  policing
policeman
  policemen
policewoman
  policewomen
policy
  policies
policyholder
polio
poliomyelitis
polish
  polishes
  polished
  polishing
Polish
polite
politic
political
politically

politician
politicise
  politicises
  politicised
  politicising
politicize
  politicizes
  politicized
  politicizing
politicking
politico
  politicos
politics
polity
  polities
polka
poll (= vote → pole)
  polls
  polled
  polling
pollard
pollen
pollinate
  pollinates
  pollinated
  pollinating
pollination
pollster
pollutant
pollute
  pollutes
  polluted
  polluting
polluter
pollution
polo
polonaise
polony
poltergeist
polyanthus
polyester
polygamist
polygamous
polygamy
polyglot
polygon
polygonal
polygraph
polyhedron
  polyhedra *or*
  polyhedrons
polymath
polymer
polymorphous

polynomial
polyp
polypropylene
polystyrene
polysyllabic
polysyllable
polytechnic
polytheism
polythene
polyunsaturated
polyurethane
pomade
pomander
pomegranate
pomegranite =
  pomegranate
pomelo
  pomelos
pommel
pommy
  pommies
pomp
pompadour
pompom
pompon
pomposity
pompous
pompously
ponce
poncey
poncho
  ponchos
pond
ponder
  ponders
  pondered
  pondering
ponderous
pondweed
pong
  pongs
  ponged
  ponging
ponies
pontiff
pontifical
pontificate
  pontificates
  pontificated
  pontificating
pontoon
pony
  ponies
Pontypridd

ponytail
pooch
poodle
poof (= homosexual
  → pouf, pouffe)
poofter
pooh
pool
  pools
  pooled
  pooling
Poona
poop
pooper-scooper
poor (= not rich
  → paw, pore, pour)
poorhouse
poorly
pop
  pops
  popped
  popping
popcorn
pope
popedom
popgun
poplar
poplin
poppadom
poppadum
popped
popper
poppet
popping
poppy
  poppies
poppycock
pops
populace
popular
popularise
  popularises
  popularised
  popularising
popularity
popularize
  popularizes
  popularized
  popularizing
popularly
populate
  populates
  populated
  populating

population
populous
porcelain
porch
porcine
porcupine
pore (pore in the skin;
  study text closely
  → paw, poor, pour)
  pores
  pored
  poring
pork
porker
porky
  porkier
  porkiest
  porkies
porn (= pornography
  → pawn)
porno
pornographic
pornography
porosity
  porosities
porous
porpoise
  porpoise or
  porpoises
porridge
porringer
port
portable
Portakabin™
portal
portcullis
portend
  portends
  portended
  portending
portent
portentous
porter
portfolio
  portfolios
porthole
portico
  porticoes or
  porticos
portion
portliness
portly
  portlier
  portliest

portmanteau
  portmanteaus or
  portmanteaux
portrait
portraiture
portray
  portrays
  portrayed
  portraying
portrayal
Port-Salut
Portugal
~~Portugese~~ =
  Portuguese
Portuguese
pose
  poses
  posed
  posing
poser
~~posess~~ = possess
~~posession~~ = possession
poseur
posh
posit
  posits
  posited
  positing
position
positive
positron
posse
possess
  possesses
  possessed
  possessing
possessed
possession
possessive
possessor
posset
possibility
  possibilities
possible
possibly
possum
post
  posts
  posted
  posting
postage
postal
postbag
postbox

postcard
postcode
poster
posterior
posterity
postern
postgraduate
posthaste
posthumous
postilion
postillion
posting
Post-it™
postman
  postmen
postmark
postmaster
postmortem
postpone
  postpones
  postponed
  postponing
postponement
postscript
postulant
postulate
  postulates
  postulated
  postulating
posture
postwoman
  postwomen
posy
  posies
pot
  pots
  potted
  potting
potable
potash
potassic
potassium
potato
  potatoes
potboiler
potency
  potencies
potent
potentate
potential
pother
pothole
potholing
potion

potluck
potpourri
  potpourris
potsherd
pottage
potted
potter
  potters
  pottered
  pottering
pottery
  potteries
pottiness
potty
  potties
  pottier
  pottiest
pouch
pouf (= seat → poof)
pouffe (= seat
  → poof)
poultice
poultry (= chickens
  → paltry)
pounce
  pounces
  pounced
  pouncing
pounce
pound
  pounds
  pounded
  pounding
pour (= dispense
  liquid → paw, poor,
  pore)
  pours
  poured
  pouring
poussin
pout
  pouts
  pouted
  pouting
poverty
pow
POW
powder
  powders
  powdered
  powdering
power
powerboat
powerboating

powerful
powerhouse
Powys
powwow
pox
poxy
  poxier
  poxiest
practicable
practical
practice (noun)
~~practicle~~ = practical
~~practicly~~ = practically
practise (verb)
  practises
  practised
  practising
practitioner
pragmatic
pragmatism
prairie
praise
  praises
  praised
  praising
praiseworthy
praline
pram
prance
  prances
  pranced
  prancing
prandial
prang
  prangs
  pranged
  pranging
prank
prankster
prat
prattle
  prattles
  prattled
  prattling
prawn
pray (= talk to God
  → prey)
  prays
  prayed
  praying
prayer
pre try pro
preach
  preaches

preached
preaching
preacher
preamble
prebend
prebendary
precancerous
precarious
precaution
precautionary
precede
  precedes
  preceded
  preceding
precedence
precedent
~~proceed~~ = precede
precept
preceptor
precinct
precious
precipice
precipitance
precipitancy
precipitant
precipitate
  precipitates
  precipitated
  precipitating
precipitation
precipitous
precis
  precis
precise
precision
preclude
  precludes
  precluded
  precluding
preclusion
preclusive
precocious
preconception
precondition
precursor
predator
predatory
predecessor
predestination
predeterminate
predicament
predicate
predict
  predicts

predicted
predicting
predictability
predictable
predictably
prediction
predictor
predilection
predisposition
predominance
predominant
predominate
pre-empt
  pre-empts
  pre-empted
  pre-empting
pre-emption
pre-emptive
pre-emptively
preen
  preens
  preened
  preening
prefab
preface
prefatory
prefect
prefer
  prefers
  preferred
  preferring
preferable
~~preference~~ =
  preference
~~prefered~~ = preferred
preference
preferential
prefix
pregnancy
  pregnancies
pregnant
prehensile
prehistoric
prehistory
prejudice
prejudicial
prelate
preliminary
  preliminaries
prelude
premature
premeditate
  premeditates
  premeditated

premeditating
premenstrual
premier
premiere
premise
premises
premium
  premiums
premonition
preoccupation
preoccupied
prep
preparation
preparatory
prepare
  prepares
  prepared
  preparing
~~preperation~~ =
  preparation
preponderance
preposition
prepossessing
preposterous
prequel
prerequisite
prerogative
presage
  presages
  presaged
  presaging
Presbyterian
presbytery
  presbyteries
preschool
prescience
prescribe (= give
  medicine → proscribe)
  prescribes
  prescribed
  prescribing
prescription
prescriptive
presence
present
  presents
  presented
  presenting
presentability
presentable
presentably
presentation
presenter
presently

presents
preservation
preservative
preserve
  preserves
  preserved
  preserving
preserver
preset
preshrunk
preside
  presides
  presided
  presiding
presidency
president
presidential
press
  presses
  pressed
  pressing
pressure
pressurise
  pressurises
  pressurised
  pressurising
pressurize
  pressurizes
  pressurized
  pressurizing
prestidigitation
prestige
prestigious
presto
presumable
presumably
presume
  presumes
  presumed
  presuming
presumption
presumptuous
presuppose
  presupposes
  presupposed
  presupposing
presupposition
pretence
pretend
  pretends
  pretended
  pretending
pretender
pretentious

preterite
preternatural
pretext
prettify
  prettifies
  prettified
  prettifying
prettily
prettiness
pretty
pretzel
prevail
  prevails
  prevailed
  prevailing
prevalent
prevaricate
  prevaricates
  prevaricated
  prevaricating
prevarication
prevaricator
~~prevelant~~ = prevalent
prevent
  prevents
  prevented
  preventing
preventable
preventably
preventative
preventible
preventibly
prevention
preventive
preview
previous
previously
prewar
prey (= hunt down
  → pray)
  preys
  preyed
  preying
price
  prices
  priced
  pricing
priceless
pricey
  pricier
  priciest
prick
  pricks
  pricked

pricking
prickle
prickles
prickled
prickling
prickliness
prickly
pricklier
prickliest
pride (= vanity
  → pried)
pried (= was nosy
  → pride)
pries (= is nosy
  → prise, prize)
priest
priesthood
prig
prim
  primmer
  primmest
primacy
  primacies
primaeval
primarily
primary
  primaries
primate
~~primative~~ = primitive
prime
  primes
  primed
  priming
primer
primetime
primeval
primitive
primmer
primmest
primogenitor
primogeniture
primordial
primp
  primps
  primped
  primping
primrose
prims
primula
Primus℗
prince
princely
princess
principal (= chief

→ principle)
principality
  principalities
principle (= moral
  rule → principal)
principled
print
  prints
  printed
  printing
printable
printer
prior
prioress
prioritise
  prioritises
  prioritised
  prioritising
prioritize
  prioritizes
  prioritized
  prioritizing
priority
  priorities
priory
  priories
prise (= force open
  → prize)
  prises
  prised
  prising
prism
prison
prisoner
prissily
prissiness
prissy
  prissier
  prissiest
pristine
privacy
private
privation
privatise
  privatises
  privatised
  privatising
privatize
  privatizes
  privatized
  privatizing
~~privalage~~ = privilege
~~priveledge~~ = privilege
privet

privilage = privilege
priviledge = privilege
privilege
privileged
prize (= value
  → pries, prise)
  prizes
  prized
  prizing
prize (= reward
  → pries, prise)
prizefight
prizewinner
pro
  pros (professionals
  → prose)
probability
  probabilities
probable
probably
probate
probation
probationary
probationer
probe
  probes
  probed
  probing
probity
problem
problematic
problematically
probly = probably
proboscis
  proboscises
procede = proceed
procedural
procedure
proceed
  proceeds
  proceeded
  proceeding
proceeds
proceedure =
  procedure
process
  processes
  processed
  processing
procession
processional
processor
proclaim
  proclaims

proclaimed
proclaiming
proclamation
proclivity
proclivities
procrastinate
  procrastinates
  procrastinated
  procrastinating
procrastination
procrastinator
procreate
  procreates
  procreated
  procreating
proctor
procurator
procure
  procures
  procured
  procuring
prod
  prods
  prodded
  prodding
prodigal
prodigious
prodigy
  prodigies
produce
  produces
  produced
  producing
producer
product
production
productive
productivity
profane
profanity
  profanities
profess
  professes
  professed
  professing
profession
professional
professionalism
professor
professorial
proffer
  proffers
  proffered
  proffering

proesor = professor
proessor = professor
proficiency
proficient
profile
profit (= gain
  → prophet)
  profits
  profited
  profiting
profitable
profiterole
profligacy
profligate
profound
profundity
profuse
profusion
progenitor
progeny
  progenies
progesterone
progestogen
prognosis
  prognoses
prognostic
program (= of a PC
  → programme)
  programs
  programmed
  programming
programmable
programme (= of a TV
  or radio → program)
  programmes
  programmed
  programming
programmer
progress
  progresses
  progressed
  progressing
progression
progressive
prohibit
  prohibits
  prohibited
  prohibiting
prohibition
prohibitive
project
  projects
  projected
  projecting

projectile
projection
projectionist
projector
prolapse
proletarian
proletariat
proliferate
  proliferates
  proliferated
  proliferating
proliferation
prolific
prolifically
prologue
prolong
  prolongs
  prolonged
  prolonging
prom
promenade
prominence
prominent
promiscous =
  promiscuous
promiscuity
promiscuous
promise
  promises
  promised
  promising
promissory
promontory
  promontories
promote
  promotes
  promoted
  promoting
promoter
promotion
promotional
prompt
  prompts
  prompted
  prompting
prone
prong
pronged
pronominal
pronoun
pronounce
  pronounces
  pronounced
  pronouncing

pronounceable
pronounced
pronouncement
~~pronounciation~~ =
   pronunciation
pronto
pronunciation
proof
proofread
  proofreads
  proofread
  proofreading
prop
  props
  propped
  propping
propaganda
propagate
  propagates
  propagated
  propagating
propagator
propane
propel
  propels
  propelled
  propelling
propellant
propellent
propeller
~~propellor~~ = propeller
propensity
  propensities
proper
propertied
property
  properties
prophecy (noun)
  prophecies
prophesy (verb)
  prophesies
  prophesied
  prophesying
prophet (= seer
  → profit)
prophetic
prophetically
prophylactic
prophylaxis
propinquity
propitiate
  propitiates
  propitiated
  propitiating

propitiation
propitious
proponent
proportion
proportional
proportionate
proposal
propose
  proposes
  proposed
  proposing
proposer
proposition
propound
  propounds
  propounded
  propounding
propping
proprietary
proprietor
proprietress
propriety
props
propulsion
pros (= professionals
  → prose)
prosaic
prosaically
proscenium
  proscenia or
  prosceniums
prosciutto
proscribe (= prohibit
  → prescribe)
  proscribes
  proscribed
  proscribing
proscription
proscriptive
prose (= writing
  → pros)
prosector
prosecute
  prosecutes
  prosecuted
  prosecuting
~~prosecuter~~ =
  prosecutor
prosecution
prosecutor
proselytism
prosodic
prosody
prospect

prospective
prospectively
prospector
prospectus
  prospectuses
prosper
  prospers
  prospered
  prospering
prosperity
prosperous
prostaglandin
prostate
prosthesis
  prostheses
prostitute
  prostitutes
  prostituted
  prostituting
prostrate
  prostrates
  prostrated
  prostrating
prostration
protagonist
protect
  protects
  protected
  protecting
protection
protectionism
protectionist
protective
protector
protectorate
protégé (male)
protégée (female)
protein
protest
  protests
  protested
  protesting
Protestant
protestation
protester
protocol
proton
protoplasm
prototype
protozoan
protozoon
  protozoa
protract
  protracts

protracted
protracting
protractedly
protractile
protractor
protrude
  protrudes
  protruded
  protruding
protrusion
protuberance
protuberant
protuberantly
proud
prove
  proves
  proved
  proved or
  proven
  proving
provenance
Provençal (= from
  Provence)
Provençale (= style of
  cooking)
proverb
proverbial
proves
provide
  provides
  provided
  providing
providence
provident
providential
provider
province
provincial
proving
provision
provisional
proviso
  provisoes or
  provisos
provisorily
provisory
provocation
provocative
provoke
  provokes
  provoked
  provoking
provolone
provost

prow
prowess
prowl
  prowls
  prowled
  prowling
proximity
proxy
  proxies
prude
prudence
prudent
prudential
prudish
prudishly
prune
  prunes
  pruned
  pruning
prurient
pruritus
Prussian
pry
  pries (= is nosy
    → prise, prize)
  pried (= was nosy
    → pride)
  prying
PS
psalm
psephologist
psephology
pseud
pseudo
pseudocarp
pseudonym
pseudonymous
pseudopodium
  pseudopodia
psittacosis
psoriasis
psuedonym =
  pseudonym
psych
  psyches
  psyched
  psyching
psyche
psychedelia
psychedelic
psychedelically
psychiatric
psychiatrist
psychiatry

psychic
psycho
  psychos
psychoanalyse
  psychoanalyses
  psychoanalysed
  psychoanalysing
psychoanalysis
psychoanalyst
psychoanalytic
psychobabble
psychological
psychologically
psychologist
psychology
psychopath
psychosis
  psychoses
psychosocial
psychosomatic
psychotherapy
psychotic
psychotically
PT
PTA
ptarmigan
pterodactyl
pto or PTO
Ptolemy
pub
puberty
pubes
pubescence
pubescent
pubic
pubis
public
publican
publication
publicise
  publicises
  publicised
  publicising
publicist
publicity
publicize
  publicizes
  publicized
  publicizing
publicly
publish
  publishes
  published
  publishing

publisher
puce
puck
pucker
  puckers
  puckered
  puckering
pud
pudding
puddle
pudendum
  pudenda
pudgily
pudginess
pudgy
  pudgier
  pudgiest
pueblo
  pueblos
puerile
puerperal
puff
  puffs
  puffed
  puffing
puffball
puffily
puffin
puffiness
puffy
  puffier
  puffiest
pug
pugilism
pugnacious
pugnacity
puke
  pukes
  puked
  puking
pukka
pull
  pulls
  pulled
  pulling
pullet
pulley
pullover
pulmonary
pulp
  pulps
  pulped
  pulping
pulpit

pulsar
pulsate
  pulsates
  pulsated
  pulsating
pulsation
pulse
pulverise
  pulverises
  pulverised
  pulverising
pulverize
  pulverizes
  pulverized
  pulverizing
puma
pumice
pummel
  pummels
  pummelled
  pummelling
pump
  pumps
  pumped
  pumping
pumpernickel
pumpkin
pun
  puns
  punned
  punning
punch
  punches
  punched
  punching
punchball
punchbowl
punchily
punchiness
punchy
  punchier
  punchiest
punctilious
punctual
punctuate
  punctuates
  punctuated
  punctuating
punctuation
puncture
  punctures
  punctured
  puncturing
pundit

pungent
punish
  punishes
  punished
  punishing
punishable
punishment
punitive
Punjabi
punk
punned
punnet
punning
puns
punt
punter
puniness
puny
  punier
  puniest
pup
pupa
  pupae *or*
  pupas
pupate
  pupates
  pupated
  pupating
pupation
pupil
puppet
puppeteer
puppetry
puppy
  puppies
purchase
  purchases
  purchased
  purchasing
purda
purdah

pure
purebred
puree
purée
  purées
  puréed
  puréeing
purely
purgative
purgatorial
purgatory
purge
  purges
  purged
  purging
puri
purify
  purifies
  purified
  purifying
Purim
puritan
puritanical
purity
purl (= stitch
  → pearl)
purloin
  purloins
  purloined
  purloining
purple
purport
  purports
  purported
  purporting
purportedly
purpose
purposeful
purposefully
purposely
purposive

purr
purrs
purred
purring
purse
purses
pursed
pursing
purser
pursue
  pursues
  pursued
  pursuing
pursuit
purveyor
pus
push
  pushes
  pushed
  pushing
pushcart
pushchair
pusher
pushily
pushiness
pushover
pushy
  pushier
  pushiest
pusillanimous
puss
pussy
  pussies
pussycat
pussyfoot
  pussyfoots
  pussyfooted
  pussyfooting
pustular
pustule
put

puts
put
putting
putative
putrefaction
putrefy
  putrefies
  putrefied
  putrefying
putrid
puts
putsch
putt
putter
putting
putty
  putties
puzzle
  puzzles
  puzzled
  puzzling
puzzlement
puzzler
PVC
Pwhlheli
pygmy
  pygmies
pyjama
pyjamas
pylon
pyramid
pyramidal
pyre
Pyrex™
pyrotechnics
Pythagoras (theorem)
python
pzazz

Q

Qatar
quack
  quacks
  quacked
  quacking
quackery
quad
quadrangle
quadrant
quadraphonic
quadrat
quadrate
quadratic
quadrilateral
quadrille
quadrillion
quadrillionth
quadriplegia
quadriplegic
quadruped
quadruple
quadruplet
quaff
  quaffs
  quaffed
  quaffing
quagga
  quagga or
  quaggas
quagmire
quail
  quail or
  quails
quaint
quake
  quakes
  quaked
  quaking
Quaker
quakily
quakiness
quaky
  quakier
  quakiest
qualification
qualifier

qualify
  qualifies
  qualified
  qualifying
qualitative
quality
  qualities
qualm
quandary
  quandaries
quango
  quangos
quantifier
quantify
  quantifies
  quantified
  quantifying
quantitative
quantity
  quantities
quantum
quarantine
quark
quarrel
  quarrels
  quarrelled
  quarrelling
quarrelsome
quarrier
quarry
  quarries
  quarried
  quarrying
quart
quarter
  quarters
  quartered
  quartering
quarterback
quarterdeck
quarterfinal
quarterly
quartermaster
quarters
quartet
quartile

quarto
quartz
quartzite
quasar
quash
  quashes
  quashed
  quashing
quatercentenary
  quatercentenaries
quaternary
  quaternaries
quatrain
quatrefoil
quaver
  quavers
  quavered
  quavering
quay (= for boats
  → key)
quayside
queasily
queasiness
queasy
  queasier
  queasiest
queen
queenly
queensize
queer
quell
  quells
  quelled
  quelling
quench
  quenches
  quenched
  quenching
quenelle
querulous
query
  queries
quest
question
  questions
  questioned

questioning
questionable
~~questionaire~~ =
  questionnaire
questionnaire
~~queu~~ = queue
queue (= wait → cue)
  queues
  queued
  queuing
quibble
  quibbles
  quibbled
  quibbling
quiche
quick
quicken
  quickens
  quickened
  quickening
quickie
quickly
quicklime
quicksand
quickset
quicksilver
quicksilver
quickstep
quid
quiescence
quiescent
quiet
quieten
  quietens
  quietened
  quietening
quietly
quietude
quietus
quiff
quill
quilling
quilt
quilting
quince
quincentenary

199

quincentenaries
quincentennial
quinine
quinquagenarian
quinquecentenary
  quinquecentenaries
quinquennial
quintessence
quintessential
quintet
quintuple
quintuplet
quintuplicate
quip

quips
quipped
quipping
quire (= of paper
  → choir, coir)
quirk
quisling
quit
  quits
  quit *or*
  quitted
  quitting
quite
quitter

quiver
  quivers
  quivered
  quivering
quiverful
quixotic
quiz
  quizzes
  quizzed
  quizzing
quizmaster
quizzical
quo *try* qua
quoit

quoits
quorate
quorum
quotable
quotation
quote
  quotes
  quoted
  quoting
quotidian
quotient
Qur'an

R

ra try wra
rabbi
  rabbis
rabbinate
rabbinic
rabbit
  rabbits
  rabbited
  rabbiting
rabble
rabid
rabidity
rabies
RAC
raccoon
  raccoons
race
  races
  raced
  racing
racecard
racecourse
racegoer
racehorse
raceme
racer
races
racetrack
racial
racialism
racialist
racially
racier
raciest
racily
raciness
racing
racism
racist
rack
  racks
  racked
  racking
racket (= noise
  → racquet)
racketeer

racoon
  racoons
  racoon
racquet (= tennis bat
  → racket)
racy
  racier
  raciest
rad
radar
raddled
radial
radian
radiance
radiant
radiate
  radiates
  radiated
  radiating
radiation
radiator
radical (=
  fundamental
  → radicle)
radicalism
radically
radicchio
radicle (= root
  → radical)
radii
radio
  radios
radioactive
radioactivity
radiocarbon
radiochemistry
radiocommunication
radiogram
radiograph
radiographic
radiography
radio-immuno-assay
radioisotope
radioisotopic
radiological
radiology

radioluminescence
radiopager
radiophone
radiophonic
radiophony
radioscope
radioscopic
radioscopy
radiosensitive
radiosonde
radiotelegram
radiotelegraph
radiotelegraphy
radiotelemetry
radiotelephone
radiotelephony
radioteletype
radiotherapy
radiothermy
radiotoxic
radish
  radishes
radium
radius
  radii or
  radiuses
radix
  radices or
  radixes
radon
RAF
raffia
raffish
raffle
  raffles
  raffled
  raffling
raft
rafter
rag
  rags
  ragged
  ragging
ragbag
rage
  rages

raged
raging
ragged
raggedy
ragging
raggle-taggle
raglan
ragout
ragtag
ragtime
raid
  raids
  raided
  raiding
rail
  rails
  railed
  railing
railcar
railcard
railhead
railing
raillery
  railleries
railroad
  railroads
  railroaded
  railroading
railway
railwayman
  railwaymen
raiment
rain (= drop water
  → reign, rein)
  rains
  rained
  raining
rainbow
raincoat
rainfall
rainforest
rainier
rainiest
rainily
raininess
rainmaker

rainproof
rains
rainstorm
rainwater
rainwear
rainy
  rainier
  rainiest
raise (= lift → raze)
  raises
  raised
  raising
raisin
raita
raj
raja
rajah
rake
  rakes
  raked
  raking
rakee
raki
rakish
Raleigh, Sir Walter
rallentando
rally
  rallies
  rallied
  rallying
rally
  rallies
rallycross
ram
  rams
  rammed
  ramming
Ramadan
ramble
  rambles
  rambled
  rambling
rambler
rambunctious
rambutan
ramekin
ramequin
ramification
ramjet
ramming
ramp
rampage
  rampages
  rampaged

rampaging
rampant
rampart
ramrod
rams
ramshackle
ran
ranch
rancher
ranchero
  rancheros
rancho
  ranchos
rancid
rancidity
rancour
rand
randier
randiest
randily
randiness
random
randomise
  randomises
  randomised
  randomising
randomize
  randomizes
  randomized
  randomizing
randy
  randier
  randiest
ranee
rang
range
  ranges
  ranged
  ranging
rangefinder
ranger
rangily
ranginess
rangy
  rangier
  rangiest
rani
rank
  ranks
  ranked
  ranking
rankle
  rankles
  rankled

rankling
ransack
  ransacks
  ransacked
  ransacking
ransom
rant
  rants
  ranted
  ranting
rap
  raps
  rapped (= hit
    → rapt, wrapped)
  rapping
rapacious
rapacity
rape
  rapes
  raped
  raping
rapeseed
Raphael
rapid
rapidity
rapids
rapier
rapine
rapist
rapped (= hit → rapt,
    wrapped)
rappel
  rappels
  rappelled
  rappelling
rapper
rapping
rapport
rapporteur
raps
rapscallion
rapt (= entranced
    → rapped, wrapped)
rapture
rapturous
rare
rarebit
rarefaction
rarefied
rarely
raring
rarity
  rarities
rasberry = raspberry

rascal
rash
rasher
rasp
  rasps
  rasped
  rasping
raspberry
  raspberries
Rasta
Rastafarian
raster
rat
  rats
  ratted
  ratting
ratable
ratafia
ratatouille
ratbag
ratchet
rate
  rates
  rated
  rating
rateable
ratepayer
rates
ratfink
rather
ratify
  ratifies
  ratified
  ratifying
rating
ratio
  ratios
ration
  rations
  rationed
  rationing
rational
rationale
rationalise
  rationalises
  rationalised
  rationalising
rationalism
rationality
rationalize
  rationalizes
  rationalized
  rationalizing
rationally

rats
ratsbane
rattan
ratted
ratter
rattily
rattiness
ratting
rattle
  rattles
  rattled
  rattling
rattler
rattlesnake
rattly
  rattlier
  rattliest
ratty
  rattier
  rattiest
raucous
raunchiness
raunchily
raunchy
  raunchier
  raunchiest
ravage
  ravages
  ravaged
  ravaging
rave
  raves
  raved
  raving
ravel
  ravels
  ravelled
  ravelling
raven
ravening
ravenous
raver
ravine
raving
ravioli
ravish
  ravishes
  ravished
  ravishing
raw
rawboned
rawhide
Rawlplug™
ray

rayon
raze (= demolish a
  building → raise)
  razes
  razed
  razing
razee
razor
razzle-dazzle
re try wre
re
RE
reach
  reaches
  reached
  reaching
react
  reacts
  reacted
  reacting
reactance
reactant
reaction
reactionary
  reactionaries
reactivate
  reactivates
  reactivated
  reactivating
reactivation
reactive
reactivity
reactor
read (= study text
  → reed)
  reads
  read
  reading
readable
readably
reader
readership
readier
readies
readiest
readily
readiness
reading
readjust
  readjusts
  readjusted
  readjusting
reads
ready

readier
readiest
reagent
real (= true → reel)
realise
  realises
  realised
  realising
realism
realist
realistic
realistically
reality
  realities
realize
  realizes
  realized
  realizing
really
realm
realpolitik
realtor
realy = really
ream
reap
  reaps
  reaped
  reaping
reaper
rear
  rears
  reared
  rearing
rearguard
rearm
  rearms
  rearmed
  rearming
rearmament
rearmost
rearrange
  rearranges
  rearranged
  rearranging
rearward
rearwards
reason
  reasons
  reasoned
  reasoning
reasonable
reasoning
reassure
  reassures

reassured
reassuring
rebarbative
rebate
rebec
rebeck
rebel
  rebels
  rebelled
  rebelling
rebelion = rebellion
rebellion
rebellious
rebelliously
rebirth
reborn
rebound
rebuff
  rebuffs
  rebuffed
  rebuffing
rebuke
  rebukes
  rebuked
  rebuking
rebus
rebut
  rebuts
  rebutted
  rebutting
rebuttal
recalcitrance
recalcitrant
recall
  recalls
  recalled
  recalling
recant
  recants
  recanted
  recanting
recantation
recap
  recaps
  recapped
  recapping
recapitulate
  recapitulates
  recapitulated
  recapitulating
recapitulation
recapture
  recaptures
  recaptured

recapturing
recce
　recces
recceing
reccommend =
　recommend
recede
　recedes
　receded
　receding
receeding = receding
receipt
receivable
receive
　receives
　received
　receiving
receiver
receivership
recent
receptacle
reception
receptionist
receptive
receptivity
receptor
recess
recession
recessional
recessionary
recessive
recharge
　recharges
　recharged
　recharging
rechargeable
recherché
recidivism
recidivist
reciept = receipt
recieve = receive
recipe
recipience
recipient
reciprocal
reciprocality
reciprocally
reciprocate
　reciprocates
　reciprocated
　reciprocating
reciprocation
reciprocative
reciprocator

reciprocatory
reciprocity
recitable
recital
recitation
recite
　recites
　recited
　reciting
reckless
reckon
　reckons
　reckoned
　reckoning
reckoner
reclaim
　reclaims
　reclaimed
　reclaiming
reclaimable
reclamation
reclinable
recline
　reclines
　reclined
　reclining
recliner
recluse
reclusion
reclusive
recognise
　recognises
　recognised
　recognising
recognition
recognitive
recognitory
recognize
　recognizes
　recognized
　recognizing
recoil
　recoils
　recoiled
　recoiling
recollect
　recollects
　recollected
　recollecting
recollection
recomend =
　recommend
recommend
　recommends

recommended
recommending
recommendation
recommendatory
recompense
reconcilable
reconcile
　reconciles
　reconciled
　reconciling
reconciliation
reconciliatory
recondite
recondition
　reconditions
　reconditioned
　reconditioning
reconize = recognize
reconnaisance =
　reconnaissance
reconnaissance
reconnoitre
　reconnoitres
　reconnoitred
　reconnoitring
reconsider
　reconsiders
　reconsidered
　reconsidering
reconsideration
reconstituent
reconstitute
　reconstitutes
　reconstituted
　reconstituting
reconstruct
　reconstructs
　reconstructed
　reconstructing
record
　records
　recorded
　recording
recordable
recorder
recording
recount
　recounts
　recounted
　recounting
recoup
　recoups
　recouped
　recouping

recoupable
recouperate =
　recuperate
recoupment
recourse
recover
　recovers
　recovered
　recovering
recoverability
recoverable
recoverer
recovery
　recoveries
recreation
recreational
recriminate
　recriminates
　recriminated
　recriminating
recrimination
recriminative
recriminatory
recruit
　recruits
　recruited
　recruiting
recruitable
recruiter
recruitment
rectal
rectangle
rectangular
rectangularity
rectify
　rectifies
　rectified
　rectifying
rectilinear
rectitude
recto
　rectos
rector
rectory
　rectories
rectum
　recta or
　rectums
recumbent
recuperate
　recuperates
　recuperated
　recuperating
recuperation

recur
  recurs
  recurred
  recurring
recurrence
recurrent
recurrently
recycle
  recycles
  recycled
  recycling
recyclable
red
redbreast
redbrick
redcoat
redcurrant
redden
  reddens
  reddened
  reddening
redder
reddest
reddish
Redditch
redeem
  redeems
  redeemed
  redeeming
redeemability
redeemable
redeemably
Redeemer
redemption
redeploy
  redeploys
  redeployed
  redeploying
redevelop
  redevelops
  redeveloped
  redeveloping
redhead
rediculous = ridiculous
redneck
redo
  redoes
  redid
  redone
  redoing
redolent
redouble
  redoubles
  redoubled

redoubling
redoubt
redoubtable
redoubtably
redraft
redress
  redresses
  redressed
  redressing
reds
redshank
redskin
redstart
reduce
  reduces
  reduced
  reducing
reducibility
reducible
reducibly
reductase
reduction
reductive
redundancy
  redundancies
redundant
reduplication
reduplicative
redwing
redwood
reed (= grass → read)
reediness
reedy
  reedier
  reediest
reef
reefer
reek (= smell
  → wreak)
  reeks
  reeked
  reeking
reel (= dance; spool
  → real)
  reels
  reeled
  reeling
reeve
ref
refectory
  refectories
refer
  refers
  referred

referring
referal = referral
refered = referred
referee
reference
referendum
  referenda or
  referendums
referent
referential
refering = referring
referral
referrence = reference
refill
refillable
refinancing
refine
  refines
  refined
  refining
refined
refinement
refiner
refinery
  refineries
refit
reflation
reflect
  reflects
  reflected
  reflecting
reflection
reflective
reflectivity
reflector
reflex
reflexive
reflexivity
reflexology
reflux
reform
  reforms
  reformed
  reforming
reformer
refractable
refraction
refractive
refractivity
refractor
refractory
refrain
  refrains
  refrained

refraining
refrence = reference
refresh
refreshes
refreshed
refreshing
refresher
refreshment
refridgerator =
  refrigerator
refrigerant
refrigerate
refrigerates
refrigerated
refrigerating
refrigeration
refrigerator
refuel
  refuels
  refuelled
  refuelling
refuge
refugee
refulgence
refulgent
refund
  refunds
  refunded
  refunding
refundable
refurbish
  refurbishes
  refurbished
  refurbishing
refurbishment
refusal
refuse
  refuses
  refused
  refusing
refusenik
refutability
refutable
refutation
refute
  refutes
  refuted
  refuting
regain
  regains
  regained
  regaining
regal

regale
  regales
  regaled
  regaling
regalia
regality
regard
  regards
  regarded
  regarding
regardless
regatta
regency
  regencies
regenerate
  regenerates
  regenerated
  regenerating
regeneration
regenerative
regenerator
regent
reggae
regicide
regime
regimen
regiment
region
regional
regionalism
register
  registers
  registered
  registering
registrant
registrar
registration
registry
  registries
regress
  regresses
  regressed
  regressing
regression
regressive
regret
  regrets
  regretted
  regretting
regretful
regrettable
regrettably
regroup
  regroups

regrouped
regrouping
regular
regularly
regulate
  regulates
  regulated
  regulating
regulation
regulator
regulo
regurgitate
  regurgitates
  regurgitated
  regurgitating
regurgitation
rehabilitate
  rehabilitates
  rehabilitated
  rehabilitating
rehabilitation
rehash
  rehashes
  rehashed
  rehashing
rehearsal
rehearse
  rehearses
  rehearsed
  rehearsing
reheat
  reheats
  reheated
  reheating
rehoboam
Reich
Reigate
reign (= rule → rain, rein)
  reigns
  reigned
  reigning
reimburse
  reimburses
  reimbursed
  reimbursing
rein (= straps → rain, reign)
reincarnation
reindeer
  reindeer
reinforce
  reinforces
  reinforced

reinforcing
reinstate
  reinstates
  reinstated
  reinstating
reiterate
  reiterates
  reiterated
  reiterating
reiteration
reiterative
reject
  rejects
  rejected
  rejecting
rejection
rejig
  rejigs
  rejigged
  rejigging
rejoice
  rejoices
  rejoiced
  rejoicing
rejoin
  rejoins
  rejoined
  rejoining
rejoinder
rejuvenate
  rejuvenates
  rejuvenated
  rejuvenating
rejuvenation
relapse
  relapses
  relapsed
  relapsing
relate
  relates
  related
  relating
relation
relational
relations
relationship
relative
relatively
relativity
relax
  relaxes
  relaxed
  relaxing
relaxant

relaxation
relaxed
relay
  relays
  relayed
  relaying
release
  releases
  released
  releasing
relegate
  relegates
  relegated
  relegating
~~releive~~ = relieve
relent
  relents
  relented
  relenting
relentless
relentlessly
relevant
~~relevent~~ = relevant
reliability
reliable
reliably
reliance
reliant
relic
relict
relief
relieve
  relieves
  relieved
  relieving
religion
religionist
religiosity
religious
religiously
~~religous~~ = religious
relinquish
  relinquishes
  relinquished
  relinquishing
reliquary
  reliquaries
relish
  relishes
  relished
  relishing
relivable
relive
  relives

relived
reliving
~~rellevant~~ = relevant
relocate
  relocates
  relocated
  relocating
reluctance
reluctant
rely
  relies
  relied
  relying
remain
  remains
  remained
  remaining
remainder
remains
remake
  remakes
  remade
  remaking
remand
  remands
  remanded
  remanding
remark
  remarks
  remarked
  remarking
remarkable
remarkably
rematch
Rembrandt van Rijn
remediable
remediably
remedial
remedially
remedy
  remedies
remember
  remembers
  remembered
  remembering
remembrance
remind
  reminds
  reminded
  reminding
reminder
reminisce
  reminisces
  reminisced

reminiscing
reminiscence
reminiscent
remiss
remission
remit
  remits
  remitted
  remitting
remittance
remnant
remonstrance
remonstrate
  remonstrates
  remonstrated
  remonstrating
remonstrative
remorse
remorseful
remorseless
remote
remould
remount
  remounts
  remounted
  remounting
removable
removably
removal
remove
  removes
  removed
  removing
remunerate
  remunerates
  remunerated
  remunerating
remuneration
remunerative
remunerator
renaissance
renal
renascence
renascent
rend
  rends
  rent
  rending
render
  renders
  rendered
  rendering
rendezvous
  rendezvous

rendition
rends
renegade
renege
  reneges
  reneged
  reneging
renew
  renews
  renewed
  renewing
renewable
renewal
rennet
renounce
  renounces
  renounced
  renouncing
renovate
  renovates
  renovated
  renovating
renown
renowned
rent
  rents
  rented
  renting
rental
renter
renunciation
reorganise
  reorganises
  reorganised
  reorganising
rep
repair
  repairs
  repaired
  repairing
repairable
repairer
reparable
reparation
repartee
repast
repatriate
  repatriates
  repatriated
  repatriating
repatriation
repay
  repays
  repaid

repaying
repayable
repayment
repeal
  repeals
  repealed
  repealing
repeat
  repeats
  repeated
  repeating
repeatability
repeatable
repeated
repeatedly
repeater
repel
  repels
  repelled
  repelling
~~repellant~~ = repellent
repellent
repeller
repent
  repents
  repented
  repenting
repentance
repentant
~~repentence~~ =
  repentance
repenter
repercussion
repertoire
repertory
  repertories
repetition
repetitious
repetitive
rephrase
  rephrases
  rephrased
  rephrasing
repine
  repines
  repined
  repining
~~repitition~~ = repetition
replace
  replaces
  replaced
  replacing
replaceable
replacement

replay
replenish
  replenishes
  replenished
  replenishing
replenishment
replete
replica
replicate
  replicates
  replicated
  replicating
replication
replier
reply
  replies
  replied
  replying
report
  reports
  reported
  reporting
reportable
reportage
reportedly
reporter
repose
  reposes
  reposed
  reposing
repository
  repositories
repossess
  repossesses
  repossessed
  repossessing
repossession
reprehensible
represent
  represents
  represented
  representing
representation
representational
representative
representitive =
  representative
repress
  represses
  repressed
  repressing
repression
repressive
reprieve

reprieves
reprieved
reprieving
reprimand
  reprimands
  reprimanded
  reprimanding
reprint
  reprints
  reprinted
  reprinting
reprisal
reprise
repro
  repros
reproach
  reproaches
  reproached
  reproaching
reproachful
reprobate
reproduce
  reproduces
  reproduced
  reproducing
reproduction
reproductive
reprographic
reprography
reproof
reproval
reprove
  reproves
  reproved
  reproving
reptile
reptilian
republic
republican
repudiate
  repudiates
  repudiated
  repudiating
repudiation
repugnance
repugnant
repulse
repulsion
repulsive
reputable
reputation
repute
reputed
reputedly

request
  requests
  requested
  requesting
requiem
require
  requires
  required
  requiring
requirement
requisite
requisition
reredos
rerun
  reruns
  reran
  rerunning
resalable
resale
resaleable
rescind
  rescinds
  rescinded
  rescinding
rescue
  rescues
  rescued
  rescuing
research
  researches
  researched
  researching
researcher
resemblance
resemble
  resembles
  resembled
  resembling
resent
  resents
  resented
  resenting
resentful
resentment
reservable
reservation
reserve
  reserves
  reserved
  reserving
reserved
reservist
reservoir
reset

resets
reset
resetting
resevoir = reservoir
reshuffle
reside
  resides
  resided
  residing
residence
residency
  residencies
resident
residential
residual
residue
residuum
  residua
resign
  resigns
  resigned
  resigning
resignation
resigned
resilience
resilient
resin
resist
  resists
  resisted
  resisting
resistance
resistant
resistence = resistance
resistible
resistibly
resistor
resit
  resits
  resat
  resitting
resoluble
resolute
resolution
resolvable
resolve
  resolves
  resolved
  resolving
resonance
resonant
resonate
  resonates
  resonated

resonating
resonator
resorption
resort
resound
  resounds
  resounded
  resounding
resource
resourceful
respect
  respects
  respected
  respecting
respectability
respectable
respectably
respectful
respective
respiration
respirator
respiratory
respire
  respires
  respired
  respiring
respite
~~resplendant~~ =
  resplendent
resplendence
resplendent
respond
  responds
  responded
  responding
respondent
response
~~responsability~~ =
  responsibility
responsibility
responsible
responsibly
responsive
rest
  rests
  rested
  resting
~~restaraunt~~ = restaurant
restate
  restates
  restated
  restating
restatement
restaurant

~~restauranteur~~ =
  restaurateur
~~restraunt~~ = restaurant
restaurateur
restful
resting
restitution
restive
restless
restoration
restorative
restore
  restores
  restored
  restoring
restorer
restrain
  restrains
  restrained
  restraining
restrained
restraint
restrict
  restricts
  restricted
  restricting
restriction
restrictive
result
  results
  resulted
  resulting
resultant
resume (= carry on
  → résumé)
  resumes
  resumed
  resuming
résumé (= summary
  → resume)
resumption
resurgence
resurgent
resurrect
  resurrects
  resurrected
  resurrecting
resurrection
resuscitate
  resuscitates
  resuscitated
  resuscitating
resuscitation
retail

retails
retailed
retailing
retain
  retains
  retained
  retaining
retainable
retainer
retake
  retakes
  retook
  retaken
  retaking
retaliate
  retaliates
  retaliated
  retaliating
retaliation
retaliative
retaliatory
retard
  retards
  retarded
  retarding
retardant
retarded
retarder
retch (= vomit
  → wretch)
  retches
  retched
  retching
retention
retentive
rethink
  rethinks
  rethought
  rethinking
reticent
retina
  retinae *or*
  retinas
retinue
retire
  retires
  retired
  retiring
retirement
retiring
retort
  retorts
  retorted
  retorting

retrace
  retraces
  retraced
  retracing
retract
  retracts
  retracted
  retracting
retractability
retractable
retraction
retractor
retread
retreat
  retreats
  retreated
  retreating
retrenchment
retrial
retribution
retrievable
retrievably
retrieval
retrieve
  retrieves
  retrieved
  retrieving
retriever
retroactive
retroflex
retrograde
retrorocket
retrospect
retrospection
retrospective
retrospectively
retroussé
retrovirus
retsina
return
  returns
  returned
  returning
returnable
returner
reunion
reunite
  reunites
  reunited
  reuniting
rev
  revs
  revved
  revving

revaluation
revalue
  revalues
  revalued
  revaluing
revamp
  revamps
  revamped
  revamping
reveal
  reveals
  revealed
  revealing
reveille
revel
  revels
  revelled
  revelling
revelant = relevant
revelation
revelry
  revelries
revenge
  revenges
  revenged
  revenging
revengeful
revenue
reverberate
  reverberates
  reverberated
  reverberating
reverberation
revere
  reveres
  revered
  revering
reverence
reverend
reverent
reverential
reverie
reversal
reverse
  reverses
  reversed
  reversing
reversi
reversibility
reversible
reversibly
reversion
revert
  reverts

reverted
reverting
review (= look at
  → revue)
  reviews
  reviewed
  reviewing
reviewer
revile
  reviles
  reviled
  reviling
revise
  revises
  revised
  revising
revision
revisionism
revisionist
revitalisation
revitalise
  revitalises
  revitalised
  revitalising
revitalization
revitalize
  revitalizes
  revitalized
  revitalizing
revival
revivalism
revivalist
revive
  revives
  revived
  reviving
revocable
revocation
revokably
revoke
  revokes
  revoked
  revoking
revolt
  revolts
  revolted
  revolting
revolution
revolutionary
revolutionise
  revolutionises
  revolutionised
  revolutionising
revolutionize

revolutionizes
revolutionized
revolutionizing
revolve
  revolves
  revolved
  revolving
revolver
revs
revue (= a show
  → review)
revulsion
revved
revving
reward
  rewards
  rewarded
  rewarding
rewind
  rewinds
  rewound
  rewinding
rewrite
  rewrites
  rewrote
  rewritten
  rewriting
Reykjavik
Rhamadhan
rhapsodic
rhapsodically
rhapsodise
  rhapsodises
  rhapsodised
  rhapsodizing
rhapsodize
  rhapsodizes
  rhapsodized
  rhapsodizing
rhapsody
  rhapsodies
rhea
rheostat
rheotropic
rheotropism
rhesus
rhetoric
rhetorical
rhetorically
rhetorician
rheumatic
rheumatically
rheumatics
rheumatism

rheumatoid
rheumy (watery
  → roomy)
Rhine
rhinestone
rhinitis
rhino
  rhino or
  rhinos
rhinoceros
  rhinoceros or
  rhinoceroses
rhinocerous =
  rhinoceros
rhinoplasty
rhizome
rho (= Greek letter
  → roe, row)
rhos (= Greek
  letters → rose,
  rows)
rhododendron
rhombic
rhombohedral
rhombohedron
rhomboid
rhombus
  rhombi or
  rhombuses
Rhondda
rhubarb
rhyme (= sound like
  → rime)
  rhymes
  rhymed
  rhyming
rhythm
rhythmical
rhythmically
ri try wri
rib
  ribs
  ribbed
  ribbing
ribald
ribaldry
riband
ribband
ribbed
ribbing
ribbon
ribcage
riboflavin
riboflavine

ribs
rice
ricer
rich
  richer
  richest
riches
rick
  ricks
  ricked
  ricking
rickets
rickety
rickshaw
ricochet
  ricochets
  ricocheted or
  ricochetted
  ricocheting or
  ricochetting
ricotta
rictus
  rictus or
  rictuses
rid
  rids
  rid or
  ridded
  ridding
riddance
ridden
riddle
ride
  rides
  rode (= travelled
   upon → road)
  ridden
  riding
rider
rides
ridge
ridicule
  ridicules
  ridiculed
  ridiculing
ridiculous
ridiculously
riding
rien = rein
riesling
rife
riff
riffle
  riffles

riffled
riffling
riffraff
rifle
  rifles
  rifled
  rifling
rift
rig
  rigs
  rigged
  rigging
rigadoon
rigamarole
rigatoni
rigger (= workman
  → rigor, rigour)
right (= opposite of
  left; correct → rite,
  write)
  rights
  righted
  righting
  rightable
  righten
  rightens
  rightened
  rightening
  righteous
  righteously
  rightful
  rightfully
  rightish
  rightist
  rightly
  righto
  rightward
  rightwards
rigid
rigidity
rigmarole
rigor (= rigidity
  → rigger, rigour)
rigorous
rigorously
rigour (= harshness
  → rigger, rigor)
rile
  riles
  riled
  riling
rim
Rimbaud, Arthur
rime (= frost

  → rhyme)
rimmed
rind
ring
  rings
  rang
  rung
  ringing
ringdove
ringed
ringer
ringleader
ringlet
ringmaster
ringside
ringworm
rink
rinse
  rinses
  rinsed
  rinsing
Rio de Janeiro
rioja
riot
  riots
  rioted
  rioting
riotous
riotously
rip
  rips
  ripped
  ripping
RIP
ripcord
ripe
ripen
  ripens
  ripened
  ripening
riposte
ripped
ripper
ripping
ripple
  ripples
  rippled
  rippling
ripsnorter
riptide
rise
  rises
  rose (= got up
   → rhos, rows)

risen
rising
riser
risibility
risible
risibly
risk
  risks
  risked
  risking
riskily
riskiness
risky
  riskier
  riskiest
risotto
risqué
rissole
rite (= ceremony
  → right, write)
ritual
ritually
ritzily
ritziness
ritzy
  ritzier
  ritziest
rival
rivalry
river
rivet
riveting
rivetting = riveting
rivulet
Riyadh
roach
road (= street
  → rode)
roadblock
roadhouse
roadie
roadroller
roadrunner
roadster
roadway
roadworthy
roam
  roams
  roamed
  roaming
roan
roar
  roars
  roared

roaring
roast
  roasts
  roasted
  roasting
rob
  robs
  robbed
  robbing
robbery
  robberies
robe
robin
robot
robotic
robs
robust
roc (= legendary bird)
rock (= stone; sway)
  rocks
  rocked
  rocking
rockabilly
rocker
rockery
  rockeries
rocket
  rockets
  rocketed
  rocketing
rockily
rockiness
rock'n'roll
rock'n'roller
rocky
  rockier
  rockiest
rococco = rococo
rococo
rod
rode (= travelled
  upon → road)
rodent
rodeo
  rodeos
roe (= deer; fish eggs
  → rho, row)
roebuck
roentgen
rogue
roguish
roguishly
roil
  roils

roiled
roiling
roister
  roisters
  roistered
  roistering
role or
  rôle (= part)
roll (= bread; turn
  over)
  rolls
  rolled
  rolling
rollbar
roller
rollercoaster
rollicking
rollmop
rollneck
roly-poly
roman (= type)
Roman (= of or from
  Rome)
romance
Romania
romantic
romantically
romanticise
  romanticises
  romanticised
  romanticising
romanticize
  romanticizes
  romanticized
  romanticizing
romp
  romps
  romped
  romping
rompers
röntgen
roo (= baby kangaroo
  → roux, rue)
rood (= found in a
  church → rude, rued)
roof
roofing
roofs
rooftop
rook
rookery
  rookeries
rookie
room

roomate = roommate
roomful
roomily
roominess
roommate
roomy (= spacious
  → rheumy)
  roomier
  roomiest
roost
  roosts
  roosted
  roosting
rooster
root (= part of a plant
  → route)
  roots
  rooted
  rooting
rootle
  rootles
  rootled
  rootling
rootless
rope
  ropes
  roped
  roping
ropey
  ropier
  ropiest
ropily
ropiness
ropy
  ropier
  ropiest
Roquefort
rosary
  rosaries
rose (= flower
  → rhos, rows)
rosé (= wine)
roseate
rosebud
rosehip
rosemary
roseola
rosery
  roseries
rosette
rosewood
rosier
rosiest
rosily

rosin
rosiness
roster
rostrum
  rostra or
  rostrums
rosy
  rosier
  rosiest
rot
  rots
  rotted
  rotting
rotary
rotatable
rotate
  rotates
  rotated
  rotating
rotation
rotational
rotator
rotatory
rote (= way of
  learning → wrote)
rotgut
rotisserie
rotogravure
rotted
rotten
rotter
rotting
Rottweiler
rotund
rotunda
rotundity
rouble
roué
rouge
rough (= not smooth
  → ruff)
roughage
roughen
  roughens
  roughened
  roughening
roughly
roughneck
roughshod
roulade
roulette
round
  rounds
  rounded

rounding
roundabout
rounded
rounder
rounders
roundly
roundup
roundworm
rouse
　rouses
　roused
　rousing
roust
　rousts
　rousted
　rousting
rout
　routs
　routed
　routing
route (= direct
　→ root)
　routes
　routed
　routeing
routemarch
routine
roux (= sauce → roo,
　rue)
rove
　roves
　roved
　roving
rover
row (= propel a boat
　→ rho, roe)
　rows (= propels a
　boat → rhos, rose)
　rowed (= propelled
　a boat → road,
　rode)
　rowing
rowan
rowboat
rowdily
rowdiness
rowdy
　rowdier
　rowdiest
rowlock
royal
royalist

royalty
　royalties
rozzer
RSJ
RSVP
rub
　rubs
　rubbed
　rubbing
rubber
rubbery
rubbing
rubbish
rubble
rubdown
rubella
rubicund
rubric
rubs
ruby
　rubies
ruche
　ruching
ruck
　rucks
　rucked
　rucking
rucksack
ruckus
　ruckuses
ruction
rudder
ruddily
ruddiness
ruddy
　ruddier
　ruddiest
rude
rudely
rudiment
rudimentary
rue (= regret → roo,
　roux)
　rues (= regrets
　→ ruse)
　rued (= regretted
　→ rood, rude)
　ruing
rueful
ruff
ruffian
ruffle

ruffles
ruffled
ruffling
rufous
rug
rugby
rugged
rugger
ruin
　ruins
　ruined
　ruining
ruination
ruing
ruinous
rule
　rules
　ruled
　ruling
ruler
rum
rumble
　rumbles
　rumbled
　rumbling
~~rumbustuous~~ =
　rumbustious
ruminant
ruminate
　ruminates
　ruminated
　ruminating
rummage
rummer
rummest
rummy
rumour
rump
rumple
　rumples
　rumpled
　rumpling
rumpus
　rumpuses
run
　runs
　ran
　run
　running
runabout
runaway
rundown

rune
rung (= rung of a
　ladder → wrung)
runner
running
runny
　runnier
　runniest
runoff
runs
runt
runway
rupee
rupture
rural
ruse (= plan → rues)
rush
　rushes
　rushed
　rushing
rushes
rusk
russet
Russia
Russian
rust
rustic
rusticity
rustier
rustiest
rustily
rustiness
rustle
　rustles
　rustled
　rustling
rustler
rustproof
rusty
　rustier
　rustiest
rut
　ruts
　rutted
　rutting
rutabaga
ruthless
Rwanda
rye (= grass → wry)
~~rythm~~ = rhythm
~~rythmn~~ = rhythm

S

Sabbath
sabbatical
sabin
sable
sabot
sabotage
  sabotages
  sabotaged
  sabotaging
saboteur
sabra
sabre
sac
saccharin
saccharine
sacerdotal
sacerdotalism
sachet (= envelope
  → sashay)
sack
  sacks
  sacked
  sacking
sackbut
sackcloth
~~sacrafice~~ = sacrifice
sacral
sacrament
sacramental
sacramentalism
sacramentality
sacred
~~sacreligious~~ =
  sacrilegious
sacrifice
sacrificial
sacrilege
sacrilegious
sacristan
sacristy
  sacristies
sacroiliac
sacrosanct
sacrum
  sacra
sad

sadden
sadder
saddest
saddle
  saddles
  saddled
  saddling
saddleback
saddlebag
saddlecloth
saddler
saddlery
sadism
sadistic
sadistically
sadomasochism
safari
safe
safeguard
safekeeping
safety
safflower
saffron
~~saftey~~ = safety
~~safty~~ = safety
sag
  sags
  sagged
  sagging
saga
sagacious
sagacity
sage
sagebrush
sagittal
Sagittarius
sago
saguaro
  saguaros
Sahara
sahib
said
sail (= travel by boat
  → sale)
  sails
  sailed

sailing
sailboard
sailboarding
sailboat
sailcloth
sailfish
sailor
sailplane
saint
sainted
Saint-Émilion
sainthood
sake (= for her sake)
saké (= rice wine)
saki
salaam
salacious
salad
salamander
salami
salaried
salary
  salaries
sale (= goods for
  purchase → sail)
saleable
~~salery~~ = salary
salesclerk
salesgirl
saleslady
  salesladies
salesman
  salesmen
salesmanship
saleswoman
  saleswomen
salic
salient
saline
salinity
Salisbury
saliva
salivary
salivate
  salivates
  salivated

salivating
sallow
sally
  sallies
  sallied
  sallying
salmagundi
salmagundy
salmon
salmonella
salmonellosis
salon
saloon
salopettes
salsa
salsify
salt
  salts
  salted
  salting
saltcellar
saltier
saltiest
saltiness
saltpetre
saltwater
saltworks
salty
  saltier
  saltiest
salubrious
salutary
salutation
salutatory
salute
  salutes
  saluted
  saluting
salvable
salvage
  salvages
  salvaged
  salvaging
salvation
salve
  salves

salved
salving
salver
salvo
  salvoes *or*
  salvos
Salzburg
Samaritan
samarium
samba
same
samey
samizdat
Samoan
samosa
samovar
Samoyed
sampan
samphire
sample
  samples
  sampled
  sampling
sampler
samurai
  samurai
sanatorium
  sanatoria *or*
  sanatoriums
sancta
sanctify
  sanctifies
  sanctified
  sanctifying
sanctimonious
sanction
  sanctions
  sanctioned
  sanctioning
sanctitude
sanctity
sanctuary
  sanctuaries
sanctum
  sancta *or*
  sanctums
sand
sandal
sandalwood
sandbank
sandblast
  sandblasts
  sandblasted
  sandblasting

sandbox
sandfly
  sandflies
  sandier
  sandiest
  sandiness
Sandinista
sandman
sandpaper
sandpiper
sandpit
sandshoe
sandstone
sandstorm
sandwich
  sandwiches
~~sandwitch~~ = sandwich
sandworm
sandy
  sandier
  sandiest
sane
sang
sang-froid
sangria
sanguine
sanguineous
sanguinity
sanitarily
sanitariness
sanitary
sanitation
sanitise
  sanitises
  sanitised
  sanitising
sanitize
  sanitizes
  sanitized
  sanitizing
~~sanitorium~~ =
  sanatorium
sanity
sank
sans-culotte
sansevieria
Sanskrit
sans serif
Santa
sap
  saps
  sapped
  sapping
sapient

sapling
~~saphire~~ = sapphire
sapper
Sapphic
sapphire
sapphism
sapping
Sappho
saps
Saracen
Sarajevo
sarcasm
sarcastic
sarcastically
sarcoma
sarcophagus
sardine
Sardinian
sardonic
sardonically
sardonicism
sari
  saris
sarnie
sarong
sarsaparilla
sarsen
sartorial
Sartre, Jean-Paul
sash
sashay (= walk along
  → sachet)
  sashays
  sashayed
  sashaying
sashimi
Saskatchewan (state)
Saskatoon (city)
sassafras
sassily
sassiness
sassy
  sassier
  sassiest
sat
satai
~~satalite~~ = satellite
Satan
satanic
satanically
Satanism
satay
satchel
sate

sates
sated
sating
sateen
~~satelite~~ = satellite
satellite
satiable
satiate
  satiates
  satiated
  satiating
satin
satinet
satinette
satinwood
satire
satirical
satirise
  satirises
  satirised
  satirising
satirist
satirize
  satirizes
  satirized
  satirizing
satisfaction
satisfactory
satisfy
  satisfies
  satisfied
  satisfying
satrap
satsuma
~~sattelite~~ = satellite
saturable
saturant
saturate
  saturates
  saturated
  saturating
saturation
Saturday
Saturn
saturnine
satyr
sauce (= dressing for
  food → source)
saucepan
saucer
saucily
sauciness
saucy
  saucier

sauciest
Saudi Arabia
sauerbraten
sauerkraut
sauna
saunter
  saunters
  sauntered
  sauntering
saurian
saurischian
sauropod
sauropodous
sausage
sauté
  sautés
  sautéed
  sautéeing or
  sautéing
Sauternes
savage
savagery
savanna
savannah
savant
save
  saves
  saved
  saving
saveloy
saver (= person who
  saves → savour)
saviour (= rescuer)
Saviour (= Jesus
  Christ)
savoir-faire
savour (= enjoy
  → saver)
  savours
  savoured
  savouring
savoury
savoy
savvy
  savvier
  savviest
saw (= cut → soar,
  sore)
  saws
  sawed
  sawn
  sawing
sawbill
sawdust

sawfly
sawhorse
sawmill
sawtooth
sawyer
sax
saxifrage
Saxon
saxophone
saxophonist
say
  says
  said
  saying
scab
  scabs
  scabbed
  scabbing
scabbard
scabbily
scabbiness
scabby
  scabbier
  scabbiest
scabies
scabious
scabrous
scad
  scad or
  scads
scaffold
scaffolding
scalable
scalar
scald
  scalds
  scalded
  scalding
scale
  scales
  scaled
  scaling
scalene
scalier
scaliest
scaliness
scallawag
scallion
scallop
scallywag
scaloppine
  scaloppini
scalp
  scalps

scalped
  scalping
scalpel
scaly
  scalier
  scaliest
scam
scamp
scamper
  scampers
  scampered
  scampering
scampi
scan
  scans
  scanned
  scanning
scandal
scandalise
  scandalises
  scandalised
  scandalising
scandalize
  scandalizes
  scandalized
  scandalizing
scandalmonger
Scandinavian
scandium
scanned
scanner
scanning
scans
scansion
scant
scantily
scantiness
scantling
  scantlings
scanty
  scantier
  scantiest
scape
scapegoat
scapegrace
scapula
scapular
scar
  scars
  scarred
  scarring
scarab
scarce
scarcity

scare
  scares
  scared
  scaring
scarecrow
scaredy-cat
scaremonger
scarf
  scarfs or
  scarves
scarier
scariest
scarlatina
scarlet
scarp
scarper
  scarpers
  scarpered
  scarpering
scarring
scars
scarves
scary
  scarier
  scariest
scat
  scats
  scatted
  scatting
scathe
scathing
scatological
scatologist
scatology
scatter
  scatters
  scattered
  scattering
scatterbrain
  scattering
scattily
scattiness
scatty
  scattier
  scattiest
scavenge
  scavenges
  scavenged
  scavenging
scavenger
scedule = schedule
sceince = science
sceme = scheme
scenario

scenarios
scene (= view
 → seen)
scenery
scenic
scent (= smell
 → sent)
sceptic
sceptre
schedule
 schedules
 scheduled
 scheduling
schema (= plan
 → schemer)
 schemata
schematic
schematically
schematise
 schematises
 schematised
 schematising
schematize
 schematizes
 schematized
 schematizing
scheme
 schemes
 schemed
 scheming
schemer (= person
 who schemes
 → schema)
scherzando
scherzo
schism
schismatic
schizoid
schizophrenia
schizophrenic
schlep
 schleps
 schlepped
 schlepping
schmaltz
schmalz
schnapps
schnaps
schnauzer
schnitzel
scholar
scholarship
scholastic
scholastically

school
 schools
 schooled
 schooling
schoolboy
schoolgirl
schoolhouse
schoolmarm
schoolmaster
schoolmistress
schoolteacher
schooner
schuss
sciatic
sciatica
science
scientific
scientist
Scientology
sci-fi
scimitar
scintillate
 scintillates
 scintillated
 scintillating
scintillation
scion
scissor
 scissors
 scissored
 scissoring
scissors
sclera
sclerite
scleritic
sclerotic
scoff
 scoffs
 scoffed
 scoffing
scold
 scolds
 scolded
 scolding
scollop
sconce
scone
scoop
 scoops
 scooped
 scooping
scoot
 scoots
 scooted

scooting
scooter
scope
scorbutic
scorch
 scorches
 scorched
 scorching
scorcher
score
 scores
 scored
 scoring
scoreboard
scorecard
scorn
 scorns
 scorned
 scorning
Scorpio
scorpion
Scot
scotch
 scotches
 scotched
 scotching
scot-free
Scottish
scoundrel
scour
 scours
 scoured
 scouring
scourge
Scouse
scout
 scouts
 scouted
 scouting
scoutmaster
scowl
 scowls
 scowled
 scowling
scrabble
 scrabbles
 scrabbled
 scrabbling
scrag
scraggly
scraggy
 scraggier
 scraggiest
scram

scramble
 scrambles
 scrambled
 scrambling
scrambler
scrap
 scraps
 scrapped
 scrapping
scrapbook
scrape
 scrapes
 scraped
 scraping
scrapheap
scrapie
 scrapped
 scrapping
scrappy
 scrappier
 scrappiest
scraps
scratch
 scratches
 scratched
 scratching
scrawl
 scrawls
 scrawled
 scrawling
scrawnily
scrawniness
scrawny
 scrawnier
 scrawniest
scream
 screams
 screamed
 screaming
scree
screech
 screeches
 screeched
 screeching
screed
screen
 screens
 screened
 screening
screenplay
screenwriter
screw
 screws
 screwed

screwing
screwball
screwdriver
screwworm
screwy
  screwier
  screwiest
scribble
  scribbles
  scribbled
  scribbling
scribe
scrimmage
scrimp
  scrimps
  scrimped
  scrimping
scrimshank
scrimshaw
script
scriptural
scripture
scriptwriter
scrivener
scrofula
scrofulous
scroll
  scrolls
  scrolled
  scrolling
scrollwork
scrotum
  scrota or
  scrotums
scrounge
  scrounges
  scrounged
  scrounging
scrub
  scrubs
  scrubbed
  scrubbing
scrubby
  scrubbier
  scrubbiest
scrubbiness
scrubland
scruff
scruffily
scruffiness
scruffy
  scruffier
  scruffiest
scrum

scrummage
scrumptious
scrumpy
scrunch
  scrunches
  scrunched
  scrunching
scruple
scrupulous
scrutable
scrutineer
scrutinise
  scrutinises
  scrutinised
  scrutinising
scrutinize
  scrutinizes
  scrutinized
  scrutinizing
scrutiny
  scrutinies
scry
  scries
  scried
  scrying
scuba
scud
  scuds
  scudded
  scudding
scuff
  scuffs
  scuffed
  scuffing
scuffle
  scuffles
  scuffled
  scuffling
scull
scullery
  sculleries
scullion
sculpt
  sculpts
  sculpted
  sculpting
~~sculpter~~ = sculptor
sculptor
~~sculptur~~ = sculpture
sculpture
scum
scumbag
scurf
scurrility

scurrilous
scurry
  scurries
  scurried
  scurrying
scurvy
scuttle
scuzziness
scuzzy
  scuzzier
  scuzziest
scythe
  scythes
  scythed
  scything
se try sce
sea (= ocean
  → see)
seaboard
seaborne
seacoast
seadog
seafarer
seafaring
seafood
seafront
seagoing
seagull
seal
  seals
  sealed
  sealing
sealant
sealer
sealskin
seam (= join → seem)
seaman
  seamen
seamanship
seaminess
seamstress
  seamstresses
seamy
  seamier
  seamiest
seance or
  séance
seaplane
seaport
seaquake
sear (burn → seer,
  sere)
  sears
  seared

searing
search
  searches
  searched
  searching
searchlight
seascape
seashell
seashore
seasick
seaside
season
  seasons
  seasoned
  seasoning
seasonable
seasonably
seasonal
seat
  seats
  seated
  seating
seaward
seawards
seaweed
seaworthiness
seaworthy
sebaceous
seborrhoea
sebum
sec
secant
secateurs
secede
  secedes
  seceded
  seceding
secession
secessionism
secessionist
secluded
seclusion
seclusive
second
secondarily
secondary
  secondaries
secondly
secondment
~~secondry~~ = secondary
secrecy
secret
secretarial
secretariat

secretary
  secretaries
secrete
  secretes
  secreted
  secreting
~~secretery~~ = secretary
secretin
secretion
secretive
secretor
secretory
sect
sectarian
section
sector
sectorial
secular
securable
secure
  secures
  secured
  securing
security
  securities
sedan
sedate
sedation
sedative
Sedbergh
sedentary
Seder
sedge
sediment
sedimentary
sedimentation
sedition
seditionary
seditious
seduce
  seduces
  seduced
  seducing
seducer
seduction
seductive
sedulity
sedulous
see (= look at → sea)
  sees
  saw (= looked at
    → sore)
  seen (= sighted
    → scene)

seeing
seed (= of a plant
  → cede)
seedbed
seedcake
seedcase
seedily
seediness
seedling
seedy
  seedier
  seediest
seeing
seek (= look for
  → Sikh)
  seeks
  sought (= looked
    for → sort)
  seeking
seem (= appear
  → seam)
  seems
  seemed
  seeming
seen (= sighted
  → scene)
seep
  seeps
  seeped
  seeping
seepage
seer (prophet → sear,
  sere)
seersucker
sees (= looks at
  → seize)
seesaw
seethe
  seethes
  seethed
  seething
segment
segmental
segmentary
segmentation
segregable
segregate
  segregates
  segregated
  segregating
segregation
segregationist
~~seige~~ = siege
seigneur

seismic
seismograph
seismography
seismologic
seismologist
seismology
~~seive~~ = sieve
seize (= grab → sees)
  seizes
  seized
  seizing
seizure
seldom
select
  selects
  selected
  selecting
selection
selective
selectivity
selector
selenite
selenium
self
  selves
selfish
selfless
selfsame
sell
  sells
  sold
  selling
seller
Sellotape℠
sellout
selvage
selvedge
selves
semantic
semantically
semantics
semaphore
semblable
semblance
semen
semester
semi
  semis
semiannual
semiaquatic
semiarid
semiautomatic
semibreve
semicentennial

semicircle
semicircular
semiconductor
semiconscious
semidetached
semidiurnal
semifinal
semifinalist
semifluid
semiliquid
semiliterate
semilunar
seminal
seminar
seminarian
seminary
  seminaries
semiology
semiotic
semiotician
semiotics
semipermeable
semiporcelain
semiprecious
semiprofessional
semiquaver
semis
semiskilled
semisolid
Semite
Semitic
semitone
semitropical
semivocal
semivowel
semolina
sempstress
senate
senator
senatorial
send
  sends
  sent (= dispatched
    → scent)
  sending
Senegal
~~senery~~ = scenery
senile
senility
senior
seniority
senna
señor
  señores or

señors
señora
señorita
sensate
sensation
sensational
sensationalise
　sensationalises
　sensationalised
　sensationalising
sensationalism
sensationalist
sensationalistic
sensationalize
　sensationalizes
　sensationalized
　sensationalizing
sensationally
sense
　senses
　sensed
　sensing
senseless
sensibility
　sensibilities
sensible
sensitise
　sensitises
　sensitised
　sensitising
sensitive
sensitivity
　sensitivities
sensitize
　sensitizes
　sensitized
　sensitizing
sensor
sensorimotor
sensory
sensual
sensualism
sensualist
sensuality
sensuous
sent (= dispatched
　→ scent)
~~sentance~~ = sentence
sentence
　sentences
　sentenced
　sentencing
sententious
sentience

sentient
sentiment
sentimental
sentimentalise
　sentimentalises
　sentimentalised
　sentimentalising
sentimentalism
sentimentality
sentimentalize
　sentimentalizes
　sentimentalized
　sentimentalizing
sentinel
sentry
　sentries
sepal
sepaloid
sepalous
separable
separate
　separates
　separated
　separating
separation
separatist
separator
~~seperate~~ = separate
sepia
sepsis
September
septet
septette
septic
septicaemia
septicemia
septuagenarian
sepulchral
sepulchre
sequel
sequence
sequencer
sequencing
sequential
sequester
　sequesters
　sequestered
　sequestering
sequestrable
sequestrate
　sequestrates
　sequestrated
　sequestrating
sequestration

sequestrator
sequin
sequoia
sera
seraph
Serb
Serbian
Serbo-Croat
Serbo-Croatian
sere (= dried up
　→ sear, seer)
serenade
　serenades
　serenaded
　serenading
serendipity
serene
serenely
serenity
serf
~~sergant~~ = sergeant
serge (= fabric
　→ surge)
sergeant
serial (= TV serial
　→ cereal)
serialise
　serialises
　serialised
　serialising
serialize
　serializes
　serialized
　serializing
series
　series
serif
sermon
serpent
serrate
serrated
serried
serum
sera
servant
serve
　serves
　served
　serving
server
~~servicable~~ =
　serviceable
service
　services

serviced
servicing
serviceable
services
serviette
servile
servility
serving
servitude
servo
　servos
servomechanical
servomechanism
servomotor
sesame
session
set
　sets
set
　setting
setback
setoff
setscrew
sett
settee
setter
setting
settle
　settles
　settled
　settling
settlement
settler
setup
seven
Sevenoaks
seventeen
seventeenth
seventh
seventhly
seventieth
seventy
　seventies
sever
　severs
　severed
　severing
severable
several
severance
severe
severely
severity
~~sevral~~ = several

sew (= stitch → so,
  sow)
  sews
  sewed
  sewn
  sewing
sewage
sewer
sewerage
sex
sexagenarian
sexagesimal
sexangular
sexcentenary
  sexcentenaries
sexed
sexier
sexiest
sexily
sexiness
sexism
sexist
sexless
sextant
sextet
sextette
sexton
sextuple
sextuplet
sexual
sexuality
sexy
  sexier
  sexiest
Seychelles
shabby
  shabbier
  shabbiest
shack
shackle
shade
  shades
  shaded
  shading
shadily
shadiness
shadow
  shadows
  shadowed
  shadowing
shadowy
shady
  shadier
  shadiest

shaft
  shafts
  shafted
  shafting
shag
  shags
  shagged
  shagging
  shaggy
  shaggier
  shaggiest
shah
shake (= shake hands
  → sheik, sheikh)
  shakes
  shook
  shaken
  shaking
  shakedown
  shaken
  shaker
  shakes
Shakespear =
  Shakespeare
Shakespeare, William
Shakespearean
Shakespearian
Shakspeare =
  Shakespeare
shakily
shakiness
shaking
shaky
  shakier
  shakiest
shale
shall
shallot
shallow
shalt
sham
shaman
shamanic
shamanism
shamble
  shambles
  shambled
  shambling
shambolic
shame
  shames
  shamed
  shaming
shamefaced

shameful
shameless
shampoo
shamrock
shandy
  shandies
shank
shan't
shanty
  shanties
shantytown
shape
  shapes
  shaped
  shaping
shapeless
shard
share
  shares
  shared
  sharing
sharecropper
sharefarmer
shareholder
shareware
shark
sharkskin
sharp
sharpen
  sharpens
  sharpened
  sharpening
sharpshooter
shashlick
shashlik
shatter
  shatters
  shattered
  shattering
shatterproof
shave
  shaves
  shaved
  shaven
  shaving
shaver
shawl
she
sheaf
  sheaves
shear (= cut → sheer)
  shears
  sheared
  sheared or

shorn
  shearing
  shearling
  shears
  shearwater
sheath
sheathe
  sheathes
  sheathed
  sheathing
sheaves
shed
  sheds
  shed
  shedding
she'd
sheep
  sheep
  sheepdog
  sheepfold
  sheepish
  sheepskin
sheer (= steep
  → shear)
sheet
Sheffield
sheik (= head of tribe
  → shake)
sheikdom
sheikh (= head of
  tribe → shake)
sheikhdom
Sheila
sheild = shield
shekel
shelf
  shelves
shell
  shells
  shelled
  shelling
she'll
shellac
shellfire
shellfish
shellproof
shelter
  shelters
  sheltered
  sheltering
shelve
  shelves
  shelved
  shelving

sheperd = shepherd
shepherd
shepherdess
sheppard = shepherd
sherbet
sheriff
sherrif = sheriff
Sherpa
  Sherpa *or*
  Sherpas
sherry
  sherries
she's
shiatsu
shibboleth
shied
shiek = sheik
shield
  shields
  shielded
  shielding
shier
shies
shiest
shift
  shifts
  shifted
  shifting
shiftily
shiftiness
shiftless
shiftwork
shifty
  shiftier
  shiftiest
Shiite
shiksa
shillelagh
shilling
shillyshally
  shillyshallies
  shillyshallied
  shillyshallying
shily
shimmer
  shimmers
  shimmered
  shimmering
shin
shinbone
shindig
shine
  shines
  shined *or*

shone
shining
shingle
shingles
shininess
shiny
  shinier
  shiniest
ship
  ships
  shipped
  shipping
shipboard
shipbuilder
shipload
shipmaster
shipmate
shipment
shipowner
shipped
shipper
shipping
ships
shipshape
shipway
shipworm
shipwreck
shipwright
shipyard
shire
shirk
  shirks
  shirked
  shirking
shirr
  shirrs
  shirred
  shirring
shirt
shirtsleeve
shirty
  shirtier
  shirtiest
shit
  shits
  shat *or*
  shitted
  shitting
shiver
  shivers
  shivered
  shivering
shivery
shoal

shock
  shocks
  shocked
  shocking
shocker
shockheaded
shockproof
shod
shoddily
shoddiness
shoddy
  shoddier
  shoddiest
shoe (= footwear
  → shoo)
  shoes
  shod
  shoeing
shoeblack
Shoeburyness
shoehorn
shoelace
shoeshine
shoestring
shoetree
shofar
  shofars *or*
  shofroth
shogun
sholder = shoulder
shone
shoo (= go away!
  → shoe)
  shoos
  shooed
  shooing
shook
shoot (= fire; film
  → chute)
  shoots
  shot
  shooting
shop
  shops
  shopped
  shopping
shopkeeper
shoplifter
shopper
shopsoiled
shoptalk
shopwalker
shopworn
shore (= beach

→ sure)
shoreless
shoreline
shoreward
shoreweed
shorn
short
shortage
shortbread
shortcake
shortcircuit
shortcoming
shorten
  shortens
  shortened
  shortening
shortfall
shorthand
shorthorn
shortly
shorts
shortstop
shot
shotgun
should
shoulder
  shoulders
  shouldered
  shouldering
shouldn't
shout
  shouts
  shouted
  shouting
shove
  shoves
  shoved
  shoving
shovel
  shovels
  shovelled
  shovelling
shovelful
show
  shows
  showed
  shown
  showing
showcase
showdown
shower
  showers
  showered

showering	Shrove Tuesday	sickening	sift
showerproof	shrub	sickle	sifts
showgirl	shrubbery	sickliness	sifted
showground	shrubberies	sickly	sifting
showier	shrug	sicklier	sigh
showiest	shrugs	sickliest	sighs (= breathes a
showily	shrugged	sickroom	sigh → size)
showiness	shrugging	side (= left side	sighed
showing	shrunk	→ sighed)	sighing
showjumping	shrunken	sideband	sight (= seeing
showman	shudder	sideboard	→ cite, site)
showmen	shudders	sideboards	sights
shown	shuddered	sideburns	sighted
showpiece	shuddering	sidecar	sighting
showroom	shuffle	sidekick	sightless
shows	shuffles	sidelight	sightliness
showy	shuffled	sideline	sightly
showier	shuffling	sidelines	sightlier
showiest	shun	sidelined	sightliest
shrank	shuns	sidelining	sightsee
shrapnel	shunned	sidelines	sightsees
shred	shunning	sidelong	sightsaw
shreds	shunt	sidereal	sightseen
shred *or*	shunts	sideroad	sightseeing
shredded	shunted	sideshow	sightseer
shredding	shunting	sideslip	sigma
shrew	shush	sidestep	sign (= emblem
shrewd	shushes	sidestroke	→ sine)
Shrewsbury	shushed	sideswipe	signs
shriek	shushing	sidetrack	signed
shrieks	shut	sidetracks	signing
shrieked	shuts	sidetracked	signal
shrieking	shut	sidetracking	signals
shrift	shutting	sidewalk	signalled
shrike	shutdown	sideways	signalling
shrill	shuteye	sidewinder	signatory
shrimp	shutout	siding	signatories
shrink	shutter	sidle	signature
shrinks	shuttle	sidles	signet (= ring or seal
shrank *or*	shuttlecock	sidled	→ cygnet)
shrunk	shy	sidling	significance
shrunk *or*	shies	Sidney (name)	significant
shrunken	shied	siege	signification
shrinking	shying	siemens	~~significent~~ = significant
shrinkage	si try sci	~~sience~~ = science	signify
shrivel	Siamese	sienna	signifies
shrivels	sibling	sierra	signified
shrivelled	sic (= as written)	Sierra Leone	signifying
shrivelling	six try psych	siesta	signor
Shropshire	sick (= ill)	sieve	signori *or*
shroud	sickbay	sieves	signors
shrouds	sicken	sieved	signora
shrouded	sickens	sieving	signoras *or*
shrouding	sickened	~~sieze~~ = seize	signore

signorina
  signorinas *or*
  signorine
signpost
Sikh (= follower of
  Sikhism → seek)
silage
sild
silence
  silences
  silenced
  silencing
silencer
silent
silhouette
silica
silicon
silicone
silk
silken
silkily
silkiness
silkweed
silkworm
silky
  silkier
  silkiest
sill
silliness
silly
  sillier
  silliest
silo
  silos
silouette = silhouette
silt
silver
silverfish
silverside
silversmith
silverware
silverweed
silvery
simian
similar
similarity
simile
  similes
similer = similar
similitude
simitar
simlar = similar
simmer
  simmers

simmered
simmering
simper
simpers
simpered
simpering
simple
simpleton
simplicity
simplify
  simplifies
  simplified
  simplifying
simplistic
simplistically
simply
simulate
  simulates
  simulated
  simulating
simulation
simulcast
simultaneity
simultaneous
simultanious =
    simultaneous
sin try syn
sin
  sins
  sinned
  sinning
since
sincere
sincerely
sincerity
sincerly = sincerely
sine (= of an angle
  → sign)
sinecure
sinew
sinewy
sinful
sing
  sings
  sang
  sung
  singing
Singapore
singe
  singes
  singed
  singeing
singer
single

singlet
singleton
singly
sings
singsong
singular
singularity
sinister
sink
  sinks
  sank *or*
  sunk
  sunk *or*
  sunken
  sinking
sinkhole
sinks
sinuous
sinus
sinusitis
Sioux
sip
  sips
  sipped
  sipping
siphon
sir
sire
siren
sis
sisal
sissors = scissors
sissy
  sissies
sister
sisterhood
sisterliness
sisterly
sit
  sits
  sat
  sitting
sitar
sitcom
site (= place → cite,
  sight)
  sites
  sited
  siting
situate
  situates
  situated
  situating
situation

six
sixfold
sixpence
sixteen
sixteenth
sixth
sixthly
sixtieth
sixty
  sixties
sizable
size (= measure
  → sighs)
  sizes
  sized
  sizing
sizeable
sizzle
  sizzles
  sizzled
  sizzling
ska
skate
  skates
  skated
  skating
skateboard
skater
skedaddle
skein
skeleton
sketch
  sketches
  sketched
  sketching
sketchbook
sketchily
sketchiness
sketchy
  sketchier
  sketchiest
skew
skewbald
skewer
skewwhiff
ski
  skis
  skied
  skiing
skid
  skids
  skidded
  skidding
skidlid

skidpan
skidproof
skied
skier
skies
skiff
skiffle
skiing
skilful
skilfull = skilful
skill
skilled
skillet
skim
  skims
  skimmed
  skimming
skimp
  skimps
  skimped
  skimping
skimpily
skimpiness
skimpy
  skimpier
  skimpiest
skims
skin
  skins
  skinned
  skinning
skinflint
skinful
sking = skiing
skinhead
skinny
  skinnier
  skinniest
skint
skintight
skip
  skips
  skipped
  skiping
skipjack
skiplane
skipper
skirmish
skirt
  skirts
  skirted
  skirting
skis
skit

skittle
skive
  skives
  skived
  skiving
skiver
skivvy
  skivvies
skua
skulduggery
skulk
  skulks
  skulked
  skulking
skull
skullcap
skunk
sky
  skies
skydive
  skydives
  skydived
  skydiving
skydiver
skydiving
skyjack
skylark
skylight
skyline
skyrocket
skysail
skyscape
skyscraper
skyward
skywards
skywriting
slab
slack
slacken
  slackens
  slackened
  slackening
slacks
slag
  slags
  slagged
  slagging
slain
slalom
slam
  slams
  slammed
  slamming
slammer

slander
  slanders
  slandered
  slandering
slang
slant
  slants
  slanted
  slanting
slantwise
slap
  slaps
  slapped
  slapping
slapdash
slaphappy
slapshot
slapstick
slash
  slashes
  slashed
  slashing
slat
slate
slatted
slattern
slaughter
  slaughters
  slaughtered
  slaughtering
slaughterhouse
slave
  slaves
  slaved
  slaving
slaver
slavery
slavish
slay (= kill → sleigh)
  slays
  slew
  slain
slaying
Sleaford
sleaze
sleazy
sledge
  sledges
  sledged
  sledging
sledgehammer
sleek
sleep
  sleeps

slept
sleeping
sleeper
sleepily
sleepiness
sleepwalk
  sleepwalks
  sleepwalked
  sleepwalking
sleepy
  sleepier
  sleepiest
sleepyhead
sleet
sleeve
sleigh (= sledge
  → slay)
sleight (= of hand
  → slight)
slender
slept
sleuth
slew
slewed
slice
  slices
  sliced
  slicing
slicer
slick
slide
  slides
  slid
  sliding
slieght = sleight
slight (= small
  → sleight)
slily
slim
  slims
  slimmed
  slimming
slime
slimily
sliminess
slimmer
slimy
  slimier
  slimiest
sling
  slings
  slung
  slinging
slingback

225

slingshot
slink
  slinks
  slunk
  slinking
slinkily
slinkiness
slinky
  slinkier
  slinkiest
slip
  slips
  slipped
  slipping
slipcase
slipcover
slipknot
slipnoose
slipover
slippage
slipped
slipper
slipperiness
slippery
slippiness
slipping
slippy
  slippier
  slippiest
slipsheet
slipshod
slipstream
slipway
slit
  slits
  slit
  slitting
slither
  slithers
  slithered
  slithering
sliver
slob
slobber
  slobbers
  slobbered
  slobbering
sloe (= berry → slow)
slog
  slogs
  slogged
  slogging
slogan
sloop

slop
  slops
  slopped
  slopping
slope
  slopes
  sloped
  sloping
sloppily
sloppiness
sloppy
  sloppier
  sloppiest
slosh
  sloshes
  sloshed
  sloshing
slot
  slots
  slotted
  slotting
sloth
slothful
slouch
  slouches
  slouched
  slouching
slough
  sloughs
  sloughed
  sloughing
Slovak
Slovakia
Slovenia
slovenly
slow (= reduce speed
  → sloe)
  slows
  slowed
  slowing
slowcoach
slowpoke
slowworm
sludge
slug
sluggish
sluice
  sluices
  sluiced
  sluicing
sluicegate
sluiceway
slum
  slums

slummed
  slumming
slumber
  slumbers
  slumbered
  slumbering
slump
  slumps
  slumped
  slumping
slung
slunk
slur
  slurs
  slurred
  slurring
slurp
  slurps
  slurped
  slurping
slurry
slush
slushiness
slushy
  slushier
  slushiest
slut
sly
  slyer
  slyest
smack
  smacks
  smacked
  smacking
smacker
  smacking
small
smallholding
smallpox
smarmily
smarminess
smarmy
  smarmier
  smarmiest
smart
  smarts
  smarted
  smarting
smarty-pants
smash
  smashes
  smashed
  smashing
smashing

smattering
smear
  smears
  smeared
  smearing
smell
  smells
  smelled or
  smelt
  smelling
smelliness
smelly
  smellier
  smelliest
smelt
  smelts
  smelted
  smelting
smelter
smile
  smiles
  smiled
  smiling
smiler
smirk
  smirks
  smirked
  smirking
smithereens
smithy
  smithies
smitten
smock
  smocking
smog
smoke
  smokes
  smoked
  smoking
smokehouse
smokeless
smoker
smokestack
smokily
smokiness
smoky
  smokier
  smokiest
smooth
  smooths
  smoothed
  smoothing
smoothly
smoothy

smoothies
smorgasbord
smother
smothers
smothered
smothering
smoulder
smoulders
smouldered
smouldering
smudge
smudges
smudged
smudging
smug
smugger
smuggest
smuggle
smuggles
smuggled
smuggling
smuggler
smut
snack
snaffle
snag
snags
snagged
snagging
snail
snake
snakes
snaked
snaking
snakebite
snakeskin
snakily
snakiness
snaky
snakier
snakiest
snap
snaps
snapped
snapping
snapdragon
snappy
snappier
snappiest
snapshot
snare
snares
snared
snaring

snarl
snarls
snarled
snarling
snatch
snatches
snatched
snatching
snazzily
snazziness
snazzy
snazzier
snazziest
sneak
sneaks
sneaked
sneaking
sneakily
sneakiness
sneakers
sneer
sneers
sneered
sneering
sneeze
sneezes
sneezed
sneezing
snide
sniff
sniffs
sniffed
sniffing
sniffle
sniffles
snifter
snigger
sniggers
sniggered
sniggering
snip
snips
snipped
snipping
snipe
snipes
sniped
sniping
sniper
snippet
snivel
snivels
snivelled
snivelling

snob
snog
snogs
snogged
snogging
snook
snooker
snoop
snoops
snooped
snooping
snooper
snooty
snootier
snootiest
snooze
snoozes
snoozed
snoozing
snore
snores
snored
snoring
snorkel
snort
snorts
snorted
snorting
snot
snotty
snout
snow
snows
snowed
snowing
snowball
snowberry
snowberries
snowcap
Snowdon
snowdrift
snowdrop
snowfall
snowfield
snowflake
snowman
snowmen
snowmobile
snowplough
snowshoe
snowstorm
snowy
snowier
snowiest

snub
snubs
snubbed
snubbing
snuff
snuffs
snuffed
snuffing
snuffbox
snuffle
snug
snugger
snuggest
snuggle
snuggles
snuggled
snuggling
so (= very much
→ sew, sow)
soak
soaks
soaked
soaking
soap
soapbark
soapberry
soapberries
soapbox
soapily
soapiness
soapstone
soapsuds
soapy
soapier
soapiest
soar (= fly → saw,
sore)
soars
soared
soaring
sob
sobs
sobbed
sobbing
sober
sobriety
sobriquet
soccer
~~soceity~~ = society
sociable
social
socialisation
socialise
socialises

socialised
socialising
socialism
socialist
socialite
socialization
socialize
  socializes
  socialized
  socializing
societal
society
  societies
sociobiology
socioeconomic
sociolinguistics
sociological
sociology
sociometric
sociometry
sociopolitical
sock
socket
sod
soda
sodden
sodium
sodomy
sofa
soft
softball
soften
  softens
  softened
  softening
softener
softhearted
softie
softness
software
softwood
softy
  softies
soggily
sogginess
soggy
  soggier
  soggiest
soigné
soil
  soils
  soiled
  soiling
soirée

sojourn
solace
solar
sold
solder
  solders
  soldered
  soldering
soldier
sole (= only → soul)
solecism
solely
~~solemly~~ = solemnly
solemn
solicit
  solicits
  solicited
  soliciting
solicitor
solicitous
solicitude
solid
solidarity
solidify
  solidifies
  solidified
  solidifying
solidus
  solidi
soliloquise
  soliloquises
  soliloquised
  soliloquising
  soliloquist
soliloquize
  soliloquizes
  soliloquized
  soliloquizing
soliloquy
  soliloquies
solitaire
solitarily
solitariness
solitary
solitude
solo
  solos
soloist
solstice
solubility
  solubilities
soluble
solution
solve

solves
solved
solving
solvency
solvent
Somalia
sombre
sombrero
some (= a few → sum)
somebody
someday
somehow
someone
somersault
Somerset
something
sometime
sometimes
somewhat
somewhere
somnambulist
somnolent
son (= child → sun)
sonar
sonata
song
songster
songwriter
sonic
sonics
sonnet
sonny (= boy
  → sunny)
  sonnies
sonorous
soon
soot
soothe
  soothes
  soothed
  soothing
soothsayer
sootily
sootiness
sooty
  sootier
  sootiest
sop
~~sophamore~~ =
  sophomore
sophisticated
sophistication
soporific
soppily

soppiness
sopping
soppy
  soppier
  soppiest
soprano
sorbet
sorcerer
sorcery
sordid
sore (= hurting
  → saw, soar)
sorghum
sorrel
sorrow
sorry
sort (= divide
  → sought)
  sorts
  sorted
  sorting
sortie
sosh try soci
sot
sou
soubriquet
~~souce~~ = source
soufflé
souffléed
sough
sought (= looked for
  → sort)
souk
soul (= spirit → sole)
soulful
soulless
sound
  sounds
  sounded
  sounding
soundboard
soundbox
soundings
soundless
soundproof
soundtrack
soup
soupçon
sour
  sours
  soured
  souring
source (= origin
  → sauce)

sourdough
sourpuss
sourwood
sousaphone
souse
　souses
　soused
　sousing
south
South Africa
Southampton
southeast
southeasterly
southerly
southern
southernly
southward
southwards
southwest
southwesterly
souvenir
sou'wester
sovereign
sovereignty
　sovereignties
sovereign = sovereign
Soviet
sow (= plant seeds
　→ sew, so)
　sows
　sowed
　sowed or
　sown
　sowing
Soweto
sozzled
spa
space
　spaces
　spaced
　spacing
spacecraft
spacelab
spaceless
spaceman
　spacemen
spaceship
spacesuit
spacewalk
spacial
spacious
spade
spadework
spagetti = spaghetti

spaghetti
Spain
span
　spans
　spanned
　spanning
spangle
Spaniard
spaniel
Spanish
spank
　spanked
　spanks
　spanking
spanned
spanner
spanning
spar
　spars
　sparred
　sparring
spare
　spares
　spared
　sparing
sparerib
spark
　sparks
　sparked
　sparking
sparkle
　sparkles
　sparkled
　sparkling
sparkler
sparrow
sparrowgrass
sparrowhawk
sparse
spasm
spasmodic
spastic
spat
spate
spatial
spatter
　spatters
　spattered
　spattering
spatula
spawn
　spawns
　spawned
　spawning

spay
　spays
　spayed
　spaying
speach = speech
speak
　speaks
　spoke
　spoken
　speaking
speakeasy
　speakeasies
speaker
spear
　spears
　speared
　spearing
spearfish
spearhead
spearmint
special
specialise
　specialises
　specialised
　specialising
specialism
specialist
speciality
　specialities
specialize
　specializes
　specialized
　specializing
speciall = special
specialty
speciel = special
species
　species
specific
specifically
specification
specificly = specifically
specify
　specifies
　specified
　specifying
speciman = specimen
specimen
specious
speck
speckle
specs
spectacle
spectacles

spectacular
spectacularly
spectate
　spectates
　spectated
　spectating
spectator
spectre
spectrum
　spectra
speculate
　speculates
　speculated
　speculating
speculation
speculative
speculator
speculum
　specula or
　speculums
speech
speechify
　speechifies
　speechified
　speechifying
speed
　speeds
　sped or
　speeded
　speeding
speedboat
speedily
speediness
speedo
　speedos
speedometer
speedway
speedwell
speedy
　speedier
　speediest
spell
　spells
　spelled or
　spelt
　spelling
spellbind
　spellbinds
　spellbound
　spellbinding
spellbound
spelled
speller
spells

spelt
spend
  spends
  spent
  spending
spendthrift
Spenserian
sperm
spermaceti
spermatozoon
  spermatozoa
spesh try speci
spew
  spews
  spewed
  spewing
sphagnum
sphere
spherical
spheroid
sphincter
sphingosine
sphinx
  sphinges or
  sphinxes
spic
spice
  spices
  spiced
  spicing
spicily
spiciness
spick-and-span
spicy
  spicier
  spiciest
spider
spied
spiel
spies
spigot
spike
  spikes
  spiked
  spiking
spikily
spikiness
spiky
  spikier
  spikiest
spill
  spills
  spilled or
  spilt

spilling
spillage
spin
  spins
  spun
  spinning
spinach
spinal
spindle
spindly
  spindlier
  spindliest
spindrift
spine
spineless
spininess
spinney
spinster
spiny
  spinier
  spiniest
spiral
spire
spirit
spirited
spiritless
spiritous
spiritual
spiritualism
spirituality
spit
  spits
  spat or
  spit
  spitting
spite
spiteful
spittle
spittoon
spiv
splash
  splashes
  splashed
  splashing
splashback
splashboard
splashdown
splashily
splashiness
splashy
  splashier
  splashiest
splat
splatter

splatters
splattered
splattering
splay
spleen
splendid
splendour
splice
  splices
  spliced
  splicing
splint
splinter
  splinters
  splintered
  splintering
split
  splits
  split
  splitting
splodge
splurge
  splurges
  splurged
  splurging
splutter
  splutters
  spluttered
  spluttering
spoil
  spoils
  spoiled or
  spoilt
  spoiling
spoilage
spoiler
spoils
spoilsport
spoilt
spoke
spoken
sponge
  sponges
  sponged
  sponging
sponger
spongily
sponginess
spongy
  spongier
  spongiest
sponser = sponsor
sponsor
spontaneity

spontaneous
spontaneously
spontanious =
  spontaneous
spoof
spook
spookily
spookiness
spooky
  spookier
  spookiest
spool
  spools
  spooled
  spooling
spoon
  spoons
  spooned
  spooning
spoonbill
spoonerism
spoonful
spoor (= tracks
  → spore)
sporadic
sporadically
sporangium
  sporangia
spore (= cell
  → spoor)
sporran
sport
  sports
  sported
  sporting
sportily
sportiness
sportsman
  sportsmen
sportsperson
  sportspeople
sportswear
sportswoman
  sportswomen
sporty
  sportier
  sportiest
spot
  spots
  spotted
  spotting
spotless
spotlight
spotter

spottily
spottiness
spotty
　spottier
　spottiness
spouse
spout
　spouts
　spouted
　spouting
sprain
　sprains
　sprained
　spraining
sprang
sprat
sprawl
　sprawls
　sprawled
　sprawling
spray
　sprays
　sprayed
　spraying
spread
　spreads
　spread
　spreading
spreadsheet
spree
sprig
sprightliness
sprightly
　sprightlier
　sprightliest
spring
　springs
　sprang *or*
　sprung
　springing
springboard
springbok
springily
springiness
springtime
springy
　springier
　springiest
sprinkle
　sprinkles
　sprinkled
　sprinkling
sprinkler
sprint

sprints
sprinted
sprinting
sprite
spritzer
sprocket
sprout
　sprouts
　sprouted
　sprouting
spruce
sprung
spry
spud
spume
spun
spunk
spur
　spurs
　spurred
　spurring
spurious
spurn
　spurns
　spurned
　spurning
spurs
spurt
　spurts
　spurted
　spurting
Sputnik
sputum
spy
　spies
　spied
　spying
spyglass
spyhole
squab
　squab *or*
　squabs
squabble
　squabbles
　squabbled
　squabbling
squad
squadron
squalid
squall
squalor
squander
　squanders
　squandered

squandering
square
　squares
　squared
　squaring
squarely
squash
　squashes
　squashed
　squashing
squashily
squashiness
squashy
　squashier
　squashiest
squat
　squats
　squatted
　squatting
squatter
squaw
squawk
　squawks
　squawked
　squawking
squeak
　squeaks
　squeaked
　squeaking
squeal
　squeals
　squealed
　squealing
squeamish
squeegee
squeeze
　squeezes
　squeezed
　squeezing
squelch
　squelches
　squelched
　squelching
squib
squid
　squid *or*
　squids
squiggle
squint
　squints
　squinted
　squinting
squire
squirm

squirms
squirmed
squirming
squirrel
squirt
　squirts
　squirted
　squirting
squish
　squishes
　squished
　squishing
squo *try* squa
Sri Lanka
St Neots
St Petersburg
stab
　stabs
　stabbed
　stabbing
~~stabalize~~ = stabilize
stabilise
　stabilises
　stabilised
　stabilising
stabiliser
stability
stabilize
　stabilizes
　stabilized
　stabilizing
stabilizer
stable
stabling
~~stablize~~ = stabilize
stabs
staccato
stack
　stacks
　stacked
　stacking
stadium
　stadia *or*
　stadiums
staff
　staffs *or*
　staves
stag
stage
　stages
　staged
　staging
stagecoach
stagecraft

stagehand
stager
stagflation
stagger
　staggers
　staggered
　staggering
stagnant
stagnate
　stagnates
　stagnated
　stagnating
stagnation
staid (= sedate
　→ stayed)
stain
　stains
　stained
　staining
Staines (town)
stainless
stair (= steps
　→ stare)
staircase
stairway
stairwell
stake (= bet; fence;
　rod → steak)
　stakes
　staked
　staking
stakeout
stalactite
stalagmite
stale
stalemate
Stalinism
stalk (= part of
　a plant
　→ stork)
　stalks
　stalked
　stalking
stall
　stalls
　stalled
　stalling
stallholder
stallion
stalwart
stamen
　stamens or
　stamina
stamina

stammer
stammers
stammered
stammering
stamp
　stamps
　stamped
　stamping
stampede
stance
stanch
stanches
stanched
stanching
stand
　stands
　stood
　standing
standard
standardise
standardises
standardised
standardising
standardize
standardizes
standardized
standardizing
standing
standoffish
standoffishly
standpipe
standpoint
stands
standstill
stank
Stanley
stanza
stapes
　stapedes or
　stapes
staphylococcus
　staphylococci
staple
　staples
　stapled
　stapling
stapler
star
　stars
　starred
　starring
starboard
starch
　starches

starched
starching
starchily
starchiness
starchy
　starchier
　starchiest
stardom
stardust
stare (= look hard at
　→ stair)
　stares
　stared
　staring
starfish
starflower
stargaze
　stargazes
　stargazed
　stargazing
stargazer
stark
starkers
starlet
starlight
starling
starlit
starred
starrily
starriness
starring
starry
　starrier
　starriest
stars
start
　starts
　started
　starting
starter
startle
　startles
　startled
　startling
starvation
starve
　starves
　starved
　starving
stash
stasis
state
　states
　stated

stating
statecraft
stateless
stateliness
stately
　statelier
　stateliest
statement
stateroom
stateside
static
station
stationary (= not
　moving)
stationer
stationery (= writing
　paper, etc.)
statistic
statistical
statistician
statistics
statue
statuesque
statuette
stature
status
statute
statutory
staunch
　staunches
　staunched
　staunching
stave
　staves
　staved or
　stove
　staving
staves
stay
　stays
　stayed (= remained
　→ staid)
　staying
stayer
stead
steadfast
steadily
steadiness
steady
　steadies
　steadied
　steadying
　steadier
　steadiest

steak (= meat
  → stake)
steakhouse
steal (rob → steel)
  steals
  stole
  stolen
  stealing
stealth
stealthily
stealthiness
stealthy
  stealthier
  stealthiest
steam
  steams
  steamed
  steaming
steamboat
steamer
steamily
steaminess
steamroller
steamship
steamy
  steamier
  steamiest
steed
steel (= metal
  → steal)
  steels
  steeled
  steeling
steeliness
steelworks
steelyard
steep
  steeps
  steeped
  steeping
steeple
steeplechase
steeplejack
steer
  steers
  steered
  steering
steerage
stegosaur
stellar
stellate
stem
  stems
  stemmed

stemming
stench
stencil
stenography
stentorian
step (= footstep
  → steppe)
  steps
  stepped
  stepping
stepbrother
stepchild
  stepchildren
stepdaughter
stepfather
Stephen
Stephenson, George
stepladder
stepmother
steppe (= plain
  → step)
stepsister
stepson
stereo
  stereos
stereophonic
stereophonically
stereoscopic
stereoscopically
stereotype
sterile
sterilisation
sterilise
  sterilises
  sterilised
  sterilising
sterility
sterilization
sterilize
  sterilizes
  sterilized
  sterilizing
sterling
stern
sternum
  sterna or
  sternums
steroid
stertorous
stethoscope
stetson
stevedore
Steven
Stevenson, R.L.

stew
  stews
  stewed
  stewing
steward
stewardess
stick
  sticks
  stuck
  sticking
sticker
stickily
stickiness
stickleback
stickler
sticky
  stickier
  stickiest
sties
stiff
stiffen
  stiffens
  stiffened
  stiffening
stifle
  stifles
  stifled
  stifling
stigma
  stigmas or
  stigmata
stigmatise
  stigmatises
  stigmatised
  stigmatising
stigmatize
  stigmatizes
  stigmatized
  stigmatizing
stile (= steps
  → style)
stiletto
  stilettos
still
  stills
  stilled
  stilling
stillbirth
stillborn
stilleto = stiletto
stilletto = stiletto
stilly
stilt
stilted

Stilton
stimulant
stimulate
  stimulates
  stimulated
  stimulating
stimulus
  stimuli
sting
  stings
  stung
  stinging
stingily
stinginess
stingray
stingy
  stingier
  stingiest
stink
  stinks
  stank or
  stunk
  stinking
stinkweed
stint
stipend
stipendiary
stipulate
  stipulates
  stipulated
  stipulating
stir
  stirs
  stirred
  stirring
Stirling
stirrer
stirrup
stitch
  stitches
  stitched
  stitching
stoat
stock
  stocks
  stocked
  stocking
stockade
stockbreeder
stockbroker
stockfish
stockholder
Stockholm
stockier

stockiest
stockily
stockiness
stocking
stockist
stockjobber
stockpile
  stockpiles
  stockpiled
  stockpiling
stockpot
stockroom
stocks
stocktaking
stocky
  stockier
  stockiest
stockyard
stodge
stodginess
stodgy
  stodgier
  stodgiest
stoic
stoke
  stokes
  stoked
  stoking
stoker
stole
stolen
stolid
stoma
  stomata
stomach
  stomachs
  stomached
  stomaching
stomachache
stomp
  stomps
  stomped
  stomping
stone
  stones
  stoned
  stoning
stonechat
stonecrop
stonecutter
stonefish
stonefly
  stoneflies
stoneground

stonemason
stonewall
  stonewalls
  stonewalled
  stonewalling
stoneware
stonewashed
stonework
stonily
stoniness
stony
  stonier
  stoniest
stood
stooge
stook
stool
stoop
  stoops
  stooped
  stooping
stop
  stops
  stopped
  stopping
stopcock
~~stoped~~ = stopped
stopgap
stoplight
stopoff
stopover
stoppage
stopper
stopping
stops
stopwatch
storage
store
  stores
  stored
  storing
storehouse
storekeeper
storeroom
storey (= floor of a
  building → story)
storeyed
stork (= bird → stalk)
storm
  storms
  stormed
  storming
  stormbound
  stormproof

stormily
storminess
stormy
  stormier
  stormiest
story (= tale
  → storey)
  stories
storyboard
storybook
storyteller
stout
stouthearted
stove
stovepipe
stow
  stows
  stowed
  stowing
stowage
stowaway
straddle
  straddles
  straddled
  straddling
strafe
  strafes
  strafed
  strafing
straggle
  straggles
  straggled
  straggling
straight (= not
  crooked → strait)
straightaway
straighten
  straightens
  straightened
  straightening
straightforward
straightjacket
strain
  strains
  strained
  straining
strainer
strait (= sea
  → straight)
straitjacket
strand
strange
stranger
strangle

strangles
strangled
strangling
stranglehold
strap
  straps
  strapped
  strapping
straphanger
strapless
Strasbourg
strata
stratagem
strategic
strategically
strategist
strategy
  strategies
stratocumulus
  stratocumuli
stratosphere
stratum
  strata *or*
  stratums
straw
strawberry
  strawberries
strawflower
stray
  strays
  strayed
  straying
streak
  streaks
  streaked
  streaking
streakily
streakiness
streaky
  streakier
  streakiest
stream
  streams
  streamed
  streaming
streamer
streamlined
~~strech~~ = stretch
street
streetcar
streetlight
streetwalker
streetwise
strength

strengthen
  strengthens
  strengthened
  strengthening
strenth = strength
strenuous
strenuously
streptococcus
  streptococci
stress
  stresses
  stressed
  stressing
stressful
stressfully
stretch
  stretches
  stretched
  stretching
stretcher
stretchiness
stretchmarks
stretchy
  stretchier
  stretchiest
strewn
stricken
strickly = strictly
stricly = strictly
strict
stricture
stride
  strides
  strode
  stridden
  striding
strident
strife
strike
  strikes
  struck
  striking
striker
striking
string
  strings
  strung
  stringing
stringed
stringent
stringiness
stringy
  stringier
  stringiest

strip
  strips
  stripped
  stripping
stripe
striped
stripling
stripper
striptease
stripy
  stripier
  stripiest
strive
  strives
  strove
  striven
  striving
strobe
strode
stroganoff
stroke
  strokes
  stroked
  stroking
stroll
  strolls
  strolled
  strolling
strong
strongbox
stronghold
strongman
  strongmen
strongpoint
strongroom
strontium
stroppy
  stroppier
  stroppiest
strove
struck
structural
structure
structured
strudel
struggle
  struggles
  struggled
  struggling
strum
  strums
  strummed
  strumming
strumpet

strung
strut
  struts
  strutted
  strutting
strychnine
stub
  stubs
  stubbed
  stubbing
stubble
stubborn
stucco
stuck
stud
studded
student
studio
  studios
studious
study
  studies
  studied
  studying
stuff
  stuffs
  stuffed
  stuffing
stuffily
stuffiness
stuffy
  stuffier
  stuffiest
stultify
  stultifies
  stultified
  stultifying
stumble
  stumbles
  stumbled
  stumbling
stump
stun
  stuns
  stunned
  stunning
stung
stunk
stunt
stupefaction
stupefy
  stupefies
  stupefied
  stupefying

stupendous
stupid
stupidity
stupify = stupefy
stupor
sturdily
sturdiness
sturdy
  sturdier
  sturdiest
sturgeon
stutter
  stutters
  stuttered
  stuttering
sty (= shed for pigs)
  sties
stye (= infection)
style (= fashion
  → stile)
  styles
  styled
  styling
stylish
stylist
stylus
  styli *or*
  styluses
styrene
suave
sub
  subs
  subbed
  subbing
subalpine
subaltern
subantarctic
subaqua
subaquatic
subaqueous
subarctic
subatomic
subbed
subbing
subconscious
subconsciously
subcontinent
subcontinental
subcontract
  subcontracts
  subcontracted
  subcontracting
subcontractor
subcortex

subcortical
subculture
subcutaneous
subdivide
  subdivides
  subdivided
  subdividing
subdivision
subdue
  subdues
  subdued
  subduing
subedit
  subedits
  subedited
  subediting
subeditor
subgroup
subheading
subhuman
subject
  subjects
  subjected
  subjecting
subjection
subjective
subjugate
  subjugates
  subjugated
  subjugating
subjunctive
sublet
  sublets
  sublet
  subletting
sublieutenant
sublimate
  sublimates
  sublimated
  sublimating
sublimation
sublime
subliminal
subliminally
submarine
submariner
submerge
  submerges
  submerged
  submerging
submersible
submersion
submission
submissive

submit
submits
submitted
submitting
subnormal
subnuclear
suboceanic
subordinate
subordinates
subordinated
subordinating
subordination
subplot
subpoena
subpoenas
subpoened
subpoenaing
subpopulation
subregion
subscribe
subscribes
subscribed
subscribing
subscriber
subscription
subsequent
subservience
subservient
subset
subside
subsides
subsided
subsiding
subsidence
subsidiary
subsidiaries
subsidise
subsidises
subsidising
subsidised
subsidize
subsidizes
subsidized
subsidizing
subsidy
subsidies
subsist
subsists
subsisted
subsisting
subsistence
subsoil
subsolar
subsonic

substance
substancial =
  substantial
substandard
substantial
substantially
substitute
  substitutes
  substituted
  substituting
substitution
substrata
subsume
  subsumes
  subsumed
  subsuming
subtenant
subterfuge
subterranean
subtitle
subtle
subtlety
subtotal
subtract
  subtracts
  subtracted
  subtracting
subtracter
subtraction
subtropical
suburb
suburban
suburbia
subversion
subversive
subway
subzero
succede = succeed
succeed
  succeeds
  succeeded
  succeeding
succesful = successful
succesive = successive
suceed = succeed
sucessful = successful
sucessive = successive
success
successful
successfully
successfulness
succession
successive
successively

successor
succinct
Succoth
succour (= help
  → sucker)
succulent
succumb
  succumbs
  succumbed
  succumbing
such
suck
  sucks
  sucked
  sucking
sucker (= something
  that sucks
  → succour)
suckle
  suckles
  suckled
  suckling
sucrose
suction
Sudan
sudden
suds
sue
  sues
  sued
  suing
suede
suet
suffer
  suffers
  suffered
  suffering
sufferable
sufferage = suffrage
sufferance
suffice
sufficiant = sufficient
sufficiency
sufficient
suffix
suffocate
  suffocates
  suffocated
  suffocating
Suffolk
suffrage
suffragette
suffragist
suffused

suficient = sufficient
sugar
sugary
suggest
  suggests
  suggested
  suggesting
suggestible
suggestion
suggestive
suggestively
suicidal
suicide
suing
suit
  suits
  suited
  suiting
suitable
suitcase
suite (= set of
  furniture → sweet)
suitor
sukiyaki
Sukkoth
sulk
  sulks
  sulked
  sulking
sulkily
sulkiness
sulky
  sulkier
  sulkiest
sullen
sully
  sullies
  sullied
  sullying
sulphate
sulphide
sulphite
sulphur
sultan
sultana
sultrily
sultriness
sultry
  sultrier
  sultriest
sum (= add up
  → some)
  sums
  summed

summing
sumary = summary
summarise
  summarises
  summarised
  summarising
summarize
  summarizes
  summarized
  summarizing
summary
  summaries
summarily
summed
summer
summerhouse
summertime
summery
summing
summit
summon
  summons
  summoned
  summoning
summons
  summonses
sumo
sump
sumptious = sumptuous
sumptuous
sun (= planet → son)
sunbathe
  sunbathes
  sunbathed
  sunbathing
sunbeam
sunbird
sunbonnet
sunbow
sunburn
sunburned or
sunburnt
sunburst
sundae (= dessert)
  sundaes
Sunday (= day of the
  week)
sunder
sundew
sundial
sundown
sundowner
sundress
sundry

sundries
sunfast
sunfish
sunflower
sung
sunglass
sunglasses
sunglow
sungrebe
sunhat
sunk
sunken
sunken
sunlight
sunned
sunnily
sunniness
sunning
sunny (= warm
  → sonny)
  sunnier
  sunniest
sunrise
sunroof
suns
sunset
sunshade
sunshine
sunspot
sunstar
sunstone
sunstroke
sunsuit
suntan
suntrap
sunup
sunward
sunwards
sup
  sups
  supped
  supping
super
superannuation
superb
supercede = supersede
supercharge
  supercharges
  supercharged
  supercharging
supercharger
supercilious
supercomputer
superduper

superficial
superficiality
superfluity
superfluous
superglue
supergrass
superhero
  superheros
superhuman
superimpose
  superimposes
  superimposed
  superimposing
superintendant =
  superintendent
superintendent
superior
superiority
superlative
superlatively
superman
  supermen
supermarket
supernatural
supernova
  supernovas or
  supernovae
supernumerary
superordinate
superpower
supersede
  supersedes
  superseded
  superseding
supersonic
superstar
supersticion =
  superstition
superstition
superstitious
superstore
supertanker
supertax
supervise
  supervised
  supervises
  supervising
superviser = supervisor
supervision
supervisor
superwoman
  superwomen
supine
supose = suppose

supped
supper
supping
supplant
　supplants
　supplanted
　supplanting
supple
supplement
supplementary
supplier
suppliment =
　supplement
supply
　supplies
　supplied
　supplying
support
　supports
　supported
　supporting
supporter
supportive
suppose
　supposes
　supposed
　supposing
suppose to = supposed
　to
supposition
suppository
　suppositories
suppress
　suppresses
　suppressed
　suppressing
suppression
supremacy
supreme
supremo
　supremos
supress = suppress
suprise = surprise
sups
surcharge
　surcharges
　surcharged
　surcharging
sure (= certain
　→ shore)
surely
surety
　sureties
surf

surfs
surfed
surfing
surface
　surfaces
　surfaced
　surfacing
surfactant
surfboard
surfeit
surfing
surfit = surfeit
surge (= move
　forward → serge)
surgeon
surgery
　surgeries
surgical
surlily
surliness
surly
　surlier
　surliest
surmise
　surmises
　surmised
　surmising
surmount
　surmounts
　surmounted
　surmounting
surmountable
surname
surpass
　surpasses
　surpassed
　surpassing
surplice
surplus
surprise
　surprises
　surprised
　surprising
surprisedly
surprisingly
surreal
surrealism
surrealist
surrender
　surrenders
　surrendered
　surrendering
surreptitious
surrogacy

surrogate
surround
　surrounds
　surrounded
　surrounding
　surroundings
surveilance =
　surveillance
surveillance
survey
　surveys
　surveyed
　surveying
surveyer = surveyor
surveyor
survivable
survival
survive
　survives
　survived
　surviving
survivor
susceptable =
　susceptible
susceptible
susceptibly
suseptible =
　susceptible
sushi
suspect
　suspects
　suspected
　suspecting
suspence = suspense
suspend
　suspends
　suspended
　suspending
suspender
suspense
suspension
suspicion
suspicious
suspiciously
suss
　susses
　sussed
　sussing
sustain
　sustains
　sustained
　sustaining
sustainable
sustenance

suttee
suture
svelte
swab
　swabs
　swabbed
　swabbing
swaddle
　swaddles
　swaddled
　swaddling
Swaffham
swag
swagger
　swaggers
　swaggered
　swaggering
swallow
　swallows
　swallowed
　swallowing
swam
swami
　swamies or
　swamis
swamp
　swamps
　swamped
　swamping
swan
swank
swanky
　swankier
　swankiest
Swansea
swap
　swaps
　swapped
　swapping
swarm
　swarms
　swarmed
　swarming
swarthily
swarthiness
swarthy
　swarthier
　swarthiest
swashbuckling
swastika
swat
swats
　swatted
　swatting

swatch
swath
  swaths
swathe
  swathes
swatter
sway
  sways
  swayed
  swaying
Swaziland
swear
  swears
  swore
  sworn
  swearing
swearword
sweat
  sweats
  sweated
  sweating
sweatband
sweater
sweatily
sweatiness
sweatshirt
sweatshop
sweaty
  sweatier
  sweatiest
swede
Sweden
Swedish
sweep
  sweeps
  swept
  sweeping
sweepstake
sweet
sweetbread
sweetbriar
sweeten
  sweetens
  sweetened
  sweetening
sweetener
sweetheart
sweetie
sweetmeat
swell
  swells
  swelled
  swollen
  swelling

sweltering
swept
swerve
  swerves
  swerved
  swerving
swift
swig
  swigs
  swigged
  swigging
swill
  swills
  swilled
  swilling
swim
  swims
  swam
  swum
  swimming
  swimmingly
  swimsuit
swindle
  swindles
  swindled
  swindling
swine
  swine *or*
  swines
swineherd
swing
  swings
  swung
  swinging
  swingeing
swipe
  swipes
  swiped
  swiping
swirl
  swirls
  swirled
  swirling
swish
switch
  switches
  switched
  switching
switchblade
Switzerland
swivel
  swivels
  swivelled
  swivelling

swizzle
swollen
swoon
  swoons
  swooned
  swooning
swoop
  swoops
  swooped
  swooping
swoosh
swop
  swops
  swopped
  swopping
sword
swordfish
swore
sworn
swot
swum
swung
sycamore
sycophant
sycophantic
Sydney (city)
s̶y̶l̶a̶b̶u̶s̶ = syllabus
syllable
syllabub
syllabus
  syllabi *or*
  syllabuses
syllogism
sylph
sylvan
symbiosis
symbol
symbolic
symbolise
  symbolises
  symbolised
  symbolising
symbolism
symbolize
  symbolizes
  symbolized
  symbolizing
s̶y̶m̶e̶t̶r̶i̶c̶a̶l̶ =
  symmetrical
symmetric
symmetrical
symmetry
  symmetries
sympathetic

sympathise
  sympathises
  sympathised
  sympathising
sympathize
  sympathizes
  sympathized
  sympathizing
sympathy
  sympathies
symphony
  symphonies
symposium
symptom
synagogue
synapse
syncromesh
synchronise
  synchronises
  synchronised
  synchronising
synchronize
  synchronizes
  synchronized
  synchronizing
syncopate
syncope
s̶y̶n̶c̶r̶o̶n̶o̶u̶s̶ =
  synchronous
syndicate
syndrome
synod
s̶y̶n̶o̶n̶i̶m̶ = synonym
synonym
synonymous
synopsis
  synopses
syntax
synthesizer
synthetic
syphilis
syphon
Syria
Syrian
syringe
syrup
system
systematic
systemic
systole
systolic
Szechuan

T

ta
tab
tabard
Tabasco™
tabby
  tabbies
tabernacle
tabla
tablature
table
  tables
  tabled
  tabling
tableau
  tableaus *or*
  tableaux
tablecloth
tablespoon
tablespoonful
  tablespoonfuls
tablet
tableware
tabloid
taboo
  taboos
tabor
tabour
tabu
  tabus
tabular
tabulate
  tabulates
  tabulated
  tabulating
tabulator
tacheometer
tacheometric
tacheometry
tachogram
tachograph
tachometer
tachometric
tachometry
tachycardia
tachycardiac
tachymeter

tacit
taciturn
tack
  tacks
  tacked
  tacking
tackier
tackiest
tackiness
tackle
  tackles
  tackled
  tackling
tacky
  tackier
  tackiest
taco
  tacos
tact
tactic
tactical
tactician
tactics
tactile
tad
tadpole
tael
taffeta
tag
  tags
  tagged
  tagging
tagliatelle
tahini
Tahiti
taiga
tail (= follow → tale)
  tails
  tailed
  tailing
tailback
tailboard
tailgate
taillight
tailor
tailorbird

tailpiece
tailpipe
tailplane
tails
tailskid
tailspin
tailwind
taint
  taints
  tainted
  tainting
Taipei
Taiwan
Tajikistan
take
  takes
  took
  taken
  taking
takeaway
takeoff
takeout
takeover
taker
takes
taking
talc
  talcs
  talced *or*
  talcked
  talcing *or*
  talcking
tale (= story → tail)
talent
talipes
talisman
talk (= speak → torc,
  torque)
  talks
  talked
  talking
talkative
talkie
tall
tallboy
tallis

tallith
  tallithes *or*
  tallitoth
tallow
tally
  tallies
  tallied
  tallying
tally-ho
Talmud
Talmudist
talon
talus
  tali *or*
  taluses
tam
tamale
tamarind
tamarisk
tambour
tambourine
tame
  tames
  tamed
  taming
Tamil
  Tamil *or*
  Tamils
tam-o'-shanter
tamp
  tamps
  tamped
  tamping
tamper
tampion
tampon
tan
  tans
  tanned
  tanning
tandem
tandoori
tang
tangelo
  tangelos
tangent

tangentally
tangential
tangentially
tangerine
tangible
tangier
tangiest
tangle
  tangles
  tangled
  tangling
tango
  tangos
  tangoes
  tangoed
  tangoing
tangram
tangy
  tangier
  tangiest
tank
tankage
tankard
tanker
tankful
tanned
tanner
tannery
  tanneries
tannic
tannin
tanning
tansy
  tansies
tantalise
  tantalises
  tantalised
  tantalising
tantalize
  tantalizes
  tantalized
  tantalizing
tantalum
tantalus
tantamount
tantara
tantrum
Tanzania
Tao
Taoiseach
Taoism
tap
  taps
  tapped

tapping
tapas
tape
  tapes
  taped
  taping
taper
  tapers
  tapered
  tapering
tapestry
  tapestries
tapeworm
tapioca
tapir
tapped
tappet
tapping
taproom
taproot
taps
tar
  tars
  tarred
  tarring
taradiddle
taramasalata
tarantella
tarantula
  tarantulae *or*
  tarantulas
tardily
tardiness
tardy
  tardier
  tardiest
tare (= weed; weight
  → tear)
target
  targets
  targeted
  targeting
targetted = targeted
targetting = targeting
tariff
tarmac
tarn
tarnish
  tarnished
  tarnished
  tarnishing
taro (= plant)
  taros
tarot (= cards)

tarpaulin
tarpon
  tarpon *or*
  tarpons
tarradiddle
tarragon
tariff = tariff
tarriff = tariff
tarring
tarry
  tarries
  tarried
  tarrying
tars
tarsal
tarsus
  tarsi
tart
tartan
tartar
tartare
Tartarean
tartaric
tartlet
tartrate
tartrazine
task
Tasmania
tassel
taste
  tastes
  tasted
  tasting
tasteful
tasteless
taster
tastily
tastiness
tasty
  tastier
  tastiest
tat
ta-ta
tatami
Tatar
tatoo = tattoo
tatter
tattiness
tatting
tattle
  tattles
  tattled
  tattling
tattoo

tattoos
tattooed
tattooing
tattooer
tattooist
tatty
  tattier
  tattiest
tau
taught (= instructed
  → taut, tort)
taunt
  taunts
  taunted
  taunting
taupe
Taurus
taut (= tense
  → taught, tort)
tauten
  tautens
  tautened
  tautening
tautological
tautologous
tautology
  tautologies
tavern
taverna
taw
tawdrily
tawdriness
tawdry
  tawdrier
  tawdriest
tawniness
tawny
taws
tawse
tax
  taxes
  taxed
  taxing
taxable
taxation
taxi
  taxies *or*
  taxis
  taxied
  taxiing *or*
  taxying
taxicab
taxidermy
taximeter

taxing
taxis
taxiway
taxonomic
taxonomist
taxonomy
taxpayer
taxying
tayberry
  tayberries
TB
Tchaikovsky
TCP℠
tea (= drink → tee)
teabread
teacake
teach
  teaches
  taught
  teaching
teacher
teacup
teacupful
  teacupfuls
teahouse
teak
teakettle
teal
  teal or
  teals
team (= group
  → teem)
  teams
  teamed
  teaming
teamster
teamwork
teapot
tear (= teardrop; rip
  → tare, tier)
  tears
  tore
  torn
  tearing
tearaway
teardrop
tearful
tear-jerker
tearoom
tears
tease
  teases
  teased
  teasing

teasel
teaser
teashop
teaspoon
teaspoonful
  teaspoonfuls
teat
teazel
teazle
tech.
technic
technical
technicality
  technicalities
technician
Technicolor℠
technicolour
technics
technique
technocracy
  technocracies
technocrat
technography
technological
technologist
technology
  technologies
technophobia
technostructure
tecnical = technical
tectonic
tectonics
teddy
  teddies
tedious
tedium
tee (= hit golf ball
  → tea)
  tees
  teed
  teeing
teem (= pour with
  rain → team)
  teems
  teemed
  teeming
teem
teenage
teenager
teens
teensy-weensy
teeny
teenybopper
teeny-weeny

teepee
tees
teeter
  teeters
  teetered
  teetering
teeth
teethe
  teethes
  teethed
  teething
teetotal
teetotalism
teetotaller
teetotally
Teignmouth
telecast
  telecasts
  telecasted
  telecasting
telecommunication
telecommunications
telecommuting
telegenic
telegram
telegrammatic
telegraph
telegrapher
telegraphic
telegraphically
telegraphist
telegraphy
telekinesis
telekinetic
telemark
telemarketing
telemeter
telemetric
telemetry
telencephalic
telencephalon
teleology
telepathic
telepathy
telephone
  telephones
  telephoned
  telephoning
telephonic
telephonist
telephony
teleport
teleprinter
teleprocessing

telesales
telescience
telescope
telescopic
telescopy
telesoftware
telethon
teletypewriter
televangelist
televise
  televises
  televised
  televising
television
televisual
teleworking
telewriter
telex
tell
  tells
  told
  telling
teller
telltale
tellurian
telly
  tellies
temerity
temp
temper
  tempers
  tempered
  tempering
tempera
temperament
temperamental
temperance
temperary = temporary
temperate
temperature
tempered
temperment =
  temperament
temperture =
  temperature
tempest
tempestuous
tempi
template
temple
tempo
  tempi or
  tempos
temporal

temporary
temporise
  temporises
  temporised
  temporising
temporize
  temporizes
  temporized
  temporizing
temprature =
  temperature
tempt
  tempts
  tempted
  tempting
temptation
temptress
tempura
ten
tenable
tenacious
tenacity
tenancy
  tenancies
tenant
tench
tend
  tends
  tended
  tending
tendancy = tendency
tendencious
tendency
  tendencies
tendentious
tender
  tenders
  tendered
  tendering
tenderfoot
tenderhearted
tenderise
  tenderises
  tenderised
  tenderising
tenderiser
tenderize
  tenderizes
  tenderized
  tenderizing
tenderizer
tenderloin
tendon
tendril

tenement
tenent = tenant
Tenerife
Tenessee = Tennessee
tenet
tenfold
tenner (= ten-pound
  note → tenor)
Tennesee = Tennessee
  Tennessee
tennis
tenon
tenor (= voice
  → tenner)
tenpin
  tenpins
tense
  tenses
  tensed
  tensing
tensile
tensimeter
tensiometer
tension
tensor
tent
tentacle
tentative
tenterhook
tenth
tenthly
tenuous
tenure
tepee
tepid
tequila
terbium
tercentenary
  tercentenaries
tercentennial
terestrial = terrestrial
teriyaki
term
termagant
terminable
terminal
terminate
  terminates
  terminated
  terminating
termination
terminator
terminological
terminology

terminologies
terminus
  termini or
  terminuses
termite
tern (= bird → turn)
ternary
terra
terrace
terracing
terracotta
terrain
terrapin
terrazzo
terrestial = terrestrial
terrestrial
terrible
terribly
terrier
terrific
terrifically
terrify
  terrifies
  terrified
  terrifying
terrine
territorial
territory
  territories
terror
terrorise
  terrorises
  terrorised
  terrorising
terrorism
terrorist
terrorize
  terrorizes
  terrorized
  terrorizing
terry
terse
tertial
tertiary
tessellate
  tessellates
  tessellated
  tessellating
tessellation
tessera
  tesserae
test
  tests
  tested

testing
testa
  testae
testament
testate
testator
tester
testes
testicle
testicular
testify
  testifies
  testified
  testifying
testimonial
testimony
  testimonies
testiness
testis
  testes
testosterone
testy
  testier
  testiest
tetanus
tetchily
tetchiness
tetchy
  tetchier
  tetchiest
tête-à-tête
tether
  tethers
  tethered
  tethering
tetragon
tetragonal
tetragram
tetrahedron
  tetrahedra or
  tetrahedrons
tetralogy
  tetralogies
tetraplegia
Teutonic
Tewkesbury
text
textbook
textile
textual
texture
Thai
Thailand
thalamus

thalami
thalidomide
Thames
than
thank
  thanks
  thanked
  thanking
thankful
thankless
thanksgiving
that
thatch
  thatches
  thatched
  thatching
thaw
  thaws
  thawed
  thawing
the
theatre
theatrical
theatricality
theatricals
theatrics
thee
theft
theif = thief
their (= belonging to
  them → there,
  they're)
theirs
theism
theistic
them
thematic
thematically
theme
themself
themselves
then
thence
thenceforth
thenceforward
theocracy
  theocracies
theodolite
theologian
theological
theologist
theology
  theologies
theorem

theoretical
theoretician
theorise
  theorises
  theorised
  theorising
theorize
  theorizes
  theorized
  theorizing
theory
  theories
theosophical
theosophism
theosophist
theosophy
therapeutic
therapeutics
therapist
therapy
  therapies
there (= not here
  → their, they're)
thereabouts
thereafter
thereby
therefor = therefore
therfore = therefore
therefore
therein
thereof
thereon
thereto
thereupon
therewith
therm
thermal
thermistor
thermocouple
thermodynamic
thermodynamics
thermometer
thermonuclear
thermoplastic
Thermos®
thermostat
thermotropism
thesarus = thesaurus
thesaurus
  thesauri or
  thesauruses
these
thesis
  theses

theta
they
they'd
they'll
they're (= they are
  → their, there)
they've
thiamine
thick
thicken
  thickens
  thickened
  thickening
thicket
thickness
thickset
thief
  thieves
thieve
  thieves
  thieved
  thieving
thigh
thighbone
thimble
thimbleful
thin
  thins
  thinned
  thinning
thine
thing
thingamabob
thingumabob
thingumajig
thingummy
think
  thinks
  thought
  thinking
thinned
thinner
thinnest
thinning
thins
third
thirdly
thirst
thirstily
thirstiness
thirsty
  thirstier
  thirstiest
thirteen

thirteenth
thirtieth
thirty
  thirties
this
thistle
thistledown
thither
thoght = thought
Thomas
thong
thoracic
thorax
  thoraces or
  thoraxes
thorn
thornily
thorniness
thorny
  thornier
  thorniest
thorough
thoroughbred
thoroughfare
thoroughgoing
thoroughly
those
thou
though
thought
thoughtful
thoughtless
thousand
thousandth
thousend = thousand
thrall
thrash
  thrashes
  thrashed
  thrashing
thread
  threads
  threaded
  threading
threadbare
threadworm
threat
threaten
  threatens
  threatened
  threatening
three
threefold
threescore

threesome
threnodies
threnodist
threnody
  threnodies
thresh
  threshes
  threshed
  threshing
thresher
~~threshhold~~ = threshold
threshold
threw (= cast away
  → through)
thrice
thrift
thriftily
thriftiness
thrifty
  thriftier
  thriftiest
thrill
  thrills
  thrilled
  thrilling
thriller
thrive
  thrives
  thrived or
  throve
  thrived or
  thriven
  thriving
throat
throatily
throatiness
throaty
  throatier
  throatiest
throb
  throbs
  throbbed
  throbbing
throes (= death
  throes → throws)
thrombosis
throne (= monarch's
  chair → thrown)
throng
  throngs
  thronged
  thronging
throttle
  throttles

throttled
throttling
through
throughout
throughput
throve
throw
  throws (= projects
  something
    → throes)
  threw
  thrown (= thrown
  out → throne)
  throwing
throwaway
throwback
thrum
  thrums
  thrummed
  thrumming
~~through~~ = through
thrush
thrust
  thrusts
  thrust
  thrusting
thud
  thuds
  thudded
  thudding
thug
thumb
  thumbs
  thumbed
  thumbing
thumbnail
thumbscrew
thumbtack
thump
  thumps
  thumped
  thumping
thunder
  thunders
  thundered
  thundering
thunderbolt
thunderclap
thundercloud
thunderous
thundershower
thunderstorm
thunderstruck
Thursday

thus
thwack
thwart
  thwarts
  thwarted
  thwarting
thy
thyme (= herb
  → time)
thymus
  thymi or
  thymuses
thyroid
thyself
tiara
tiaraed
tibia
  tibiae or
  tibias
tic (= twitch)
tick (= of a clock)
  ticks
  ticked
  ticking
ticker
ticket
ticking
tickle
  tickles
  tickled
  tickling
tickler
ticklish
ticktack
tick-tack-toe
ticktock
tidal
tidbit
tiddler
tiddly
tiddlywink
tiddlywinks
tide (= wait → tied)
  tides
  tided
  tiding
tidemark
tidewater
tidily
tidiness
tidings
tidy
  tidies
  tidied

tidying
tidier
tidiest
tie
  ties
  tied (= drew;
  joined → tide)
tieback
tiebreaker
~~tieing~~ = tying
tiepin
tier (= layer → tear)
ties
tiff
tiffin
tiger
tight
tighten
  tightens
  tightened
  tightening
tightfisted
tightknit
tightrope
tights
tigress
tike
tikka
tilde
tile
  tiles
  tiled
  tiling
till
  tills
  tilled
  tilling
tillage
tiller
tilt
  tilts
  tilted
  tilting
timbal
timbale
timber (= wood
  → timbre)
timbered
timberyard
timbre (= tone
  → timber)
time
  times
  timed

timing
timecard
timekeeper
timeless
timeliness
timely
timelier
timeliest
timepiece
timer
timesaving
timescale
timetable
timeworn
timid
timidity
timing
timorous
timpani
tin
tins
tinned
tinning
tincture
tinder
tinderbox
tine
tined
tinfoil
ting
ting-a-ling
tinge
tinges
tinged
tingeing or
tinging
tingle
tingles
tingled
tingling
tinier
tiniest
tinker
tinkers
tinkered
tinkering
tinkle
tinkles
tinkled
tinkling
tinned
tinner
tinnily
tinniness

tinning
tinnitus
tinny
tinnier
tinniest
tinpot
tins
tinsel
tinsmith
tint
tints
tinted
tinting
tintype
tinware
tinwork
tinworks
tiny
tinier
tiniest
tip
tips
tipped
tipping
tipical = typical
tipper
Tipperary
tipple
tipples
tippled
tippling
tippler
tips
tipsily
tipsiness
tipstaff
tipster
tipsy
tipsier
tipsiest
tiptoe
tiptoes
tiptoed
tiptoeing
tiptop
tirade
tire (= grow tired
→ tyre)
tires
tired
tiring
tireless
tiresome
tisane

tissue
tit
titanic
titanium
titbit
titchy
titchier
titchiest
titfer
tithe
tithing
Titian
titillate
titillates
titillated
titillating
titivate
titivates
titivated
titivating
title
titles
titled
titling
titleholder
titmouse
titmice
titrant
titrate
titration
titre
titter
titters
tittered
tittering
tittivate
tittivates
tittivated
tittivating
tittle-tattle
titular
tizz
tizzy
tizzies
T-junction
TNT
to (= opposite of from
→ too, two)
toad
toadflax
toadstool
toady
toadies
toadied

toadying
toast
toasts
toasted
toasting
toaster
toastmaster
toastmistress
toasty
tobacco
tobaccoes or
tobaccos
tobacconist
tobaco = tobacco
toboggan
toboggans
tobogganed
tobogganing
tobogganer
tobogganist
toby
toccata
tocsin
tod
today
toddle
toddles
toddled
toddling
toddler
toddy
toddies
toe (= touch with part
of the foot → tow)
toes
toed
toeing
toecap
toehold
toenail
toerag
toff
toffee
toft
tofu
tog
togs
togged
togging
toga
togaed
together
togetherness
toggle

Togo
togs
toil
   toils
   toiled
   toiling
toile
toilet
toiletry
   toiletries
toilette
token
tokenism
Tokyo
tolbutamide
told
tolerable
tolerance
tolerant
tolerate
   tolerates
   tolerated
   tolerating
toleration
toll
   tolls
   tolled
   tolling
tollbooth
tollgate
tollhouse
Tolstoy, Leo
toluene
tom
tomahawk
tomato
   tomatoes
tomb
tombola
tomboy
tombstone
tome
tomfoolery
tommy
   tommies
tommyrot
tomography
tomorrow
tomtit
ton (= weight
   → tonne, tun)
tonal
tonality
tone

tones
toned
toning
toneless
toner
tong
tongs
tongue
   tongues
   tongued
   tonguing
tonic
tonicity
tonight
tonnage
tonne (= metric ton
   → ton, tun)
tonsil
tonsilitis = tonsillitis
tonsillectomy
   tonsillectomies
tonsillitis
tonsorial
tonsure
too (= also;
   excessively → to,
   two)
toodle-oo
took
tool (= hammer, etc.
   → tulle)
tooling
toot
   toots
   tooted
   tooting
tooth
toothache
toothbrush
toothed
toothily
toothiness
toothpaste
toothpick
toothsome
toothy
   toothier
   toothiest
tootle
   tootles
   tootled
   tootling
   tootsies
top

tops
topped
topping
topaz
topcoat
tope
   topes
   toped
   toping
topiary
topic
topical
topicality
topknot
topless
topnotch
topographer
topographic
topography
topological
topologist
topology
topped
topper
topping
topple
   topples
   toppled
   toppling
tops
topside
topsoil
topspin
topsy-turvy
toque
tor
Torah
torc (= metal band
   → talk, torque)
torch
   torches
   torched
   torching
torchbearer
tore
toreador
torment
   torments
   tormented
   tormenting
tormenter
tormentor
torn
tornado

tornadoes or
tornados
tornament =
   tournament
torpedo
   torpedoes
   torpedoed
   torpedoing
torpid
torpidity
torpor
Torquay
torque (= force
   → talk, torc)
torrent
torrential
torrid
torsion
torso
   torsi or
   torsos
tort (= legal term
   → taught, taut)
torte (= cake)
tortellini
tortoise
tortoiseshell
tortuous
torture
   tortures
   tortured
   torturing
torturous = tortuous
Tory
   Tories
tosh
toss
   tosses
   tossed
   tossing
tosser
tot
   tots
   totted
   totting
total
   totals
   totalled
   totalling
totalisator
totaliser
totalitarian
totalitarianism
totality

totalities
totalizator
totalizer
tote
  totes
  toted
  toting
totem
tots
totted
totter
totting
toucan
touch
  touches
  touched
  touching
touchdown
touché
touchily
touchiness
touching
touchline
touchpaper
touchstone
touchy
  touchier
  touchiest
tough
toughen
  toughens
  toughened
  toughening
toughness
Toulouse-Lautrec
toupee
tour
  tours
  toured
  touring
tourer
tourism
tourist
touristic
touristy
tournament
tournedos
  tournedos
tournement =
  tournament
tourniquet
tousle
  tousles
  tousled

tousling
tout
  touts
  touted
  touting
tow (= pull → toe)
  tows
towed
towing
toward
towards
towbar
towboat
Towcester
towel
  towels
  towelled
  towelling
towelling
tower
  towers
  towered
  towering
towhead
towing
town
township
townspeople
towpath
towrope
toxaemia
toxaemic
toxic
toxicity
toxicological
toxicology
toxin
toxoplasmosis
toy
  toys
  toyed
  toying
trace
  traces
  traced
  tracing
tracer
tracery
  traceries
trachea
  tracheae
tracheostomy
  tracheostomies
tracheotomy

tracheotomies
tracing
track
  tracks
  tracked
  tracking
tracksuit
tract
tractable
tractate
traction
tractor
trade
  trades
  traded
  trading
trademark
trader
tradescantia
tradesman
  tradesmen
tradespeople
tradeswoman
  tradeswomen
tradgedy = tragedy
trading
tradition
traditional
traditionalism
traditionalist
traditionalistic
traditionally
traduce
  traduces
  traduced
  traducing
traducement
traducer
traffic
tragacanth
tragedian
tragedy
  tragedies
tragic
tragically
tragicomedy
  tragicomedies
trail
  trails
  trailed
  trailing
trailblazer
trailer
train

trains
trained
training
trainee
trainer
trainers
traipse
  traipses
  traipsed
  traipsing
trait
traitor
trajectory
  trajectories
tra-la
tra-la-la
tram
tramcar
tramline
trammel
  trammels
  trammelled
  trammelling
tramp
  tramps
  tramped
  tramping
trample
  tramples
  trampled
  trampling
trampoline
trance
tranche
tranquil
tranquility =
  tranquillity
tranquillise
  tranquillises
  tranquillised
  tranquillising
tranquilliser
tranquillity
tranquillize
  tranquillizes
  tranquillized
  tranquillizing
tranquillizer
transact
  transacts
  transacted
  transacting
transaction
transactional

transactor
transalpine
transatlantic
transceiver
transcend
　transcends
　transcended
　transcending
transcendence
transcendency
transcendent
transcendental
transcendentalism
transcendingly
transcontinental
　transcibing
transducer
transept
transfer
　transfers
　transferred
　transferring
transferable
~~transfered~~ =
　transferred
transference
transferential
transferrable
transferrer
transfiguration
transfigure
　transfigures
　transfigured
　transfiguring
transfigurement
transfix
　transfixes
　transfixed
　transfixing
transfixion
transform
　transforms
　transformed
　transforming
transformable
transformation
transformer
transfuse

transfuses
transfused
transfusing
transfuser
transfusion
transgress
　transgresses
　transgressed
　transgressing
transgression
transgressor
transhipment
transhumance
transient
transistor
transit
transition
transitional
transitive
transitorily
transitoriness
transitory
translatable
translate
　translates
　translated
　translating
translation
translator
transliterate
　transliterates
　transliterated
　transliterating
translucence
translucency
translucent
transmissibility
transmissible
transmission
transmit
　transmits
　transmitted
　transmitting
transmittable
transmittance
transmittancy
transmitter
transmittible
transmogrification
transmogrify
　transmogrifies
　transmogrified
　transmogrifying
transmutability

transmutable
transmutably
transmutation
transmutative
transmute
　transmutes
　transmuted
　transmuting
transmuter
transom
transparence
transparency
　transparencies
transparent
transpire
　transpires
　transpired
　transpiring
transplant
　transplants
　transplanted
　transplanting
transplantable
transponder
transport
　transports
　transported
　transporting
transportable
transportation
transporter
transpose
　transposes
　transposed
　transposing
transsexual
transshipment
transubstantiation
transversal
transversally
transverse
transvestism
transvestite
transvestitism
trap
　traps
　trapped
　trapping
trapeze
trapezium
　trapezia or
　trapeziums
trapezius
　trapeziuses

trapezohedral
trapezohedron
　trapezohedra or
　trapezohedrons
trapezoid
trapped
trapper
trapping
trappings
Trappist
traps
trash
trashy
　trashier
　trashiest
trattoria
trauma
traumatic
traumatically
traumatise
　traumatises
　traumatised
　traumatising
traumatize
　traumatizes
　traumatized
　traumatizing
travail
travel
　travels
　travelled
　travelling
traveller
travelogue
traverse
　traverses
　traversed
　traversing
travesty
　travesties
trawl
　trawls
　trawled
　trawling
trawler
tray
treacherous
treachery
　treacheries
treacle
tread
　treads
trod
　trod or

trodden
treading
treadle
treadmill
treadwheel
treason
treasure
　treasures
　treasured
　treasuring
treasurer
treasury
　treasuries
treat
　treats
　treated
　treating
treatise
treatment
treaty
　treaties
treble
　trebles
　trebled
　trebling
~~trecherous~~ =
　treacherous
tree
treen
trefoil
trek
　treks
　trekked
　trekking
trellis
tremble
　trembles
　trembled
　trembling
trembler
tremendous
tremolo
　tremolos
tremor
tremulous
trench
trenchant
trencher
trenches
trend
trendily
trendiness
trendsetter
trendy

trendier
trendiest
Treorchy
trepan
trepans
trepanned
trepanning
trepanner
trepidation
trespass
　trespasses
　trespassed
　trespassing
tress
trestle
trews
triad
triage
trial
triangle
triangular
triangulate
　triangulates
　triangulated
　triangulating
triangulation
Triassic
triathlon
tribalism
tribe
tribulation
tribunal
tribune
tributary
　tributaries
tribute
trice
tricentenary
　tricentenaries
tricentennial
triceps
triceratops
trichologist
trichology
trick
　tricks
　tricked
　tricking
trickery
　trickeries
trickier
trickiest
trickily
trickiness

trickle
　trickles
　trickled
　trickling
tricksiness
tricksy
　tricksier
　tricksiest
tricky
　trickier
　trickiest
tricolour
tricot
tricycle
trident
tried
triennial
triennium
　triennia or
　trienniums
trier
tries
triffid
trifle
　trifles
　trifled
　trifling
trigger
trigonometric
trigonometry
trihedral
trihedron
　trihedra or
　trihedrons
trike
trilateral
trilby
　trilbies
trilingual
trilithic
trilithon
trill
　trills
　trilled
　trilling
trillion
trilogy
　trilogies
trim
　trimmer
　trimmest
　trims
　trimmed
　trimming

trimaran
trimester
trimonthly
trims
trinitrotoluene
trinity
　trinities
trinket
trio
　trios
trip
　trips
　tripped
　tripping
tripartite
tripe
triplane
triple
　triples
　tripled
　tripling
triplet
triplicate
tripod
tripos
tripped
tripper
tripping
trips
triptane
triptych
tripwire
trireme
trisection
trisector
trite
triumph
　triumphs
　triumphed
　triumphing
triumphal
triumphalism
triumphant
triumvirate
trivet
trivia
trivial
trivialise
　trivialises
　trivialised
　trivialising
triviality
　trivialities
trivialize

trivializes
trivialized
trivializing
triweekly
trochee
trod
trodden
troglodyte
troika
Trojan
troll
trolley
trolleybus
trollop
trombone
trombonist
troop (= display
soldiers, etc.
→ troupe)
troops
trooped
trooping
trooper (= soldier
→ trouper)
troopship
trope
trophy
trophies
tropic
tropical
tropism
tropistic
troposphere
trot
trots
trotted
trotting
troth
trots
trotter
troubadour
trouble
troubles
troubled
troubling
troublemaker
troubleshooter
troublesome
trough
trounce
trounces
trounced
trouncing
troupe (= company of

actors → troop)
trouper (= troupe
member → trooper)
trouser
trousers
trousseau
trousseaus or
trousseaux
trout
trout
trowel
truant
truce
truck
trucks
trucked
trucking
trucker
truckle
truckload
truculent
trudge
trudges
trudged
trudging
true
truelove
~~truely~~ = truly
truer
truest
truffle
trug
truism
truistic
truly
trump
trumps
trumped
trumping
trumpery
trumperies
trumpet
trumpets
trumpeted
trumpeting
trumpeter
trumps
truncate
truncates
truncated
truncating
truncheon
trundle
trundles

trundled
trundling
trunk
trunks
Truro
truss
trusses
trussed
trussing
trussing
trust
trusts
trusted
trusting
trustee
trustworthily
trustworthiness
trustworthy
trusty
trustier
trustiest
truth
truthful
try
tries
tried
trying
trying
tryout
trypsin
tryptophan
tryst
tsar
tsarina
tsetse
T-shirt
T-square
tub
tuba
tubae or
tubas
tubal
tubbiness
tubby
tubbier
tubbiest
tube
tuber
tubercle
tubercular
tuberculin
tuberculosis
tuberculous
tuberose

tuberous
tubing
tubs
tubular
tuck
tucks
tucked
tucking
tucker
Tuesday
tuffet
tuft
tufted
tug
tugs
tugged
tugging
tugboat
tuition
tulip
tulle (= fabric → tool)
tum
tumble
tumbles
tumbled
tumbling
tumbledown
tumbler
tumbleweed
tumbrel
tumbril
tumefacient
tumefaction
tumescence
tumescent
tummy
tummies
tumour
tumult
tumultuous
tumulus
tun (= beer cask
→ ton, tonne)
tuna
tuna or
tunas
tundra
tune
tunes
tuned
tuning
tuneful
tuneless
tuner

tungsten
tunic
Tunisia
tunnage
tunnel
  tunnels
  tunnelled
  tunnelling
tunny
  tunnies *or*
  tunny
tuns
tup
  tups
  tupped
  tupping
tuppence
tuppenny
turban
turbid
turbidity
turbine
turbocharger
turbofan
turbogenerator
turbojet
turboprop
turbosupercharger
turbot
turbulence
turbulent
turd
tureen
turf
  turfs *or*
  turves
  turfs
  turfed
  turfing
turgid
turkey
Turkey
Turkish
Turkmenistan
turmeric
turmoil
turn (= move round
  → tern)
  turns
  turned
  turning
turnabout
turnaround
turncoat

turner
turnip
turnkey
turnout
turnover
turnpike
turnround
turnstile
turntable
turpentine
turpitude
turps
turquoise
turret
turreted
turtle
turtledove
turtleneck
turves
tush
tushery
tusk
tusked
tusker
tussle
  tussles
  tussled
  tussling
tussock
tut
  tuts
  tutted
  tutting
tutee
tutelage
tutor
tutorial
tuts
tutted
tutti-frutti
tutting
tutu
tuxedo
  tuxedos
TV
twaddle
twain
twang
  twangs
  twanged
  twanging
twat
tweak
  tweaks

tweaked
tweaking
twee
tweed
tweedy
  tweedier
  tweediest
tweet
  tweets
  tweeted
  tweeting
tweeter
tweezers
twelfth
~~twelth~~ = twelfth
twelve
twelvemonth
~~twelveth~~ = twelfth
twentieth
twenty
  twenties
twerp
twice
Twickenham
twiddle
  twiddles
  twiddled
  twiddling
twig
  twigs
  twigged
  twigging
twilight
twilit
twill
twin
  twins
  twinned
  twinning
twine
twinge
twinkle
  twinkles
  twinkled
  twinkling
twinset
twirl
  twirls
  twirled
  twirling
twirp
twist
  twists
  twisted

twisting
twister
twit
twitch
  twitches
  twitched
  twitching
twitter
  twitters
  twittered
  twitting
twixt
two (= number → to,
  too)
twofold
twopence
twopenny
twosome
Twyford
tycoon
tying
tyke
tymbal
tympan
tympani
tympanic
tympanist
tympanum
  tympana *or*
  tympanums
Tyne and Wear
type
  types
  typed
  typing
typecast
typeface
typescript
typesetter
typewriter
typhoid
typhoon
typhus
typical
typify
  typifies
  typified
  typifying
typist
typographer
typography
typology
tyrannical
tyrannise

tyrannises
tyrannised
tyrannising
tyrannize
tyrannizes

tyrannized
tyrannizing
tyrannosaur
tyranny
tyrannies

tyrant
~~tyrany~~ = tyranny
tyre (= on a wheel
    → tire)
Tyrone

~~tyrrany~~ = tyranny
tzar
tzarina
tzatziki

U

ubiquitous
U-boat
udder
uf *try* euph
UFO
ufologist
ufology
Uganda
ugh
ugli
  uglies *or*
  uglis
uglily
ugliness
ugly
  uglier
  ugliest
uh-huh
uh-uh
ukelele
Ukraine
Ukrainian
ukulele
ulcer
ulceration
ulcerous
ulna
  ulnae *or*
  ulnas
ulterior
ultimate
ultimatum
  ultimata *or*
  ultimatums
ultra
ultramarine
ultramodern
ultrared
ultrasonic
ultrasound
ultraviolet
ululate
  ululates
  ululated
  ululating
um

umber
umbilical
umbilicus
  umbilici
umbilicus
umbrage
umbrella
umlaut
umpire
  umpires
  umpired
  umpiring
umpteen
unabated
unable
unaccompanied
unaccountable
unaccustomed
unadvised
unadvisedly
unaffected
unalienable
unalloyed
unanimity
unanimous
unanswerable
unanswerably
unappetising
unappetizing
unapproachable
unarguable
unarguably
unarmed
unashamed
unashamedly
unasked
unassailable
unassuming
unattached
unattended
unatural = unnatural
unauthorised
unauthorized
unavoidable
unaware
unawares

unbalanced
unbearable
unbearably
unbeatable
unbeaten
unbecoming
unbeknown
unbelievable
unbeliever
unbelieving
unbending
unbiased
unbiassed
unbidden
unborn
unbowed
unbridled
unbroken
unburden
  unburdens
  unburdened
  unburdening
unbutton
  unbuttons
  unbuttoned
  unbuttoning
uncalled-for
uncannily
uncanniness
uncanny
uncap
  uncaps
  uncapped
  uncapping
uncared-for
unceasing
unceremonious
uncertain
uncertainty
  uncertainties
uncharted
unchristian
uncircumcised
uncivilised
uncivilized
unclassified

uncle
unclean
unclear
uncoil
  uncoils
  uncoiled
  uncoiling
uncomfortable
uncomfortably
uncommercial
uncommitted
uncommon
uncommunicative
uncompromising
unconcerned
unconditional
unconditioned
unconnected
unconscionable
unconscionably
unconscious
unconsious =
  unconscious
unconstitutional
uncontrollable
unconventional
uncoordinated
uncork
  uncorks
  uncorked
  uncorking
uncouple
  uncouples
  uncoupled
  uncoupling
uncouth
uncover
  uncovers
  uncovered
  uncovering
unction
unctuous
uncurl
  uncurls
  uncurled
  uncurling

undaunted
undecided
undemonstrative
undeniable
under
underachieve
  underachieves
  underachieved
  underachieving
underage
underarm
underbelly
undercarriage
undercharge
  undercharges
  undercharged
  undercharging
underclass
underclothes
underclothing
undercover
undercurrent
underdeveloped
underdog
underdone
underestimate
  underestimates
  underestimated
  underestimating
underfoot
undergarment
undergo
  undergoes
  underwent
  undergone
  undergoing
undergraduate
underground
undergrowth
underhand
underline
  underlines
  underlined
  underlining
underling
underlying
undermine
  undermines
  undermined
  undermining
underneath
undernourish
  undernourishes
  undernourishing

underpants
underpass
underpin
  underpins
  underpinned
  underpinning
underprivileged
underrate
  underrates
  underrated
  underrating
undersecretary
  undersecretaries
undershirt
underside
undersigned
undersized
understand
  understands
  understood
  understanding
understudy
  understudies
  understudied
  understudying
undertake
  undertakes
  undertook
  undertaken
  undertaking
undertaker
undertaking
undertone
undertow
underwater
underwear
underweight
underworld
underwrite
  underwrites
  underwrote
  underwritten
  underwriting
underwriter
undescended
undesirable
undetermined
undid
undistinguished
undo
  undoes
  undid
  undone
  undoing

undoubted
undoubtedly
undoubtly =
  undoubtedly
undress
  undresses
  undressed
  undressing
undue
undulant
undulate
  undulates
  undulated
  undulating
undulation
undulatory
unduly
undying
unearned
unearth
  unearths
  unearthed
  unearthing
unearthliness
unearthly
unease
uneasily
uneasiness
uneasy
unecessary =
  unnecessary
uneconomic
uneconomical
unemployable
unemployed
unemployment
unequal
unequalled
unequally
unequivocal
unerring
uneven
uneventful
unexceptionable
unexceptional
unexpected
unexperienced
unfailing
unfair
unfairly
unfaithful
unfamiliar
unfamiliarity
unfasten

unfastens
unfastened
unfastening
unfathomable
unfathomably
unfavourable
unfavourably
unfazed
unfeeling
unfertilised
unfit
unflappable
unflinching
unfold
  unfolds
  unfolded
  unfolding
unforgettable
unfortunate
unfounded
unfriendliness
unfriendly
unfurl
  unfurls
  unfurled
  unfurling
ungainliness
ungainly
ungrateful
ungrudging
unguent
unhappily
unhappiness
unhappy
unhealthily
unhealthiness
unhealthy
unheard-of
unhesitating
unhesitatingly
unhoped-for
unhurried
unicorn
unicycle
unidirectional
unification
uniform
uniformity
unify
  unifies
  unified
  unifying
unilateral
unimproved

uninspired
unintelligent
uninterested
union
uniqe = unique
unique
unisex
unison
unit
Unitarian
unitary
unite
  unites
  united
  uniting
United Kingdom
United States of
  America
unity
universal
universe
university
  universities
unjust
unkempt
unkind
unknowingly
unknown
unlace
  unlaces
  unlaced
  unlacing
unlawful
unleaded
unleash
  unleashes
  unleashed
  unleashing
unleavened
unless
unlicensed
unlikable
unlike
unlikeable
unlikeliness
unlikely
unlimited
unlisted
unload
  unloads
  unloaded
  unloading
unlock
  unlocks

unlocked
unlocking
unlooked-for
unluckily
unluckiness
unlucky
unmade
unmanned
unmarked
unmarried
unmentionable
unmentionably
unmerciful
unmistakable
unmistakeable =
  unmistakable
unmitigated
unnamed
unnatural
unnecessarily
unnecessary
unoccupied
unofficial
unorganised
unorganized
unorthodox
unpack
  unpacks
  unpacked
  unpacking
unpaid
unparalleled
unpasteurised
unpasteurized
unpick
  unpicks
  unpicked
  unpicking
unpleasant
unplug
  unplugs
  unplugged
unpopular
unprecedented
unpredictable
unpremeditated
unprepared
unprincipled
unprintable
unproductive
unprofessional
unprofitable
unprofitably
unputdownable

unqualified
unquestionable
unquestionably
unquote
unravel
  unravels
  unravelled
  unravelling
unread
unreadable
unreal
unreasonable
unreasonably
unrecognisable
unrecognizable
unrefined
unrelenting
unremitting
unrequited
unreserved
unreservedly
unrest
unrestrained
unripe
unrivalled
unroll
  unrolls
  unrolled
  unrolling
unruffled
unruliness
unruly
unsaid
unsaturated
unsavoury
unscathed
unscientific
unscratched
unscrupulous
unseasonable
unseasonably
unseemliness
unseemly
unseen
unselfish
unshakable
unshakably
unshakeable
unshakeably
unsightliness
unsightly
unskilful
unskilled
unsociable

unsociably
unsophisticated
unsound
unsparing
unsparingly
unspeakable
unspeakably
unspecialised
unspecialized
unspoiled
unspoilt
unspoken
unstable
unsteadily
unsteadiness
unsteady
unstoppable
unstoppably
unstructured
unstuck
unstudied
unsubstantial
unsung
unsupportable
unsure
unsuspected
unsuspecting
unswerving
untangle
  untangles
  untangled
  untangling
untenable
unthinkable
unthinkably
unthinking
unthought-of
untidily
untidiness
untidy
untie
  unties
  untied
  untying
until
untill = until
untimeliness
untimely
untitled
unto
untold
untouchable
untouched
untoward

untried
untrue
untruthful
untuck
　untucks
　untucked
　untucking
unused
unusual
unvarnished
unveil
　unveils
　unveiled
　unveiling
unwaged
unwanted (= not
　wanted → unwonted)
unwarily
unwariness
unwarranted
unwarily
unwariness
unwary
unwelcome
unwell
unwieldly = unwieldy
unwieldy
unwilling
unwind
　unwinds
　unwinded
　unwound
　unwinding
unwise
unwitting
unwonted (= unusual
　→ unwanted)
unworldliness
unworldly
unwrap
　unwraps
　unwrapped
　unwrapping
unwritten
unzip
　unzips
　unzipped
　unzipping
up
　ups
　upped
　upping
upbeat
upbraid

upbraids
upbraided
upbraiding
upbringing
upcoming
update
　updates
　updated
　updating
updraught
upend
　upends
　upended
　upending
upfront
upgrade
　upgrades
　upgraded
　upgrading
uph try euph
upheaval
upheld
uphill
uphold
　upholds
　upheld
　upholding
upholster
　upholsters
　upholstered
　upholstering
upholsterer
upholstery
upholstry = upholstery
upkeep
uplifting
upmost
upon
upped
upper
uppercut
uppermost
upping
uppish
uppity
upright
uprising
upriver
uproar
uproarious
uproot
　uproots
　uprooted
　uprooting

ups
upsadaisy
upscale
upset
　upsets
　upset
　upsetting
upshot
upside-down
upsilon
upstage
　upstages
　upstaged
　upstaging
upstairs
upstanding
upstart
upstream
upstretched
upsurge
upswing
upsy-daisy
uptake
uptight
upturn
upward
upwards
upwind
ur try eur
uranium
Uranus
urban
urbane
urchin
Urdu
urea
ureter
urethra
　urethrae or
　urethras
urethral
urge
　urges
　urged
　urging
urgency
urgent
uric
urinal
urinary
urinate
　urinates
　urinated
　urinating

urine
urn (= container
　→ earn)
urogenital
urology
ursine
urticaria
Uruguay
us
USA
usable
usage
usally = usually
use
　uses
　used
　using
useable
useful
useless
user
useage = usage
usefull = useful
useing = using
use to = used to
usful = useful
usher
　ushers
　ushered
　ushering
usherette
usual
usualy = usually
usurer
usurious
usurp
　usurps
　usurped
　usurping
usurper
usury
　usuries
utensil
uterine
uterus
　uteri
utilise
　utilises
　utilised
　utilising
utilitarian
utilitarianism
utility
　utilities

utilize	Utopian	utterance	uvulas *or*
utilizes	utter	utterly	uvulae
utilized	utters	uttermost	uvular
utilizing	uttered	U-turn	uxorious
utmost	uttering	uvula	Uzbekistan

V

vac
vacancy
  vacancies
vacant
vacate
  vacates
  vacated
  vacating
vacation
vaccinate
  vaccinates
  vaccinated
  vaccinating
vaccination
vaccine
vaccum = vacuum
vacccuum = vacuum
vacillate
  vacillates
  vacillated
  vacillating
vacum = vacuum
vacuous
vacuum
vagabond
vagary
  vagaries
vagina
vaginal
vagrancy
vagrant
vain (= proud → vane, vein)
vainglory
valance
vale (= valley → veil)
valediction
valedictory
valency
  valencies
valentine
valet
valiant
valid
validate
validity

valley
valour
valuable
valuation
valuble = valuable
value
  values
  valued
  valuing
valuer
valve
vamoose
vamp
vampire
van
Vancouver
vandal
vandalise
  vandalises
  vandalised
  vandalising
vandalism
vandalize
  vandalizes
  vandalized
  vandalizing
vane (= weather vane → vain, vein)
Van Gogh, Vincent
vanguard
vanilla
vanish
  vanishes
  vanished
  vanishing
vanity
  vanities
vanquish
  vanquishes
  vanquished
  vanquishing
vantage
vapid
vapidity
vaporise
  vaporises

vaporised
vaporising
vaporize
  vaporizes
  vaporized
  vaporizing
vapour
vareity = variety
variable
variance
variant
variation
variaty = variety
varicoloured
varicose
varied
variegated
varies
varietal
variety
  varieties
varigated = variegated
various
varlet
varmint
varnish
  varnishes
  varnished
  varnishing
vary
  varies
  varied
  varying
vascular
vase
Vaseline™
vasectomy
  vasectomies
vassal
vast
vat
VAT
vaudeville
vault (= jump over → volt)
  vaults

vaulted
vaulting
vaunt
  vaunts
  vaunted
  vaunting
VCR
V-E Day
veal
vector
veer
  veers
  veered
  veering
veg
vegan
vegetable
vegetarian
vegetarianism
vegetate
  vegetates
  vegetated
  vegetating
vegetation
vegetative
veggie
vegtable = vegetable
vehement
vehical = vehicle
vehicle
vehicular
veil (= draw a cover over → vale)
veiled
vein (= blood carrier → vane)
Velcro™
veld
veldt
vellum
velocipede
velocity
  velocities
velodrome
velour
velours

velvet
velveteen
venal
vend
  vends
  vended
  vending
vendetta
vendor
veneer
venerable
veneration
venereal
Venezuela
vengance = vengeance
vengeance
vengeful
vengence = vengeance
venial
venison
venom
venous
vent
  vents
  vented
  venting
ventilate
  ventilates
  ventilated
  ventilating
ventilation
ventilator
ventral
ventricle
ventriloquism
ventriloquist
venture
  ventures
  ventured
  venturing
venturesome
venue
veracious
veracity
veranda
verandah
verb
verbal
verbalise
  verbalises
  verbalised
  verbalising
verbalize
  verbalizes

verbalized
verbalizing
verbatim
verbena
verbiage
verbose
verbosity
verdict
verdigris
verge
  verges
  verged
  verging
verger
verification
verify
  verifies
  verified
  verifying
verisimilitude
veritable
vermicelli
vermilion
vermin
verminous
vermouth
vernacular
vernal
verruca
  verrucae *or*
  verrucas
versatile
versatility
verse
versed
version
verso
versus
vertebra
  vertebrae
vertebrate
vertex
  vertexes *or*
  vertices
vertical
vertigo
verve
very
vesicle
vespers
Vespucci, Amerigo
vessel
vest
vestal

vested
vestibule
vestige
vestigial
vestment
vestry
  vestries
Vesuvius
vet
  vets
  vetted
  vetting
veteran
veterinarian
veterinary
vetinary = veterinary
veto
  vetoes
  vetoed
  vetoing
vex
  vexes
  vexed
  vexing
vexation
vexatious
via
viable
viaduct
vial try viol
vial (= small bottle
  → vile, viol)
viand
vibes
vibrant
vibrate
  vibrates
  vibrated
  vibrating
vibration
vibrato
vibrator
vicar
vicarage
vicarious
vice
vichyssoise
vicinity
  vicinities
vicious
victim
victimised
victimized
victor

Victoria
Victorian
victorious
victory
  victories
victual
victualler
victuals
video
  videos
  videoed
  videoing
videodisk
videotext
vie
  vies
  vied
  vying
viel = veil
Vietnam
view
  views
  viewed
  viewing
viewer
vigil
vigilance
vigilant
vigilante
vignette
vigorous
vigour
Viking
vilage = village
vile (= horrible
  → vial, viol)
villa
village
villager
villain (= baddie
  → villein)
villainous
villainy
villan = villain
villein (= serf
  → villain)
villi
villous (adj.)
villus (noun)
  villi
vim
vinagrette = vinaigrette
vinaigrette
vindicate

vindicates
vindicated
vindicating
vindication
vindictive
vindictively
vine
vinegar
vineyard
viniculture
vino
  vinos
vintage
vintner
vinyl
viol (= instrument
  → vial, vile)
viola
violate
  violates
  violated
  violating
violence
violent
violet
violin
violincello = violoncello
violinist
violoncello
  violoncellos
VIP
viper
virago
  viragoes *or*
  viragos
viral
Virgil
virgin
virginal
virginity
virile
virility
virtual
virtually
virtue
virtuoso
virtuous
virulence
virulent
virus
visa

visage
vis-à-vis
viscose
viscosity
viscount
viscountess
viscous
visibility
visible
vision
visionary
  visionaries
visit
  visits
  visited
  visiting
visitor
visor
vista
visual
visualise
  visualises
  visualised
  visualising
visualize
  visualizes
  visualized
  visualizing
vital
vitality
  vitalities
vitamin
viticulture
vitreous
vitriol
vitriolic
vituperation
vituperative
viva
vivacious
vivacity
  vivacities
vivarium
  vivaria *or*
  vivariums
vivid
viviparous
vivisection
vixen
viz
vizier

vizor
vocabulary
  vocabularies
vocal
vocalic
vocalise
  vocalises
  vocalised
  vocalising
vocalist
vocalize
  vocalizes
  vocalized
  vocalizing
vocation
vocational
vocative
vociferous
vodka
vogue
voice
  voices
  voiced
  voicing
void
voile
volatile
vol-au-vent
volcanic
volcano
  volcanoes *or*
  volcanos
vole
volition
volley
  volleys
  volleyed
  volleying
volleyball
volt (= unit of
  potential → vault)
voltage
voltameter
volte-face
  volte-faces
voltmeter
voluble
volume
volumeter
volumetric
volumetry

voluminous
voluntarily
voluntary
volunteer
  volunteers
  volunteered
  volunteering
voluptious =
  voluptuous
voluptuous
vomit
  vomits
  vomited
  vomiting
Vonnegut, Kurt
voodoo
  voodoos
voracious
voracity
vortex
  vortexes *or*
  vortices
vote
  votes
  voted
  voting
voter
votive
vouch
  vouches
  vouched
  vouching
voucher
vow
  vows
  vowed
  vowing
vowel
voyage
voyeur
voyeurism
vulgar
vulgarism
vulgarity
  vulgarities
vulnerability
vulnerable
vulpine
vulture
vulva
vying

W

wa try wha
wackily
wackiness
wacky
  wackier
  wackiest
wad
wadding
waddle
  waddles
  waddled
  waddling
wade (= walk in
  water → weighed)
  wades
  waded
  wading
wader
waders
wafer
waffle
  waffles
  waffled
  waffling
waft
  wafts
  wafted
  wafting
wag
  wags
  wagged
  wagging
wage
waggle
  waggles
  waggled
  waggling
waggon
wagon
wagon-lit
  wagons-lits
wags
wagtail
waif
wail (= cry → whale)
  wails

wailed
wailing
wainscot
waist (= part of the
  body → waste)
waistband
waistcoat
waistline
wait (= watch for;
  remain → weight)
  waits
  waited
  waiting
waiter
waitress
waive (= cancel a fee,
  etc. → wave)
  waives
  waived
  waiving
waiver (=
  relinquishment
  → waver)
wake
  wakes
  woke
  woken
  waking
wakeful
waken
  wakens
  wakened
  wakening
walk
  walks
  walked
  walking
walkabout
walkie-talkie
  walkie-talkies
walkout
walkover
walkway
walky-talky
  walky-talkies
wall

wallaby
  wallabies
Wallasey
walled
wallet
wallflower
wallop
  wallops
  walloped
  walloping
wallow
  wallows
  wallowed
  wallowing
wallpaper
wally
  wallies
walnut
walrus
Walsall
waltz
  waltzes
  waltzed
  waltzing
wampum
wan
wand
wander
  wanders
  wandered
  wandering
wanderlust
wane
  wanes
  waned
  waning
wangle
  wangles
  wangled
  wangling
wank
  wanks
  wanked
  wanking
wanker
want

wants
wanted
wanting
wanton
war
  wars
  warred (= fought
  → ward)
  warring
waranty = warranty
warble
  warbles
  warbled
  warbling
warbler
ward (= hospital room
  → warred)
warden
warder
wardrobe
warehouse
wares (= goods
  → wears)
warf = wharf
warfare
Warhol, Andy
warhorse
warier
wariest
warily
wariness
warlike
warlock
warlord
warm
warmonger
warmth
warn
  warns
  warned
  warning
warpath
warped
warplane
warrant
  warrants

warranted
warranting
warrantor
warranty
  warranties
warren
~~warrent~~ = warrant
warring
warrior
wart
wary
  warier
  wariest
Warwick
Warwickshire
was
wash
  washes
  washed
  washing
washable
washbasin
washer
washout
washy
wasn't
wasp
waspish
wassail
wastage
waste (= rubbish;
  squander → waist)
  wastes
  wasted
  wasting
wastebasket
wasteful
wasteland
wastepaper
waster
watch
  watches
  watched
  watching
watchable
watchdog
watchful
watchstrap
water
  waters
  watered
  watering
waterborne
watercolour

watercress
waterfall
waterfowl
wateriness
waterlogged
watermelon
waterproof
watertight
waterworks
watery
watt (= unit of power
  → what)
wattage
wattle
Waugh, Evelyn
wave (= signal by
  hand → waive)
  waves
  waved
  waving
waveband
wavelength
waver (= hesitate
  → waiver)
  wavers
  wavered
  wavering
wavily
waviness
wavy
  wavier
  waviest
wawl try wal
wax
  waxes
  waxed
  waxing
waxiness
waxwing
waxwork
waxy
  waxier
  waxiest
way (= road → weigh,
  whey)
waylay
  waylays
  waylaid
  waylaying
wayside
wayward
WC
we try whe
we (= us → wee)

weak (= feeble
  → week)
weaken
  weakens
  weakened
  weakening
weakling
weak-willed
weal (= mark on the
  skin → we'll, wheel)
weald
wealth
wealthily
wealthiness
wealthy
  wealthier
  wealthiest
wean
  weans
  weaned
  weaning
weapon
weaponry
wear
  wears (= is clothed
  → wares)
  wore
  worn
  wearing
wearable
wearily
weariness
wearisome
weary
  wearies
  wearied
  wearying
  wearier
  weariest
weasel
weather (= climate;
  survive → whether
  weathers
  weathered
  weathering
weathercock
weave (= make cloth
  → we've)
  weaves
  wove
  woven
  weaving
weaver
web

webbed
webbing
website
wed
  weds
  wed or
  wedded
  wedding
we'd (= we had; we
  would → weed)
~~Wednesday~~ =
  Wednesday
wedge
  wedges
  wedged
  wedging
wedlock
Wednesday
~~Wednesday~~ =
  Wednesday
wee (= tiny → we)
  wees (= urinates
  → wheeze)
  weed (= urinated
  → we'd, weed)
  weeing
weed (= plant;
  remove weeds
  → we'd, weed)
  weeds
  weeded
  weeding
weedily
weediness
weedkiller
weedy
  weedier
  weediest
week (= seven days
  → weak)
weekday
weekend
weekly
weeny
weeny-bopper
weep
  weeps
  wept
  weeping
weepiness
weepy
  weepier
  weepiest
weevil

weigh (= measure
  weight of → way,
  whey)
  weighs
  weighed
  weighing
weighbridge
weight (= heavy
  object → wait
weightily
weightiness
weighting
weightlifting
weighty
  weightier
  weightiest
weir (= dam on a river
  → we're)
weird
weirdo
welcome
  welcomes
  welcomed
  welcoming
weld
  welds
  welded
  welding
welfare
well
we'll (= we will
  → weal, wheel)
wellbeing
wellfare = welfare
wellies
wellingtons
wellspring
welly
  wellies
Welsh
welt
welterweight
wench
wend
  wends
  wended
  wending
went
wept
were (= they were
  out → whirr)
we're (= we are
  → weir)
weren't

werewolf
  werewolves
west
westerly
western
Westmorland
westward
westwards
wet
  wets
  wet or
  wetted
  wetting
wetter
wettest
we've (= we have
  → weave)
Weybridge
Weymouth
whack
  whacks
  whacked
  whacking
whale (= large
  mammal → wail)
whalebone
whaler
whaling
wham
wharf
  wharfs or
  wharves
what (= question
  → watt)
whatever
whatnot
whatsit
whatsoever
wheat
wheaten
wheatmeal
wheedle
  wheedles
  wheedled
  wheedling
wheel (= roll along
  → weal, we'll)
  wheels
  wheeled
  wheeling
wheelbarrow
wheelchair
wheeler-dealer
wheelie

wheeze (= pant
  → wees)
  wheezes
  wheezed
  wheezing
whelk
whelp
when
whenever
where
whereabouts
whereas
whereat
whereby
whereever = wherever
wherein
whereof
whereon
whereupon
wherever
wherewithal
whet
  whets
  whetted
  whetting
whether (= if
  → weather)
whew
whey (= made with
  curds → way, weigh)
which (= question
  → witch)
whichever
whicker
whiff
whiffy
while (= during
  → wile)
whilst
whim
whimper
  whimpers
  whimpered
  whimpering
whimsical
whine (= moan
  → wine)
  whines
  whined (= moaned
  → wind)
  whining
whinge
  whinges
  whinged

whinging
whinny
  whinnies
  whinnied
  whinnying
whip
  whips
  whipped
  whipping
whiplash
whippet
whir (= noise
  → were)
  whirs
  whirred
  whirring
whirls
  whirled (= spun
  → world)
  whirling
whirligig
whirlpool
whirlwind
whirr (= noise
  → were)
  whirrs
  whirred (= made
  a noise → word)
  whirring
whirls
whisk
  whisks
  whisked
  whisking
whisker
whiskey (= Irish)
whisky (= Scotch)
whisper
  whisper
  whispered
  whispering
whist
whistle
  whistles
  whistled
  whistling
whistler
whit (= jot → wit)
white
whitebait
whiten
  whitens
  whitened
  whitening

whitening
whiteout
whitewash
whither (= where to
 → wither)
whiting
Whitsun
whitter
whittle
 whittles
 whittled
 whittling
whiz
 whizzes
 whizzed
 whizzing
whizz
 whizzes
 whizzed
 whizzing
who
whoa
who'd
whoever
whole (= complete
 → hole)
wholefood
wholehearted
wholely = wholly
wholemeal
wholesale
wholesome
who'll
wholly (= completely
 → holy)
whom
whomever
whomsoever
whoop (= shout
 → hoop)
 whoops
 whooped
 whooping
whoopee
whoosh
whopping
whore (= prostitute
 → hoar)
whorl
whorled
who's (= who is)
whose (= of who)
why
wi try whi

wick
wicked
wicker
wickerwork
wicket
wicketkeeper
widdershins
wide
widen
 widens
 widened
 widening
widespread
widget
Widnes
widow
widower
width
widthwise
wiegh = weigh
wieght = weight
wield
 wields
 wielded
 wielding
wieldy
wier = weir
wierd = weird
wife
 wives
wig
wiggle
 wiggles
 wiggled
 wiggling
Wight, Isle of
wigwam
wild
wildcat
Wilde, Oscar
wildebeest
wilderness
wildfire
wildfowl
wildlife
wile (= trickery
 → while)
wilful
wilier
wiliest
wiliness
will
 wills
 willed

willing
willfull = wilful
will-o'-the-wisp
willow
willowy
willpower
willy-nilly
wilt
 wilts
 wilted
 wilting
wily
 wilier
 wiliest
wimp
wimple
win
 wins
 won (= came first
 → one)
 winning
wince
 winces
 winced
 wincing
winceyette
winch
 winches
 winched
 winching
wind (= turn
 → whined)
 winds
 winded
 wound
 winding
windcheater
windfall
windier
windiest
windily
windiness
windlass
windmill
window
windowpane
windowsill
windpipe
windscreen
windshield
windsock
Windsor
windsurfing
windswept

windy
 windier
 windiest
wine (= drink
 → whine)
wineglass
wineglassful
winery
 wineries
wing
winger
wingspan
wink
 winks
 winked
 winking
winkle
winner
winning
Winnipeg
winnow
 winnows
 winnowed
 winnowing
wins
winsome
winter
wintertime
wintrier
wintriest
wintry
wipe
 wipes
 wiped
 wiping
wipeout
wiper
wire
 wires
 wired
 wiring
wireless
wiring
wiry
 wirier
 wiriest
Wisconsin
wisdom
wise
wisecrack
wish
 wishes
 wished
 wishing

wishbone
wishful
wishy-washy
wisp
wispily
wispiness
wispy
  wispier
  wispiest
wistaria
wisteria
wistful
wit (= repartee
  → whit)
witch (= magic
  woman → which)
witchcraft
witch hazel
with
withdraw
  withdraws
  withdrew
  withdrawn
  withdrawing
withdrawal
wither (= droop
  → whither)
withhold
  withholds
  withheld
  withholding
within
wit~~hold~~ = withhold
without
withstand
  withstands
  withstood
  withstanding
witless
witness
  witnesses
  witnessed
  witnessing
witticism
wittily
wittiness
witty
  wittier
  wittiest
wives
wizard
wizardry
wizened
wo try wa

woad
wobble
  wobbles
  wobbled
  wobbling
  wobbly
wod try wad
Wodehouse, P.G.
wodge
woe
woebegone
woeful
wog
woggle
wok
woke
woken
wold
wolf
  wolves
wolfhound
woman
  women
womanish
womankind
womanly
womb
wombat
women
womenfolk
won (= came first
  → one)
wonder
  wonders
  wondered
  wondering
wonderful
wonderment
wondrous
wonky
  wonkier
  wonkiest
wont (= as is my
  wont)
won't (= will not)
woo
  woos
  wooed
  wooing
wood (= forest
  → would)
woodcarving
woodcutter
wooded

wooden
woodier
woodiest
woodlark
woodlouse
  woodlice
woodpecker
woodshed
woodwind
woodwork
woodworm
woody
  woodier
  woodiest
wooed
woof
  woofs
  woofed
  woofing
woofer
wooing
wool
Woolf, Virginia
woollen
woolliness
woolly
  woollier
  woolliest
woolsack
woos
woozily
wooziness
woozy
  woozier
  wooziest
wop
Worcester
wor try wa
word (= group of
  letters → whirred)
wordily
wordiness
wording
wordless
wordy
  wordier
  wordiest
wore
work
  works
  worked
  working
workable
workaholic

workbench
worker
workforce
workload
workmanship
workmate
workplace
workshop
workshy
worktop
world (= globe
  → whirled)
worldly
worldwide
worm
  worms
  wormed
  worming
wormcast
wormery
  wormeries
wormwood
wormy
  wormier
  wormiest
worn
worrisome
worry
  worries
  worried
  worrying
worse
worsen
  worsens
  worsened
  worsening
worship
  worships
  worshipped
  worshipping
worshipful
worst
worsted
worth
worthily
worthiness
worthless
worthwhile
worthy
  worthier
  worthiest
would (= question
  → wood)
wouldn't

wound
  wounds
  wounded
  wounding
wove
woven
wow
wrack
wraith
wrangle
  wrangles
  wrangled
  wrangling
wrap
  wraps
  wrapped (= covered → rapt)
  wrapping
wraparound
wrapover
wrapper
wrath
wrathful
wreak (= make havoc → reek)

wreaks
wreaked
wreaking
wreath
wreathe
  wreathes
  wreathed
  wreathing
wreck
  wrecks
  wrecked
  wrecking
wren
wrench
wrestle
  wrestles
  wrestled
  wrestling
wrestling
wretch
wretched
Wrexham
wriggle
  wriggles
  wriggled

  wriggling
wring (= squeeze → ring)
  wrings
  wrung
  wringing
wringer
wrinkle
  wrinkles
  wrinkled
  wrinkling
wrist
wristband
wristwatch
writ
write (= form words with a pen → right, rite)
  writes
  wrote (= formed words → rote)
  written
  writing
~~writeing~~ = writing
~~writen~~ = written

writer
writhe
  writhes
  writhed
  writhing
writing
written
~~writting~~ = writing
wrong
  wrongs
  wronged
  wronging
wrongdoer
wrongful
wrought
wrung (= squeezed → rung)
wry (= ironic → rye)
wun try one
wur try wor
wych-elm
Wymondham
Wyoming
wyvern

X

Xanadu
xanthan
Xavier
x-axis
X-chromosome
xenon
xenophile
xenophobe
xenophobia

Xerox™
  Xeroxes
  Xeroxed
  Xeroxing
Xhosa
  Xhosa *or*
  Xhosas
xi
  xis

X-rated
XML
x-ray
  x-rays
  x-rayed
  x-raying
X-ray
  X-rays
  X-rayed

  X-raying
xylan
xylem
xylene
xylocarp
xylophone
xylophonic
xylophonist
xylose

Y

yacht
  yachts
  yachted
  yachting
yachtsman
  yachtsmen
yackety-yak
yah
yahoo
  yahoos
yahooism
Yahweh
yak
  yaks
  yakked
  yakking
Yakut
yam
yammer
  yammers
  yammered
  yammering
yank
  yanks
  yanked
  yanking
Yankee
yap
  yaps
  yapped
  yapping
Yarborough
yard
yardage
yardarm
Yardie
yardstick
Yarmouth
yarmulke
yarn
yarrow
yashmac
yashmak
yaw (= pitch → yore,
  your, you're)
  yaws

yawed
  yawing
yawl
yawn
  yawns
  yawned
  yawning
Y-chromosome
ye
yea
yeah
year
yearbook
yearling
yearlong
yearn
  yearns
  yearned
  yearning
yeast
  yeastily
  yeastiness
  yeasty
  yeastier
  yeastiest
Yeats, W.B.
yeild = yield
yell
  yells
  yelled
  yelling
yellow
  yellows
  yellowed
  yellowing
yellowbird
yellowhammer
yellowtail
yelp
  yelps
  yelped
  yelping
Yemen
yen
yeoman
  yeomen

yeomanry
Yeovil
yep
yes
yeshiva
  yeshivahs or
  yeshivoth
yesterday
yesteryear
yet
yeti
yew (= tree → you)
Y-fronts
Yiddish
yield
  yields
  yielded
  yielding
yin
yippee
ylang-ylang
YMCA
yo
yob
yobbos
yobs
yodel
  yodels
  yodelled
  yodelling
yoga
yogh
yoghourt
yoghurt
yogi
yogic
yogurt
yoke (= join → yolk)
  yokes
  yoked
  yoking
yokel
yolk (= part of an egg
  → yoke)
yomp
  yomps

yomped
  yomping
yon
yonder
yonks
yoo-hoo
yore (= long ago
  → yaw, your, you're)
yorker
Yoruba
you (= not me → yew)
you'd
you'll (= you will
  → yule)
young
youngster
your (= belonging to
  you → yaw, yore,
  you're)
you're (= you are
  → yaw, yore, your)
yours
yourself
  yourselves
youth
youthful
you've
yowl
  yowls
  yowled
  yowling
yo-yo
  yo-yos
  yo-yoed
  yo-yoing
ytterbia
ytterbite
ytterbium
yttria
yttrium
yuan
  yuan
yucca
yuck
yuckily
yuckiness

yucky
  yuckier
  yuckiest
Yugoslav
Yugoslavia
yuk

yukkily
yukkiness
yukky
  yukkier
  yukkiest
yule (= Christmas

→ you'll)
yummy
  yummier
  yummiest
yum-yum
yup

yuppie
yuppy
  yuppies
yurt
Yvonne

Z

zabaglione
Zaïre
Zambezi
Zambia
zanily
zaniness
zany
  zanier
  zaniest
Zanzibar
zap
  zaps
  zapped
  zapping
zapping
zappy
  zappier
  zappiest
zarzuela
zeal
zealot
zealotry
zealous
zebec
zebeck
zebra
zebu
zed
zemstvo
  zemstvos
Zen
zenana

zenith
zeolite
zeolitic
zephyr
zeppelin
zero
  zeroes *or*
  zeros
  zeroes
  zeroed
  zeroing
zest
zeta
zeugma
zidovudine
ziggurat
zigzag
zilch
zillion
  zillion *or*
  zillions
Zimbabwe
zimmer
zinc
zincate
zincite
Zinfandel
zing
  zings
  zinged
  zinging
zink = zinc

zinnia
Zion
Zionism
zip
  zips
  zipped
  zipping
zipper
zippy
  zippier
  zippiest
zircalloy
zircon
zirconium
zit
zither
zloty
  zloty *or*
  zlotys
zodiac
zodiacal
Zoë
Zohar
zombie
  zombies
zonal
zonate
zonation
zone
  zones
  zoned
  zoning

zonked
zoo
zoological
zoologist
zoology
zoom
  zooms
  zoomed
  zooming
Zoroastrian
Zoroastrianism
zounds
zucchetto
  zucchettos
zucchini
  zucchini *or*
  zucchinis
Zulu
  Zulus *or*
  Zulu
zwieback
zwitterion
zygospore
zygote
zygotene
zygotic
zygotically
zymotic
zymotically